PLAYFAIR
CRICKET ANNUAL
1985

38th edition

EDITED BY GORDON ROSS

Statistics by
Barry McCaully, Brian Heald and Brian Croudy

P. C. A. 1985—1

KU-236-102

PICK THE BEST CURRENT ENGLAND ONE-DAY TEAM (all of whom have played in the NatWest Trophy) TO OPPOSE THE TEAM OF OVERSEAS PLAYERS CHOSEN IN LAST YEAR'S COMPETITION (see page 56)

£1400 TO BE WON

Prizes: 1st: £450 2nd: £300 3rd: £225 4th: £175
Plus twenty-five prizes of £10 each

How to enter: Pick the best NatWest Bank Trophy team from the 40 cricketers shown below who played in the competition in the first four seasons. Then write in 20 words if you think there is too much one-day cricket. Give a reason for your opinion.

Write the names on the entry form on the opposite page with your name and address and post to the address shown.

Your Choice
The 21 players who appeared for England last summer – Jonathon Agnew, Paul Allott, Ian Botham, Chris Broad, Nick Cook, Norman Cowans, Paul Downton, Richard Ellison, Neil Foster, Graeme Fowler, Mike Gatting, David Gower, Allan Lamb, Andy Lloyd, Geoff Miller, Pat Pocock, Derek Pringle, Derek Randall, Chris Tavaré, Paul Terry, Bob Willis. These six who went on the winter tour – Chris Cowdrey, Phil Edmonds, Bruce French, Vic Marks, Martyn Moxon, Tim Robinson. Plus – Bill Athey, David Bairstow, Kim Barnett, Mark Benson, John Emburey, Graham Gooch, Trevor Jesty, Alan Knott, Wayne Larkins, John Lever, Les Taylor, Derek Underwood, Peter Willey.

Rules
Judging: Each entry will be considered by a panel of cricket experts and the entry which, in the opinion of the judges, constitutes the best NatWest Trophy team will be adjudged the winner. The decision of the judges is final and binding; no correspondence will be entered into. Employees of Macdonald & Co (Publishers) Ltd and their families are not eligible to compete.
Proof of entry: All entries must be on the entry form provided. Proof of posting is not proof of entry.

ENTRY FORM

Your team in batting order, with a captain:

1

2

3

4

5

6

7

8

9

10

11

Write in no more than 20 words if you think there is too much one-day cricket. Give a reason for your opinion.

Closing date: 12.00 noon Wednesday, 18 September 1985

Your name and address:

....

....

....

Post to: The Editor, Playfair Cricket Annual Competition, Queen Anne Press, Macdonald & Co (Publishers) Ltd, Maxwell House, 74 Worship Street, London EC2A 2EN

This won't be a bouncer!
7th Sept 19 85
60-00-00
National Westminster Bank PLC
Pay NatWest Trophy Winners
or order
Seventeen thousand pounds only
£17,000
per pro NATIONAL WESTMINSTER BANK PLC
000000 60-0000 00000000
NatWest
The Action Bank

WEST INDIAN SUMMER
By Gordon Ross

The summer of 1984 in England belonged unconditionally to West Indies. It was a fast bowler's summer, when England were destroyed to the tune of five nothing – not the first time, of course, that fast bowlers have won Test matches. Len Hutton placed his faith in pace on the famous 1954–55 tour of Australia when Frank Tyson (probably bowling faster than he did before or after), along with Fred Trueman and Brian Statham, wrecked Australia. There was Miller and Lindwall, Hall and Griffith, but as far as history goes, five of them were never used in such spells that two were always fresh. It was indeed high quality bowling, and nothing should be taken away from West Indies' bowling, batting or fielding, or one of the most popular captains in the history of Test cricket. Yet it would be remiss of anyone passing judgement on England's performance not to mention what everyone considered an absolute excess of the short-pitched ball which perpetually threatened injury – and serious injury – to batsmen. It was, if I remember correctly, as respected an authority as Mike Brearley who took the view that cricket is a game where courage is paramount and batsmen should learn to get on with it. But a bouncer's function is surely to create in the batsman's mind an uncertainty as to what is coming next, and so unsettle him in his concentration. It was not intended to be used liberally for the sole purpose of intimidation. Tony Lewis wrote in the *Sunday Telegraph*: 'The memory of last summer in England was of a helmeted, arm-padded, rib-padded anonymous procession of batsmen doing their best not to get their skulls cracked or being caught off the bat handle.'

Surely one leading question to be asked is: 'Is this what the modern cricketing public want, or would they prefer to see great batsmen playing their shots in a battle of their respective skills against great bowlers, using the occasional bouncer for the purpose for which it was originally intended?'

Two young England players were seriously hurt, Andy Lloyd at Edgbaston and Paul Terry at Old Trafford. Whether or not the particular ball which did the damage was lethal is not the point at issue. It was the state of mind of young batsmen inexperienced at Test level having been subjected to a succession of short-pitched balls whistling around their heads.

It may well be argued, particularly by Australians, that England started this sort of thing as a means of curbing Bradman's activities back in the 'thirties. They were given some of this medicine in return by Dennis Lillee and Jeff Thomson in Australia in 1974 when a few nerves were shattered, and not with players who, in the normal course of events, were given to apprehension. In looking at the situation today it is irrelevant who started it, or who carried it on, particularly as the days when no bowler would think of bouncing a number 11 batsmen are over. A famous current Test bowler has said that if the batsman is wearing a helmet for protection, then he will bowl short to anyone, from number one to 11.

No, what we have to look at now are its ramifications in cricket today; yesterday doesn't matter. You cannot blame umpires for not taking a much firmer line to control intimidatory bowling unless clear instructions are given by the International Boards of Control. For this, the International Cricket Conference must stand and be counted. Its record over the years is not one of positive action, because each and every member is looking to the needs of his own country, just as a politician will consider first the demands of his own constituency. Are the West Indian delegates likely to urge a restriction in short-pitched bowling when they have the best fast bowlers in the world, and performing as they are allowed to do now, can scythe down all opposition that stand in their path? Australia's winter victory over West Indies was significant, and nothing should be taken away from Australia, but psychologically for West Indies it came at a time when the series had already been won, and the urge to win might not have been quite as great as if the series had yet to be settled. It still doesn't change the rational thinking on cricket's major problem at the present time.

Another problem which refuses to go away is the slow over-rate. Here the Test and County Cricket Board cannot be accused of dragging its feet. Even more severe penalties have been introduced for 1985. County teams who fail to bowl an average of 18·5 overs an hour will subject themselves to stringent financial penalties. A less severe fining system which operated from 1978 to 1983 was scrapped and replaced in 1984 by the introduction of 117 overs per day minimum. This has now been reduced to 112 overs, but teams will not be allowed to bowl more than 22 overs an hour, so as to eliminate the possibility of farce in trying to push the day's over-rate up in matches where a result cannot be achieved.

One or two counties will cringe at the thought of this in relation to what they achieved last summer; possibly as many as five of them would have been paying the Board five-figure sums for not even reaching seventeen overs an hour. The figure for the new penalties set at 18·5 overs an hour would have had quite a few struggling in 1984. Half of the money is paid by the players, so there is small wonder that the County Captains opposed the scheme; they were, however, over-ruled.

The summer of 1985 holds much brighter prospects for the follower of English cricket. The renaissance began in India with the Second Test, and continued with Fowler and Gatting committing their names to the history books for what is likely to be a very long time to come. Jubilation, certainly, but the Indian attack on good batting wickets was no more than moderate, and is unlikely to lead to complacency on anyone's part.

Having said that, there is no reason at all why England, at long last able to field its full quota of players, should not beat Australia. Fowler and Robinson have certainly provided food for thought for when the triumphant return of Graham Gooch is contemplated. If anyone wants to criticise Fowler's style from the aesthetic point of view they can, but the most carping critic could not fault his determined ability to accumulate runs, and his tremendous guts. Throw in his fielding, and it would be difficult to put him out of any side. It will be nice for the Selectors to experience keen competition for places. But let us be wary of one thing – saying that Australia are not a very good team. We have said this quite often before with disastrous results. It is a very open series, and it will be interesting to see when they open their books, just what the bookmakers think about it!

The change of circumstances in 1985 could make a change or two in the honours winners from 1984. The West Indians will now be back with their Counties, so once again you must fancy Somerset for one title or another. Essex, that fine side who won the Britannic Assurance Championship and The John Player Special League, look like losing Foster and Gooch on a regular basis to Test matches. Middlesex could possibly lose three if Edmonds retains his place with Gatting and Downton, but this should not affect Middlesex setting out to retain the NatWest Trophy when their Test players will be available. All in all, it looks a happier summer than 1984, except that it will do well to produce a better summer's weather – what a vital part the weather plays in the game of cricket.

Pakistan v England 1983-84

FIRST TEST MATCH

PLAYED AT KARACHI, 2, 3, 4, 6 MARCH
PAKISTAN WON BY 3 WICKETS

ENGLAND

C.L. Smith c Wasim b Sarfraz	28	lbw b Sarfraz	5
M.W. Gatting b Tauseef	26	lbw b Sarfraz	4
D.I. Gower lbw b Qadir	58	c Mohsin b Tauseef	57
A.J. Lamb c Ramiz b Sarfraz	4	c Anil b Qadir	20
D.W. Randall b Qadir	8	b Qadir	16
I.T. Botham c Ramiz b Qadir	22	b Tauseef	10
V.J. Marks c Ramiz b Sarfraz	5	b Qadir	1
†R.W. Taylor lbw b Qadir	4	c Mohsin b Tauseef	19
N.G.B. Cook c Salim b Sarfraz	9	c Mohsin b Wasim	5
*R.G.D. Willis c Wasim b Qadir	6	c Tauseef b Wasim	2
N.G. Cowans not out	1	not out	0
Extras (LB6, NB5)	11	(B6, LB6, NB8)	20
Total	**182**		**159**

PAKISTAN

Mohsin Khan c Botham b Cook	54	b Cook	10
Qasim Omar lbw b Cook	29	c Botham b Cook	7
Ramiz Raja b Smith b Cook	1	c Botham b Marks	1
Zaheer Abbas c Lamb b Botham	0	b Cook	8
Salim Malik lbw b Willis	74	run out	11
Wasim Raja c Cowans b Cook	3	c Cowans b Cook	0
†Anil Dalpat c Taylor b Willis	12	not out	16
Abdul Qadir c Lamb b Botham	40	b Cook	7
Sarfraz Nawaz c Botham b Cook	8	not out	4
Tauseef Ahmed not out	17		
Azeem Hafeez c Willis b Cook	24		
Extras (LB5, NB10)	15	(B1, NB1)	2
Total	**277**	**(7 wkts)**	**66**

BOWLING

PAKISTAN	O	N	R	W		O	M	R	W
Azeem	11	3	21	0	—	8	3	14	0
Sarfraz	25.5	8	42	4	—	15	1	27	2
Tauseef	24	11	33	1	—	21	6	37	3
Wasim	3	2	1	0	—	3.3	1	2	2
Qadir	31	12	74	5	—	31	4	59	3

ENGLAND	O	M	R	W		O	M	R	W
Willis	17	6	33	2	—	2	0	13	0
Cowans	12	3	34	0	—	2.3	1	10	0
Botham	30	5	90	2	—	—	—	—	—
Cook	30	12	65	6	—	14	8	18	5
Marks	13	4	40	1	—	12	5	23	1

FALL OF WICKETS

	ENG 1st	PAK 1st	ENG 2nd	PAK 2nd
1st	41	67	6	17
2nd	90	79	21	18
3rd	94	80	63	26
4th	108	96	94	38
5th	154	105	121	38
6th	159	138	128	40
7th	164	213	128	59
8th	165	229	157	—
9th	180	240	159	—
10th	182	277	159	—

SECOND TEST MATCH

PLAYED AT FAISALABAD 12, 13, 14, 16, 17 MARCH
MATCH DRAWN

PAKISTAN

Mohsin Khan c Lamb b Dilley	20	b Dilley	2
Mudassar Nazar c Gatting b Cook	12	lbw b Foster	4
Qasim Omar c Gatting b Foster	16	c Taylor b Dilley	17
Salim Malik c Lamb b Cook	116	c sub (Cowans) b Marks	76
*Zaheer Abbas lbw b Gatting	68	not out	32
Wasim Raja b Marks	112	not out	5
Abdul Qadir c Foster b Dilley	50		
†Anil Dalpat lbw b Dilley	8		
Sarfraz Nawaz not out	16		
Tauseef Ahmed not out	1		
Azeem Hafeez did not bat			
Extras (LB11, W2, NB17)	30	(LB1)	1
Total (8 wkts dec)	449	(4 wkts)	137

ENGLAND

C.L. Smith b Sarfraz	66
M.W. Gatting c Salim b Tauseef	75
D.W. Randall b Sarfraz	65
A.J. Lamb b Anil b Azeem	19
*D.I. Gower st Anil b Mudassar	152
G. Fowler c Qasim b Wasim	57
†R.W. Taylor c Salim b Qadir	0
V.J. Marks b Sarfraz	83
G.R. Dilley not out	2
N.G.B. Cook not out	1
N.A. Foster did not bat	
Extras (B10, LB4, NB12)	26
Total (8 wkts dec)	546

BOWLING

ENGLAND	O	M	R	W	O	M	R	W
Foster	30	7	109	1	5	1	10	1
Dilley	28	6	101	3	9	0	41	2
Cook	54	14	133	2	16	6	38	0
Marks	27	9	59	1	8	2	26	1
Gatting	3	0	17	1	2	0	18	0
Fowler	—	—	—	—	1	0	3	0
PAKISTAN								
Azeem	19	3	71	1	—			
Sarfraz	49	11	129	3	—			
Wasim	26	6	61	1	—			
Qadir	51	14	124	1	—			
Tauseef	30	8	96	1	—			
Mudassar	14	1	39	1	—			

FALL OF WICKETS

	PAK	ENG	PAK
	1st	1st	2nd
1st	35	127	6
2nd	53	163	6
3rd	70	214	56
4th	200	245	123
5th	323	361	—
6th	416	361	—
7th	430	528	—
8th	433	545	—
9th	—	—	—
10th	—	—	—

THIRD TEST MATCH

PLAYED AT LAHORE, 19, 20, 21, 23, 24 MARCH
MATCH DRAWN

ENGLAND

C.L. Smith c Salim b Sarfraz	18	run out		15
M.W. Gatting lbw b Sarfraz	0	run out		53
*D.I. Gower c Anil b Mohsin Kamal	9	not out		173
A.J. Lamb c Ramiz b Qadir	29	c & b Qadir		6
D.W. Randall c Salim b Qadir	14	c Salim b Qadir		0
G. Fowler c Qasim b Abdul Qadir	58	c Anil b Mohsin		19
V.J. Marks c Mohsin Khan b Qadir	74	c sub (Akram) b Qadir		55
†R.W. Taylor lbw b Qadir	1	b Sarfraz		5
N.A. Foster lbw b Qadir	6	lbw b Qadir		0
N.G.B. Cook c Anil b Sarfraz	3			
N.G. Cowans not out	3	st Anil b Qadir		3
Extras (B4, LB5, W9, NB8)	26	(B6, LB3, W1, NB5)		15
Total	**241**	(9 wkts dec)		**344**

PAKISTAN

Mohsin Khan lbw Foster	1	c Smith b Cowans		104
Shoaib Mohammad lbw b Cowans	7	c Gatting b Cowans		80
Qasim Omar c Fowler b Foster	73	run out		0
Salim Malik b Marks	38	c Gatting b Cowans		7
Ramiz Raja c Smith b Foster	26	not out		6
Wasim Raja c Gower b Cowans	12	lbw b Cowans		0
*Zaheer Abbas not out	82	c Gatting b Cowans		5
Abdul Qadir c Taylor b Foster	3			
†Anil Dalpat c Gower b Foster	2			
Sarfraz Nawaz c Gatting b Smith	90	not out		10
Mohsin Kamal c Gower b Cook	0			
Extras (LB9)	9	(LB5)		5
Total	**343**	(6 wkts)		**217**

BOWLING

PAKISTAN	O	M	R	W		O	M	R	W	FALL OF WICKETS			
										ENG	PAK	ENG	PAK
Mohsin Kamal	15	0	66	1	—	17	3	59	1	1st	1st	2nd	2nd
Sarfraz	22.5	5	49	4	—	27.4	1	112	1	1st	5	9	35	173
Qadir	30	7	84	5	—	42	5	110	5	2nd	20	13	38	175
Wasim	11	4	16	0	—	21	5	48	0	3rd	47	99	175	187
ENGLAND					—					4th	77	138	189	197
Cowans	29	5	89	2	—	14	2	42	5	5th	83	151	189	199
Foster	32	8	67	5	—	15	4	44	0	6th	203	166	308	199
Cook	45	12	117	1	—	18.3	2	73	0	7th	205	175	309	
Marks	20	4	59	1	—	10	1	53	0	8th	222	181	327	
Smith	1	0	2	1	—	1	1	0	0	9th	237	342	344	
					—					10th	241	343	—	—

TEST MATCH AVERAGES

PAKISTAN

	M	I	NO	Runs	HS	Avge	100	50	Ct	St
Sarfraz Nawaz	3	5	3	128	90	64.00	—	1	—	—
Salim Malik	3	6	0	322	116	53.66	1	2	6	—
Zaheer Abbas	3	6	2	195	82*	48.75	—	2	—	—
Shoaib Mohammed	1	2	0	87	80	43.50	—	1	—	—
Mohsin Khan	3	6	0	191	104	31.88	1	1	4	—
Wasim Raja	3	6	1	132	112	26.40	1	—	2	—
Abdul Qadir	3	4	0	100	50	25.00	—	1	1	—
Azeem Hafeez	2	1	0	24	24	24.00	—	—	—	—
Qasim Omar	3	6	0	142	73	23.66	—	1	2	—
Tauseef Ahmed	2	2	2	18	17*	—	—	—	1	—
Anil Dalpat	3	4	1	38	16*	12.66	—	—	5	2
Ramiz Raja	2	4	1	34	26	11.33	—	—	4	—
Mudassar Nazar	1	2	0	16	12	8.00	—	—	—	—
Mohsin Kamal	1	1	0	0	0	0.00	—	—	—	—

	Overs	Mdns	Runs	Wkts	Avge	Best	5 wI	10 wM
Abdul Qadir	185	42	451	19	23.73	5/74	3	1
Sarfraz Nawaz	137.2	26	359	14	25.64	4/42	—	—
Tauseef Ahmed	75	25	166	5	33.20	3/37	—	—
Mudassar Nazar	14	1	39	1	39.00	1/39	—	—
Wasim Raja	64.3	18	128	3	42.66	1/61	—	—
Mohsin Kamal	32	3	125	2	62.50	1/59	—	—
Azeem Hafeez	38	9	106	1	106.00	1/71	—	—

ENGLAND

	M	I	NO	Runs	HS	Avge	100	50	Ct	St
D.I. Gower	3	5	1	449	173	112.25	2	2	3	—
G. Fowler	2	3	0	134	58	44.66	—	2	1	—
V.J. Marks	3	5	0	218	83	43.60	—	3	—	—
M.W. Gatting	3	5	0	158	75	31.60	—	2	6	—
C.L. Smith	3	5	0	132	66	26.40	—	1	3	—
D.W. Randall	3	5	0	103	65	20.60	—	1	—	—
I.T. Botham	2	2	0	32	22	16.00	—	—	4	—
A.J. Lamb	3	5	0	78	29	15.60	—	—	4	—
N.G. Cowans	2	4	3	7	3*	7.00	—	—	2	—
N.G.B. Cook	3	4	1	18	9	6.00	—	—	—	—
R.W. Taylor	3	5	0	29	19	5.80	—	—	3	—
R.G.D. Willis	1	2	0	8	6	4.00	—	—	1	—
N.A. Foster	2	2	0	6	6	3.00	—	—	1	—
G.R. Dilley	1	1	1	2	2	—	—	—	—	—

	Overs	Mdns	Runs	Wkts	Avge	Best	5 wI	10 wM
C.L. Smith	2	1	2	1	2.00	1/2	—	—
R.G.D. Willis	19	6	46	2	23.00	2/33	—	—
N.G. Cowans	57.3	11	175	7	25.00	5/42	1	—
G.R. Dilley	37	6	142	5	28.40	3/101	—	—
N.G.B. Cook	178.3	54	444	14	31.71	6/56	2	1
N.A. Foster	82	20	230	7	32.85	5/67	1	—
M.W. Gatting	5	0	35	1	35.00	1/17	—	—
I.T. Botham	30	5	90	2	45.00	2/90	—	—
V.J. Marks	90	24	260	4	65.00	1/23	—	—
G. Fowler	1	0	3	0	—	—	—	—

West Indies v Australia 1983-84

FIRST TEST MATCH

PLAYED AT GEORGETOWN, 2, 3, 4, 6, 7 MARCH
MATCH DRAWN

AUSTRALIA

S.B. Smith c Dujon b Garner	3	c Dujon b Garner	12
K.C. Wessels c Lloyd b Garner	4	c Lloyd b Daniel	20
G.M. Ritchie c Davis b Harper	78	lbw b Garner	3
*K.J. Hughes b Garner	18	c Haynes b Daniel	0
A.R. Border b Garner	5	run out	54
D.W. Hookes c Dujon b Harper	32	b Garner	10
†W.B. Phillips c Greenidge b Harper	16	b Daniel	76
G.F. Lawson c Richards b Harper	11	not out	35
T.G. Hogan not out	42	lbw b Davis	18
T.M. Alderman lbw b Garner	1	not out	3
R.M. Hogg lbw b Garner	52	b Davis	6
Extras (B2, LB3, W1, NB11)	17	(B10, LB15, NB11)	36
Total	**279**	**(9 wkts dec)**	**273**

WEST INDIES

C.G. Greenidge c Wessels b Lawson	16	not out	120
D.L. Haynes lbw b Hogg	60	not out	103
R.B. Richardson lbw b Lawson	19		
I.V.A. Richards c Phillips b Hogg	8		
H.A. Gomes c Border b Wessels	10		
*C.H. Lloyd c Phillips b Alderman	36		
†P.J. Dujon b Hogan	21		
R.A. Harper b Hogan	10		
J. Garner not out	16		
W.W. Davis c Ritchie b Hogan	11		
W.W. Daniel lbw b Lawson	4		
Extras (LB7, NB12)	19	(B10, LB13, NB4)	27
Total	**230**	**(0 wkt)**	**250**

BOWLING

WEST INDIES	O	M	R	W		O	M	R	W	FALL OF WICKETS			
											AUS	WI	AUS
Garner	27.2	10	75	6	—	24	5	67	3		1st	1st	2nd
Daniel	12	3	60	0	—	27	4	86	3	1st	6	29	37
Davis	19	2	45	0	—	14	3	35	2	2nd	23	72	41
Harper	24	7	56	4	—	15	4	27	0	3rd	55	93	42
Gomes	15	1	35	0	—	11	2	25	0	4th	63	110	50
Richards	5	2	3	0	—	6	2	8	0	5th	139	154	60
AUSTRALIA					—					6th	166	181	185
Lawson	20.4	4	59	3	—	18	0	54	0	7th	180	191	209
Alderman	21	3	64	1	—	11	0	43	0	8th	181	203	248
Hogg	12	0	44	2	—	13	0	56	0	9th	182	225	263
Hogan	25	9	56	4	—	19	2	74	0	10th	279	230	—

SECOND TEST MATCH
PLAYED AT PORT OF SPAIN 16, 17, 18, 20, 21 MARCH
MATCH DRAWN

AUSTRALIA

K.C. Wessels c Gomes b Garner	4	lbw b Garner	4
†W.B. Phillips c Dujon b Garner	4	run out	0
G.M. Ritchie b Garner	1	b Small	26
*K.J. Hughes c Dujon b Garner	24	lbw b Marshall	33
A.R. Border not out	98	not out	100
D.W. Hookes b Garner	23	c Richardson b Gomes	21
D.M. Jones c & b Richards	48	b Richards	5
C.F. Lawson c & b Daniel	14	b Marshall	20
T.G. Hogan c Greenidge b Daniel	0	c Logie b Daniel	38
R.M. Hogg c Marshall b Daniel	11	c Garner b Richards	9
T.M. Alderman c Richardson b Garner	1	not out	21
Extras (B6, LB4, NB17)	27	(B6, LB1, W1, NB14)	22
Total	**255**	**(9 wkts)**	**299**

WEST INDIES

C.G. Greenidge c Phillips b Hogg	24
D.L. Haynes run out	53
R.B. Richardson c Wessels b Alderman	23
*I.V.A. Richards c Phillips b Alderman	76
H.A. Gomes b Lawson	3
A.L. Logie lbw b Hogan	97
†P.J. Dujon b Hogan	130
M.D. Marshall lbw b Lawson	10
J. Garner not out	24
W.W. Daniel not out	6
M.A. Small did not bat	
Extras (B7, LB12, W2, NB1)	22
Total (8 wkts dec)	**468**

BOWLING

WEST INDIES	O	M	R	W		O	M	R	W	FALL OF WICKETS		
											AUS	*WI*	*AUS*
Garner	28.1	9	60	6	—	15	4	35	1		*1st*	*1st*	*2nd*
Marshall	19	2	73	0	—	22	3	73	2	1st	4	35	1
Daniel	15	3	40	3	—	9	3	11	1	2nd	7	93	35
Small	10	3	24	0	—	14	2	51	1	3rd	16	124	41
Gomes	10	0	33	0	—	27	5	53	1	4th	50	129	114
Richards	10	4	15	1	—	25	5	65	2	5th	85	229	115
Logie					—	0.1	0	4	0	6th	185	387	153
AUSTRALIA										7th	233	430	162
Lawson	32	3	132	2	—	—	—	—	—	8th	233	462	196
Hogg	31	2	103	1	—	—	—	—	—	9th	253	—	238
Alderman	35	9	91	2	—	—	—	—	—	10th	255	—	—
Hogan	28	3	123	2	—	—	—	—	—				

THIRD TEST MATCH

AUSTRALIA

S.B. Smith c Dujon b Marshall	10	b Marshall		7
G.M. Wood c Dujon b Holding	68	lbw b Garner		20
G.M. Ritchie c & b Harper	57	c Haynes b Marshall		0
*K.J. Hughes c Dujon b Holding	20	c Lloyd b Holding		25
A.R. Border c Richardson b Marshall	38	c Dujon b Holding		8
D.W. Hookes c Dujon b Garner	30	b Holding		9
T.G. Hogan b Garner	40	c Richardson b Holding		2
†W.B. Phillips c Dujon b Garner	120	b Marshall		1
G.F. Lawson b Baptiste	10	c Harper b Marshall		5
R.M. Hogg c Garner b Harper	3	not out		0
T.M. Alderman not out	2	b Marshall		0
Extras (B14, LB8, NB9)	31	(B1, LB6, NB11)		18
Total	**429**			**97**

WEST INDIES

C.G. Greenidge run out	64	not out	10
D.L. Haynes b Hogg	145	not out	11
R.B. Richardson not out	131		
I.V.A. Richards b Lawson	6		
E.A.E. Baptiste b Lawson	11		
†P.J. Dujon b Alderman	2		
*C.H. Lloyd b Hogg	76		
M.D. Marshall b Hogg	10		
R.A. Harper b Hogg	19		
J. Garner c Phillips b Hogg	9		
M.A. Holding c Smith b Hogg	0		
Extras (LB25, NB11)	36		
Total	**509**	(0 wkt)	21

BOWLING

WEST INDIES	O	M	R	W		O	M	R	W	FALL OF WICKETS			
											AUS	*WI*	*AUS*
Garner	33.5	6	110	3	—	8	4	9	1		*1st*	*1st*	*2nd*
Marshall	26	2	83	2	—	15.5	1	42	5	1st	11	132	13
Holding	30	5	94	2	—	15	4	24	0	2nd	114	277	13
Baptiste	17	5	34	1	—	3	0	14	0	3rd	158	289	63
Harper	43	9	86	2	—	2	1	1	0	4th	171	313	65
AUSTRALIA										5th	223	316	68
Lawson	33.2	4	150	2	—	2	1	3	0	6th	263	447	80
Alderman	42.4	6	152	1	—	1.4	0	18	0	7th	307	465	85
Hogg	32.4	4	77	6	—	—	—	—	—	8th	330	493	85
Hogan	34	8	97	0	—	—	—	—	—	9th	366	509	92
Border	3	1	8	0	—					10th	429	509	97

FOURTH TEST MATCH

PLAYED AT ST. JOHN'S, ANTIGUA, 7, 8, 9, 11 APRIL
WEST INDIES WON BY AN INNINGS AND 36 RUNS

AUSTRALIA

W.B. Phillips	c Dujon b Garner	5	b Gardner	22
G.M. Ritchie	c Holding b Marshall	6	c Dujon b Garner	23
A.R. Border	c Dujon b Baptiste	98	c Greenidge b Baptiste	19
*K.J. Hughes	c Marshall b Harper	24	c Richards b Marshall	29
D.M. Jones	b Harper	1	C Dujon b Garner	11
D.W. Hookes	c Richardson b Baptiste	51	c Greenidge b Holding	29
†R.D. Woolley	c Dujon b Baptiste	13	lbw b Marshall	8
T.G. Hogan	c Harper b Holding	14	c Baptiste b Garner	6
G.F. Lawson	b Holding	4	not out	17
J.N. Maguire	not out	15	b Marshall	0
C.G. Rackemann	b Holding	12	b Garner	0
Extras	(B5, LB4, NB10)	19	(B19, LB7, NB10)	36
Total		**262**		**200**

WEST INDIES

C.G. Greenidge	c Ritchie b Lawson	0
D.L. Haynes	b Lawson	21
R.B. Richardson	c Woolley b Rackemann	154
I.V.A. Richards	c Woolley b Rackemann	178
†P.J. Dujon	c Hughes b Rackemann	28
*C.H. Lloyd	c Jones b Rackemann	38
M.D. Marshall	c Hookes b Maguire	6
E.A.E. Baptiste	b Maguire	6
R.A. Harper	c Ritchie b Maguire	27
J. Garner	c Hogan b Rackemann	10
M.A. Holding	not out	3
Extras	(B13, LB13, NB1)	27
Total		**498**

BOWLING

WEST INDIES	O	M	R	W		O	M	R	W	FALL OF WICKETS			
											AUS	WI	AUS
Marshall	18	2	70	1	—	17	5	51	3		1st	1st	2nd
Garner	18	5	34	1	—	20.5	2	83	5	1st	14	0	50
Holding	19.5	3	42	3	—	14	2	22	1	2nd	14	43	57
Harper	19	4	58	2	—	6	0	24	0	3rd	67	351	97
Baptiste	17	2	42	3	—	8	2	14	1	4th	78	390	116
Richards	5	0	7	0	—					5th	201	405	150
AUSTRALIA					—					6th	208	426	167
Lawson	29	4	125	2	—					7th	217	442	176
Rackemann	42.4	8	160	5	—					8th	224	468	185
Maguire	44	9	122	3	—					9th	246	491	185
Hogan	30	9	65	0	—					10th	262	498	200

FIFTH TEST MATCH
PLAYED AT KINGSTON, 28, 29, 30 APRIL, 1 MAY
WEST INDIES WON BY 10 WICKETS

AUSTRALIA

†W.B. Phillips c Dujon b Garner	12	b Garner	2
S.B. Smith c Greenidge b Marshall	9	absent hurt	—
A.R. Border c Dujon b Marshall	41	not out	60
G.M. Ritchie c Dujon b Marshall	5	b Holding	8
*K.J. Hughes c Harper b Holding	19	c Greenidge b Marshall	23
D.W. Hookes b Harper	36	c Dujon b Marshall	7
G.R.J. Matthews st Dujon b Harper	7	b Holding	7
T.G. Hogan c & b Garner	25	b Marshall	10
G.F. Lawson c Harper b Garner	15	b Marshall	4
R.M. Hogg not out	1	b Marshall	14
J.N. Maguire b Baptiste	9	b Garner	0
Extras (B8, LB4, W1, NB7)	20	(B17, LB4, NB4)	25
Total	**199**		**160**

WEST INDIES

C.G. Greenidge c Ritchie b Hogan	127	not out	32
D.L. Haynes b Hogan	60	not out	15
R.B. Richardson c Phillips b Lawson	0		
I.V.A Richards run out	2		
*C.H. Lloyd c Phillips b Lawson	20		
†P.J. Dujon c Phillips b Maguire	23		
M.D. Marshall c Hookes b Maguire	19		
E.A.E. Baptiste c Lawson b Maguire	27		
R.A. Harper c Phillips b Maguire	0		
J. Garner c Phillips b Lawson	7		
M.A. Holding not out	0		
Extras (B1, LB11, NB8)	20	(B2, LB3, NB3)	8
Total	**305**	**(0 wkt)**	**55**

BOWLING

WEST INDIES	O	M	R	W		O	M	R	W	FALL OF WICKETS		
											AUS	WI	AUS
Marshall	18	4	37	3	—	23	3	51	5		1st	1st	2nd
Garner	17	4	41	3	—	16.3	6	28	2		1st	22	162	7
Holding	12	2	43	1	—	11	4	20	2	2nd	23	169	15
Baptiste	11	3	40	1	—	6	3	11	0	3rd	34	174	27
Harper	20	8	26	2	—	9	2	25	0	4th	73	213	89
Richards	—	—	—	—	—	2	0	4	0	5th	113	228	109
AUSTRALIA					—					6th	124	260	125
Lawson	30	6	91	3	—	5	0	24	0	7th	142	274	131
Hogg	16	2	67	0	—	5.2	0	18	0	8th	181	274	159
Hogan	30	8	68	2	—	—	—	—	—	9th	190	297	160
Maguire	16.4	2	57	4	—	1	0	8	0	10th	199	305	—
Matthews	2	0	10	0	—	—	—	—	—				

Sri Lanka v New Zealand 1983–84

FIRST TEST MATCH

PLAYED AT KANDY, 9, 10, 11, 13, 14 MARCH (NO PLAY)
NEW ZEALAND WON BY 165 RUNS

NEW ZEALAND

*G.P. Howarth c de Alwis b John	62	16w b John		60
J.G. Wright lbw b John	45	c de Alwis b John		4
J.F. Reid c Kaluperuma b Amerasinghe	26	Cranatunga b de Silva		30
M.D. Crowe c Ratnayake b de Silva	26	st de Alwis b de Silva		8
J.J. Crowe c sub b John	20	c Amerasinghe b Kaluperuma		9
J.V. Coney lbw b Ratnayake	25	not out		3
R.J. Hadlee c Ratnayake b John	29	c sub b Kaluperuma		27
† I.D.S. Smith b Ranatunga	30	not out		31
B.L. Cairns c de Alwis b Ranatunga	0	c Wettimuny b de Silva		2
J.G. Bracewell c de Silva b John	2	c Amerasinghe b John		21
S.L. Boock not out	4			
Extras (B1, LB1, W5)	7	(B2, LB1, W3)		6
Total	**276**	(8 wkts dec)		**201**

SRI LANKA

S. Wettimuny c Coney b Hadlee	0	c Smith b Hadlee		5
E.R.N.S. Fernando c Hadlee b Boock	29	lbw b Hadlee		2
S.M.S. Kaluperuma c Howarth b Bracewell	18	c J.J. Crowe b Boock		5
R.J. Ratnayake c Smith b Hadlee	6	lbw b Boock		12
*L.R.D. Mendis c Bracewell b Hadlee	5	b Hadlee		0
R.S. Madugalle c M.D. Crowe b Hadlee	33	c Bracewell b Hadlee		2
A. Ranatunga c Bracewell b Cairns	20	c & b Bracewell		51
D.S. de Silva b Bracewell	11	c Coney b Boock		0
†R.G. de Alwis lbw b Boock	26	c Howarth b Boock		19
V.B. John not out	0	c Wright b Boock		0
A.M.J.G. Amerasinghe run out	34	not out		0
Extras (LB2, NB4)	6	(LB1)		1
Total	**215**			**97**

BOWLING

SRI LANKA	O	N	R	W		O	M	R	W	FALL OF WICKETS			
											NZ	SL	NZ	SL
John	29.1	7	86	5	—	17.5	1	73	3		1st	1st	2nd	2nd
Ratnayake	15	4	45	1	—	—	—	—	—	1st	97	0	14	3
Ranatunga	9	3	17	2	—	4	0	14	0	2nd	124	38	75	12
de Silva	29	6	69	1	—	21	2	59	3	3rd	163	55	111	12
Amerasinghe	12	3	45	1	—	8	2	32	0	4th	189	55	126	14
Kaluperuma	6	3	7	0	—	4	0	17	2	5th	210	61	133	18
NEW ZEALAND										6th	236	89	137	18
Hadlee	20.5	7	35	4	—	7	4	8	4	7th	266	120	167	55
Cairns	18	3	71	1	—	4	1	6	0	8th	266	132	167	97
M.D. Crowe	3	1	4	0	—	—	—	—	—	9th	272	155	—	97
Boock	23	7	63	2	—	9	3	28	5	10th	276	215	—	97
Bracewell	15	4	36	2	—	7	1	54	1					

SECOND TEST MATCH
PLAYED AT COLOMBO, 16, 17, 18, 20, 21 MARCH
MATCH DRAWN

SRI LANKA

S. Wettimuny c Coney b Chatfield	26	c Hadlee b Chatfield	65
E.R.N.S. Fernando b M.D. Crowe	8	c J.J. Crowe b Hadlee	0
S.M.S. Kaluperuma b Boock	23	c Wright b Hadlee	2
R.L. Dias run out	16	b Cairns	108
*L.R.D. Mendis b Hadlee	1	b Chatfield	36
R.S. Madugalle not out	44	c J.J. Crowe b Chatfield	36
A. Ranatunga c Smith b Cairns	6	run out	7
J.R. Ratnayeke lbw b Hadlee	22	c & b Hadlee	12
D.S. de Silva c Coney b Cairns	0	not out	13
†R.G. de Alwis c Smith b Cairns	2	b Chatfield	2
V.B. John c Smith b Cairns	0	not out	3
Extras (B5, LB7, W8, NB6)	26	(LB4, NB1)	5
Total	**174**	**(9 wkts dec)**	**289**

NEW ZEALAND

*G.P. Howarth b John	24	c Kaluperuma b John	10
J.G. Wright c Dias b John	20	c de Silva b Ranatunga	48
J.F. Reid c de Alwis b John	7	lbw b John	0
J.J. Crowe b Ratnayeke	50	c de Alwis b Ranatunga	16
J.V. Coney c John b de Silva	30	not out	20
R.J. Hadlee b Ratnayeke	19		
S.L. Boock c Madugalle b Ratnayeke	4		
M.D. Crowe c Kaluperuma b Ratnayeke	0	not out	19
†I.D.S. Smith c Kaluperuma b Ratnayeke	7		
B.L. Cairns lbw b de Silva	14		
E.J. Chatfield not out	9		
Extras (B4, LB6, W1, NB3)	14	(B4, LB4, NB2)	10
Total	**198**	**(4 wkts)**	**123**

BOWLING

NEW ZEALAND	O	M	R	W		O	M	R	W
Hadlee	22	12	27	2	—	30	13	58	3
Cairns	24.5	6	47	4	—	22	3	79	1
Chatfield	20	7	35	1	—	29	9	78	4
M.D. Crowe	13	5	21	1	—				
Boock	7	2	18	1	—	42	16	65	0
Coney	—					4	3	24	1
SRI LANKA									
John	24	1	89	3	—	21	11	26	2
Ratnayeke	21	8	42	5	—	21	11	17	0
Kaluperuma	1	0	3	0	—	6	3	10	0
Ranatunga	4	1	11	0	—	18	7	29	2
de Silva	14.3	6	39	2	—	19	10	31	0
Madugalle	—					1	1	0	0

FALL OF WICKETS

	SL 1st	NZ 1st	SL 2nd	NZ 2nd
1st	25	38	3	10
2nd	66	53	13	10
3rd	68	66	176	48
4th	69	127	209	89
5th	99	151	234	—
6th	111	166	244	—
7th	152	166	245	—
8th	153	171	278	—
9th	165	178	282	—
10th	174	198	—	—

THIRD TEST MATCH
PLAYED AT COLOMBO, 24, 25, 26, 28, 29 MARCH
NEW ZEALAND WON BY AN INNINGS AND 61 RUNS

SRI LANKA

S. Wettimuny b Hadlee	4	c Coney b Hadlee	2
S.M.S. Kaluperuma b Hadlee	16	c Coney b Hadlee	18
J.R. Ratnayeke lbw b Hadlee	0	b Boock	2
R.L. Dias c Smith b Chatfield	10	absent hurt	—
*L.R.D. Mendis c J.J. Crowe b Chatfield	19	b Boock	10
R.S. Madugalle not out	89	c Wright b Bracewell	38
A. Ranatunga c sub (Edgar) b Chatfield	37	c Wright b Boock	50
D.S. de Silva c Smith b Hadlee	17	c Smith b Hadlee	1
†R.G. de Alwis c Boock b Hadlee	28	c Bracewell b Hadlee	10
A.M.J.G. Amerasinghe c Wright b Chatfield	15	b Hadlee	5
V.B. John c & b Chatfield	12	not out	0
Extras (LB4, NB5)	9	(LB1, NB5)	6
Total	**256**		**142**

NEW ZEALAND

*G.P. Howarth lbw b Ratnayeke	7
J.G. Wright c de Alwis b Ratnayeke	18
J.F. Reid c & b Amerasinghe	180
M.D. Crowe c de Alwis b Ratnayeke	45
S.L. Boock b John	35
J.J. Crowe lbw b John	18
J.V. Coney c de Alwis b Amerasinghe	92
R.J. Hadlee c Kaluperuma b de Silva	0
†I.D.S. Smith b John	42
J.G. Bracewell c Kaluperuma b de Silva	0
E.J. Chatfield not out	1
Extras (B4, LB10, W2, NB5)	21
Total	**459**

BOWLING

NEW ZEALAND	O	M	R	W		O	M	R	W
Hadlee	22	4	73	5	—	16	7	29	5
Chatfield	22	5	63	5	—	9	2	27	0
M.D. Crowe	6	2	22	0	—	5	2	13	0
Boock	20	9	51	0	—	16	2	32	3
Bracewell	9	2	31	0	—	11	4	35	1
Coney	3	0	7	0	—				
SRI LANKA									
John	37	8	99	3					
Ratnayeke	40	9	128	3					
Ranatunga	16	5	18	0					
de Silva	42	4	95	2					
Amerasinghe	30	4	73	2					
Kaluperuma	10	2	25	0					

FALL OF WICKETS

	SL 1st	NZ 1st	SL 2nd
1st	4	13	6
2nd	4	32	63
3rd	22	132	63
4th	32	214	79
5th	63	253	101
6th	182	387	105
7th	222	391	136
8th	227	426	138
9th	249	436	142
10th	256	459	—

England v West Indies 1984

FIRST CORNHILL TEST MATCH

PLAYED AT EDGBASTON, 14, 15, 16 JUNE

WEST INDIES WON BY AN INNINGS AND 180 RUNS

ENGLAND

G. Fowler c Dujon b Garner	0	lbw b Garner	7
T.A. Lloyd retired hurt	10	absent hurt	—
D.W. Randall b Garner	0	c Lloyd b Garner	1
*D.I. Gower c Harper b Holding	10	c Dujon b Garner	12
A.J. Lamb c Lloyd b Baptiste	15	c Richards b Marshall	13
I.T. Botham c Garner b Harper	64	lbw b Garner	38
G. Miller c Dujon b Garner	22	c Harper b Marshall	11
D.R. Pringle c Dujon b Holding	4	not out	46
†P.R. Downton lbw b Garner	33	c Greenidge b Harper	56
N.G.B. Cook c Lloyd b Marshall	2	run out	9
R.G.D. Willis not out	10	c Dujon b Garner	22
Extras (B8, LB5, W8)	21	(B1, LB5, W4, NB10)	20
Total	**191**		**235**

WEST INDIES

C.G. Greenidge lbw b Willis	19
D.L. Haynes lbw b Willis	8
H.A. Gomes c Miller b Pringle	143
I.V.A. Richards c Randall b Cook	117
†P.J. Dujon c Gower b Miller	23
*C.H. Lloyd c Pringle b Botham	71
M.D. Marshall lbw b Pringle	2
R.A. Harper b Pringle	14
E.A.E. Baptiste not out	87
M.A. Holding c Willis b Pringle	69
J. Garner c Lamb b Pringle	0
Extras (B6, LB17, W2, NB28)	53
Total	**606**

BOWLING

WEST INDIES	O	N	R	W		O	M	R	W	FALL OF WICKETS			
Marshall	14	4	37	1	—	23	7	65	2		*ENG*	*WI*	*ENG*
Garner	14.3	2	53	4	—	23.5	7	55	5		*1st*	*1st*	*2nd*
Holding	16	4	44	2	—	12	3	29	0	1st	1	34	17
Baptiste	11	3	28	1	—	5	1	18	0	2nd	5	35	21
Harper	4	1	8	1	—	13	3	48	1	3rd	45	241	37
ENGLAND					—					4th	49	294	65
Willis	25	3	108	2	—	—	—	—	—	5th	89	418	127
Botham	34	7	127	1	—	—	—	—	—	6th	103	418	138
Pringle	31	5	108	5	—	—	—	—	—	7th	168	421	181
Cook	38	6	127	1	—	—	—	—	—	8th	173	455	193
Miller	15	1	83	1	—	—	—	—	—	9th	191	605	235
										10th	—	606	—

SECOND CORNHILL TEST MATCH

PLAYED AT LORD'S 28, 29, 30 JUNE, 2, 3, JULY
WEST INDIES WON BY 9 WICKETS

ENGLAND

G. Fowler c Harper b Baptiste	106	lbw b Small	11
B.C. Broad c Dujon b Marshall	55	c Harper b Garner	0
*D.I. Gower lbw b Marshall	3	c Lloyd b Small	21
A.J. Lamb lbw b Marshall	23	c Dujon b Marshall	110
M.W. Gatting lbw b Marshall	1	lbw b Marshall	29
I.T. Botham c Richards b Baptiste	30	lbw b Garner	81
†P.R. Downton not out	23	lbw b Small	4
G. Miller run out	0	b Harper	9
D.R. Pringle lbw b Garner	2	lbw b Garner	8
N.A. Foster c Harper b Marshall	6	not out	9
R.G.D. Willis b Marshall	2		
Extras (B4, LB14, W2, NB15)	35	(B4, LB7, W1, NB6)	18
Total	**286**	**(9 wkts dec)**	**300**

WEST INDIES

C.G. Greenidge c Miller b Botham	1	not out	214
D.L. Haynes lbw b Botham	12	run out	17
H.A. Gomes c Gatting b Botham	10	not out	92
I.V.A. Richards lbw b Botham	72		
*C.H. Lloyd lbw b Botham	39		
†P.J. Dujon c Fowler b Botham	8		
M.D. Marshall c Pringle b Willis	29		
E.A.E. Baptiste c Downton b Willis	44		
R.A. Harper c Gatting b Botham	8		
J. Garner c Downton b Botham	6		
M.A. Small not out	3		
Extras (LB5, W1, NB7)	13	(B4, LB4, NB13)	21
Total	**245**	**(1 wkt)**	**344**

BOWLING

WEST INDIES	O	M	R	W		O	M	R	W
Garner	32	10	67	1	—	30.3	3	91	3
Small	9	0	38	0	—	12	2	40	3
Marshall	36.5	10	85	6	—	22	6	85	2
Baptiste	20	6	36	2	—	26	8	48	0
Harper	8	0	25	0	—	8	1	18	1
ENGLAND					—				
Willis	19	5	48	2	—	15	5	48	0
Botham	27.4	6	103	8	—	20.1	2	117	0
Pringle	11	0	54	0	—	8	0	44	0
Foster	6	2	13	0	—	12	0	69	0
Miller	2	0	14	0	—	11	0	45	0

FALL OF WICKETS

	ENG	WI	ENG	WI
	1st	1st	2nd	2nd
1st	101	1	5	57
2nd	106	18	33	—
3rd	183	35	36	—
4th	185	138	88	—
5th	243	147	216	—
6th	248	173	230	—
7th	251	213	273	—
8th	255	231	290	—
9th	264	241	300	—
10th	286	245	—	—

THIRD CORNHILL TEST MATCH

PLAYED AT HEADINGLEY 12, 13, 14, 16 JULY
WEST INDIES WON BY 8 WICKETS

ENGLAND

G. Fowler lbw b Garner	10	c & b Marshall	50
B.C. Broad c Lloyd b Harper	32	c Baptiste b Marshall	2
V.P. Terry c Harper b Holding	8	lbw b Garner	1
*D.I. Gower lbw b Garner	2	c Dujon b Harper	43
A.J. Lamb b Harper	100	lbw b Marshall	3
I.T. Botham c Dujon b Baptiste	45	c Dujon b Garner	14
†P.R. Downton c Lloyd b Harper	17	c Dujon b Marshall	27
D.R. Pringle c Haynes b Holding	19	lbw b Marshall	2
P.J.W. Allott b Holding	3	lbw b Marshall	4
N.G.B. Cook b Holding	1	c Lloyd b Marshall	0
R.G.D. Willis not out	4	not out	5
Extras (B4, LB7, NB18)	29	(LB6, NB2)	8
Total	**270**		**159**

WEST INDIES

C.G. Greenidge c Botham b Willis	10	c Terry b Cook	49
D.L. Haynes b Allott	18	c Fowler b Cook	43
H.A. Gomes not out	104	not out	2
I.V.A. Richards c Pringle b Allott	15	not out	22
*C.H. Lloyd c Gower b Cook	48		
†P.J. Dujon lbw b Allott	26		
E.A.E. Baptiste c Broad b Allott	0		
R.A. Harper c Downton b Allott	0		
M.A. Holding c Allott b Willis	59		
J. Garner run out	0		
M.D. Marshall c Botham b Allott	4		
Extras (LB3, NB15)	18	(LB2, NB13)	15
Total	**302**	(2 wkts)	**131**

BOWLING

WEST INDIES	O	M	R	W		O	M	R	W	FALL OF WICKETS				
											ENG	WI	ENG	WI
Garner	30	11	73	2	—	16	7	37	2		1st	1st	2nd	2nd
Marshall	6	4	6	0	—	26	9	53	7	1st	13	16	10	106
Holding	29.2	8	70	4	—	7	1	31	0	2nd	43	43	13	108
Baptiste	13	1	45	1	—	—	—	—	—	3rd	53	78	104	—
Harper	19	6	47	3	—	16	8	30	1	4th	87	148	106	—
ENGLAND										5th	172	201	107	—
Willis	18	1	123	2	—	8	1	40	0	6th	236	206	135	—
Allott	26.5	7	61	6	—	7	2	24	0	7th	237	206	138	—
Botham	7	0	45	0	—	—	—	—	—	8th	244	287	140	—
Pringle	13	3	26	0	—	8.3	2	25	0	9th	254	290	146	—
Cook	9	1	29	0	—	9	2	27	2	10th	270	302	159	—

FOURTH CORNHILL TEST MATCH

PLAYED AT OLD TRAFFORD, 26, 27, 28, 30, 31 JULY
WEST INDIES WON BY AN INNINGS AND 64 RUNS

WEST INDIES

C.G. Greenidge c Downton b Pocock	223	
D.L. Haynes c Cowans b Botham	2	
H.A. Gomes c Botham b Allott	30	
I.V.A. Richards c Cook b Allott	1	
*C.H. Lloyd c Downton b Allott	1	
†P.J. Dujon c Downton b Botham	101	
W.W. Davis b Pocock	77	
E.A.E. Baptiste c Downton b Pocock	6	
R.A. Harper not out	39	
M.A. Holding b Cook	0	
J. Garner c Terry b Pocock	7	
Extras (B4, LB6, W2, NB1)	13	
Total	**500**	

ENGLAND

G. Fowler b Baptiste	38	b Holding	0
B.C. Broad b Davis	42	lbw b Harper	21
V.P. Terry b Garner	7	absent hurt	—
*D.I. Gower c Dujon b Baptiste	4	not out	57
A.J. Lamb not out	100	b Harper	9
I.T. Botham c Garner b Baptiste	6	c Haynes b Harper	1
†P.R. Downton c Harper b Garner	0	b Harper	24
P.J.W. Allott c Gomes b Davis	26	b Garner	14
N.G.B. Cook b Holding	13	c Dujon b Garner	0
P.I. Pocock b Garner	0	c Garner b Harper	0
N.G. Cowans b Garner	0	b Harper	14
Extras (B5, LB21, NB18)	44	(B9, LB3, W1, NB3)	16
Total	**280**		**156**

BOWLING

ENGLAND	O	M	R	W		O	M	R	W	FALL OF WICKETS			
											WI	ENG	ENG
Botham	29	5	100	2	—						1st	1st	2nd
Cowans	19	2	76	0	—								
Allott	28	9	76	3	—					1st	11	90	0
Cook	39	6	114	1	—					2nd	60	112	39
Pocock	45.3	14	121	4	—					3rd	62	117	77
WEST INDIES					—					4th	70	138	99
Garner	22.2	7	51	4	—	12	4	25	2	5th	267	147	101
Davis	20	2	71	2	—	3	1	6	0	6th	437	228	125
Harper	23	10	33	0	—	28.4	12	57	6	7th	443	257	127
Holding	21	2	50	1	—	11	2	21	1	8th	470	278	128
Baptiste	19	8	31	3	—	11	5	29	0	9th	471	278	156
Richards					—	1	0	2	0	10th	500	280	—

FIFTH CORNHILL TEST MATCH

PLAYED AT THE OVAL, 9, 10, 11, 13, 14 AUGUST

WEST INDIES WON BY 172 RUNS

WEST INDIES

C.G. Greenidge lbw b Botham	22	c Botham b Agnew	34
D.L. Haynes b Allott	10	b Botham	125
H.A. Gomes c Botham b Ellison	18	c Tavaré b Ellison	1
I.V.A. Richards c Allott b Botham	8	lbw b Agnew	15
†P.J. Dujon c Tavaré b Botham	3	c Lamb b Ellison	49
*C.H. Lloyd not out	60	c Downton b Ellison	36
M.D. Marshall c Gower b Ellison	0	c Lamb b Botham	12
E.A.E. Baptiste c Fowler b Allott	32	c Downton b Allott	5
R.A. Harper b Botham	18	c Downton b Allott	17
M.A. Holding lbw b Botham	0	lbw b Botham	30
J. Garner c Downton b Allott	6	not out	10
Extras (B1, LB4, W7, NB1)	13	(LB12)	12
Total	**190**		**346**

ENGLAND

G. Fowler c Richards b Baptiste	31	c Richards b Marshall	7
B.C. Broad b Garner	4	c Greenidge b Holding	39
P.I. Pocock c Greenidge b Marshall	0	c & b Holding	0
C.J. Tavaré c Dujon b Holding	16	c Richards b Garner	49
*D.I. Gower c Dujon b Holding	12	lbw b Holding	7
A.J. Lamb lbw b Marshall	12	c Haynes b Holding	1
I.T. Botham c Dujon b Marshall	14	c Marshall b Garner	54
†P.R. Downton c Lloyd b Garner	16	lbw b Garner	10
R.M. Ellison not out	20	c Holding b Garner	13
P.J.W. Allott b Marshall	16	c Lloyd b Holding	4
J.P. Agnew b Marshall	5	not out	2
Extras (B2, LB4, NB10)	16	(LB2, W1, NB13)	16
Total	**162**		**202**

BOWLING

ENGLAND	O	M	R	W		O	M	R	W	FALL OF WICKETS			
											WI	*ENG*	*WI*	*ENG*
Agnew	12	3	46	0	—	14	1	51	2		*1st*	*1st*	*2nd*	*2nd*
Allott	17	7	25	3	—	26	1	96	2	1st	19	10	51	15
Botham	23	8	72	5	—	22.3	2	103	3	2nd	45	22	52	75
Ellison	18	3	34	2	—	26	7	60	3	3rd	64	45	69	88
Pocock	—	—	—	—	—	8	3	24	0	4th	64	64	132	90
WEST INDIES					—					5th	67	83	214	135
Garner	18	6	37	2	—	18.4	5	51	4	6th	70	84	237	
Marshall	17.5	5	35	5	—	22	5	71	1	7th	124	116	264	
Holding	13	2	55	2	—	13	2	43	5	8th	154	133	293	
Baptiste	12	4	19	1	—	8	3	11	0	9th	154	156	329	
Harper	1	1	0	0	—	8	5	10	0	10th	190	162	346	

24

TEST MATCH AVERAGES

ENGLAND

	M	I	NO	Runs	HS	Avge	100	50	Ct	St
A.J. Lamb	5	10	1	386	110	42.88	3	—	3	—
I.T. Botham	5	10	0	347	81	34.70	—	3	5	—
R.M. Ellison	1	2	1	33	20*	33.00	—	—	—	—
C.J. Tavaré	1	2	0	65	49	32.50	—	—	2	—
G. Fowler	5	10	0	260	106	26.00	1	1	3	—
B.C. Broad	4	8	0	195	55	24.37	—	1	1	—
P.R. Downton	5	10	1	210	56	23.33	—	1	10	—
R.G.D. Willis	3	5	3	43	22	21.50	—	—	1	—
D.I. Gower	5	10	1	171	57*	19.00	—	1	3	—
D.R. Pringle	3	6	1	81	46*	16.20	—	—	3	—
N.A. Foster	1	2	1	15	9*	15.00	—	—	—	—
M.W. Gatting	1	2	0	30	29	15.00	—	—	2	—
P.J.W. Allott	3	6	0	67	26	11.16	—	—	2	—
G. Miller	2	4	0	42	22	10.50	—	—	2	—
T.A. Lloyd	1	1	1	10	10*	—	—	—	—	—
J.P. Agnew	1	1	0	7	5	7.00	—	—	—	—
N.G. Cowans	1	2	0	14	14	7.00	—	—	1	—
V.P. Terry	2	3	0	16	8	5.33	—	—	2	—
N.G.B. Cook	3	6	0	25	13	4.16	—	—	1	—
D.W. Randall	1	2	0	1	1	0.50	—	—	1	—
P.I. Pocock	2	4	0	0	0	0.00	—	—	—	—

	Overs	Mdns	Runs	Wkts	Avge	Best	5 wI	10 wM
R.M. Ellison	44	10	94	5	18.80	3/60	—	—
P.J.W. Allott	104.5	26	282	14	20.14	6/61	1	—
I.T. Botham	163.2	30	667	19	35.10	8/103	2	—
P.I. Pocock	53.3	17	145	4	36.25	4/121	—	—
J.P. Agnew	26	4	97	2	48.50	2/51	—	—
D.R. Pringle	71.3	10	257	5	51.40	5/108	1	—
N.G.B. Cook	95	15	297	5	59.40	2/27	—	—
R.G.D. Willis	85	15	367	6	61.16	2/48	—	—
G. Miller	28	1	142	1	142.00	1/83	—	—
N.G. Cowans	19	2	76	0	—	—	—	—
N.A. Foster	18	2	82	0	—	—	—	—

WEST INDIES

	Overs	Mdns	Runs	Wkts	Avge	Best	5 wI	10 wM
M.D. Marshall	167.4	50	437	24	18.20	7/53	3	—
J. Garner	217.5	60	540	29	18.62	5/55	1	—
R.A. Harper	128.4	47	276	13	21.23	6/57	1	—
M.A. Holding	122.2	24	343	15	22.86	5/43	1	—
M.A. Small	21	2	78	3	26.00	3/40	—	—
E.A.E. Baptiste	125	39	265	8	33.12	3/31	—	—
W.W. Davis	23	3	77	2	38.50	2/71	—	—
I.V.A. Richards	1	0	2	0	—	—	—	—

WEST INDIES

	M	I	NO	Runs	HS	Avge	100	50	Ct	St
C.G. Greenidge	5	8	1	572	223	81.71	2	—	3	—
H.A. Gomes	5	8	3	400	143	80.00	2	1	1	—
W.W. Davis	1	1	0	77	77	77.00	—	1	—	—
C.H. Lloyd	5	6	1	255	71	51.00	—	2	9	—
I.V.A. Richards	5	7	1	250	117	41.66	1	1	5	—
P.J. Dujon	5	6	0	210	101	35.00	1	—	16	—
E.A.E. Baptiste	5	6	1	174	87*	34.80	—	1	1	—
M.A. Holding	4	5	0	158	69	31.60	—	2	2	—
D.L. Haynes	5	8	0	235	125	29.37	1	—	3	—
R.A. Harper	5	6	1	96	39*	19.20	—	—	8	—
M.D. Marshall	4	5	0	47	29	9.40	—	—	2	—
J. Garner	5	6	1	29	10*	5.80	—	—	3	—
M.A. Small	1	1	1	3	3*	—	—	—	—	—

LEADING CAREER AVERAGES

The following are the abbreviated figures of the leading batsmen and bowlers based on their career averages, and fielders and wicket-keepers based on the number of their catches and dismissals. The figures are complete to the end of the 1984 season and the full career records will be found in the main tables. The qualification for inclusion for batsmen and bowlers is 100 innings and 100 wickets respectively. Only those players likely to play first-class county cricket in 1985 have been included.

BATTING AND BOWLING

BATSMEN	Runs	Avge	BOWLER	Wkts	Avge
G. Boycott	45,777	56.44	J. Garner	665	17.74
Javed Miandad	20,416	52.89	M.D. Marshall	709	18.28
Zaheer Abbas	33,844	52.47	R.J. Hadlee	977	18.77
I.V.A. Richards	24,089	49.26	D.L. Underwood	2,301	19.78
M.D. Crowe	5,359	45.41	G.S. Le Roux	587	20.25
A.J. Lamb	15,058	48.57	M. Hendrick	770	20.50
C.H. Lloyd	29,865	49.20	S.T. Clarke	634	20.87
A.I. Kallicharran	28,096	45.21	R.W. Hanley	398	20.91
C.G. Greenidge	26,492	45.20	W.W. Daniel	670	21.22
M.W. Gatting	12,833	44.09	C.E.B. Rice	712	21.97
D.L. Amiss	39,118	43.85	Imran Khan	995	22.10
G.A. Gooch	18,963	42.14			

FIELDING AND WICKET-KEEPING

FIELDERS	Ct	WICKET-KEEPERS	Total	Ct	St
K.W.R. Fletcher	586	A.P.E. Knott	1,290	1,158	132
C.T. Radley	485	D.L. Bairstow	886	770	116
J.A. Ormrod	396	G. Sharp	635	548	87
J.F. Steele	393	G.W. Humpage	448	396	52
C.G. Greenidge	387	I.J. Gould	443	381	62
D.L. Amiss	374	B.N. French	418	377	41

England v Sri Lanka 1984

PLAYED AT LORD'S, 23, 24, 25, 27, 28 AUGUST
MATCH DRAWN
SRI LANKA

S. Wettimuny c Downton b Allott	190	c Gower b Botham	13
†S.A.R. Silva lbw b Botham	8	not out	102
R.S. Madugalle b Ellison	5	b Botham	3
R.L. Dias c Lamb b Pocock	32	lbw b Botham	38
A. Ranatunga b Agnew	84	lbw b Botham	0
*L.R.D. Mendis c Fowler b Pocock	111	c Fowler b Botham	94
P.A. de Silva c Downton b Agnew	16	c Downton b Pocock	3
A.L.F. de Mel not out	20	c Ellison b Botham	14
J.R. Ratnayeke not out	5	not out	7
D.S. de Silva did not bat			
V.B. John did not bat			
Extras (B2, LB8, W2, NB8)	20	(B5, LB4, NB11)	20
Total (7 wkts dec)	491	(7 wkts dec)	294

ENGLAND

G. Fowler c Madugalle b John	25
B.C. Broad c Silva b de Mel	86
C.J. Tavaré c Ranatunga b D.S. de Silva	14
*D.I. Gower c Silva b de Mel	55
A.J. Lamb c Dias b John	107
I.T. Botham c sub (Vonhagt) b John	6
R.M. Ellison c Ratnayeke b D.S. de Silva	41
†P.R. Downton c Dias b de Mel	10
P.J.W. Allott b de Mel	0
P.I. Pocock c Silva b John	2
J.P. Agnew not out	1
Extras (B5, LB7, W5, NB6)	23
Total	370

BOWLING

ENGLAND	O	M	R	W		O	M	R	W	FALL OF WICKETS			
											SL	ENG	SL
Agnew	32	3	123	2	—	11	3	54	0		1st	1st	2nd
Botham	29	6	114	1	—	27	6	90	6	1st	17	49	19
Ellison	28	6	70	1	—	7	0	36	0	2nd	43	105	27
Pocock	41	17	75	2	—	29	10	78	1	3rd	144	190	111
Allott	36	7	89	1	—	1	0	2	0	4th	292	210	118
Lamb	—	—	—	—	—	1	0	6	0	5th	442	218	118
Tavaré	—	—	—	—	—	3	3	0	0	6th	456	305	216
Fowler	—	—	—	—	—	1	0	8	0	7th	464	354	276
SRI LANKA					—					8th	—	354	—
de Mel	37	10	110	4	—	—	—	—	—	9th	—	369	—
John	39.1	12	98	4	—	—	—	—	—	10th	—	370	—
Ratnayeke	22	5	50	0	—	—	—	—	—				
D.S. de Silva	45	16	85	2	—	—	—	—	—				
Ranatunga	1	1	0	0	—	—	—	—	—				
Madugalle	3	0	4	0	—	—	—	—	—				

Pakistan v India 1984-85

FIRST TEST MATCH

PLAYED AT LAHORE 17, 18, 19, 21, 22 OCTOBER MATCH DRAWN

PAKISTAN

Mohsin Khan b Chetan Sharma	4	
Mudassar Nazar c Gavaskar b Chetan Sharma	15	
Qasim Omar c Amarnath b Shastri	46	
Javed Miandad c Amarnath b Chetan Sharma	34	
*Zaheer Abbas not out	168	
Salim Malik c & b Shastri	45	
Wasim Raja c Amarnath b Kapil Dev	3	
†Ashraf Ali c Gavaskar b Gaekwad	65	
Tauseef Ahmed c Gavaskar b Maninder Singh	10	
Jalaluddin lbw b Shastri	2	
Azeem Hafeez not out	17	
Extras (LB7, W1, NB11)	19	
Total (9 wkts dec)	**428**	

INDIA

*S.M. Gavaskar c Salim b Azeem	48	lbw b Jalaluddin	37
A.D. Gaekwad b Jalaluddin	4	c Salim b Tauseef	60
D.B. Vengsarkar c Ashraf b Azeem	41	c Mudassar b Azeem	28
M. Amarnath b Wasim	36	not out	101
S.M. Patil c Salim b Azeem	0	b Jalaluddin	7
R.J. Shastri lbw b Azeem	0	lbw b Salim	71
Kapil Dev lbw b Azeem	3	not out	33
R.M.H. Binny lbw b Mudassar	0	lbw b Wasim	13
†S.M.H. Kirmani c sub (Ramiz) b Mudassar	2		
Chetan Sharma b Azeem	4		
Maninder Singh not out	4		
Extras (B2, LB7, W1, NB4)	14	(B6, LB7, W4, NB4)	21
Total	**156**	(6 wkts)	**371**

BOWLING

INDIA	O	M	R	W	O	M	R	W	FALL OF WICKETS			
										PAK	IND	PAK
Kapil Dev	30	4	104	1	—	—	—	—		1st	1st	2nd
Chetan Sharma	29	2	94	3	—	—	—	—	1st	6	7	85
Binny	8	1	20	0	—	—	—	1	2nd	54	94	114
Maninder Singh	40	10	90	1	—	—	—	—	3rd	100	112	148
Shastri	46	13	90	3	—	—	—	—	4th	110	114	164
Amarnath	4	0	19	0	—	—	—	—	5th	195	114	290
Gaekwad	1	0	4	1	—	—	—	—	6th	212	119	315
PAKISTAN					—				7th	354	120	—
Jalaluddin	17	5	41	1	24	3	61	2	8th	384	130	—
Azeem	23	7	46	6	43	12	114	1	9th	397	135	—
Mudassar	16	2	31	2	14	3	34	0	10th	—	156	—
Tauseef	13	3	19	0	50	19	93	1				
Wasim	5.3	0	10	1	19	4	46	1				
Salim	—	—	—	—	5	2	6	1				
Javed	—	—	—	—	1	0	4	0				

SECOND TEST MATCH
PLAYED AT FAISALABAD 24, 25, 26, 28, 29 OCTOBER
MATCH DRAWN

INDIA

*S.M. Gavaskar c Qasim b Abdul	35
A.D. Gaekwad c & b Manzoor	74
D.B. Vengsarkar c Mohsin b Abdul	5
M. Amarnath hit wicket b Azeem	37
S.M. Patil c Zaheer b Mudassar	127
R.J. Shastri c Ashraf b Abdul	139
Kapil Dev c Ashraf b Azeem	16
S. Madan Lal c Ashraf b Azeem	0
†S.M.H. Kirmani c sub (Shoaib) b Azeem	6
N.S. Yadav c Salim b Abdul	29
Chetan Sharma not out	18
Extras (B1, LB6, NB7)	14
Total	**500**

PAKISTAN

Mohsin Khan c Gavaskar b Chetan Sharma	59
Mudassar Nazar c Kirmani b Yadav	199
Qasim Omar c Yadav b Gaekwad	210
Javed Miandad st Kirmani b Shastri	16
*Zaheer Abbas c Kirmani b Madan Lal	26
Salim Malik not out	102
Manzoor Elahi run out	26
†Ashraf Ali not out	9
Abdul Qadir did not bat	
Jalaluddin did not bat	
Azeem Hafeez did not bat	
Extras (B7, LB6, W1, NB13)	27
Total (6 wkts)	**674**

BOWLING

PAKISTAN	O	M	R	W	O	M	R	W	FALL OF WICKETS
Jalaluddin	34	5	103	0	—	—	—	—	*IND* *PAK*
Azeem	44	9	137	4	—	—	—	—	*1st* *1st*
Mudassar	21	3	74	1	—	—	—	—	1st 88 141
Manzoor	25	5	74	1	—	—	—	—	2nd 100 391
Abdul	38	8	104	4	—	—	—	—	3rd 148 430
Salim	1	0	1	0	—	—	—	—	4th 170 494
INDIA					—				5th 370 603
Kapil Dev	5	0	22	0	—	—	—	—	6th 412 650
Chetan Sharma	32	0	139	1	—	—	—	—	7th 420 —
Madan Lal	27	2	94	1	—	—	—	—	8th 441 —
Yadav	74	16	196	1	—	—	—	—	9th 461 —
Shastri	50	14	99	1	—	—	—	—	10th 505 —
Gaekwad	27	5	75	1	—	—	—	—	
Amarnath	8.5	0	36	0	—	—	—	—	

Pakistan v New Zealand 1984-85

FIRST TEST MATCH

PLAYED AT LAHORE 16, 17, 18, 19, 20 NOVEMBER
PAKISTAN WON BY 6 WICKETS

NEW ZEALAND

J.J. Crowe c Anil b Mudassar		0	c & b Iqbal	43
B.A. Edgar b Mudassar		3	lbw b Azeem	26
M.D. Crowe c Qasim b Abdul		55	c sub (Ramiz) b Iqbal	33
J.G. Wright c Anil b Azeem		1	run out	65
J.F. Reid lbw b Mudassar		2	b Abdul	6
*J.V. Coney c Mohsin b Iqbal		7	c Anil b Azeem	26
E.J. Gray c sub (Ramiz) b Iqbal		12	c Mudassar b Abdul	6
†I.D.S. Smith c Iqbal b Azeem		41	not out	11
D.A. Stirling b Iqbal		16	c Anil b Iqbal	10
S.L. Boock c Javed b Iqbal		13	c Javed b Abdul	0
E.J. Chatfield not out		6	c Qasim b Iqbal	0
Extras (B1)		1	(B8, LB2, W1, NB4)	15
		—		—
Total		**157**		**241**

PAKISTAN

Mudassar Nazar c Reid b Stirling		26	b Boock	16
Mohsin Khan c Reid b Gray		58	c & b Gray	38
Qasim Omar c J.J. Crowe b Boock		13	lbw b Stirling	20
Javed Miandad c Reid b Gray		11	not out	48
*Zaheer Abbas c M.D. Crowe b Boock		43	c Smith b Gray	31
Salim Malik lbw b Stirling		10	not out	24
Abdul Qadir c Coney b Chatfield		14		
†Anil Dalpat b M.D. Crowe		11		
Iqbal Qasim c Coney b Chatfield		22		
Azeem Hafeez c Boock b Chatfield		11		
Tauseef Ahmed not out		0		
Extras (NB2)		2	(LB4)	4
		—		—
Total		**221**	(4 wkts)	**181**

BOWLING

PAKISTAN	O	M	R	W		O	M	R	W	FALL OF WICKETS				
											NZ	PAK	NZ	PAK
Mudassar	11	5	8	3	—	10	1	30	0		1st	2nd	2nd
Azeem	18	9	40	2	—	13	5	37	2	1st	0	54	66	33
Abdul	21	6	58	1	—	26	4	82	3	2nd	11	84	123	77
Iqbal	22.4	10	41	4	—	29.5	10	65	4	3rd	28	103	138	77
Tauseef	2	0	9	0	—	4	0	17	0	4th	31	114	140	138
N. ZEALAND										5th	50	144	208	—
Stirling	27	7	71	4	—	15.1	2	60	1	6th	76	165	209	—
M.D. Crowe	7	1	21	1						7th	108	188	220	—
Gray	8	1	19	2	—	18	0	45	2	8th	124	189	220	—
Chatfield	28.2	7	57	3	—	13	7	12	0	9th	146	212	235	—
Boock	24	7	53	2	—	17	2	56	1	10th	157	221	241	—
Coney					—	2	1	4	0					

SECOND TEST MATCH

PLAYED AT HYDERABAD 25, 26, 27, 29 NOVEMBER
PAKISTAN WON BY 7 WICKETS

NEW ZEALAND

J.G. Wright c Anil b Iqbal	18	c Anil b Iqbal	22
B.A. Edgar c Salim b Abdul	11	lbw b Mudassar	1
M.D. Crowe b Abdul	19	st Anil b Iqbal	21
J.F. Reid b Azeem	106	lbw b Abdul	21
*J.V. Coney c Manzoor b Abdul	6	b Iqbal	5
J.J. Crowe c Salim b Zaheer	39	lbw b Iqbal	57
†I.D.S. Smith c Iqbal b Zaheer	6	c Mudassar b Azeem	34
E.J. Gray lbw b Mudassar	25	c Qasim b Iqbal	5
J.G. Bracewell c Mudassar b Abdul	0	c & b Abdul	0
D.A. Stirling not out	11	b Abdul	11
S.L. Boock lbw b Abdul	12	not out	4
Extras (B13, NB1)	14	(B1, LB4, NB3)	8
Total	**267**		**189**

PAKISTAN

Mudassar Nazar c M.D. Crowe b Bracewell	28	c Coney b Boock	106
Mohsin Khan c Gray b Boock	9	b M.D. Crowe	2
Qasim Omar c Coney b Boock	45	lbw b M.D. Crowe	0
Javed Miandad c J.J. Crowe b Boock	104	not out	103
†Anil Dalpat b Bracewell	1		
*Zaheer Abbas st Smith b Boock	2		
Salim Malik b Boock	1		
Manzoor Elahi c J.J. Crowe b Boock	19	not out	4
Abdul Qadir lbw b Boock	11		
Iqbal Qasim c J.J. Crowe b Bracewell	8		
Azeem Hafeez not out	0		
Extras (LB2)	2	(B5, LB7, W3)	15
Total	**230**	**(3 wkts)**	**230**

BOWLING

PAKISTAN	O	M	R	W		O	M	R	W	FALL OF WICKETS			
										NZ	PAK	NZ	PAK
										1st	1st	2nd	2nd
Mudassar	7	4	14	1	—	5	2	8	1	1st 30	26	2	14
Azeem	18	4	29	1	—	8	3	33	1	2nd 30	50	34	14
Iqbal	33	6	80	1	—	24.1	7	79	5	3rd 74	153	58	226
Abdul	40.3	11	108	5	—	18	3	59	3	4th 88	154	71	—
Manzur	2	1	2	0	—	—	—	—	—	5th 150	159	80	—
Zaheer	8	1	21	2	—	1	0	5	0	6th 164	169	125	—
N. ZEALAND										7th 237	191	149	—
Stirling	3	1	11	0	—	4	0	26	0	8th 239	215	149	—
M.D. Crowe	3	0	8	0	—	8	1	29	2	9th 243	230	167	—
Coney	10	4	8	0	—	4	1	9	0	10th 267	230	189	—
Boock	37	12	87	7	—	23.4	4	69	1				
Bracewell	16.1	3	44	3	—	13	2	36	0				
Gray	22	4	70	0	—	11	0	49	0				

THIRD TEST MATCH
PLAYED AT KARACHI 10, 11, 12, 14, 15 DECEMBER
MATCH DRAWN

PAKISTAN

Mudassar Nazar c Smith b Stirling	5	c McEwan b Stirling	0
Shoaib Mohammad c Smith b Stirling	31	c McEwan b Boock	34
Qasim Omar lbw b Boock	45	c & b M.D. Crowe	17
Javed Miandad c Smith b M.D. Crowe	13	c J.J. Crowe b Boock	58
*Zaheer Abbas c Smith b Stirling	14	c Smith b Bracewell	3
Salim Malik c & b M.D. Crowe	50	not out	119
Wasim Raja lbw b Stirling	51	not out	60
Abdul Qadir c Wright b Boock	7		
†Anil Dalpat b Boock	52		
Iqbal Qasim not out	45		
Azeem Hafeez lbw b Boock	0		
Extras (B5, LB6, W1, NB3)	15	(B2, LB8, NB7)	17
Total	**328**	**(5 wkts)**	**308**

NEW ZEALAND

J.G. Wright c Anil b Iqbal	107
B.A. Edgar run out	15
J.F. Reid c Iqbal b Azeem	97
M.D. Crowe lbw b Wasim	45
J.J. Crowe c Javed b Azeem	62
*J.V. Coney c & b Iqbal	16
P.E. McEwan not out	40
†I.D.S. Smith c Salim b Iqbal	0
D.A. Stirling c Qasim b Iqbal	7
J.G. Bracewell c Anil b Azeem	30
S.L. Boock c Anil b Azeem	0
Extras (B1, LB5, NB1)	7
Total	**426**

BOWLING

N. ZEALAND	O	M	R	W		O	M	R	W
Stirling	29	5	88	4	—	14	1	82	1
M.D. Crowe	21	4	81	2	—	10	3	26	1
McEwan	4	1	6	0	—	2	0	7	0
Boock	41	19	83	4	—	30	10	83	2
Coney	5	3	5	0	—				
Bracewell	20	5	54	0	—	33	11	83	1
J.J. Crowe					—	2	0	9	0
Wright	—	—	—	—	—	1	0	1	0
Reid	—	—	—	—	—	2	0	7	0
PAKISTAN					—				
Mudassar	15.4	4	45	0	—	—	—	—	—
Azeem	46.4	9	132	4	—	—	—	—	—
Iqbal	57	13	133	4	—	—	—	—	—
Wasim	33	8	97	1	—	—	—	—	—
Zaheer	5.2	1	13	0	—	—	—	—	—

FALL OF WICKETS

	PAK	NZ	PAK
	1st	1st	2nd
1st	14	83	5
2nd	80	163	37
3rd	92	258	119
4th	102	292	126
5th	124	338	130
6th	204	352	—
7th	226	353	—
8th	315	361	—
9th	319	426	—
10th	328	426	—

Australia v West Indies 1984-5

FIRST TEST MATCH

PLAYED AT PERTH 9, 10, 11, 12 NOVEMBER
WEST INDIES WON BY AN INNINGS AND 112 RUNS

WEST INDIES

C.G. Greenidge c Rackemann b Alderman	30
D.L. Haynes c Yallop b Hogg	56
R.B. Richardson b Alderman	0
H.A. Gomes b Hogg	127
I.V.A. Richards c Phillips b Alderman	10
*C.H. Lloyd c Phillips b Alderman	0
†P.J. Dujon c Phillips b Alderman	139
M.D. Marshall c Hughes b Hogg	21
M.A. Holding c Wood b Alderman	1
J. Garner c Phillips b Hogg	17
C.A. Walsh not out	9
Extras (B1, LB1, NB4)	6
Total	**416**

AUSTRALIA

K.C. Wessels c Holding b Garner	13	c Lloyd b Garner	0
J. Dyson c Lloyd b Marshall	0	b Marshall	30
G.M. Wood c Lloyd b Garner	6	c Richardson b Walsh	56
A.R. Border c Dujon b Holding	15	c Haynes b Marshall	6
*K.J. Hughes c Marshall b Holding	4	lbw b Marshall	37
G.N. Yallop c Greenidge b Holding	2	c Haynes b Walsh	1
†W.B. Phillips c Marshall b Holding	22	c Dujon b Garner	16
G.F. Lawson c Dujon b Marshall	1	not out	38
R.M. Hogg b Holding	0	b Marshall	0
C.G. Rackemann c Richardson b Holding	0	b Garner	0
T.M. Alderman not out	0	c Richardson b Holding	23
Extras (B4, LB2, NB7)	13	(LB7, NB14)	21
Total	**76**		**228**

BOWLING

AUSTRALIA	O	M	R	W	O	M	R	W	FALL OF WICKETS			
										WI	AUS	AUS
Lawson	24	3	79	0	—	—	—	—		*1st*	*1st*	*2nd*
Rackemann	28	3	106	0	—	—	—	—	1st	83	1	4
Hogg	32	6	101	4	—	—	—	—	2nd	83	18	94
Alderman	39	12	128	6	—	—	—	—	3rd	89	28	107
WEST INDIES									4th	104	40	107
Marshall	15	5	25	2	21	4	68	4	5th	104	46	124
Garner	7	0	24	2	16	5	52	3	6th	186	55	166
Holding	9.2	3	21	6	11.3	1	53	1	7th	335	58	168
Walsh	—	—	—	—	20	4	43	2	8th	337	63	168
Gomes	—	—	—	—	1	0	1	0	9th	387	63	169
Richards	—	—	—	—	1	0	4	0	10th	416	76	228

Dujon retired hurt at 155-5 and resumed at 186-6.

33

SECOND TEST MATCH

PLAYED AT BRISBANE, 23, 24, 25, 26 NOVEMBER
WEST INDIES WON BY 8 WICKETS

AUSTRALIA

J. Dyson	c Dujon b Holding	13	c Dujon b Marshall		21
K.C. Wessels	b Garner	0	c Gomes b Walsh		61
G.M. Wood	c Marshall b Walsh	20	c Richardson b Holding		3
A.R. Border	c Lloyd b Marshall	17	c sub (Harper) b Holding		24
*K.J. Hughes	c Marshall b Garner	34	lbw b Holding		4
D.C. Boon	c Richardson b Marshall	11	c Holding b Marshall		51
†W.B. Phillips	c Dujon b Walsh	44	c sub (Harper) b Holding		54
G.F. Lawson	b Garner	14	c Richards b Marshall		14
T.M. Alderman	c Lloyd b Walsh	0	c Richardson b Marshall		1
R.G. Holland	c Dujon b Garner	6	b Marshall		0
R.M. Hogg	not out	0	not out		21
	Extras (B4, LB1, NB11)	16	(B4, LB5, NB8)		17
	Total	**175**			**271**

WEST INDIES

C.G. Greenidge	c Border b Lawson	44			
D.L. Haynes	b Alderman	21	b Lawson		7
R.B. Richardson	c Phillips b Alderman	138	c Alderman b Hogg		9
H.A. Gomes	b Holland	13	not out		9
I.V.A. Richards	c Boon b Lawson	6	not out		3
†P.J. Dujon	c Phillips b Holland	14			
*C.H. Lloyd	c Hughes b Alderman	114			
M.D. Marshall	b Lawson	57			
M.A. Holding	b Lawson	1			
J. Garner	not out	0			
C.A. Walsh	c Phillips b Lawson	0			
	Extras (B2, LB6, NB8)	16	(LB2)		2
	Total	**424**	(2 wkts)		**26**

BOWLING

WEST INDIES	O	M	R	W		O	M	R	W	FALL OF WICKETS				
											AUS	WI	AUS	WI
Garner	18.4	5	67	4	—	20	4	80	0		1st	1st	2nd	2nd
Marshall	14.4	5	39	2	—	34	7	82	5	1st	1	36	88	6
Holding	6.2	2	9	1	—	30	7	92	4	2nd	33	99	88	18
Walsh	16	5	55	3	—	5	2	7	0	3rd	33	129	99	—
Richards					—	1	0	1	0	4th	81	142	106	—
AUSTRALIA										5th	97	184	131	—
Lawson	30.4	8	116	5	—	5	0	10	1	6th	102	336	212	—
Alderman	29	10	107	3	—	—	—	—	—	7th	122	414	236	—
Hogg	21	3	71	0	—	4.1	0	14	1	8th	136	423	236	—
Holland	27	5	97	2	—	—	—	—	—	9th	173	424	271	—
Border	5	0	25	0	—	—	—	—	—	10th	175	424	271	—

THIRD TEST MATCH
PLAYED AT ADELAIDE, 7, 8, 9, 10, 11 DECEMBER
WEST INDIES WON BY 191 RUNS

WEST INDIES

C.G. Greenidge c Hogg b Lawson	95	lbw b Lawson	4
D.L. Haynes c Hughes b Hogg	0	c Wood b Lawson	50
R.B. Richardson c Border b Lawson	8	lbw b Hogg	3
H.A. Gomes c Rixon b Lawson	60	not out	120
I.V.A. Richards c Rixon b Lawson	0	c Rixon b Hogg	42
*C.H. Lloyd b Lawson	78	c Rixon b Lawson	6
†P.J. Dujon lbw b Lawson	77	c Boon b Holland	32
M.D. Marshall c Rixon b Lawson	9		
R.A. Harper c Rixon b Lawson	9	c Rixon b Hogg	26
J. Garner not out	8		
C.A. Walsh b Holland	0		
Extras (B5, LB4, NB3)	12	(LB2, NB7)	9
Total	**356**	**(7 wkts dec)**	**292**

AUSTRALIA

G.M. Wood c Greenidge b Harper	41	c Dujon b Harper	19
J. Dyson c Dujon b Walsh	8	lbw b Marshall	5
K.C. Wessels b Marshall	98	c Dujon b Harper	70
†S.J. Rixon c Richards b Marshall	0	lbw b Harper	16
K.J. Hughes c Dujon b Marshall	0	b Marshall	2
*A.R. Border c Garner b Marshall	21	b Marshall	18
D.C. Boon c Dujon b Marshall	12	c Harper b Garner	9
G.F. Lawson c Dujon b Garner	49	c Dujon b Marshall	2
R.G. Holland c Haynes b Walsh	2	not out	7
R.M. Hogg not out	7	b Harper	7
T.M. Alderman c Richardson b Marshall	10	b Marshall	18
Extras (B2, LB8, NB26)	36	(B7, LB7, NB4)	18
Total	**284**		**173**

BOWLING

AUSTRALIA	O	M	R	W		O	M	R	W	FALL OF WICKETS				
											WI	AUS	WI	AUS
Lawson	40	7	112	8	—	24	6	69	3		1st	1st	2nd	2nd
Hogg	28	7	75	1	—	21	2	77	3	1st	4	28	4	22
Alderman	19	8	38	0	—	12	1	66	0	2nd	25	91	39	70
Holland	30.2	5	109	1	—	18.1	1	54	1	3rd	157	91	45	78
Wessels	5	0	13	0	—	—	—	—	—	4th	157	122	121	97
Border	—	—	—	—	—	4	0	24	0	5th	172	138	218	126
WEST INDIES										6th	322	145	225	150
Marshall	26	8	69	5	—	15.5	4	38	5	7th	331	232	292	153
Garner	26	5	61	2	—	16	2	58	1	8th	328	241	—	153
Walsh	24	8	88	2	—	4	0	20	0	9th	355	265	—	170
Harper	21	4	56	1	—	15	6	43	4	10th	356	284	—	173

FOURTH TEST MATCH

PLAYED AT MELBOURNE 22, 23, 24, 26, 27 DECEMBER
MATCH DRAWN

WEST INDIES

C.G. Greenidge c Bennett b Lawson	10	lbw b Lawson
D.L. Haynes c Border b Lawson	13	b McDermott
R.B. Richardson b McDermott	51	b Lawson
H.A. Gomes c Matthews b McDermott	68	c Bennett b McDermott
I.V.A. Richards c Hughes b Matthews	208	lbw b McDermott
†P.J. Dujon b McDermott	0	not out
C.H. Lloyd c Lawson b Matthews	19	not out
M.D. Marshall c Rixon b Hogg	55	
R.A. Harper c & b Hogg	5	
J. Garner lbw b Lawson	8	
C.A. Walsh not out	18	
Extras (B1, LB11, NB12)	24	(B4, LB9, NB5)
Total	**479**	**(5 wkts dec)**

(second innings scores: lbw b Lawson 1; b McDermott 63; b Lawson 3; c Bennett b McDermott 18; lbw b McDermott 0; not out 49; not out 34; Extras 18; Total 186)

AUSTRALIA

G.M. Wood lbw b Garner	12	c Dujon b Garner
A.M.J. Hilditch b Harper	70	b Gomes
K.C. Wessels c Dujon b Marshall	90	b Garner
K.J. Hughes c Dujon b Walsh	0	lbw b Garner
*A.R. Border c Richards b Walsh	35	c Dujon b Richards
G.R.J. Matthews b Marshall	5	b Harper
†S.J. Rixon c Richardson b Marshall	0	c Richardson b Harper
M.J. Bennett not out	22	not out
G.F. Lawson c Walsh b Garner	8	b Walsh
C.J. McDermott b Marshall	0	
R.M. Hogg lbw b Marshall	19	
Extras (B5, LB7, W1, NB22)	35	(B6, LB2, NB9)
Total	**296**	**(8 wkts)**

(second innings scores: c Dujon b Garner 5; b Gomes 113; b Garner 0; lbw b Garner 0; c Dujon b Richards 41; b Harper 2; c Richardson b Harper 17; not out 3; b Walsh 0; Extras 17; Total 198)

BOWLING

	O	M	R	W		O	M	R	W
AUSTRALIA									
Lawson	37	9	108	3	—	19	4	54	2
Hogg	27	2	96	2	—	14	3	40	0
McDermott	27	2	118	3	—	21	6	65	3
Bennett	20	0	78	0	—	3	0	12	0
Matthews	14.3	2	67	2	—	—	—	—	—
Wessels	—	—	—	—	—	1	0	2	0
WEST INDIES									
Marshall	31.5	6	86	5	—	20	4	36	0
Garner	24	6	74	2	—	19	1	49	3
Walsh	21	5	57	2	—	18	4	44	1
Harper	14	1	58	1	—	22	4	54	2
Richards	1	0	9	0	—	6	2	7	1
Gomes	—	—	—	—	—	2	2	0	1

FALL OF WICKETS

	WI 1st	AUS 1st	WI 2nd	AUS 2nd
1st		38	2	17
2nd	30	161	12	17
3rd	153	163	63	17
4th	154	220	63	128
5th	154	238	100	131
6th	223	238	—	162
7th	362	240	—	198
8th	426	253	—	198
9th	426	253		
10th	479	296		

FIFTH TEST MATCH

PLAYED AT SYDNEY 30, 31 DECEMBER, 1, 2 JANUARY
AUSTRALIA WON BY AN INNINGS AND 55 RUNS

AUSTRALIA

A.M.J. Hilditch c Dujon b Holding	2
G.M. Wood c Haynes b Gomes	45
K.C. Wessels b Holding	173
G.M. Ritchie run out	37
*A.R. Border c Greenidge b Walsh	69
D.C. Boon b Garner	49
†S.J. Rixon c Garner b Holding	20
M.J. Bennett c Greenidge b Garner	23
G.F. Lawson not out	5
C.J. McDermott c Greenidge b Walsh	4
R.G. Holland did not bat	
Extras (B7, LB20, NB17)	44
Total (9 wkts dec)	**471**

WEST INDIES

C.G. Greenidge c Rixon b McDermott	18	b Holland	12
D.L. Haynes c Wessels b Holland	34	lbw b McDermott	3
R.B. Richardson b McDermott	2	c Wood b Bennett	26
H.A. Gomes c Bennett b Holland	28	c Wood b Lawson	8
I.V.A. Richards c Wessels b Holland	15	b Bennett	58
*C.H. Lloyd c Wood b Holland	33	c Border b McDermott	72
†P.J. Dujon c Hilditch b Bennett	22	c & b Holland	8
M.D. Marshall st Rixon b Holland	0	not out	32
M.A. Holding c McDermott b Bennett	0	c Wessels b Holland	0
J. Garner c Rixon b Holland	0	c Rixon b Bennett	8
C.A. Walsh not out	1	c Bennett b Holland	4
Extras (LB3, NB7)	10	(B2, LB12, NB8)	22
Total	**163**		**253**

BOWLING

WEST INDIES	O	M	R	W	O	M	R	W
Marshall	37	2	111	0	—	—	—	—
Garner	31	5	101	2	—	—	—	—
Holding	31	7	74	3	—	—	—	—
Walsh	38.2	1	118	2	—	—	—	—
Gomes	12	2	29	1	—	—	—	—
Richards	7	2	11	0	—	—	—	—
AUSTRALIA								
Lawson	9	1	27	0	6	1	14	1
McDermott	9	0	34	2	12	0	56	2
Bennett	22.4	7	45	2	33	9	79	3
Holland	22	7	54	6	33	8	90	4

FALL OF WICKETS

	AUS	WI	AUS	WI
	1st	1st	2nd	
1st	12	26	7	
2nd	126	34	31	
3rd	338	72	46	
4th	342	103	93	
5th	350	106	153	
6th	392	160	180	
7th	450	160	231	
8th	463	160	231	
9th	471	160	244	
10th	—	163	253	

India v England 1984-85

FIRST TEST MATCH

PLAYED AT BOMBAY 28, 29 NOVEMBER, 1, 2, 3 DECEMBER

INDIA WON BY 8 WICKETS

ENGLAND

G. Fowler c & b Sivaramakrishnan	28	lbw b Sivaramakrishnan	55
R.T. Robinson c Kirmani b Sivaramakrishnan	22	lbw b Kapil Dev	1
M.W. Gatting c & b Sivaramakrishnan	15	c Patil b Sivaramakrishnan	136
*D.I. Gower b Kapil Dev	13	c Vengsarkar b Shastri	2
A.J. Lamb c Shastri b Kapil Dev	9	st Kirmani b Sivaramakrishnan	1
C.S. Cowdrey c Kirmani b Yadav	13	c Vengsarkar b Yadav	14
R.M. Ellison b Sivaramakrishnan	1	c Vengsarkar b Yadav	0
†P.R. Downton not out	37	lbw b Sivaramakrishnan	62
P.H. Edmonds c Gaekwad b Shastri	48	c Kapil Dev b Sivaramakrishnan	0
P.I. Pocock c Kirmani b Sivaramakrishnan	8	not out	22
N.G. Cowans c Shastri b Sivaramakrishnan	0	c Vengsarkar b Sivara'krishnan	0
Extras (B1)	1	(B4, LB8, NB4)	16
Total	**195**		**317**

INDIA

*S.M. Gavaskar c Downton b Cowans	27	c Gower b Cowans	5
A.D. Gaekwad run out	24	st Downton b Edmonds	1
D.B. Vengsarkar c Lamb b Cowans	34	not out	21
M. Amarnath c Cowdrey b Pocock	49	not out	22
S.M. Patil c Gower b Edmonds	20		
R.J. Shastri c Lamb b Pocock	142		
Kapil Dev b Cowdrey	42		
†S.M.H. Kirmani c Lamb b Pocock	102		
Chetan Sharma not out	5		
N.S. Yadav not out	7		
L. Sivaramakrishnan did not bat			
Extras (B4, LB2, NB7)	13	(B2)	2
Total (8 wkts dec)	**465**	**(2 wkts)**	**51**

BOWLING

INDIA	O	M	R	W		O	M	R	W	FALL OF WICKETS				
											ENG	IND	ENG	IND
Kapil Dev	22	8	44	2	—	21	8	34	1		1st	1st	2nd	2nd
Chetan Sharma	11	4	28	0	—	9	2	39	0	1st	46	47	3	5
Shastri	17	8	23	1	—	29	8	50	1	2nd	51	59	138	7
Amarnath	3	2	1	0	—					3rd	78	116	145	—
Sivara'krishnan	31.2	10	64	6	—	46	10	117	6	4th	78	156	152	—
Yadav	12	2	34	1	—	29	9	64	2	5th	93	156	199	—
Gaekwad	—				—	1	0	4	0	6th	94	218	222	—
ENGLAND										7th	114	453	228	—
Ellison	18	3	85	0	—	—				8th	175	453	255	—
Cowans	28	6	109	2	—	5	2	18	1	9th	193	—	317	—
Edmonds	33	6	82	1	—	8	3	21	1	10th	195	—	317	—
Pocock	46	10	133	3	—	2.1	0	10	0					
Cowdrey	5	0	30	1	—									
Gatting	7	0	20	0										

PLAYED AT NEW DELHI, 12, 13, 15, 16, 17 DECEMBER
ENGLAND WON BY 8 WICKETS

INDIA

*S.M. Gavaskar	c Downton b Ellison	1	b Pocock	65
A.D. Gaekwad	b Pocock	28	c Downton b Edmonds	0
D.B. Vengsarkar	st Downton b Edmonds	24	b Cowans	1
M. Amarnath	c Gower b Pocock	42	b Edmonds	64
S.M. Patil	c Pocock b Edmonds	30	c Lamb b Edmonds	41
R.J. Shastri	c Fowler b Pocock	2	not out	25
Kapil Dev	c Downton b Ellison	60	c Lamb b Pocock	7
†S.M.H. Kirmani	c Gatting b Ellison	27	b Pocock	6
M. Prabhakar	c Downton b Ellison	25	c Downton b Cowans	5
N.S. Yadav	not out	28	c Lamb b Edmonds	1
L. Sivaramakrishnan	run out	25	c & b Pocock	0
Extras	(B1, LB12, NB2)	15	(B6, LB10, W1, NB3)	20
Total		**307**		**235**

ENGLAND

G. Fowler	c Gaekwad b Prabhakar	5	c Vengsarkar b Sivaramakrishnan	29
R.T. Robinson	c Gavaskar b Kapil Dev	160	run out	18
M.W. Gatting	b Yadav	26	not out	30
A.J. Lamb	c Vengsarkar b Yadav	52	not out	37
*D.I. Gower	lbw b Sivaramakrishnan	5		
C.S. Cowdrey	c Gavaskar b Sivaramakrishnan	38		
†P.R. Downton	c Kapil Dev b Sivaramakrishnan	74		
P.H. Edmonds	c Shastri b Sivaramakrishnan	26		
R.M. Ellison	b Sivaramakrishnan	10		
P.I. Pocock	b Sivaramakrishnan	0		
N.G. Cowans	not out	0		
Extras	(B6, LB13, NB3)	22	(B4, LB7, W2)	13
Total		**418**	(2 wkts)	**127**

BOWLING

ENGLAND	O	M	R	W		O	M	R	W
Cowans	20	5	70	0	—	13	2	43	2
Ellison	26	6	66	4	—	7	1	20	0
Edmonds	44.2	16	83	2	—	44	24	60	4
Pocock	33	8	70	3	—	38.4	9	93	4
Gatting	2	0	5	0	—	1	0	3	0
INDIA									
Kapil Dev	32	5	87	1	—	6	0	20	0
Prabhakar	21	3	68	1	—	3	0	18	0
Sivara'krishnan	49.1	17	99	6	—	8	0	41	1
Yadav	36	6	95	2	—	2	0	7	0
Shastri	29	4	44	0	—	4	0	20	0
Amarnath	2	0	6	0					
Gavaskar					—	0.4	0	10	0

FALL OF WICKETS

	IND 1st	ENG 1st	IND 2nd	ENG 2nd
1st	3	15	12	41
2nd	56	60	15	68
3rd	68	170	136	—
4th	129	181	172	—
5th	131	237	207	—
6th	140	343	214	—
7th	208	398	216	—
8th	235	411	225	—
9th	258	416	234	—
10th	307	418	235	—

THIRD TEST MATCH

PLAYED AT CALCUTTA, 31 DECEMBER, 1, 3, 4, 5 JANUARY

MATCH DRAWN

INDIA

*S.M. Gavaskar c Gatting b Edmonds	13			
A.D. Gaekwad c Downton b Cowans	18			
D.B. Vengsarkar b Edmonds	48			
M. Amarnath c Cowdrey b Edmonds	42			
M. Azharuddin c Gower b Cowans	110			
R.J. Shastri b Cowans	111	not out		7
†S.M.H. Kirmani c Fowler b Pocock	35			
M. Prabhakar not out	35	lbw b Lamb		21
Chetan Sharma not out	13			
N.S. Yadav		not out		0
L. Sivaramakrishnan did not bat				
Extras (LB8, W1, NB3)	12	(NB1)		1
Total (7 wkts dec)	437	(1 wkt)		29

ENGLAND

G. Fowler c Vengsarkar b Sivaramakrishnan	49
R.T. Robinson b Yadav	36
*D.I. Gower c Shastri b Yadav	19
P.I. Pocock c Azharuddin b Sivaramakrishnan	5
M.W. Gatting b Yadav	48
A.J. Lamb c Kirmani b Chetan Sharma	67
C.S. Cowdrey lbw b Yadav	27
†P.R. Downton not out	6
P.H. Edmonds c Gavaskar b Chetan Sharma	8
R.M. Ellison c & b Chetan Sharma	1
N.G. Cowans b Chetan Sharma	1
Extras (LB2, NB7)	9
Total	276

BOWLING

ENGLAND	O	M	R	W		O	M	R	W	FALL OF WICKETS			
											IND	ENG	IND
Cowans	41	12	103	3	—	4	1	6	0		1st	1st	2nd
Ellison	53	14	117	0		1	0	1	0				
Edmonds	47	22	72	3	—	4	3	2	0	1st	28	71	29
Pocock	52	14	108	1	—	2	1	4	0	2nd	35	98	—
Gatting	2	1	1	0						3rd	126	110	—
Cowdrey	2	0	15	0	—	4	0	10	0	4th	127	152	—
Gower	3	0	13	0	—					5th	341	163	—
Fowler	—	—	—	—	—	1	1	0	0	6th	356	229	—
Robinson	—	—	—	—	—	1	1	0	0	7th	407	261	—
Lamb	—	—	—	—	—	1	0	6	1	8th	—	270	—
INDIA										9th	—	273	—
Chetan Sharma	12.3	0	38	4	—					10th	—	276	—
Prabhakar	5	1	16	0	—								
Sivara'krishnan	28	7	90	2	—								
Yadav	32	10	86	4	—								
Shastri	23	6	44	0	—								

Robinson retired hurt at 31-0 and resumed at 71-1.

FOURTH TEST MATCH

INDIA

*S.M. Gavaskar	b Foster	17	c Gatting b Foster		3
K. Srikkanth	c Downton b Cowans	0	c Cowdrey b Foster		16
D.B. Vengsarkar	c Lamb b Foster	17	c Downton b Foster		2
M. Amarnath	c Downton b Foster	78	c Cowans b Foster		95
M. Azharuddin	b Cowdrey	48	c Gower b Pocock		105
R.J. Shastri	c Downton b Foster	2	c Cowdrey b Edmonds		33
Kapil Dev	c Cowans b Cowdrey	53	c Gatting b Cowans		49
†S.M.H. Kirmani	not out	30	c Lamb b Edmonds		75
N.S. Yadav	b Foster	2	c Downton b Cowans		5
L. Sivaramakrishnan	c Cowdrey b Foster	13	lbw b Foster		5
Chetan Sharma	c Lamb b Cowans	5	not out		17
Extras	(LB3, NB4)	7	(B1, LB4, NB2)		7
Total		**272**			**412**

ENGLAND

G. Fowler	c Kirmani b Kapil Dev	201	c Kirmani b Sivaramakrishnan		2
R.T. Robinson	c Kirmani b Sivaramakrishnan	74	not out		21
M.W. Gatting	c sub b Shastri	207	not out		10
A.J. Lamb	b Amarnath	62			
P.H. Edmonds	lbw b Shastri	36			
N.A. Foster	b Amarnath	5			
*D.I. Gower	b Kapil Dev	18			
C.S. Cowdrey	not out	3			
†P.R. Downton	not out	3			
P.I. Pocock	did not bat				
N.G. Cowans	did not bat				
Extras	(B7, LB19, NB17)	43	(LB1, W1)		2
Total	(7 wkts dec)	**652**	(1 wkt)		**35**

BOWLING

ENGLAND	O	M	R	W		O	M	R	W	FALL OF WICKETS				
											IND	*ENG*	*IND*	*ENG*
Cowans	12.5	3	39	2	—	15	1	73	2		*1st*	*1st*	*2nd*	*2nd*
Foster	23	2	104	6	—	28	3	59	5	1st	17	178	7	7
Edmonds	6	1	33	0	—	41.5	13	119	2	2nd	17	419	19	—
Cowdrey	19	1	65	2	—	5	0	26	0	3rd	45	563	22	—
Pocock	7	1	28	0	—	33	8	130	1	4th	155	599	212	—
INDIA					—					5th	167	604	259	—
Kapil Dev	36	5	131	2	—	3	0	20	0	6th	167	640	259	—
Chetan Sharma	18	0	95	0	—					7th	241	646	341	—
Sivara'krishnan	44	6	145	1	—	4	0	12	1	8th	243	—	350	—
Yadav	23	4	76	0	—					9th	263	—	361	—
Shastri	42	7	143	2	—	1	0	2	0	10th	272	—	412	—
Amarnath	12	1	36	2	—			—	—					

FIFTH TEST MATCH

PLAYED AT KANPUR 31 JANUARY, 1, 3, 4, 5 FEBRUARY
MATCH DRAWN

INDIA

*S.M. Gavaskar b Cowans	9		
K. Srikkanth c Downton b Foster	84	not out	41
M. Azharuddin c sub (Ellison) b Cowdrey	122	not out	54
M. Amarnath b Cowans	15		
D.B. Vengsarkar c Downton b Foster	137		
A. Malhotra lbw b Pocock	27		
R.J. Shastri b Edmonds	59	run out	2
Kapil Dev c Gower b Foster	42		
†S.M.H. Kirmani not out	16		
L. Sivaramakrishnan not out	16		
Gopal Sharma did not bat			
Extras (B9, LB12, W5)	26		
Total 8 wkts dec)	**553**	(0 wkt)	**97**

England

G. Fowler c Kirmani b Shastri	69		
R.T. Robinson b Kapil Dev	96	retired hurt	16
M.W. Gatting c & b Gopal Sharma	62	not out	41
A.J. Lamb c Srikkanth b Shastri	13		
*D.J. Gower lbw b Shastri	78	not out	32
C.S. Cowdrey c Kirmani b Gopal Sharma	1		
†P.R. Downton b Gopal Sharma	1		
P.H. Edmonds lbw b Kapil Dev	49		
N.A. Foster c Kirmani b Kapil Dev	8		
P.I. Pocock not out	4		
N.G. Cowans b Kapil Dev	9		
Extras (B10, LB17)	27	(LB2)	2
Total	**417**	(0 wkt)	**91**

BOWLING

ENGLAND	O	M	R	W		O	M	R	W	FALL OF WICKETS
										IND ENG IND
Cowans	36	9	115	2	—	7	0	51	0	*IST IST 2ND*
Foster	36	8	123	3	—	—	—	—	—	
Pocock	24	2	79	1	—	—	—	—	—	1st 19 156 2
Edmonds	48	16	112	1	—	—	—	—	—	2nd 169 196 —
Cowdrey	21	1	103	1	—	5	0	39	0	3rd 209 222 —
Gatting	—	—	—	—	—	1	0	7	0	4th 277 276 —
INDIA				—						5th 362 278 —
Kapil Dev	36.5	6	81	4	—	5	0	19	0	6th 457 286 —
Amarnath	4	1	6	0	—	—	—	—	—	7th 511 386 —
Gopal Sharma	60	16	115	3	—	11	4	17	0	8th 533 402 —
Sivara Krishnan	54	11	133	0	—	10	2	22	0	9th — 404 —
Shastri	32	13	52	3	—	7	2	12	0	10th — 417 —
Malhotra	2	0	3	0	—	—	—	—	—	
Spikkanth	—	—	—	—	—	2	0	11	0	
Azharuddin	—	—	—	—	—	1	0	8	0	

Robinson retired hurt at 36-0

42

Your flexible friend – a big hit wherever he goes.

♻ NatWest Access

The fastest century in NatWest.

NatWest have installed 300 Rapid Cash Tills inside branches in the London area for those who want a quick century.

The Rapid Cash Till certainly lives up to its name.

You can draw up to £100 in just 15 seconds. You can make as many withdrawals a day as you like up to a limit agreed with your branch.

You can keep a check on your money because each withdrawal is accompanied by a slip showing how much you've taken out.

All you need to use a Rapid Cash Till is a Servicecard.

The same card that you can use at over 1,400 of our Servicetills and Midland AutoBanks. So if you want a fast century, track down your nearest Rapid Cash Till. Nothing beats it.

The Action Bank

ENGLAND v AUSTRALIA
1876-77 TO 1982-83

SERIES BY SERIES

Season		Visiting Captain	P	E W	A W	D
1876-77	In Australia	James Lillywhite (E)	2	1	1	0
1878-79	In Australia	Lord Harris (E)	1	0	1	0
1880	In England	W.L. Murdoch (A)	1	1	0	0
1881-82	In Australia	A. Shaw (E)	4	0	2	2
1882	In England	W.L. Murdoch (A)	1	0	1	0

The Ashes

Season		Visiting Captain	P	E W	A W	D
1882-83	In Australia	Hon.Ivo Bligh (E)	4†	2	2	0
1884	In England	W.L. Murdoch (A)	3	1	0	2
1884-85	In Australia	A. Shrewsbury (E)	5	3	2	0
1886	In England	H.J.H. Scott (A)	3	3	0	0
1886-87	In Australia	A. Shrewsbury (E)	2	2	0	0
1887-88	In Australia	W.W. Read (E)	1	1	0	0
1888	In England	P.S. McDonnell (A)	3	2	1	0
1890	In England	W.L. Murdoch (A)	2*	0	2	0
1891-92	In Australia	W.G. Grace (E)	3	1	2	0
1893	In England	J.McC. Blackham (A)	3	1	0	2
1894-95	In Australia	A.E. Stoddart (E)	5	3	2	0
1896	In England	G.H.S. Trott (A)	3	2	1	0
1897-98	In Australia	A.E. Stoddart (E)	5	1	4	0
1899	In England	J. Darling (A)	5	0	1	4
1901-02	In Australia	A.C. MacLaren (E)	5	1	4	0
1902	In England	J. Darling (A)	5	1	2	2
1903-04	In Australia	P.F. Warner (E)	5	3	2	0
1905	In England	J. Darling (A)	5	2	0	3
1907-08	In Australia	A.O. Jones (E)	5	1	4	0
1909	In England	M.A. Noble (A)	5	1	2	2
1911-12	In Australia	J.W.H.T. Douglas (E)	5	4	1	0
1912	In England	S.E. Gregory (A)	3	1	0	2
1920-21	In Australia	J.W.H.T. Douglas (E)	5	0	5	0
1921	In England	W.W. Armstrong (A)	5	0	3	2
1924-25	In Australia	A.E.R. Gilligan (E)	5	1	4	0
1926	In England	H.L. Collins (A)	5	1	0	4
1928-29	In Australia	A.P.F. Chapman (E)	5	4	1	0
1930	In England	W.M. Woodfull (A)	5	1	2	2
1932-33	In Australia	D.R. Jardine (E)	5	4	1	0
1934	In England	W.M. Woodfull (A)	5	1	2	2
1936-37	In Australia	G.O. Allen (E)	5	2	3	0
1938	In England	D.G. Bradman (A)	4*	1	1	2
1946–47	In Australia	W.R. Hammond (E)	5	0	3	2
1948	In England	D.G. Bradman (A)	5	0	4	1
1950-51	In Australia	F.R. Brown (E)	5	1	4	0
1953	In England	A.L. Hassett (A)	5	1	0	4
1954-55	In Australia	L. Hutton (E)	5	3	1	1
1956	In England	I.W. Johnson (A)	5	2	1	2
1958-59	In Australia	P.B.H. May (E)	5	0	4	1
1961	In England	R. Benaud (A)	5	1	2	2

Season		Visiting Captain	P	E W	A W	D
1962-63	In Australia	E.R. Dexter (E)	5	1	1	3
1964	In England	R.B. Simpson (A)	5	0	1	4
1965-66	In Australia	M.J.K. Smith (E)	5	1	1	3
1968	In England	W.M. Lawry (A)	5	1	1	3
1970-71	In Australia	R. Illingworth (E)	6*	2	0	4
1972	In England	I.M. Chappell (A)	5	2	2	1
1974-75	In Australia	M.H. Denness (E)	6	1	4	1
1975	In England	I.M. Chappell (A)	4	0	1	3
1976-77	In Australia	A.W. Greig (E)	1	0	1	0
1977	In England	G.S. Chappell (A)	5	3	0	2
1978-79	In Australia	J.M. Brearley (E)	6	5	1	0
1979-80	In Australia	J.M. Brearley (E)	3	0	3	0
1980	In England	G.S. Chappell (A)	1	0	0	1
1981	In England	K.J. Hughes (A)	6	3	1	2
1982-83	In Australia	R.G.D. Willis (E)	5	1	2	2
		At Lord's	27	5	9	13
		At The Oval	28	12	5	11
		At Manchester	23	7	4	12
		At Leeds	18	5	5	8
		At Nottingham	14	3	4	7
		At Birmingham	6	2	1	3
		At Sheffield	1	0	1	0
		At Melbourne	47	17	23	7
		At Sydney	46	20	22	4
		At Adelaide	23	7	13	3
		At Brisbane	13	4	6	3
		At Perth	5	1	2	2
		In England	117	34	29	54
		In Australia	134	49	66	19
		Total	251	83	95	73

* The Test Matches at Manchester in 1890 and 1938 and the third Test match at Melbourne in 1970-71 were abandoned without a ball being bowled and are excluded from this schedule.

† The Ashes were awarded to England after a series of three matches which England won 2-1. A fourth unofficial match was played which was won by Australia, each innings being played on a different pitch.

N.B. The Ashes were not at stake in 1976-77, 1979-80 and 1980.

HIGHEST INNINGS TOTALS

England			Australia		
903-7d	The Oval	1938	729-6d	Lord's	1930
658-8d	Nottingham	1938	701	The Oval	1934
636	Sydney	1928-29	695	The Oval	1930
627-9d	Manchester	1936	659-8d	Sydney	1946-47
611	Manchester	1964	656-8d	Manchester	1964
			645	Brisbane	1946-47
			604	Melbourne	1936-37
			601-8d	Brisbane	1954-55
			600	Melbourne	1924-25

LOWEST INNINGS TOTALS

England			Australia		
45	Sydney	1886-87	36	Birmingham	1902
52	The Oval	1948	42	The Oval	1887-88
53	Lord's	1888	44	The Oval	1896
61	Melbourne	1901-02	53	Lord's	1896
61	Melbourne	1903-04	58	Brisbane	1936-37
			60	Lord's	1888
			63	The Oval	1882
			65	The Oval	1912
			66	Brisbane	1928-29

HIGHEST INDIVIDUAL INNINGS FOR ENGLAND

364	L. Hutton	at The Oval	1938
287	R.E. Foster	at Sydney	1903-04
256	K.F. Barrington	at Manchester	1964
251	W.R. Hammond	at Sydney	1928-29
240	W.R. Hammond	at Lord's	1938
231*	W.R. Hammond	at Sydney	1936-37
216*	E. Paynter	at Nottingham	1938
200	W.R. Hammond	at Melbourne	1928-29

A total of 171 centuries have been scored for England.

HIGHEST INDIVIDUAL INNINGS FOR AUSTRALIA

334	D.G. Bradman	at Leeds	1930
311	R.B. Simpson	at Manchester	1964
307	R.M. Cowper	at Melbourne	1965-66
304	D.G. Bradman	at Leeds	1934
270	D.G. Bradman	at Melbourne	1936-37
266	W.H. Ponsford	at The Oval	1934
254	D.G. Bradman	at Lord's	1930
244	D.G. Bradman	at The Oval	1934
234	S.G. Barnes	at Sydney	1946-47
234	D.G. Bradman	at Sydney	1946-47
232	D.G. Bradman	at The Oval	1930
232	S.J. McCabe	at Nottingham	1938
225	R.B. Simpson	at Adelaide	1965-66
212	D.G. Bradman	at Adelaide	1936-37
211	W.L. Murdoch	at The Oval	1884
207	K.R. Stackpole	at Brisbane	1970-71
206*	W.A. Brown	at Lord's	1938
206	A.R. Morris	at Adelaide	1950-51
201	J. Ryder	at Sydney	1924-25
201	S.E. Gregory	at Sydney	1894-95

A total of 193 centuries have been scored for Australia.

47

A CENTURY IN EACH INNINGS OF A MATCH
FOR ENGLAND

176 & 127	H. Sutcliffe	at Melbourne	1924-25
119* & 177	W.R. Hammond	at Adelaide	1928-29
147 & 103*	D.C.S. Compton	at Adelaide	1946-47

FOR AUSTRALIA

136 & 130	W. Bardsley	at The Oval	1909
122 & 124*	A.R. Morris	at Adelaide	1946-47

A CENTURY ON DEBUT IN SERIES
FOR ENGLAND

152	W.G. Grace (on Test debut)	at The Oval	1880
154*	K.S. Ranjitsinhji (on Test debut)	at Manchester	1896
287	R.E. Foster (on Test debut)	at Sydney	1903-4
119	G. Gunn (on Test debut)	at Sydney	1907-08
115	H. Sutcliffe	at Sydney	1924-25
137	M. Leyland	at Melbourne	1928-29
173	K.S. Duleepsinhji	at Lord's	1930
102	Nawab of Pataudi (on Test debut)	at Sydney	1932-33
100	L. Hutton	at Nottingham	1938
102	D.C.S. Compton	at Nottingham	1938
109	W. Watson	at Lord's	1953
112	R. Subba Row	at Birmingham	1961
120	J.H. Edrich	at Lord's	1964
174	D.W. Randall	at Melbourne	1976-77

FOR AUSTRALIA

165*	C. Bannerman (on Test debut)	at Melbourne	1876-77
107	H. Graham (on Test debut)	at Lord's	1893
104	R.A. Duff (on Test debut)	at Melbourne	1903-04
116	R.J. Hartigan (on Test debut)	at Adelaide	1907-08
104	H.L. Collins (on Test debut)	at Sydney	1920-21
110	W.H. Ponsford (on Test debut)	at Sydney	1924-25
164	A.A. Jackson (on Test debut)	at Adelaide	1928-29
112	R.N. Harvey	at Leeds	1948
101*	J.W. Burke (on Test debut)	at Adelaide	1950-51
155	K.D. Walters (on Test debut)	at Brisbane	1965-66
108	G.S. Chappell (on Test debut)	at Perth	1970-71
102	G.N. Yallop	at Brisbane	1978-79
103	D.M. Wellham (on Test debut)	at The Oval	1981
162	K.C. Wessels (on Test debut)	at Brisbane	1982-83

RECORD WICKET PARTNERSHIPS FOR ENGLAND

1st	323	J.B. Hobbs & W. Rhodes at Melbourne	1911-12
2nd	382	L. Hutton & M. Leyland at The Oval	1938
3rd	262	W.R. Hammond & D.R. Jardine at Adelaide	1928-29
4th	222	W.R. Hammond & E. Paynter at Lord's	1938
5th	206	E. Paynter & D.C.S. Compton at Nottingham	1938
6th	215	L. Hutton & J. Hardstaff at The Oval	1938
		G. Boycott & A.P.E. Knott at Nottingham	1977
7th	143	F.E. Woolley & J. Vine at Sydney	1911-12
8th	124	E.H. Hendren & H. Larwood at Brisbane	1928-29
9th	151	W.H. Scotton & W.W. Read at The Oval	1884
10th	130	R.E. Foster & W. Rhodes at Sydney	1903-04

RECORD WICKET PARTNERSHIPS FOR AUSTRALIA

1st	244	R.B. Simpson & W.M. Lawry at Adelaide	1965-66
2nd	451	W.H. Ponsford & D.G. Bradman at The Oval	1934
3rd	276	D.G. Bradman & A.L. Hassett at Brisbane	1946-47
4th	388	W.H. Ponsford & D.G. Bradman at Leeds	1934
5th	405	S.G. Barnes & D.G. Bradman at Sydney	1946-47
6th	346	J.H. Fingleton & D.G. Bradman at Melbourne	1936-37
7th	165	C. Hill & H. Trumble at Melbourne	1897-98
8th	243	C. Hill & R. J. Hartigan at Adelaide	1907-08
9th	154	S.E. Gregory & J. McC. Blackham at Sydney	1894-95
10th	127	J.M. Taylor & A.A. Mailey at Sydney	1924-25

HIGHEST RUN AGGREGATES IN A TEST RUBBER FOR:

England in England	562 (Av. 62.44)	D.C.S. Compton	1948
England in Australia	905 (Av. 113.12)	W.R. Hammond	1928-29
Australia in England	974 (Av. 139.14)	D.G. Bradman	1930
Australia in Australia	810 (Av. 90.00)	D.G. Bradman	1936-37

BEST BOWLING FIGURES FOR:

England in England	10-53	J.C. Laker at Manchester	1956
England in Australia	8-35	G.A. Lohmann at Sydney	1886-87
Australia in England	8-31	F. Laver at Manchester	1909
Australia in Australia	9-121	A.A. Mailey at Manchester	1920-21

TEN WICKETS OR MORE IN A MATCH

36 occurrences for England (the last by I.T. Botham at The Oval in 1981) and 35 occurrences for Australia (the last by G.F. Lawson at Brisbane in 1982-83).

HIGHEST WICKET AGGREGATE IN A TEST RUBBER FOR:

England in England	46 (Av. 9.60) J.C. Laker	1956
England in Australia	38 (Av. 23.18) M.W. Tate	1924-25
Australia in England	42 (Av 21.26) T.M. Alderman	1981
Australia in Australia	41 (Av. 12.85) R.M. Hogg	1978-79

HIGHEST MATCH AGGREGATE	1753-49 wkts Adelaide	1920-21
LOWEST MATCH AGGREGATE	291-40 wkts Lord's	1888

MIDDLESEX WIN THE FOURTH NATWEST TROPHY

When Derbyshire won the first NatWest Trophy off the very last ball of the day in 1981, the pundits were fairly safe in saying that this will never happen again. But history does have a habit of repeating itself, and very quickly, too. So Middlesex won off the last ball of the day in 1984 to disappoint Kent for the second year in succession (Somerset beat Kent in the 1983 Final). The name of Middlesex will be inscribed on the Trophy, yet many would say that they were not the NatWest Team of the year, and that this honour belongs to a Minor County, Shropshire, who beat Yorkshire, only the fourth time in the twenty two years of the competition that a Minor County has beaten a First-Class County, and the second time that it has happened to Yorkshire. In the Gillette Cup, Durham beat Yorkshire, Lincolnshire beat Glamorgan and Hertfordshire beat Essex. So Yorkshire were the first First-Class County to lose a Gillette Cup-tie, and the first to lose a NatWest game against a Minor County.

The fine weather that blessed every round of the 1984 competition (twenty nine matches finished on the appointed day, and there was plenty of cricket on the first day in the other two matches which did go to the second) produced some magnificent cricket and several records. There were thirteen centuries. Kallicharran's 206 for Warwickshire against Oxfordshire set three national records for one-day cricket. It produced a victory by 227 runs, the largest victory by a runs margin (previously 214). Warwickshire's score of 392-5 was the highest innings total (previously 371) and Kallicharran's 206 was the highest individual score (previously 198 not out). Kallicharran won the Man of the Match award twice, against Oxfordshire and against Surrey. So did Graham Gooch and Christopher Cowdrey, but although Oxfordshire had an unhappy time at Edgbaston overall, the Minor Counties did quite well, as apart from Shropshire's thrilling win, five Minor Counties and Ireland won Man of the Match awards in the sixteen First Round matches.

So in the first four years of the NatWest seven different Counties have reached the Final and four have won it –

Derbyshire, Surrey, Somerset and Middlesex. Perhaps the biggest surprise in this twenty-two-year-old competition is that Essex, who have done so well in all other competitions, have never once reached a Final – something which, apparently, Keith Fletcher is very anxious to put right before the sun finally sets on his distinguished career. It might have to be 1985!

1984 RESULTS

FIRST ROUND – 4 JULY

Derbyshire beat **Cumberland** by 9 wickets at Kendal
Cumberland 121 (59.2 overs) (K.J. Barnett 9.2-0-24-6). Derbyshire 124-1 (25.1 overs) (J.G. Wright 73*)
Toss: Derbyshire
Man of the Match: J.G. Wright (73*)
Adjudicator: J.H. Wardle

Northamptonshire beat **Durham** by 11 runs at Feethams, Darlington
Northamptonshire 209-8 closed (60 overs) (W. Larkins 77, S. Greensword 12-2-28-4). Durham 198 (58.5 overs)
Toss: Northamptonshire
Man of the Match: S. Greensword (34 and 12-2-28-4)
Adjudicator: C. Washbrook

Essex beat **Scotland** by 190 runs at Chelmsford
Essex 327-6 closed (60 overs) (G.A. Gooch 133 and K. S. McEwan 75 added record NatWest third wicket partnership of 179, A.W. Lilley 59*). Scotland 137 (52.3 overs) (D.L. Acfield 12-7-9-3 equalled NatWest most economical bowling analysis)
Toss: Essex
Man of the Match: G.A. Gooch (133)
Adjudicator: F.J. Titmus

Nottinghamshire beat **Glamorgan** by 6 wickets at St Helen's, Swansea
Glamorgan 147-9 closed (60 overs). Nottinghamshire 148-4 (42.2 overs) (D.W.Randall 71)
Toss: Nottinghamshire
Man of the Match: D.W. Randall (71)
Adjudicator: C.A. Milton

Somerset beat Hertfordshire by 16 runs at St Albans
Somerset 153-9 closed (60 overs). Hertfordshire 137 (59.2 overs)
Toss: Somerset
Man of the Match: B.G. Evans (46)
Adjudicator: J.M. Parks

Kent beat Berkshire by 89 runs at Canterbury
Kent 232-7 closed (60 overs) (C.S. Cowdrey 64). Berkshire 143-9 closed (60 overs)
Toss: Kent
Man of the Match: C.S. Cowdrey (64, 12-0-33-1 and 1 ct)
Adjudicator: R.T. Simpson

Lancashire beat **Buckinghamshire** by 73 runs at Old Trafford, Manchester
Lancashire 272-7 closed (60 overs) (G. Fowler 101). Buckinghamshire 199-8 closed (60 overs). (D.E. Smith 54, P.J.W. Allott 11-2-34-4)
Toss: Buckinghamshire
Man of the Match: G. Fowler (101)
Adjudicator: P.J. Sharpe

Hampshire beat **Norfolk** by 118 runs at Lakenham, Norwich
Hampshire 239-8 closed (60 overs) (M.C.J. Nicholas 63, V.P. Terry 50). Norfolk 121 (43.2 overs) (N.G. Cowley 11.2-2-24-5)
Toss: Norfolk
Man of the Match: N.G. Cowley (30 and 11.2-2-24-5)
Adjudicator: F.R. Brown

Middlesex beat **Northumberland** by 85 runs at Jesmond, Newcastle upon Tyne.
Middlesex 233-9 closed (60 overs) (C.T. Radley 64*). Northumberland 148 (54 overs) (M.E. Younger 57)
Toss: Northumberland
Man of the Match: M.E. Younger (57 and 10-3-32-0)
Adjudicator: J.B. Statham

Shropshire beat **Yorkshire** by 37 runs at St George's, Telford
Shropshire 229-5 closed (60 overs) (Mushtaq Mohammad 80, S.C. Gale 68). Yorkshire 192 (57.5 overs)
Toss: Yorkshire
Man of the Match: Mushtaq Mohammad (80, 12-1-26-3 and 1 ct)
Adjudicator: F.M. Engineer
Shropshire became the first minor county to defeat a first-class county in the NatWest Trophy competition.

Gloucestershire beat **Staffordshire** by 8 wickets at Stone
Staffordshire 151-8 closed (60 overs) (J.N. Shepherd 12-3-20-4). Gloucestershire 152-2 (37 overs) (P.W. Romaines 52, C.W.J. Athey 70*)
Toss: Staffordshire
Man of the Match: J.N. Shepherd (12-3-20-4)
Adjudicator: D. Kenyon

Surrey beat **Ireland** by 7 wickets at The Oval, London
Ireland 157-7 closed (60 overs) (S.J.S. Warke 77, J.A. Prior 50). Surrey 161-3 (48.5 overs) (G.S. Clinton 79*)
Toss: Surrey
Man of the Match: S.J.S. Warke (77)
Adjudicator: T.E. Bailey

Sussex beat **Devon** by 62 runs at Hove
Sussex 231-8 closed (60 overs) (A.M. Green 74). Devon 169-9 closed (60 overs) (J.R.T. Barclay 12-0-53-5)
Toss: Devon
Man of the Match: A.M. Green (74 and 1-0-7-0)
Adjudicator: A.V. Bedser

Warwickshire beat **Oxfordshire** by 227 runs at Edgbaston, Birmingham
Warwickshire 392-5 closed (60 overs) (K.D. Smith 101 and A.I. Kallicharran 206 added 197 for the 2nd wicket – the highest stand for any wicket in NatWest Trophy matches). Oxfordshire 165-8 closed (60 overs) (G. Ford 62, A.I. Kallicharran 12-4-32-6)
Toss: Warwickshire
Man of the Match: A.I. Kallicharran (206 and 12-4-32-6)
Adjudicator: B.L. D'Oliveira

The following national records for all limited-overs cricket were set during this match:
    Largest victory by a runs margin (previously 214)
    Highest innings total (previously 371)
    Highest individual score (previously 198*)

Leicestershire beat **Wiltshire** by 145 runs at Swindon
Leicestershire 354-7 closed (60 overs) (J.J. Whitaker 155, N.E. Briers 59, D.I. Gower 77, A.J. Spencer 12-0-82-4). Wiltshire 209-6 closed (60 overs) (J.M. Rice 75*)
Toss: Wiltshire
Man of the Match: J.J. Whitaker (155 and 1-0-5-0)
Adjudicator: R.E. Marshall

Worcestershire beat **Suffolk** by 6 wickets at Worcester
Suffolk 149 (57.3 overs) (M.J. Weston 12-5-30-4, D.N. Patel 7.2-0-22-4). Worcestershire 152-4 (39.1 overs) (T.S. Curtis 54*)
Toss: Suffolk
Man of the Match: T.S. Curtis (54* and 1 ct)
Adjudicator: T.G. Evans

SECOND ROUND – 18 JULY

Surrey beat **Essex** by 5 wickets at Chelmsford
Essex 121 (56.5 overs) (G.A. Gooch 64). Surrey 122-5 (46.1 overs)
Toss: Essex
Man of the Match: G.A. Gooch (64)
Adjudicator: R.T. Simpson

Lancashire beat **Gloucestershire** by 68 runs at Bristol
Lancashire 349-6 closed (60 overs) (G. Fowler 122, J. Abrahams 51). Gloucestershire 281 (56.2 overs) (A.W. Stovold 53, P.W. Romaines 56, P. Bainbridge 51, J. Simmons 12-2-37-5)
Toss: Gloucestershire
Man of the Match: G. Fowler (122)
Adjudicator: J.M. Parks

Kent beat **Hampshire** by 151 runs at Southampton
Kent 250-8 closed (60 overs) (D.G. Aslett 67, C.S. Cowdrey 71, E.L. Reifer 12-1-46-4). Hampshire 99 (43.3 overs) (T.M. Alderman 9.3-3-21-4)
Toss: Hampshire
Man of the Match: C.S. Cowdrey (71 and 6-0-19-1)
Adjudicator: C.A. Milton

Leicestershire beat **Derbyshire** by 120 runs at Leicester
Leicestershire 301-7 closed (60 overs) (D.I. Gower 156). Derbyshire 181 (48.4 overs). Match completed 19 July
Toss: Derbyshire
Man of the Match: D.I. Gower (156)
Adjudicator: B.L. D'Oliveira

Northamptonshire beat **Worcestershire** by 130 runs at Northampton
Northamptonshire 247-5 closed (60 overs) (A.J. Lamb 65 and R.G. Williams 94 added 150 for the fourth wicket – NatWest record). Worcestershire 117 (36 overs) (N.A. Mallender 12-3-37-7 – the second bowler to take seven wickets in a NatWest Trophy match)
Toss: Worcestershire
Man of the Match: N.A. Mallender (12-3-37-7)
Adjudicator: T.G. Evans

Middlesex beat **Nottinghamshire** by 5 runs at Trent Bridge, Nottingham
Middlesex 228 (59.5 overs) (P.R. Downton 62, M.W. Gatting 67, K. Saxelby 11.5-5-28-4). Nottinghamshire 223-8 closed (60 overs) (B.C. Broad 65, C.E.B. Rice 57)
Toss: Nottinghamshire
Man of the Match: J.E. Emburey (11 and 12-1-24-1)
Adjudicator: P. J. Sharpe

Somerset beat **Sussex** by 68 runs at Hove
Somerset 288-3 closed (60 overs) (P.M. Roebuck 98, M.D. Crowe 114). Sussex 220-9 closed (60 overs) (C.D. Mendis 55)
Toss: Sussex
Man of the Match: M.D. Crowe (114, 12-2-29-2 and 1 ct)
Adjudicator: A.V. Bedser

Warwickshire beat **Shropshire** by 103 runs at Edgbaston, Birmingham
Warwickshire 305-8 closed (60 overs) (R.I.H.B. Dyer 119, G.W. Humpage 77).
Shropshire 202 (59.4 overs) (J. Foster 56)
Toss: Warwickshire
Man of the Match: R.I.H.B. Dyer (119)
Adjudicator: F.M. Engineer

QUARTER-FINALS – 1 AUGUST

Middlesex beat **Lancashire** by 171 runs at Lord's, London
Middlesex 276-8 closed (60 overs) (G.D. Barlow 158). Lancashire 105 (29.4 overs) (W.W. Daniel 8.4-1-14-5)
Toss: Middlesex
Man of the Match: G.D. Barlow (158 – the first hundred for Middlesex in NatWest Trophy matches)
Adjudicator: A.V. Bedser

Northamptonshire beat **Leicestershire** by 3 wickets at Northampton
Leicestershire 238-9 closed (60 overs) (I.P. Butcher 81). Northamptonshire 242-7 (59.1 overs) (R.J. Boyd-Moss 88*)
Toss: Northamptonshire
Man of the Match: R.J. Boyd-Moss (88*)
Adjudicator: R.T. Simpson

Kent beat **Somerset** by 10 runs at Taunton
Kent 275-5 closed (60 overs) (M.R. Benson 96, C.J. Tavaré 103). Somerset 265-5 closed (60 overs) (P.M. Roebuck 81, N.A. Felton 87, B.C. Rose 54*)
Toss: Kent
Man of the Match: C.J. Tavaré (103)
Adjudicator: C.A. Milton

Warwickshire beat **Surrey** by 110 runs at Edgbaston
Warwickshire 305-5 closed (60 overs) (K.D. Smith 74, A. I. Kallicharran 101, D.L. Amiss 73*). Surrey 195 (51.1 overs) (D.J. Thomas 53, C.M. Old 11-1-45-4, G.W. Humpage made 4 dismissals)
Toss: Warwickshire
Man of the Match: A.I. Kallicharran (101)
Adjudicator: J.M. Parks

Middlesex beat **Northamptonshire** by 8 wickets at Lord's, London
Northamptonshire 226-6 closed (60 overs) (W. Larkins 52, R.J. Bailey 56*).
Middlesex 228-2 (54.5 overs) (W.N. Slack 79, M.W. Gatting 88*)
Toss: Middlesex
Man of the Match: W.N. Slack (79 and 12-0-49-1)
Adjudicator: J.M. Parks

Kent beat **Warwickshire** by 6 wickets at Edgbaston, Birmingham
Warwickshire 224 (59.3 overs) (A.I. Kallicharran 86). Kent 226-4 (58 overs) (M.R.
Benson 113*, R.M. Ellison 49*)
Toss: Kent
Man of the Match: M.R. Benson (113*)
Adjudicator: D.C.S. Compton

THE 1984 PICK-A-TEAM COMPETITION
(See page 2)

THE WINNING TEAM

(1) Glenn Turner, (2) Gordon Greenidge, (3) Viv Richards, (4) Zaheer
Abbas, (5) Clive Lloyd (Captain), (6) Ken McEwan, (7) Imran Khan,
(8) Richard Hadlee, (9) Malcolm Marshall, (10) Andy Roberts, (11)
Joel Garner.

There were 1,378 entries.

NATWEST BANK TROPHY FINAL

PLAYED AT LORD'S, 1 SEPTEMBER
MIDDLESEX WON BY 4 WICKETS

KENT

M.R. Benson	st Downton b Emburey	37
N.R. Taylor	b Slack	49
*C.J. Tavaré	c Downton b Daniel	28
D.G. Aslett	run out	11
C.S. Cowdrey	c Radley b Daniel	58
R.M. Ellison	not out	23
G.W. Johnson	run out	0
†S.N.V. Waterton	not out	4
D.I. Underwood	did not bat	
T.M. Alderman	did not bat	
K.B.S. Jarvis	did not bat	
Extras (B10, LB8, W3, NB1)		22
Total (60 overs) (6 wkts)		**232**

MIDDLESEX

G.D. Barlow	c Waterton b Jarvis	25
W.N. Slack	b Ellison	20
*M.W. Gatting	c Tavaré b Jarvis	37
R.O. Butcher	b Underwood	15
C.T. Radley	c Tavaré b Ellison	67
†P.R. Downton	c Cowdrey b Jarvis	40
J.E. Emburey	not out	17
P.H. Edmonds	not out	5
S.P. Hughes	did not bat	
N.G. Cowans	did not bat	
W.W. Daniel	did not bat	
Extras (LB7, W1, NB2)		10
Total (60 overs) (6 wkts)		**236**

Man of the Match: C.T. Radley
Adjudicator: C.H. Lloyd

BOWLING

MIDDLESEX	O	M	R	W		FALL OF WICKETS	
						K	M
Cowans	9	2	24	0			
Daniel	12	1	41	2	1st	96	39
Hughes	10	0	52	0	2nd	98	60
Edmonds	5	0	33	0	3rd	135	88
Slack	12	2	33	1	4th	163	124
Emburey	12	1	27	1	5th	217	211
KENT					6th	217	217
Alderman	12	0	53	0	7th	—	—
Jarvis	12	1	47	3	8th	—	—
Ellison	12	2	53	2	9th	—	—
Cowdrey	12	1	48	0	10th	—	—
Underwood	12	2	25	1			

NATWEST BANK TROPHY
PRINCIPAL RECORDS 1981–84

Highest Innings Total: 392-5 off 60 overs, Warwickshire v Oxfordshire (Birmingham) 1984.

Highest Innings Total by a Minor County: 256 off 58 overs, Oxfordshire v Warwickshire (Birmingham) 1983.

Highest Innings Total by a side batting second: 306-6 off 59.3 overs, Gloucestershire v Leicestershire (Leicester) 1983.

Highest Innings Total by a side batting first and losing: 302-5 off 60 overs, Leicestershire v Gloucestershire (Leicester) 1983.

Lowest Innings Total: 65 off 40.4 overs, Sussex v Somerset (Hove) 1983.

Lowest Innings Total by a First-Class County: 65 off 40.4 overs, Sussex v Somerset (Hove) 1983.

Biggest Victory: 227 runs: Warwickshire beat Oxfordshire (Birmingham) 1984.
There have been six victories by 9 wickets.

Highest Individual Innings: 206 A. I. Kallicharran, Warwickshire v Oxfordshire (Birmingham) 1984.

Highest Individual Innings by a Minor County Player: 119 P. A. Fowler, Oxfordshire v Warwickshire (Birmingham) 1983.

Centuries: 33 centuries have been scored in the competition.

Record Wicket Partnerships

1st	184	G.A. Gooch & B.R. Hardie, Essex v Hertfordshire (Hitchin)	1981
2nd	197	K.D. Smith & A.I. Kallicharran, Warwickshire v Oxfordshire (Birmingham)	1984
3rd	179	G.A. Gooch & K.S. McEwan, Essex v Scotland (Chelmsford)	1984
4th	150	A.J. Lamb & R.G. Williams, Northamptonshire v Worcestershire (Northampton)	1984
5th	166	M.A. Lynch & G.R.J. Roope, Surrey v Durham (Oval)	1982
6th	104	I.T. Botham & N.F.M. Popplewell, Somerset v Middlesex (Lord's)	1983
7th	160*	C.J. Richards & I.R. Payne, Surrey v Lincolnshire (Sleaford)	1983
8th	54	C.S. Cowdrey & R.M. Ellison, Kent v Essex (Chelmsford)	1983
9th	62	Asif Din & G.C. Small, Warwickshire v Surrey (Lord's)	1982
10th	81	S. Turner & R.E. East, Essex v Yorkshire (Leeds)	1982

Best Bowling: 7-32 S.P. Davis, Durham v Lancashire (Chester-le-Street) 1983.

Hat-Tricks: Nil

Most Wicket-Keeping Dismissals: 6 (5 ct 1st) R.W. Taylor, Derbyshire v Essex (Derby) 1981.

GILLETTE CUP WINNERS

1963 Sussex	1969 Yorkshire	1975 Lancashire
1964 Sussex	1970 Lancashire	1976 Northamptonshire
1965 Yorkshire	1971 Lancashire	1977 Middlesex
1966 Warwickshire	1972 Lancashire	1978 Sussex
1967 Kent	1973 Gloucestershire	1979 Somerset
1968 Warwickshire	1974 Kent	1980 Middlesex

NATWEST BANK TROPHY WINNERS

1981 Derbyshire	1982 Surrey	1983 Somerset
1984 Middlesex		

NATWEST BANK TROPHY
PRINCIPAL RECORDS 1963–1984

(including those in the former Gillette Cup)

Highest innings total: 392-5 off 60 overs, Warwickshire v Oxfordshire (Birmingham) 1984.

Highest innings total by a Minor County: 256 off 58 overs, Oxfordshire v Warwickshire (Birmingham) 1983.

Highest innings total by a side batting second: 306-6 off 59.3 overs, Gloucestershire v Leicestershire (Leicester) 1983.

Highest innings total by a side batting first and losing: 302-5 off 60 overs, Leicestershire v Gloucestershire (Leicester) 1983.

Lowest innings total: 41 off 20 overs, Cambridgeshire v Buckinghamshire (Cambridge) 1972; 41 off 19.4 overs, Middlesex v Essex (Westcliff) 1972; 41 off 36.1 overs, Shropshire v Essex (Wellington) 1974.

Lowest innings total by a side batting first and winning: 98 off 56.2 overs, Worcestershire v Durham (Chester-le-Street) 1968.

Highest individual innings: 206 A.I. Kallicharran, Warwickshire v Oxfordshire (Birmingham) 1984.

Highest individual innings by a Minor County player: 132 G. Robinson, Lincolnshire v Northumberland (Jesmond) 1971.

Centuries: 93 were scored in the Gillette Cup. 33 have been scored in the NatWest Bank Trophy.

Record Wicket Partnerships

1st	227	R.E. Marshall & B.L. Reed, Hampshire v Bedfordshire (Goldington)	1968
2nd	223	M.J. Smith & C.T. Radley, Middlesex v Hampshire (Lord's)	1977
3rd	179	G.A. Gooch & K.S. McEwan, Essex v Scotland (Chelmsford)	1984
4th	234*	D. Lloyd & C.H. Lloyd, Lancashire v Gloucestershire (Manchester)	1978
5th	166	M.A. Lynch & G.R.J. Roope, Surrey v Durham (Oval)	1982
6th	105	G.S. Sobers & R.A. White, Nottinghamshire v Worcestershire (Worcester)	1974
7th	160*	C.J. Richards & I.R. Payne, Surrey v Lincolnshire (Sleaford)	1983
8th	69	S.J. Rouse & D.J. Brown, Warwickshire v Middlesex (Lord's)	1977
9th	87	M.A. Nash & A.E. Cordle, Glamorgan v Lincolnshire (Swansea)	1974
10th	81	S. Turner & R.E. East, Essex v Yorkshire (Leeds)	1982
Hat-tricks:		J.D.F. Larter, Northamptonshire v Sussex (Northampton)	1963
		D.A.D. Sydenham, Surrey v Cheshire (Hoylake)	1964
		R.N.S. Hobbs, Essex v Middlesex (Lord's)	1968
		N.M. McVicker, Warwickshire v Lincolnshire (Birmingham)	1971

Seven wickets in an innings: 7-15 A.L. Dixon, Kent v Surrey (The Oval) in 1968; 7-30 P.J. Sainsbury, Hampshire v Norfolk (Southampton) in 1965; 7-32 S.P. Davis, Durham v Lancashire (Chester-le-Street) in 1983; 7-33 R.D. Jackman, Surrey v Yorkshire (Harrogate) in 1970; 7-37 N.A. Mallender, Northamptonshire v Worcestershire (Northampton) in 1984.

Most 'Man of the Match' awards: 7 C.H. Lloyd (Lancashire); 6 B.L. D'Oliveira (Worcestershire) and B. Wood (Lancashire); 5 M.C. Cowdrey (Kent), A.W. Greig (Sussex) and R.D.V. Knight (Gloucestershire and Surrey).

WINNERS OF THE 1984 PICK-A-TEAM COMPETITION

First Prize: £400 T.J.W. Saunders, 32 Cromwell Road, Whitefield, Manchester M25 7RQ

Second Prize: £250 Mrs E.M. Brewer, 12 Sandbach Road, Brislington, Bristol BS4 3RZ

Third Prize: £200 J. Bowen, 514 Woodway Lane, Walsgrave, Coventry CV2 2AF

Fourth Prize: £150 Miss J. E. Hayes, 48 Derby Road, Kirkby-in-Ashfield, Nottingham NG17 9BD

25 Runners-up: £10 each

W.R. Ashby, The Old Bakery, 26 Queen Street, Tintinhull, Yeovil, Somerset; N.H. Bailey, 10 Elmwood Road, Hilsea, Portsmouth, Hants PO2 9QL; Robert Usherwood, 20 Endcliffe Terrace Road, Sheffield S11 8RT; B. Edwards, 29 Mold Road, Wrexham, Clwyd LL11 2AE; Johnny Singh, 73 Maria's Pleasure, Wakenaam, Essequibo River, Guyana, South America; Peter Trussell, The Cottage, Brookledge Lane, Adlington, Cheshire; Richard Calder, Vicarage Cottage, 17 Parsons Street, Woodford Halse, Daventry, Northants NN11 6RE; Gilbert Jessop, The Master's Lodge, St John's Hospital, Bath BA1 1SL; Paul Marshall, 4 Maws Drive, Dundee, Tayside DD3 9BN; Alan Rowe, 45 Dukes Avenue, London N10 2PX; Alan Penfold, 25 Bosbury Road, Catford, London SE6 2SJ; Andrew Swindells, 43 Calton Gardens, Bath, Avon BA2 4QG; J. Goodman, 26 Downer Drive, Sarratt, Rickmansworth, Herts; G. Pickard, The Cottage, Willowgarth School, Grimethorpe, Nr Barnsley, S Yorks S72 7AJ; M. Hillman, 2 Raffles House, Brampton Grove, Hendon, London NW4 4BG; M. Tutt, 9 Robert Drive, Greasby, Wirral, Merseyside L49 1SD; M. Dancocks, 3 Sydgates, Wadborough, Worcester WR8 9HD; Michael Barrett, 26 Gebe Road, Tiptree, Colchester, Essex CO5 0TP; R.L. Collins, 26 Stangate Road, Strood, Kent MG2 2TU; A. Wright, 37 Southern Walk, Scartho, Grimsby, South Humberside; Brian Strawson, Skelton House Farm, Scothern Road, Nettleham, Lincoln; R. N. Billinghurst, 82 Ranworth Avenue, Hoddesdon, Herts EN11 9NT; C.J. Mitchell, 37 Pragnell Road, Grove Park, Lee, London SE12 0LF; David Weston, 34 Deanhouse, Netherthong, Huddersfield HD7 2UG; John Boakes, 1 Manse Road, Carnon Downs, Truro, Cornwall TR3 6JA.

The winning team will be found on page 56.

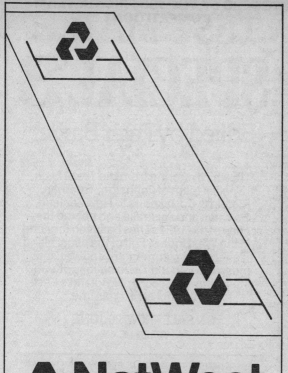

NatWest

Sponsors

TEST MATCH
SPECIAL 3

Edited by Peter Baxter

This third offering from the *Test Match Special* team of Johnston, Trueman, Blofeld & Co. takes us to New Zealand, Pakistan and Australia and behind the scenes of the 1984 series between England and the West Indies. Full of the usual blend of anecdote, commentary and statistics plus a dip into the *TMS* mailbag, it's an entertainment record of England's best-loved cricket programme.

ON SALE FROM 20 JUNE
AT £9.95

Available through bookshops or in case of difficulty direct from Marketing Services Dept., Queen Anne Press, Maxwell House, 74 Worship St, London EC2A 2EN; cash with order plus £1.40 p&p. Please make cheques payable to Macdonald & Co (Publishers) Ltd. Allow 28 days for delivery.

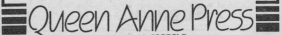

Queen Anne Press

a division of Macdonald, a BPCC PLC company

LANCASHIRE WIN EASILY IN THE BENSON & HEDGES FINAL

This Benson and Hedges Final, like so many before it, did not produce a dramatic finish of the sort that has the crowd on edge throughout the last few overs. When Warwickshire were 115 for 3 against Lancashire the match had all the makings of an exciting game of cricket; but when they were all out for 139 the result was beginning to look like a foregone conclusion. Momentarily, when Lancashire were 71 for 4, Warwickshire were back in the hunt, but it was only momentarily. David Hughes, with a wealth of one-day experience, and young Neil Fairbrother, with very little experience (but surely with a great future), were able to ward off a very moderate Warwickshire attack and win comfortably. Perhaps the greatest surprise of the day was when Peter May gave the Gold Award to John Abrahams who was out for nought and didn't bowl, something which, when historians look back in the future, they will find it very difficult to understand. The award was, however, for his captaincy. As a captain himself, and having been looking for more positive deeds from England's captains, this may be an area which particularly appealed to May. So John Abrahams holds a record which may never be broken: an award winner having failed to score or bowl!

Lancashire thus stirred up memories of their great Gillette days when they won the Gillette Cup three years in succession in 1970, 1971 and 1972, and then again in 1975. Warwickshire in Group A and Essex in Group D were the only Counties to have won all four of their Zonal matches and Essex were strong favourites to beat Lancashire at Chelmsford in the Quarter-Final. Having got through, Lancashire were not expected to beat Notts in the Semi-Final at Trent Bridge but they won quite easily by 6 wickets. Not surprisingly, Lancashire were favourites for the Final on their Quarter-Final and Semi-Final form, and they landed the odds at Lord's.

Scotland, the Minor Counties, and Combined Universities all finished at the foot of the table in their respective groups and may be expected to continue to do so. Playing so early in the season poses a problem for Scotland and Minor County players, and such things as examinations at the Universities

PERCY CHAPMAN

a biography

DAVID LEMMON

Relive the Golden Age of cricket with this new biography of one of its most attractive and controversial figures. Tracing the life of Percy Chapman from his spectacular rise to fame to his tragic decline and death, it's a must for all devotees of that magical cricketing era.

ON SALE NOW – £9.95

Available through bookshops or in case of difficulty direct from Marketing Services Dept., Queen Anne Press, Maxwell House, 74 Worship St, London EC2A 2EN; cash with order plus £1.40 p&p. Please make cheques payable to Macdonald & Co (Publishers) Ltd. Allow 28 days for delivery.

Queen Anne Press

a division of Macdonald, a BPCC PLC company

take precedence these days. Yorkshire, last season's John Player winners, had looked possible contenders at one time but unexpectedly went down to Warwickshire in the Semi-Final – a poor year for Yorkshire, to be sure.

1984 RESULTS

5 MAY

Chelmsford: Essex 222-8 (in 55 overs) beat Gloucestershire 217-9 (in 55 overs) by 5 runs
Gold Award: B.R. Hardie

Swansea: Somerset 182-7 (in 49 overs) beat Glamorgan 178-9 (in 55 overs) by 3 wickets
Gold Award: R.C. Ontong

Southampton: Hampshire 155-1 (in 47 overs) beat Combined Universities 154 (in 49.2 overs) by 9 wickets
Gold Award: C.L. Smith

Lord's: Kent 220-9 (in 55 overs) beat Middlesex 143 (in 47 overs) by 77 runs
Gold Award: R.M. Ellison

Northampton: Northamptonshire 256-3 (in 55 overs) beat Scotland 230 (in 54.3 overs) by 26 runs
Gold Award: A.J. Lamb

Nottingham: Nottinghamshire 210-7 (in 55 overs) beat Worcestershire 181 (in 52.2 overs) by 29 runs
Gold Award: B.N. French

Leeds: Yorkshire 178-3 (in 50 overs) beat Leicestershire 172-9 (in 55 overs) by 7 wickets
Gold Award: P. Willey

Bowden: Lancashire 223-4 (in 53.2 overs) beat Minor Counties 219-4 (in 55 overs) by 6 wickets
Gold Award: R.E. Hayward

12 MAY

Bristol: Gloucestershire 240-2 (in 52.5 overs) beat Hampshire 239-9 (in 55 overs) by 8 wickets
Gold Award: P.W. Romaines

Canterbury: Kent 201-7 (in 55 overs) beat Glamorgan 144 (in 53 overs) by 57 runs
Gold Award: R.M. Ellison

Manchester: Lancashire 104-3 (in 38.4 overs) beat Nottinghamshire 100 (in 50.4 overs) by 7 wickets
Gold Award: S.T. Jeffries

Leicester: Warwickshire 229-7 (in 55 overs) beat Leicestershire 202 (in 53.5 overs) by 27 runs
Gold Award: D.L. Amiss

Taunton: Sussex 279-5 (in 55 overs) beat Somerset 205 (in 53.2 overs) by 74 runs
Gold Award: J.R.T. Barclay

Worcester: Derbyshire 257-7 (in 55 overs) beat Worcestershire 257-9 (in 55 overs) by losing fewer wickets
Gold Award: D.B. D'Oliveira

Perth: Yorkshire 231-7 (in 55 overs) beat Scotland 186-8 (in 55 overs) by 45 runs
Gold Award: J.D. Love

Oxford: Surrey 194-9 (in 54.1 overs) beat Combined Universities 193-6 (in 55 overs) by 1 wicket
Gold Award: A.J.T. Miller

15 MAY

Derby: Nottinghamshire 282-4 (in 55 overs) beat Derbyshire 223 (in 51 overs) by 59 runs
Gold Award: B.C. Broad

Bristol: Combined Universities 243 (in 54.3 overs) beat Gloucestershire 216 (in 50.4 overs) by 27 runs
Gold Award: A.J.T. Miller

P.C.A. 1985—3

THE
1985 CRICKETERS' WHO'S WHO

Compiled and edited by

IAIN SPROAT

The complete cricketing companion for every enthusiast of the game. Packed with facts and information about every player who appeared for a County First XI during 1984 plus details on performances, careers and statistics, it's a unique guide to who's who and what's what in cricket!

'Compulsive reading' *Ian Botham*

'It's always in my bag'
Brian Johnston, Test Match Special

ON SALE FROM 25 APRIL
£7.95   paper

Available through bookshops or in case of difficulty direct from Marketing Services Dept., Queen Anne Press, Maxwell House, 74 Worship St, London EC2A 2EN; cash with order plus £1.40 p&p. Please make cheques payable to Macdonald & Co (Publishers) Ltd. Allow 28 days for delivery.

Queen Anne Press

a division of Macdonald a BPCC PLC company

Leicester: **Leicestershire** 243-4 (in 53 overs) beat **Northamptonshire** 239-6 (in 55 overs) by 6 wickets
Gold Award: P. Willey

Birmingham: **Warwickshire** 254 (in 55 overs) beat **Yorkshire** 247-8 (in 55 overs) by 7 runs
Gold Award: S.N. Hartley

Worcester: **Worcestershire** 209-3 (in 42.5 overs) beat **Minor Counties** 205-8 (in 55 overs) by 7 wickets
Gold Award: D.N. Patel

15, 16 MAY

Chelmsford: **Essex** 152-4 (in 39.3 overs) beat **Surrey** 150 (in 50 overs) by 6 wickets
Gold Award: S. Turner

Lord's: **Middlesex** 215-8 (in 52-4 overs) beat **Sussex** 214 (in 54.5 overs) by 2 wickets
Gold Award: C.T. Radley

16 MAY

Canterbury: **Somerset** 161-8 (in 54.4 overs) beat **Kent** 160 (in 55 overs) by 2 wickets
Gold Award: M.D. Crowe

17 MAY

Manchester: **Lancashire** 240-7 (in 53 overs) beat **Worcestershire** 237-9 (in 55 overs) by 3 wickets
Gold Award: D.N. Patel

Taunton: **Somerset** 193-3 (in 45.1 overs) beat **Middlesex** 189-9 (in 55 overs) by 7 wickets
Gold Award: N.F.M. Popplewell

Hove: **Sussex** 169-3 (in 47.3 overs) beat **Glamorgan** 165 (in 55 overs) by 7 wickets
Gold Award: G.D. Mendis

Glasgow: **Leicestershire** 207-4 (in 54.2 overs) beat **Scotland** 204-5 (in 55 overs) by 6 wickets
Gold Award: O. Henry

17, 18 MAY

Northampton: **Warwickshire** 252-8 (in 54 overs) beat **Northamptonshire** 248-8 (in 55 overs) by 2 wickets
Gold Award: A.I. Kallicharran

The Oval: **Hampshire** 223-7 (in 55 overs) beat **Surrey** 117 (in 39.1 overs) by 106 runs
Gold Award: S. Andrew

Shrewsbury: **Derbyshire** 201-6 (in 52.3 overs) beat **Minor Counties** 197-8 (in 55 overs) by 4 wickets
Gold Award: W.P. Fowler

Cambridge: **Essex** 156-4 (in 38.3 overs) beat **Combined Universities** 152-8 (in 55 overs) by 6 wickets
Gold Award: K.S. McEwan

19 MAY

Derby: **Derbyshire** 210-8 (in 55 overs) beat **Lancashire** 165-9 (in 55 overs) by 45 runs
Gold Award: R.J. Finney

Cardiff: **Glamorgan** 165-3 (in 51.4 overs) beat **Middlesex** 163 (in 52.2 overs) by 7 wickets
Gold Award: W.W. Davis

Southampton: **Essex** 254-4 (in 55 overs) beat **Hampshire** 227-8 (in 55 overs) by 27 runs
Gold Award: D.R. Pringle

Nottingham: **Nottinghamshire** 140-6 (in 38.5 overs) beat **Minor Counties** 139-8 (in 55 overs) by 4 wickets
Gold Award: R.J. Hadlee

The Oval: **Surrey** 202 (in 55 overs) beat **Gloucestershire** 164 (in 51.3 overs) by 38 runs
Gold Award: G.S. Clinton

Hove: **Sussex** 230-9 (in 54.5 overs) beat **Kent** 227-7 (in 55 overs) by 1 wicket
Gold Award: C.M. Wells

Birmingham: **Warwickshire** 262-7 (in 55 overs) beat **Scotland** 133 (in 53.1 overs) by 129 runs
Gold Award: C.M. Old

Bradford: **Yorkshire** 252-3 (in 53.3 overs) beat **Northamptonshire** 251-7 (in 55 overs) by 7 wickets
Gold Award: G. Boycott

QUARTER-FINALS – 6 JUNE

Chelmsford: Lancashire 158-6 (in 52.5 overs) beat **Essex** 157 (in 55 overs) by 4 wickets
Gold Award: J. Abrahams

Hove: Yorkshire 260-5 (in 55 overs) beat **Sussex** 223 (in 53.3 overs) by 37 runs
Gold Award: M.D. Moxon

Birmingham: Warwickshire 282-5 (in 55 overs) beat **Somerset** 216 (in 47.1 overs) by 66 runs
Gold Award: T.A. Lloyd

7 JUNE

Nottingham: Nottinghamshire 256-3 (in 55 overs) beat **Surrey** 89 (in 35.3 overs) by 167 runs
Gold Award: C.E.B. Rice

SEMI-FINALS – 20 JUNE

Leeds: Warwickshire 276-4 (in 55 overs) beat **Yorkshire** 273-8 (in 55 overs) by 3 runs
Gold Award: D.L. Bairstow

Nottingham: Lancashire 224-4 (in 52.2 overs) beat **Nottinghamshire** 223-6 (in 55 overs) by 6 wickets
Gold Award: M.R. Chadwick

ZONAL POINTS TABLE

Group A	P	W	L	Pts
Warwickshire	4	4	0	8
Yorkshire	4	3	1	6
Leicestershire	4	2	2	4
Northamptonshire	4	1	3	2
Scotland	4	0	4	0

Group B	P	W	L	Pts
Nottinghamshire	4	3	1	6
Lancashire	4	3	1	6
Derbyshire	4	3	1	6
Worcestershire	4	1	3	2
Minor Counties	4	0	4	0

Group C	P	W	L	Pts
Somerset	4	3	1	6
Sussex	4	3	1	6
Kent	4	2	2	4
Middlesex	4	1	3	2
Glamorgan	4	1	3	2

Group D	P	W	L	Pts
Essex	4	4	0	8
Surrey	4	2	2	4
Hampshire	4	2	2	4
Gloucestershire	4	1	3	2
Combined Universities	4	1	3	2

THE BENSON & HEDGES CUP FINAL
PLAYED AT LORD'S, 21 JULY
LANCASHIRE WON BY 6 WICKETS

WARWICKSHIRE

R.I.H.B. Dyer	c Maynard b Watkinson	11
P.A. Smith	c Fairbrother b Allott	0
A.I. Kallicharran	c Abrahams b Jefferies	70
D.L. Amiss	c Maynard b Watkinson	20
†G.W. Humpage	c Maynard b Allott	8
A.M. Ferreira	c & b O'Shaughnessy	4
C.M. Old	b O'Shaughnessy	5
Asif Din	c Ormrod by Jefferies	3
G.C. Small	lbw b Jefferies	2
N. Gifford	not out	2
*R.G.D. Willis	c Jefferies b Allott	2
Extras (LB4, NB8)		12
Total (50.4 overs)		139

LANCASHIRE

G. Fowler	c Humpage b Willis	7
J.A. Ormrod	c Humpage b Ferreira	24
S.J. O'Shaughnessy	c Humpage b Ferreira	22
D.P. Hughes	not out	35
*J. Abrahams	c Humpage b Smith	0
N.H. Fairbrother	not out	36
S.J. Jefferies	did not bat	
J. Simmons	did not bat	
†C. Maynard	did not bat	
M. Watkinson	did not bat	
P.J.W. Allott	did not bat	
Extras (LB6, W1, NB9)		16
Total (42.4 overs) (4 wkts)		140

Gold Award: J. Abrahams

BOWLING

Lancashire	O	M	R	W
Allott	8.4	0	15	3
Jefferies	11	2	28	3
Watkinson	9	0	23	2
O'Shaughnessy	11	1	43	2
Simmons	11	3	18	0
Warwickshire				
Willis	9	0	10	1
Small	4	0	30	0
Ferreira	11	2	26	2
Old	10.4	3	23	0
Smith	6	0	20	1
Gifford	2	1	6	0

FALL OF WICKETS		
	WA	LA
1st	1	23
2nd	48	43
3rd	102	70
4th	115	71
5th	121	—
6th	127	—
7th	132	—
8th	133	—
9th	134	—
10th	139	—

BENSON & HEDGES CUP
PRINCIPAL RECORDS

Highest innings total: 350-3 off 55 overs, Essex v Combined Universities (Chelmsford) 1979.

Highest innings total by a side batting second: 291-5 off 53.5 overs, Warwickshire v Lancashire (Manchester) 1981.

Highest innings total by a side batting first and losing: 288-9 off 55 overs, Lancashire v Warwickshire (Manchester) 1981.

Lowest completed innings total: 56 off 26.2 overs, Leicestershire v Minor Counties (Wellington) 1982.

Highest individual innings: 198* G.A. Gooch, Essex v Sussex (Hove) 1982.

Record Wicket Partnerships

1st	241	S.M. Gavaskar & B.C. Rose, Somerset v Kent (Canterbury)	1980
2nd	285*	C.G. Greenidge & D.R. Turner, Hampshire v Minor Counties (South) (Amersham)	1973
3rd	268*	G.A. Gooch & K.W.R. Fletcher, Essex v Sussex (Hove) (Chesterfield)	1982
4th	184*	D. Lloyd & B.W. Reidy, Lancashire v Derbyshire	1980
5th	134	M. Maslin & D.N.F. Slade, Minor Counties (East) v Nottinghamshire (Nottingham)	1976
6th	114	M.J. Khan & G.P. Ellis, Glamorgan v Gloucestershire (Bristol)	1975
7th	149*	J.D. Love & C.M. Old, Yorkshire v Scotland (Bradford)	1981
8th	109	R.E. East & N. Smith, Essex v Northamptonshire (Chelmsford)	1977
9th	81	J.N. Shepherd & D.L. Underwood, Kent v Middlesex (Lord's)	1975
10th	80*	D.L. Bairstow & M. Johnson, Yorkshire v Derbyshire (Derby)	1981

Hat-tricks: G.D. McKenzie, Leicestershire v Worcestershire (Worcester) 1972. K. Higgs, Leicestershire v Surrey (Lord's) 1974. A.A. Jones, Middlesex v Essex (Lord's) 1977. M.J. Procter, Gloucestershire v Hampshire (Southampton) 1977. W. Larkins, Northamptonshire v Combined Universities (Northampton) 1980. E.A. Moseley, Glamorgan v Kent (Cardiff) 1981.

Seven wickets in an innings: 7-12 W.W. Daniel, Middlesex v Minor Counties (East) (Ipswich) 1978, 7-22 J.R. Thomson, Middlesex v Hampshire (Lord's) 1981, 7-32 R.G.D. Willis, Warwickshire v Yorkshire (Birmingham) 1981.

Most 'Gold' awards: 11 B. Wood (10 for Lancashire, 1 for Derbyshire), 9 J.H. Edrich (Surrey), G.A. Gooch (Essex).

BENSON & HEDGES CUP WINNERS

1972 Leicestershire	1979 Essex
1973 Kent	1980 Northamptonshire
1974 Surrey	1981 Somerset
1975 Leicestershire	1982 Somerset
1976 Kent	1983 Middlesex
1977 Gloucestershire	1984 Lancashire
1978 Kent	

ESSEX WIN THE JOHN PLAYER

We wrote in last year's *Playfair* about the John Player: 'There can be few competitions in any sport anywhere in the world where each side's fortunes vary so much from season to season.' How this applies yet again for the 1984 season.

Yorkshire, who had been sixteenth in 1982 and first in 1983, now dropped to thirteenth. Somerset, who were second in 1983, were bracketed thirteenth with Yorkshire, and Derbyshire, who were sixth in 1983, were now relegated to bottom place. Kent, third in 1983, were bracketed ninth with Hampshire and Glamorgan. The dramatic climb up the table was made by Notts from fifteenth in 1983 to second in 1984. All this, perhaps, is characteristic of the competition, which is decided over a short period of 40 overs; and with rain involving mathematical calculations to determine a winner, luck plays a more important part than in any other competition. As against this it could be argued that the best team in the County Championship – Essex – also won the John Player. Happily for them, none of their matches ended in 'no result', whereas Sussex, who were third, had three; so did Warwickshire, but they were too far behind for it to have made any great difference.

JOHN PLAYER LEAGUE FINAL TABLE

	P	W	L	Tie	NR	Pts
Essex (6)	16	12	3	1	0	50
Nottinghamshire (15)	16	10	5	0	1	42
Sussex (4)	16	9	4	0	3	42
Lancashire (8)	16	10	6	0	0	40
Middlesex (8)	16	9	5	1	1	40
Worcestershire (11)	16	9	5	0	2	40
Warwickshire (9)	16	7	6	0	3	34
Surrey (11)	16	7	7	0	2	32
Hampshire (5)	16	7	9	0	0	28
Glamorgan (10)	16	6	8	0	2	28
Kent (3)	16	6	8	0	2	28
Northamptonshire (13)	16	6	9	0	1	26
Gloucestershire (14)	16	5	9	0	2	24
Leicestershire (11)	16	4	8	0	4	24
Somerset (2)	16	5	9	0	2	24
Yorkshire (1)	16	6	10	0	0	24
Derbyshire (6)	16	4	11	0	1	18

1983 positions in brackets.

JOHN PLAYER SPECIAL LEAGUE
PRINCIPAL RECORDS

Highest innings total: 310 for 5 off 40 overs, Essex v Glamorgan (Southend) 1983
Lowest completed innings total: 23 off 19.4 overs, Middlesex v Yorks (Leeds) 1974
Highest individual innings: 176 G.A. Gooch, Essex v Glamorgan (Southend) 1983
Record Wicket Partnerships

1st	224	J.A. Ormrod and D.N. Patel, Worcs v Hants (Southampton)	1982
2nd	273	G.A. Gooch & K.S. McEwan, Essex v Notts (Nottingham)	1983
3rd	215	W. Larkins & R.G. Williams, Northants v Worcs (Luton)	1982
4th	175*	M.J.K. Smith & D.L. Amiss, Warwicks v Yorks (Birmingham)	1970
5th	179	I.T. Botham & I.V.A. Richards, Somerset v Hants (Taunton)	1981
6th	121	C.P. Wilkins & A.J. Borrington, Derby v Warwicks (Chesterfield)	1972
7th	101	S.J. Windaybank & D.A. Graveney, Glos v Notts (Nottingham)	1981
8th	95*	D. Breakwell & K.F. Jennings, Somerset v Notts (Nottingham)	1976
9th	105	D.G. Moir & R.W. Taylor, Derby v Kent (Derby)	1984
10th	57	D.A. Graveney & J.B. Mortimore, Glos v Lancs (Tewkesbury)	1973

Four wickets in four balls: A. Ward, Derby v Sussex (Derby) 1970.
Hat-tricks (excluding above): R. Palmer, Somerset v Glos (Bristol) 1970. K.D. Boyce, Essex v Somerset (Westcliff) 1971. G.D. McKenzie, Leics v Essex (Leicester) 1972. R.G.D. Willis, Warwicks v Yorks (Birmingham) 1973. W. Blenkiron, Warwicks v Derby (Buxton) 1974. A. Buss, Sussex v Worcs (Hastings) 1974. J.M. Rice, Hants v Northants (Southampton) 1975. M.A. Nash, Glamorgan v Worcs (Worcester) 1975. A. Hodgson, Northants v Sussex (Northampton) 1976. A.E. Cordle, Glamorgan v Hants (Portsmouth) 1979. C.J. Tunnicliffe, Derby v Worcs (Derby) 1979. M.D. Marshall, Hants v Surrey (Southampton) 1981. I.V.A. Richards, Somerset v Essex (Chelmsford) 1982, P.W. Jarvis, Yorks v Derby (Derby) 1982, R.M. Ellison, Kent v Hants (Canterbury) 1983.
Eight wickets in an innings: 8-26 K.D. Boyce, Essex v Lancs (Manchester) 1971.

JOHN PLAYER LEAGUE CHAMPIONS

1969 Lancashire	1977 Leicestershire
1970 Lancashire	1978 Hampshire
1971 Worcestershire	1979 Somerset
1972 Kent	1980 Warwickshire
1973 Kent	1981 Essex
1974 Leicester	1982 Sussex
1975 Hampshire	1983 Yorkshire
1976 Kent	1984 Essex

ESSEX RETAIN THE
COUNTY CHAMPIONSHIP

Essex retained their County title in 1984, having won it in 1983 for the second time, but this bald statement of fact conceals the high drama during the final stages of 1984. It was to be Essex or Nottinghamshire, and after the long, hot summer months the ultimate winner was not decided until the final over. Notts were playing Somerset at Taunton and needed fourteen runs from the sixtieth over for the win which would produce sixteen points, enough to overtake Essex. Their last pair were at the wicket. Bore hit 4, 4, 2 off the first three balls, played defensively at the fourth, but was caught at long-off from the fifth: it was all over.

Chelmsford celebrated. Nottingham did not. For Notts it was a bitterly disappointing end to what had promised to be a golden season. They were well fancied for the Benson & Hedges and the NatWest, and were beaten at home in each competition by Lancashire and Middlesex, and were runners-up to Essex in the John Player. They could have won all four at one stage in the season: they won nothing in the end.

It was a splendid season for Essex, a fine side admirably led by Keith Fletcher. It is just surprising that although they seem well capable of winning everything else, they have never been in the Final of the Gillette Cup, and now the NatWest, in twenty two years.

In the summer of 1984 they were clearly running for the title virtually throughout the season. In early July they were second, but with a game in hand over the leaders, Fletcher was thrusting them forward at every opportunity. It is interesting that early July had very nearly set the pattern. Essex were second – but a game in hand over Leicestershire who were then top – and Notts third. At the bottom of the table Lancashire were sixteenth and Gloucestershire last, and this is how they finished. England's tragic loss of Graham Gooch by the tiresome ban was certainly a great gain for Essex, and with Pringle and Foster not called upon all the time by England, and the superb bowling of John Lever, Essex had great advantages: a balanced side with something of everything in attack and defence.

The measure of how well a side has done, of course, can be

accurately gauged by how their performances compare with the previous season. In this respect Notts can be highly pleased with themselves with second in the County Championship as opposed to fourteenth in the previous season. Middlesex dropped one place from second to third; Kent improved from seventh to fifth, and Leicestershire and Surrey finished in exactly the same position as in 1983 – fourth and eighth respectively. At the other end of the scale, the biggest fall was by Hampshire who dropped from third to fifteenth. Yorkshire were being watched very carefully by the cricketing world at large after their winter of discontent and disruption. Certainly they improved from seventeenth place to fourteenth, but then fourteenth in the County Championship table hardly calls for any sort of celebration in the light of Yorkshire's illustrious past – they have been County Champions on thirty one occasions. Overall, they were beaten by a Minor County in the NatWest; unexpectedly beaten by Warwickshire at Headingley in the Benson & Hedges Semi-Final, and fell from first to thirteenth in the John Player. Food for thought, indeed. Essex, by contrast, are the first County to win the Championship and the John Player in the same season – the two extremes of cricket skills, but both within the compass of an all-round side.

BRITANNIC ASSURANCE CHAMPIONSHIP FINAL TABLE

	P	W	L	D	Tie	Bt	Bw	Pts
1—Essex (1)	24	13	3	8	0	64	83	355
2—Nottinghamshire (14)	24	12	3	9	0	68	81	341
3—Middlesex (2)	24	8	7	9	0	63	78	269
4—Leicestershire (4)	24	8	2	14	0	60	78	266
5—Kent (7)	24	8	3	11	2	45	65	254
6—Sussex (11)	24	7	6	10	1	54	79	249
7—Somerset (10)	24	6	7	11	0	60	78	234
8—Surrey (8)	24	6	6	12	0	62	72	230
9—Warwickshire (5)	24	6	7	11	0	71	60	227
10—Worcestershire (16)	24	5	5	14	0	66	74	220
11—Derbyshire (9)	24	4	6	14	0	72	66	202
Northamptonshire (6)	24	5	9	9	1	58	56	202
13—Glamorgan (15)	24	4	2	18	0	65	71	200
14—Yorkshire (17)	24	5	4	15	0	59	55	194
15—Hampshire (3)	24	3	13	8	0	58	62	168
16—Lancashire (13)	24	1	9	14	0	49.	72	137
17—Gloucestershire (12)	24	1	10	13	0	56	61	133

Sussex total includes 12 points for a win in 1 innings match. 1983 positions in brackets.

COUNTY CHAMPIONS

The earliest winners of the title were decided usually by the least matches lost. In 1888 an unofficial points table was introduced and in 1890 the Championship was constituted officially. Since 1977 it has been sponsored by Schweppes.

Year	County	Year	County	Year	County
1864	Surrey	1898	Yorkshire	1948	Glamorgan
1865	Nottinghamshire	1899	Surrey	1949	Middlesex / Yorkshire
1866	Middlesex	1900	Yorkshire		
1867	Yorkshire	1901	Yorkshire	1950	Lancashire / Surrey
1868	Nottinghamshire	1902	Yorkshire		
1869	Nottinghamshire / Yorkshire	1903	Middlesex	1951	Warwickshire
		1904	Lancashire	1952	Surrey
1870	Yorkshire	1905	Yorkshire	1953	Surrey
1871	Nottinghamshire	1906	Kent	1954	Surrey
1872	Nottinghamshire	1907	Nottinghamshire	1955	Surrey
1873	Gloucestershire / Nottinghamshire	1908	Yorkshire	1956	Surrey
		1909	Kent	1957	Surrey
1874	Gloucestershire	1910	Kent	1958	Surrey
1875	Nottinghamshire	1911	Warwickshire	1959	Yorkshire
1876	Gloucestershire	1912	Yorkshire	1960	Yorkshire
1877	Gloucestershire	1913	Kent	1961	Hampshire
1878	Undecided	1914	Surrey	1962	Yorkshire
1879	Nottinghamshire / Lancashire	1919	Yorkshire	1963	Yorkshire
		1920	Middlesex	1964	Worcestershire
1880	Nottinghamshire	1921	Middlesex	1965	Worcestershire
1881	Lancashire	1922	Yorkshire	1966	Yorkshire
1882	Nottinghamshire / Lancashire	1923	Yorkshire	1967	Yorkshire
		1924	Yorkshire	1968	Yorkshire
1883	Nottinghamshire	1925	Yorkshire	1969	Glamorgan
1884	Nottinghamshire	1926	Lancashire	1970	Kent
1885	Nottinghamshire	1927	Lancashire	1971	Surrey
1886	Nottinghamshire	1928	Lancashire	1972	Warwickshire
1887	Surrey	1929	Nottinghamshire	1973	Hampshire
1888	Surrey	1930	Lancashire	1974	Worcestershire
1889	Surrey / Lancashire / Nottinghamshire	1931	Yorkshire	1975	Leicestershire
		1932	Yorkshire	1976	Middlesex
		1933	Yorkshire	1977	Kent / Middlesex
1890	Surrey	1934	Lancashire		
1891	Surrey	1935	Yorkshire	1978	Kent
1892	Surrey	1936	Derbyshire	1979	Essex
1893	Yorkshire	1937	Yorkshire	1980	Middlesex
1894	Surrey	1938	Yorkshire	1981	Nottinghamshire
1895	Surrey	1939	Yorkshire	1982	Middlesex
1896	Yorkshire	1946	Yorkshire	1983	Essex
1897	Lancashire	1947	Middlesex	1984	Essex

THE COUNTIES AND
THEIR PLAYERS

Compiled by Barry McCaully

with the assistance of **Brian Croudy** (averages and first-class records), **Brian Heald** (Test cricket), **Vic Isaacs** and **Nigel McCaully** (limited-overs cricket).

Abbreviations

B	Born	HSGC/	Highest score in
RHB	Right-hand bat	NW	Gillette Cup if higher
LHB	Left-hand bat		than NatWest Trophy
RF	Right-arm fast	HSJPL	Highest score John Player
RFM	Right-arm fast medium		League
RM	Right-arm medium	HSBH	Highest score Benson &
LF	Left-arm fast		Hedges Cup
LFM	Left-arm fast medium	BB	Best bowling figures
LM	Left-arm medium	BBUK	Best bowling figures in this
OB	Off-break		country
LB	Leg-break	BBTC	Best bowling figures in Test
LBG	Leg-break and googly		cricket if different from
SLA	Slow left-arm orthodox		above
SLC	Slow left-arm 'chinaman'	BBC	Best bowling figures for
WK	Wicket-keeper		County if different from
*	Not out or unfinished stand		above
HS	Highest score	BBNW	Best bowling figures
HSUK	Highest score in this		NatWest Trophy
	country	BBGC/	Best bowling figures in
HSTC	Highest score in Test	NW	Gillette Cup if better
	cricket if different from		than NatWest Trophy
	above	BBJPL	Best bowling figures John
HSC	Highest score for County if		Player League
	different from above	BBBH	Best bowling figures Benson
HSNW	Highest score NatWest		& Hedges Cup
	Trophy		

When a player is known by a name other than his first name, the name in question has been underlined.

All Test appearances are complete to 1st September 1984.

'Debut' denotes 'first-class debut' and 'Cap' means '1st XI county cap'.

Wisden 1981 indicates that a player was selected as one of *Wisden's* Five Cricketers of the Year for the year indicated.

Overseas tours on which a player played first-class cricket are listed.

Qualification for best performances: HS: 10. BB: 3 wkts.

Particulars of players who played in 1984 but have been omitted from the County sections because they are not expected to play in 1985 may be found in the Valete section on page 162.

DERBYSHIRE

Formation of present club: 1870.
Colours: Chocolate, amber and pale blue.
Badge: Rose and crown.
County Champions: 1936.
Nat West Trophy Winners: 1981.
Gillette Cup Finalists: 1969.
Best final position in John Player League: 3rd in 1970.
Benson & Hedges Cup Finalists: 1978.
Nat West Trophy Man of the Match Awards: 7.
Gillette Man of the Match Awards: 15.
Benson & Hedges Gold Awards: 31.

Secretary: R. Pearman, County Cricket Ground, Nottingham Road, Derby DE2 6DA.
Captain: K.J. Barnett.

Iain Stuart ANDERSON (Dovecliff GS, Wulfric School, Burton-on-Trent) B Derby 24/4/1960. RHB, OB. Debut 1978. 1233 runs (av. 37.36) in 1983. HS: 112 v Kent (Chesterfield) 1983. HSNW: 47 v Suffolk (Bury St. Edmunds) 1983. HSJPL: 54 v Somerset (Heanor) 1983. HSBH: 32 v Notts (Nottingham) 1983. BB: 4-35 v Australians (Derby) 1981.

Kim John BARNETT (Leek HS) B Stoke-on-Trent 17/7/1960. RHB, LB. Debut 1979. Cap 1982. Captain 1983. Played for Boland 1982-83. Tour: D.H. Robins Under-23 in New Zealand 1979-80. 1,000 runs (2) – 1,734 (av. 45.63) in 1984 best. NatWest Man of the Match: 2. HS: 144 v Middlesex (Derby) 1984. HSNW: 88 v Middlesex (Derby) 1983. HSJPL: 131* v Essex (Derby) 1984. HSBH: 34 v Notts (Nottingham) 1980 and 34 v Worcs (Worcester) 1984. BB: 4-76 v Warwicks (Birmingham) 1980. BBNW: 6-24 v Cumberland (Kensal) 1984. BBJPL: 3-39 v Yorks (Chesterfield) 1979.

Ian BROOME (Mitcham TC, Box Hill TC, Melbourne) B Bradenstoke cum Clack, Wilts 6/5/1960. RHB, RFM. Debut 1984. Played for Glos v Kent (JPL) 1980. HS: 26* v Kent (Derby) 1984. BBJPL: 3-53 v Surrey (Oval) 1984.

Roger John FINNEY (Lady Manners School, Bakewell) B Darley Dale 2/8/1960. RHB, LM. Debut 1982. BH Gold Award: 1. HS: 78 v Lancs (Buxton) 1984. HSNW: 14* v Suffolk (Bury St Edmunds) 1983. HSJPL: 50* v Worcs (Worcester) 1984. HSBH: 46 v Lancs (Derby) 1984. BB: 5-55 v Lancs (Buxton) 1984. BBJPL: 4-38 v Northants (Northampton) 1984.

William Peter FOWLER (Tawa College, Kamo HS, Otago U and Auckland U). B St. Helen's Lancs 13/3/1959. RHB, SLA. Debut and played for Northern Districts 1979-80 and 1980-81. Played for Auckland 1981-82. Debut for Derby in 1983. BH Gold Awards: 1. HS: 116 v Glamorgan (Derby) 1984. HSJPL: 51 v Northants (Northampton) 1984. HSBH: 53 v Minor Counties (Shrewsbury) 1984. BBJPL: 3-31 v Worcs (Worcester) 1984.

Alan HILL (New Mills GS, Chester College of Education) B Buxworth 29/6/1950. RHB, OB. Debut 1972. Cap 1976. Played for Orange Free State in 1976-77. Gillette Man of the Match: 1. NW Man of the Match: 1. BH Gold Award: 1. 1,000 runs (4)

77

DERBYSHIRE

– 1,352 (av. 32.97) in 1984 best. HS: 160* v Warwicks (Coventry) 1976. HSGC/NW: 72 v Middlesex (Derby) 1978. HSJPL: 120 v Northants (Buxton) 1976. HSBH: 102* v Warwicks (Ilkeston) 1978. BB: 3-5 Orange Free State v Northern Transvaal (Pretoria) 1976-77. BBJPL: 3-32 v Essex (Derby) 1984.

Michael Anthony HOLDING B Kingston, Jamaica 16/2/1954. RHB, RF. Debut for Jamaica in 1972-73. *Wisden* 1976. Played for Lancs 1981 and Tasmania 1982-83. Debut for Derby 1983. Tests: 49 for West Indies between 1975-76 and 1984. Tours: West Indies to Australia 1975-76, 1981-82, England 1976, 1980 and 1984, Australia and New Zealand 1979-80, Pakistan 1980-81, India 1983-84. International team to Pakistan 1981-82 One-day internationals: 66 for West Indies. HS: 69 West Indies v England (Birmingham) 1984. HSC: 63 v Glamorgan (Swansea) 1984. HSNW: 12* v Northants (Northampton) 1981. HSJPL: 12 v Hants (Derby) 1983. BB: 8-92 (14-149 match) West Indies v England (Oval) 1976. BBJPL: 6-74 v Glos (Manchester) 1981. BBNW: 3-35 v Hants (Southampton) 1981. BBJPL: 3-19 v Hants (Derby) 1983.

Bernard Joseph Michael MAHER (Abbotsfield and Bishopsmalt Schools, Harrow College, Loughborough U) B Hillingdon, Middlesex 11/2/1958. RHB, WK. Debut 1981. HS: 66 v Essex (Chesterfield) 1984. HSJPL: 13* v Yorks (Bradford) 1983.

Devon Eugene MALCOLM (Richmond College, Sheffield) B Kingston, Jamaica 22/2/1963. RHB, RF. Debut 1984. HS: 23 v Notts (Nottingham) 1984. BB: 3-78 v Kent (Maidstone) 1984.

Geoffrey MILLER (Chesterfield GS) B Chesterfield 8/9/1952. RHB, OB. Debut 1973. Cap 1976. Captain 1979-81. Tests: 34 between 1976 and 1984. One-day internationals: 25. Tours: India, Sri Lanka and Australia 1976-77, Pakistan and New Zealand 1977-78, Australia 1978-79 and 1979-80, West Indies 1980-81, Australia 1982-83. BH Gold Awards: 6. HS: 130 v Lancs (Manchester) 1984. HSTC: 98* v Pakistan (Lahore) 1977-78. HSGC/NW: 59* v Worcs (Worcester) 1978. HSJPL: 84 v Somerset (Chesterfield) 1980. HSBH: 88* v Minor Counties (Derby) 1982. BB: 8-70 v Leics (Coalville) 1982. BBTC: 5-44 v Australia (Sydney) 1978-79. BBNW: 3-28 v Suffolk (Bury St. Edmunds) 1983. BBJPL: 4-22 v Yorks (Huddersfield) 1978. BBBH: 3-23 v Surrey (Derby) 1979. Benefit 1985.

Dallas Gordon MOIR (Aberdeen GS) B Mtarfa, Malta 13/4/1957. RHB, SLA. Debut for Scotland 1980, for Derby 1981. HS: 107 v Warwicks (Chesterfield) 1984. HSNW: 23 v Leics (Leicester) 1984. HSBH: 44 Scotland v Lancs (Manchester) 1984. HSJPL: 79 v Kent (Derby) 1984. BB: 6-60 v Notts (Nottingham) 1984. BBJPL: 3-54 v Kent (Derby) 1984.

John Edward MORRIS (Shavington CS, Dane Bank CFE) B Crewe, Cheshire 1/4/1964. RHB, RM. Debut 1982. HS: 135 v Leics (Leicester) 1984. HSBH: 51 v Worcs (Worcester) 1984. HSJPL: 104 v Glos (Gloucester) 1984.

Ole Henrek MORTENSEN B Vejle Jutland, Denmark 29/1/1958. RHB, RFM. Debut 1983. HS: 40* v Glamorgan (Derby) 1984. BB: 6-27 v Yorks (Sheffield) 1983. BBNW: 3-16 v Suffolk (Bury St. Edmunds) 1983. BBJPL: 3-25 v Hants (Derby) 1984. BBBH: 3-30 v Lancs (Derby) 1984.

Paul Geoffrey NEWMAN (Alderman Newton's GS, Leicester) B Evington, Leicester 10/1/1959. RHB, RFM. Debut 1980. HS: 40 v Lancs (Manchester) 1984.

HSNW: 35 v Leics (Leicester) 1984. HSJPL: 24 v Yorks (Chesterfield) 1984. BB: 7-104 v Surrey (Oval) 1984. BBJPL: 4-21 v Hants (Derby) 1983. BBBH: 4-48 v Worcs (Worcester) 1982.

Bruce ROBERTS (Prince Edward, Rhodesia) B Lusaka, Zambia 30/5/1962. RHB, RM. Debut for Transvaal B in 1982-83; for Derby 1984. HS: 89 Transvaal B v Orange Free State (Johannesburg) and v Boland (Stellenbosch) 1983-84. HSUK: 80 v Leics (Chesterfield) 1984. HSJPL: 47 v Sussex (Heanor) 1984. HSBH: 11 v Lancs (Derby) 1984. BB: 4-32 Transvaal B v Orange Free State (Johannesburg) 1982-83. BBUK: 4-77 v Essex (Ilford) 1984. BBJPL: 4-29 v Lancs (Derby) 1984.

Jonathan Paul TAYLOR (Pingle School, Swadlincote) B Ashby-de-la-Zouch, Leics 8/8/1964. LHB, LFM. Debut 1984. HS: 11 v Middlesex (Derby) 1984.

Alan Esmond WARNER (Tabernacle School, St. Kitts) B Birmingham 12/5/1957. RHB, RFM. Debut for Worcs 1982. Joined Derby for 1985. HS: 67 Worcs v Warwicks (Birmingham) 1982. HSJPL: 14 Worcs v Derby (Derby) 1983. HSBH: 29* Worcs v Derby (Worcester) 1982. BB: 5-27 Worcs v Glamorgan (Worcester) 1984. BBJPL: 3-26 Worcs v Essex (Worcester) 1983.

John Geoffrey WRIGHT (Christ's College, Christchurch; Otaga University) B Darfield, New Zealand 5/7/1954. LHB, RM. Debut for Northern Districts 1975-76. Debut for Derby and Cap 1977. Tests: 31 for New Zealand between 1977-78 and 1983-84. One-day internationals: 52 for New Zealand. Tours: New Zealand to England 1978 and 1983; Australia 1980-81; D.H. Robins to Sri Lanka 1977-78; International XI to Jamaica 1982-83; New Zealand to Sri Lanka 1983-84. 1,000 runs (6) – 1,830 (av. 55.45) in 1982 best. NW Man of the Match: 1. BH Gold Awards: 3. HS: 190 v Yorks (Derby) 1982. HSTC: 141 New Zealand v Australia (Christchurch) 1981-82. HSGC/NW: 87* v Sussex (Hove) 1977. HSJPL: 108 v Warwicks (Coventry) 1983. HSBH: 102 v Worcs (Chesterfield) 1977.

NB. The following players whose particulars appeared in the 1984 Annual have been omitted: J.H. Hampshire, R.W. Taylor and C.J. Tunnicliffe.

County Averages

Britannic Assurance County Championship: Played 24, won 4, drawn 14, lost 6.
All first-class matches; Played 25, won 4, drawn 14, lost 7.

BATTING AND FIELDING

Cap		M	I	NO	RUNS	HS	Avge	100	50	Ct	St
1977	J.G. Wright	12	21	1	1201	177	60.05	2	9	10	—
1982	K.J. Barnett	24	41	3	1734	144	45.63	6	9	21	—
1976	G. Miller	20	30	5	891	130	35.64	1	5	25	—
—	J.E. Morris	15	28	1	948	135	35.11	3	3	4	—
—	I. Broome	2	4	3	35	26*	35.00	—	—	1	—
1976	A. Hill	25	44	3	1352	125	32.97	1	11	13	—
—	W.P. Fowler	22	38	8	948	116	31.60	2	7	17	—
1982	J.H. Hampshire	21	32	4	792	101*	28.28	1	4	20	—
—	B. Roberts	17	26	5	554	80	26.38	—	3	12	—
—	D.G. Moir	20	28	6	534	107	24.27	1	2	18	—
—	R.J. Finney	24	37	5	679	78	21.21	—	4	5	—
—	I.S. Anderson	14	23	1	454	79	20.63	—	1	14	—
1962	R.W. Taylor	18	22	7	303	46	20.20	—	—	27	5
—	B.J.M. Maher	7	11	2	146	66	16.22	—	1	17	—
—	O.H. Mortensen	8	8	4	63	40*	15.75	—	—	4	—
—	P.G. Newman	16	21	2	269	40	14.15	—	—	3	—
—	D.E. Malcolm	7	8	1	40	23	5.71	—	—	4	—

Played in three matches: J.P. Taylor 11,0 (2 ct).

BOWLING

	Type	O	M	R	W	Avge	Best	5 wI	10 wM
G. Miller	OB	869.3	256	2094	86	24.34	6-30	6	—
R.J. Finney	LM	584	130	1770	62	28.54	5-55	2	—
O.H. Mortensen	RFM	212.3	55	570	18	31.66	3-37	—	—
P.G. Newman	RFM	505.2	89	1717	50	34.34	7-104	1	—
D.G. Moir	SLA	822.5	206	2419	65	37.21	6-60	3	1
D.E. Malcolm	RF	156.2	24	674	16	42.12	3-78	—	—
B. Roberts	RM	277	43	1044	22	47.45	4-77	—	—

Also bowled: I.S. Anderson 55-10-176-3; K.J. Barnett 43-6-162-0; I. Broome 19.1-6-82-2; W.P. Fowler 117.3-27-398-5; J.H. Hampshire 1-1-0-0; A. Hill 50-10-191-3; J.E. Morris 11-0-73-1; J.P. Taylor 49.2-6-188-2; R.W. Taylor 6.2-1-23-1; J.G. Wright 22-2-114-1.

County Records

First-class cricket

Highest innings	For	645 v Hants (Derby)		1898
totals:	Agst	662 by Yorks (Chesterfield)		1898
Lowest innings	For	16 v Notts (Nottingham)		1879
totals:	Agst	23 by Hants (Burton-on-Trent)		1958
Highest indi-	For	274 G. Davidson v Lancs (Manchester)		1896
vidual innings:	Agst	343* P.A. Perrin for Essex (Chesterfield)		1904
Best bowling	For	10-40 W. Bestwick v Glamorgan (Cardiff)		1921
in an innings:	Agst	10-47 T.F. Smailes for Yorks (Sheffield)		1939
Best bowling	For	16-84 C. Gladwin v Worcs (Stourbridge)		1952
in a match:	Agst	16-101 G. Giffen for Australians (Derby)		1886
Most runs in a season:		2165 (av. 48.11) D.B. Carr		1959
runs in a career:		20516 (av. 31.41) D. Smith		1927-1952
100s in a season:		8 by P.N. Kirsten		1982
100s in a career:		30 by D. Smith		1927-1952
wickets in a season:		168 (av. 19.55) T.B. Mitchell		1935
wickets in a career:		1670 (av. 17.11) H.L. Jackson		1947-1963

RECORD WICKET STANDS

1st	322	H. Storer & J. Bowden v Essex (Derby)	1929
2nd	349	C.S. Elliot & J.D. Eggar v Notts (Nottingham)	1947
3rd	291	P.N. Kirsten & D.S. Steele v Somerset (Taunton)	1981
4th	328	P. Vaulkhard & D. Smith v Notts (Nottingham)	1946
5th	203	C.P. Wilkins & I.R. Buxton v Lancs (Manchester)	1971
6th	212	G.M. Lee & T.S. Worthington v Essex (Chesterfield)	1932
7th	241*	G.H. Pope & A.E.G. Rhodes v Hants (Portsmouth)	1948
8th	182	A.H.M. Jackson & W. Carter v Leics (Leicester)	1922
9th	283	A.R. Warren & J. Chapman v Warwicks (Blackwell)	1910
10th	93	J. Humphries & J. Horsley v Lancs (Derby)	1914

One-day cricket

Highest innings	NatWest Trophy	270-6 v Suffolk (Bury St. Edmund's)	1981
totals:	John Player League	272-4 v Glos (Gloucester)	1984
	Benson & Hedges Cup	284-6 v Worcs (Worcester)	1982
Lowest innings	Gillette Cup/NatWest Trophy	79 v Surrey (Oval)	1967
totals:	John Player League	70 v Surrey (Derby)	1972
	Benson & Hedges Cup	102 v Yorks (Bradford)	1975
Highest indi-	NatWest Trophy	110* P.N. Kirsten v Hants (Southampton)	1982
vidual innings:	John Player League	131* K.J. Barnett v Essex (Derby)	1984
	Benson & Hedges Cup	111* P.J. Sharpe v Glamorgan (Chesterfield)	1976
Best bowling	Gillette Cup/NatWest Trophy	6-18 T.J.P. Eyre v Sussex (Chesterfield)	1969
figures:	John Player League	6-7 M. Hendrick v Notts (Nottingham)	1972
	Benson & Hedges Cup	6-33 E.J. Barlow v Glos (Bristol)	1978

ESSEX

Formation of present club: 1876.
Colours: Blue, gold and red.
Badge: Three seaxes with word 'Essex' underneath.
County Champions: 1979, 1983 and 1984.
Gillette Cup semi-finalists: 1978.
NatWest Trophy semi-finalists: 1981.
John Player League Champions: 1981 and 1984.
Benson & Hedges Cup Winners: 1979.
Benson & Hedges Cup Finalists: 1980 and 1983.
Gillette Man of the Match Awards: 14.
NatWest Trophy Man of the Match Awards: 7.
Benson & Hedges Gold Awards: 40.

Secretary: P.J. Edwards, The County Ground, New Writtle Street, Chelmsford CM2 0PG.
Captain: K.W.R. Fletcher.
Prospects of Play Telephone No: Chelmsford matches only. Chelmsford (0245) 87921.

David Laurence ACFIELD (Brentwood School and Cambridge) B Chelmsford 24/7/1947. RHB, OB. Debut for Cambridge U and Essex 1966. Blue 1967-68. Cap 1970. Benefit 1981. HS: 42 Cambridge U v Leics (Leicester) 1967. HSC: 38 v Notts (Chelmsford) 1973. BB: 8-55 v Kent (Canterbury) 1981. BBNW: 3-9 v Scotland (Chelmsford) 1984. BBJPL: 5-14 v Northants (Northampton) 1970. Fencing Blue, Olympic International and British Champion (sabre).

David Edward EAST (Hackney Downs Sch; University of East Anglia) B Clapton 27/7/1959. No relation to R.E. East. RHB, WK. Debut 1981. Cap 1982. NW Man of the Match: 1. HS: 91 v Sussex (Hove) 1984. HSNW: 25* v Scotland (Chelmsford) 1984. HSJPL: 43 v Derby (Derby) 1982. HSBH: 33 v Glos (Chelmsford) 1984.

Raymond Eric EAST (East Bergholt Comprehensive) B Manningtree 20/6/1947. RHB, SLA. Debut 1965. Cap 1967. Played for Overseas XI v Board President's XI (Calcutta) 1980-81. Benefit 1978 (£29,000). Tour: D.H. Robins to South Africa 1973-74. Overseas XI to India 1980-81. Hat-trick: The Rest v MCC Tour XI (Hove) 1973. BH Gold Awards: 3. HS: 113 v Hants (Chelmsford) 1976. HSGC/NW: 38* v Glos (Chelmsford) 1973. HSJPL: 25* v Glamorgan (Colchester) 1976. HSBH: 54 v Northants (Chelmsford) 1977. BB: 8-30 v Notts (Ilford) 1977. BBGC/NW: 4-28 v Herts (Hitchin) 1976. BBJPL: 6-18 v Yorks (Hull) 1969. BBBH: 5-33 v Kent (Chelmsford) 1975.

Keith William Robert FLETCHER B Worcester 20/5/1944. RHB, LB. Debut 1962. Cap 1963. County Captain 1974. Benefit 1973 (£13,000). *Wisden* 1973. Testimonial: 1982 (£83,250). Tests: 59 between 1968 and 1981-82. Captain in 7 and played in 4 matches v Rest of the World in 1970. One-day internationals: 24. Tours: Cavaliers to West Indies 1964-65, MCC Under-25 to Pakistan 1966-67, International XI to India, Pakistan and Ceylon 1967-68, Ceylon and Pakistan 1968-69, Ceylon 1969-70, Australia and New Zealand 1970-71, India, Pakistan and Sri Lanka 1972-73, West Indies 1973-74, Australia and New Zealand 1974-75, India, Sri Lanka and Australia 1976-77, India and Sri Lanka 1981-82 (captain). 1,000 runs (20) – 1,890 (av. 41.08) in 1968 best. Century in each innings (111 and 102*) v Notts (Nottingham) 1976. GC Man of the Match: 1. NW Man of the Match: 1. BH Gold Awards: 7. HS: 228* v Sussex (Hastings) 1968. HSTC: 216 v New Zealand (Auckland) 1974-75. HSNW: 97 v Kent (Chelmsford) 1982. HSJPL: 99* v Notts (Ilford) 1974. HSBH: 101* v Sussex (Hove) 1982. BB: 5-41 v Middlesex (Colchester) 1979. OBE 1985.

Neil Alan FOSTER (Philip Morant Secondary CS, Colchester) B Colchester 6/5/1962. RHB, RFM. Debut 1980. Cap 1983. Tests: 6 between 1983 and 1984. One-day internationals: 8. HS: 54* v Sussex (Eastbourne) 1984. HSTC: 18* v New Zealand (Auckland) 1983-84. Tour: England to New Zealand and Pakistan 1983-84. HSJPL: 10 v Middlesex (Lord's) 1982 and 10 v Derby (Derby) 1984. BB: 6-30 England XI v Northern Districts (Hamilton) 1983-84. BBUK: 6-46 v Sussex (Ilford) 1983. BBNW: 3-19 v Dorset (Bournemouth) 1983. BBBH: 3-26 v Middlesex (Lord's) 1983.

Christopher GLADWIN (Langton Comprehensive, Newham) B East Ham 10/5/1962. LHB, RM. Debut 1981. Cap 1984. 1,396 runs (av. 33.23) in 1984. HS: 162 v Cambridge U (Cambridge) 1984. HSJPL: 75 v Middlesex (Lord's) 1984. HSBH: 41 v Surrey (Chelmsford) 1984.

Andrew Kenneth GOLDING (Colchester Royal GS and Cambridge University) B Colchester 5/10/1963. RHB, SLA. Debut 1983. Played for CU in 1984. HS: 44 Cambridge U v Worcs (Worcester) 1984.

Graham Alan GOOCH (Norlington Junior HS, Leytonstone) B Leytonstone 23/7/1953. RHB, RM. Debut 1973. Cap 1975. *Wisden* 1979. Played for Western Province 1982-83 and 1983-84. Benefit 1985. Tests: 42 between 1975 and 1981-82. One-day internationals: 37. Tours: Australia 1978-79, Australia and India 1979-80, West Indies 1980-81, India and Sri Lanka 1981-82, SAB in South Africa 1981-82. 3-year Test ban ends in 1985. Shared county record 2nd wicket partnership (321) with K.S. McEwan v Northants (Ilford) 1978. 1,000 runs (8) – 2,559 (av. 67.34) in 1984 best. Scored 1,363 (av. 54.60) in 1981-82. NW Man of the Match: 3. BH Gold Awards: 9. HS: 227 v Derby (Chesterfield) 1984. HSTC: 153 v West Indies (Kingston) 1980-81. HSNW: 133 v Scotland (Chelmsford) 1984. HSJPL: 176 v Glamorgan (Southend) 1983. HSBH: 198* v Sussex (Hove) 1982 (Competition Record). BB: 7-14 v Worcs (Ilford) 1982. BBJPL: 4-33 v Worcs (Chelmsford) 1984. BBBH: 3-24 v Sussex (Hove) 1982.

Brian Ross HARDIE (Larbert HS) B Stenhousemuir 14/1/1950. RHB, RM. Debut for Scotland 1970, for Essex 1973. Cap 1974. Benefit 1983. BH Gold Award: 1. 1,000 runs (9) – 1,522 (av. 43.48) in 1975 best. HS: 162 v Warwicks (Birmingham) 1975. HSGC/NW: 83 v Staffs (Stone) 1974. HSJPL: 108* v Yorks (Chelmsford) 1981. HSBH: 62* v Glos (Chelmsford) 1984. Brother of K.M. Hardie (Scotland).

John Kenneth LEVER (Dane County Secondary School) B Stepney 24/2/1949. RHB, LFM. Debut 1967. Cap 1970. *Wisden* 1978. Benefit: 1980 (£66,110). Played for Natal 1982-83. Tests: 20 between 1976-77 and 1981-82. One-day internationals: 22. Tours: D.H. Robins to South Africa 1972-73 and 1973-74, India, Sri Lanka and Australia 1976-77, D.H. Robins in Sri Lanka 1977-78, Pakistan and New Zealand 1977-78, Australia 1978-79, Australia and India 1979-80, India and Sri Lanka 1981-82, SAB in South Africa 1981-82. 3-year ban from Test cricket ends in 1985. Played for Overseas XI v Board President's XI (Calcutta) 1980-81. 100 wkts (4) – 116 (av. 21.98) in 1984 best. GC Man of the Match: 3. NW Man of the Match: 1. BH Gold

ESSEX

Awards: 1. HS: 91 v Glamorgan (Cardiff) 1970. HSTC: 53 v India (Delhi) 1976-77. HSNW: 15* v Surrey (Chelmsford) 1984. HSJPL: 23 v Worcs (Worcester) 1974. HSBH: 13 v Lancs (Chelmsford) 1984. BB: 8-37 v Glos (Birmingham) 1984. BBTC: 7-46 v India (Delhi) 1976-77 on debut. BBGC/NW: 5-8 v Middlesex (Westcliff) 1972. BBJPL: 5-13 v Glamorgan (Ebbw Vale) 1975. BBBH: 5-16 v Middlesex (Chelmsford) 1976.

Alan William LILLEY (Caterham HS, Ilford) B Ilford 8/5/1959. RHB, WK. Debut 1978 scoring 100* in second innings. BH Gold Award: 1. HS: 1000* v Notts (Nottingham) 1978. HSNW: 59* v Scotland (Chelmsford) 1984. HSJPL: 60 v Northants (Chelmsford) 1980. HSBH: 119 v Combined Universities (Chelmsford) 1979.

Kenneth Scott McEWAN (Queen's College, Queenstown, S.A.) B. Bedford, Cape Province, South Africa 16/7/1952. RHB, OB, WK. Played for Easter Province 1972-73 to 1978-79 and 1981-82, for T.N. Pearce's XI v West Indians (Scarborough) 1973, for Western Australia 1979-80 and 1980-81 and for Western Province 1982-83 and 1983-84. Debut for county and cap 1974. *Wisden* 1977. Shares 2nd wicket county partnership record with G.A. Gooch 1,000 runs (11) 2,176 (av. 64.00) in 1983 best. Scored 4 consecutive hundreds including two in match (102 and 116) v Warwicks (Birmingham) 1977. GC Man of the Match: 1. NW Man of the Match: 1. BH Gold Awards: 6. HS: 218 v Sussex (Chelmsford) 1977. HSGC/NW: 119 v Leics (Leicester) 1980. HSJPL: 162* v Notts (Nottingham) 1983. HSBH: 133 v Notts (Chelmsford) 1978. Benefit 1984.

Norbert PHILLIP (Dominica GS) B Bioche, Dominica 22/6/1948. RHB, RFM. Debut for Windward Islands 1969-70 and has also played for Combined Islands. Debut for county and cap 1978. Tests: 9 for West Indies between 1977-78 and 1978-79. One-day Internationals: 1. Tour: West Indies in India and Sri Lanka 1978-79. HS: 134 v Glos (Gloucester) 1978. HSTC: 47 West Indies v India (Calcutta) 1978-79. HSGC/NW: 45 v Surrey (Chelmsford) 1980. HSJPL: 95 v Glos (Colchester) 1983. HSBH: 33* v Surrey (Oval) 1982. BB: 7-33 Windward Is v Leeward Is (Roseau) 1981. BBUK: 6-4 v Surrey (Chelmsford) 1983. BBTC: 4-48 West Indies v India (Madras) 1978-79. BBNW: 4-26 v Kent (Chelmsford) 1982. BBJPL: 6-13 v Lancs (Manchester) 1982. BBBH: 4-32 v Glamorgan (Chelmsford) 1980.

Keith Rupert PONT B Wanstead 16/1/1953. RHB, RM. Debut 1970. Cap 1976. BH Gold Awards: 2. HS: 125* v Glamorgan (Southend) 1983. HSGC/NW: 39 v Somerset (Taunton) 1978. HSJPL: 55* v Warwicks (Birmingham) 1981. HSBH: 60* v Notts (Ilford) 1976. BB: 5-17 v Glamorgan (Cardiff) 1982. BBJPL: 4-22 v Warwicks (Birmingham) 1981. BBBH: 4-60 v Northants (Lord's) 1980. Brother of I.L. Pont (Notts).

Paul John PRICHARD B Billericay 7/1/1965. RHB. Debut 1984. HS: 100 v Lancs (Manchester) 1984.

Derek Raymond PRINGLE (Felsted School and Cambridge) B Nairobi, Kenya 18/9/1958. 6ft 4½in tall. RHB, RM. Debut 1978. Cap 1982. Blue 1979-80-81. University captain 1982 but did not play in University match. BH Gold Awards: 2. Tour: Australia 1982-83. Tests: 10 between 1982 and 1984. One-day Internationals: 7. HS: 127* Cambridge U v Worcs (Cambridge) 1981. HSC: 102* v Hants (Southend) 1983. HSTC: 47* v Australia (Perth) 1982-83. HSNW: 19 v Kent (Chelmsford)

1983. HSJPL: 81 v Notts (Chelmsford) 1984. HSBH: 68 Combined Universities v Somerset (Taunton) 1982. BB: 7-32 v Middlesex (Chelmsford) 1983. BBTC: 5-108 v West Indies (Birmingham) 1984. BBNW: 3-12 v Glos (Bristol) 1981. BBJPL: 3-11 v Worcs (Ilford) 1982. BBBH: 5-35 v Lancs (Chelmsford) 1984.

Stuart TURNER (Epping SM) B Chester 18/7/1943. RHB, RFM. Debut 1965. Cap 1970. Hat-trick v Surrey (Oval) 1981. Played for Natal 1976-77 and 1977-78. Benefit 1979 (£37,288). Tour: D.H. Robins to South Africa 1974–75. BH Gold Awards: 4. HS: 121 v Somerset (Taunton) 1970. HSNW: 50* v Yorks (Leeds) 1982. HSJPL: 87 v Worcs (Chelmsford) 1975. HSBH: 75* v Hants (Chelmsford) 1982. BB: 6-26 v Northants (Northampton) 1977. BBNW: 4-23 v Kent (Chelmsford) 1982. BBJPL: 5-35 v Hants (Chelmsford) 1978. BBBH: 4-19 v Combined Universities (Chelmsford) 1981.

N.B. The following players whose particulars were included in the 1984 Annual have been omitted: M.G. Hughes and R.J. Leiper.

County Averages

Britannic Assurance County Championship: Played 24 won 13 drawn 8, lost 3.
All first-class matches: Played 27, won 13, drawn 10, lost 4.

BATTING AND FIELDING

Cap		M	I	NO	RUNS	HS	Avge	100	50	Ct	St
1975	G.A. Gooch	26	45	7	2559	227	67.34	8	13	27	—
1974	K.S. McEwan	27	44	6	1755	142*	46.18	4	10	20	—
1974	B.R. Hardie	27	38	7	1077	99	34.74	—	6	27	—
1984	C. Gladwin	26	45	3	1396	162	33.23	1	9	14	—
1963	K.W.R. Fletcher	25	37	5	1056	131	33.00	3	4	22	—
—	P.J. Prichard	20	29	2	888	100	32.88	1	6	10	—
1970	S. Turner	12	13	5	197	54*	24.62	—	2	4	—
1982	D.R. Pringle	18	29	6	577	96	25.08	—	4	11	—
1983	N.A. Foster	21	25	7	341	54*	18.94	—	1	9	—
1978	N. Phillip	13	17	2	293	71	19.53	—	1	3	—
1982	D.E. East	27	37	2	510	81	14.57	—	3	76	1
1970	J.K. Lever	24	22	7	182	37	12.13	—	—	10	—
1970	D.L. Acfield	24	22	9	41	7*	3.15	—	—	10	—

Played in four matches: R.E. East 22,8 (2 ct).
Played in two matches: K.R. Pont 28,32,1 (1 ct).
Played in one match: A.W. Lilley did not bat.

BOWLING

	Type	O	M	R	W	Avge	Best	5 wI	10 wM
J.K. Lever	LFM	874.5	195	2550	116	21.98	8-37	8	3
G.A. Gooch	RM	321.1	75	850	38	22.36	4-54	—	—
N.A. Foster	RM	669.1	151	2016	87	23.17	6-79	4	—
D.R. Pringle	RM	508.4	117	1527	59	25.88	7-53	2	—
N. Phillip	RFM	275.2	48	911	34	26.79	5-48	1	—
S. Turner	RM	285	95	617	21	29.38	3-29	—	—
D.L. Acfield	OB	577.4	174	1368	46	29.73	6-44	2	—
R.E. East	SLA	152.4	48	324	11	29.45	3-24	—	—

Also bowled: D.E. East 3-0-11-0; K.W.R. Fletcher 9-2-28-0; C. Gladwin 15-1-48-0; A.W. Lilley 5.2-2-11-2; P.J. Prichard 1-0-5-0.

County Records
First-Class Cricket

Highest innings totals:	For	692 v Somerset (Taunton)	1895
	Agst	803-4 by Kent (Brentwood)	1934
Lowest innings totals	For	30 v Yorkshire (Leyton)	1901
	Agst	14 by Surrey (Chelmsford)	1983
Highest individual innings	For	343* P.A. Perrin v Derby (Chesterfield)	1904
	Agst	332 W.H. Ashdown for Kent (Brentwood)	1934
Best bowling in an innings	For	10-32 H. Pickett v Leics (Leyton)	1895
	Agst	10-40 G.E. Dennett for Glos (Bristol)	1906
Best bowling in a match	For	17-119 W. Mead v Hants (Southampton)	1895
	Agst	17-56 C.W.L. Parker for Glos (Gloucester)	1925
Most runs in a season:		2,559 (av 64.34) G.A. Gooch	1984
runs in a career		29,162 (av. 36.18) P.A. Perrin	1896-1928
100s in a season:		9 by J. O'Connor and D.J. Insole	1934 & 1955
100s in a career		71 by J. O'Connor	1921-1939
wickets in a season:		172 (av. 27.13) T.P.B. Smith	1947
wickets in a career		1610 (av. 26.68) T.P.B. Smith	1929-1951

RECORD WICKET STANDS

1st	270	A.V. Avery & T.C. Dodds v Surrey (Oval)	1946
2nd	321	G.A. Gooch & K.S. McEwan v Northants (Ilford)	1978
3rd	343	P.A. Gibb & R. Horsfall v Kent (Blackheath)	1951
4th	298	A.V. Avery & R. Horsfall v Worcs (Clacton)	1948
5th	287	C.T. Ashton & J. O'Connor v Surrey (Brentwood)	1934
6th	206	J.W.H.T. Douglas & J. O'Connor v Glos (Cheltenham)	1923
		B.R. Knight & R.A.G. Luckin v Middlesex (Brentwood)	1962
7th	261	J.W.H.T. Douglas & J. Freeman v Lancs (Leyton)	1914
8th	263	D.R. Wilcox & R.M. Taylor v Warwicks (Southend)	1946
9th	251	J.W.H.T. Douglas & S.N. Hare v Derby (Leyton)	1921
10th	218	F.H. Vigar & T.P.B. Smith v Derby (Chesterfield)	1947

One-day cricket

Highest innings totals:	Gillette Cup/NatWest Trophy	327-6 v Scotland (Chelmsford)	1984
	John Player League	310-5 v Glamorgan (Southend)	1983
	Benson & Hedges Cup	350-3 v Combined Universities (Chelmsford)	1979
Lowest innings totals:	Gillette Cup/NatWest Trophy	100 v Derby (Brentwood)	1965
	John Player League	69 v Derby (Chesterfield)	1974
	Benson & Hedges Cup	123 v Kent (Canterbury)	1973
Highest individual innings:	Gillette Cup/NatWest Trophy	176 G.A. Gooch v Glamorgan (Southend)	1983
	John Player League	125* G.A. Gooch v Hants (Colchester)	1984
	Benson & Hedges Cup	198* G.A. Gooch v Sussex (Hove)	1982
Best bowling figures:	Gillette Cup/NatWest Trophy	5-8 J.K. Lever v Middlesex (Westcliff)	1972
	John Player League	8-26 K.D. Boyce v Lancs (Manchester)	1971
	Benson & Hedges Cup	5-16 J.K. Lever v Middlesex (Chelmsford)	1976

GLAMORGAN

Formation of present club: 1888.
Colours: Blue and gold.
Badge: Gold daffodil.
County Champions (2): 1948 and 1969.
Gillette Cup finalists: 1977.
NatWest Trophy Second Round (2): 1981 and 1983.
Best final position in John Player League: 8th in 1977.
Benson & Hedges Cup quarter-finalists (5): 1972, 1973,
1977, 1978 and 1979.
Gillette Man of the Match Awards: 13.
NatWest Man of the Match Awards: 1.
Benson & Hedges Gold Awards: 25.

Secretary: P.G. Carling, 6 High Street, Cardiff CF1 2PW.
Coach: A. Jones, M.B.E.
Captain: R.C. Ontong.
Prospects of Play Telephone Nos: Cardiff (0222) 29956 or 387367
Swansea (0792) 466321.

Stephen Royston BARWICK (Cwrt Sart and Dwr-y-Felin Comprehensives) B Neath 6/9/1960. RHB, RM. Debut 1981. HS: 25 v Derby (Derby) 1984. HSJPL: 12* v Sussex (Hastings) 1982. HSBH: 18 v Kent (Canterbury) 1984. BB: 8-42 v Worcs (Worcester) 1983. BBNW: 4-14 v Hants (Bournemouth) 1981. BBJPL: 3-39 v Sussex (Ebbw Vale) 1981. BBBH: 3-28 v Somerset (Swansea) 1982.

Terry DAVIES (Townsend Secondary School, St. Albans) B St. Albans, Herts 25/10/1960. RHB, WK. Debut 1979. HS: 69* v Kent (Cardiff) 1983. HSJPL: 46* v Kent (Cardiff) 1983. HSBH: 23 v Sussex (Hove) 1984. Shared record 10th wkt county partnership (143) with S.A.B. Daniels v Glos (Swansea) 1982.

John DERRICK (Blaengwawr Comprehensive) B Cwmaman 15/1/1963. RHB, RM. Debut 1983. HS: 69* v Surrey (Swansea) 1984. HSJPL: 18* v Northants (Northampton) 1983. BB: 3-42 v Derby (Swansea) 1984.

Stephen Peter HENDERSON (Downside, Durham U and Cambridge U) B Oxford 24/9/1958. LHB, RM. Son of Derek Henderson (Oxford U 1949–50). Debut for Worcs 1977. Blue 1982-83. Debut for Glamorgan 1983. HS: 209* CU v Middx (Cambridge) 1982. HSC: 135* v Warwicks (Birmingham) 1983. HSJPL: 65* v Northants (Swansea) 1984.

Geoffrey Clark HOLMES (West Denton HS) B Newcastle-upon-Tyne 16/9/1958. RHB, RM. Debut 1978. Scored 1,039 runs (av. 29.68) in 1984. HS: 100* v Glos (Bristol) 1979. HSNW: 13 v Notts (Swansea) 1984. HSJPL: 73 v Warwicks (Birmingham) 1984. HSBH: 30 v Glos (Bristol) 1980. BB: 5-86 v Surrey (Oval) 1980. BBJPL: 5-2 v Derby (Ebbw Vale) 1984.

John Anthony HOPKINS (Trinity CE, Carmarthen) B Maesteg 16/6/1953. RHB, WK. Younger brother of J.D. Hopkins (Glamorgan and Middlesex). Debut 1970. Cap 1977. Played for Eastern Province 1981-82. 1,000 runs (7): 1,500 (av. 33.33) in 1984 best. GC Man of Match: BH Gold Awards: 4. HS: 230 v Worcs (Worcester)

GLAMORGAN

1977. HSGC/NW: 63 v Leics (Swansea) 1977. HSJPL: 130* v Somerset (Bath) 1983. HSBH: 103* v Minor Counties (Swansea) 1980.

JAVED MIANDAD KHAN (C.M.S. Secondary, Karachi) B Karachi 12/6/1957. RHB, LBG. Debut 1973-74 for Karachi Whites aged 16 years 5 months. Has played for various Karachi, Sind and Habib Bank teams in Pakistan. Played for Sussex 1976-79. Cap 1977. Debut for Glamorgan and cap 1980. *Wisden* 1981. Tests: 60 for Pakistan between 1976-77 and 1983–84, captain in 10 matches. One-day Internationals: 58 for Pakistan. Tours: Pakistan in Sri Lanka 1975-76, Australia and West Indies 1976-77, England 1978, New Zealand and Australia 1978-79, India 1979-80, Australia 1981-82 (captain), England 1982, Australia 1982-83, India 1983-84, Australia 1983-84. 1,000 runs (4) 2,083 (av. 69.43) in 1981 best including 8 centuries (both records). Also scored 1,000 runs in an overseas season 8 times. Scored 163 for Pakistan v New Zealand (Lahore) on Test debut. Century in each innings three times. GC Man of the Match: 1. BH Gold Awards: 2. HS: 311 Karachi Whites v National Bank (Karachi) 1974-75. HSUK: 212* v Leics (Swansea) 1984. HSTC: 280* Pakistan v India (Hyderabad) 1982-83. HSGC/NW: 75 Sussex v Lancs (Hove) 1978. HSJPL: 107* v Leics (Leicester) 1981. HSBH: 95 v Combined Universities (Cambridge) 1983. BB: 7-39 Habib Bank v IDBP (Lahore) 1980-81. BBUK: 4-10 Sussex v Northants (Northampton) 1977. BBTC: 3-74 Pakistan v New Zealand (Hyderabad) 1976-77.

Alan Lewis JONES (Ystalyfera GS; Cwmtawe Comprehensive; Cardiff CE) B Alltwen 1/6/1957. No relation to A. and E.W. Jones. LHB. Debut 1973 aged 16 years 99 days. Cap 1983. 1,000 runs (2): 1,811 (av. 36.95) in 1984 best. HS: 132 v Hants (Cardiff) 1984. HSNW: 36 v Hants (Swansea) 1983. HSJPL: 82 v Warwicks (Birmingham) 1982. HSBH: 36 v Worcs (Cardiff) 1979.

Hugh MORRIS (Blundell's School) B Cardiff 5/10/1963. LHB. Debut 1981. HS: 114* v Yorks (Cardiff) 1984. HSJPL: 55* v Essex (Southend) 1984. HSBH: 10 v Kent (Canterbury) 1984.

Rodney Craig ONTONG (Selbourne College, East London, SA) B Johannesburg, South Africa 9/9/1955. RHB, RFM. Played for Border 1972-73 to 1975-76. Transvaal 1976-77 and 1977-78. Northern Transvaal 1978-79 to 1981-82. Border 1982-83 to date. Debut for county 1975. Cap 1979. Captain 1984 succeeding M.W.W. Selvey in mid-season. 1,000 runs (4): 1,320 (av. 35.67) in 1984 best. NW Man of the Match: 1. BH Gold Awards: 2. HS: 204* v Middlesex (Swansea) 1984. HSGC/NW: 64 v Somerset (Cardiff) 1978. HSJPL: 100 v Northants (Abergavenny) 1982. HSBH: 81 v Somerset (Swansea) 1984. BB: 7-60 Border v Northern Transvaal (Pretoria) 1975-76. BBUK: 7-96 v Yorks (Bradford) 1984. BBNW: 4-49 v Norfolk (Norwich) 1983. BBJPL: 4-31 v Middlesex (Lord's) 1979. BBBH: 4-28 v Worcs (Cardiff) 1979.

Mark Richard PRICE (Harper Green SMS) B Liverpool, Lancs 20/4/1960. RHB, SLA. Debut 1984.

John Frederick STEELE B Stafford 23/7/1946. Younger brother of D.S. Steele of Northants. RHB, SLA. Debut 1970 for Leics. Was 12th man for England v Rest of World (Lord's) a month after making debut. Cap 1971. Joined Glamorgan for 1984. Cap 1984. Played for Natal in 1973-74, 1975-76 and 1977-78. Benefit 1983

(£33,470). Tour: D.H. Robins to South Africa 1974-75. 1,000 runs (6) – 1,347 runs (av. 31.32) in 1972 best. Shared in 1st wkt partnership record for Leics, 390 with B. Dudleston v Derby (Leicester) 1979. Gillette Man of the Match: 3, for Leics. BH Gold Awards: 4 for Leics. HS: 195 Leics v Derby (Leicester) 1971. HSGC/NW: 108* Leics v Staffs (Longton) 1975. HSJPL: 92 Leics v Essex (Leicester) 1973. HSBH: 91, Leics v Somerset (Leicester) 1974. BB: 7-29 Natal B v Griqualand West (Umzinto) 1973-74 and 7-29 Leics v Glos (Leicester) 1980. BBGC/NW: 5-19 Leics v Essex (Southend) 1977. BBJPL: 5-22 Leics v Glamorgan (Leicester) 1979. BBBH: 5-11 Leics v Worcs (Worcester) 1983.

John Gregory THOMAS (Cwmtawe Comprehensive, S. Glamorgan IHE) B Trebannws 12/8/1960. RHB, RM. Debut 1979. Played for Border 1983-84. HS: 84 v Surrey (Guildford) 1982. HSNW: 24 v Hants (Swansea) 1983. HSJPL: 37 v Notts (Nottingham) 1983. HSBH: 17 v Kent (Canterbury) 1984. BB: 5-56 v Somerset (Cardiff) 1984. BBJPL: 5-38 v Yorks (Cardiff) 1983.

Mohammad YOUNIS AHMED (Moslem HS, Lahore) B Jullunder, Pakistan 20/10/1947. LHB, LM/SLA. Younger brother of Saeed Ahmed, Pakistan Test cricketer. Debut 1961-62 for Pakistan Inter Board Schools XI v South Zone at age of 14 years 4 months. Debut for Surrey 1965. Cap 1969. Played for South Australia in 1972-73. Tours: Cavaliers to Jamaica 1969-70, Commonwealth to Pakistan 1970-71, D.H. Robins to South Africa 1973-74 and 1974-75, International Wanderers to South Africa 1974-75 and 1975-76. Debut for Worcs and cap 1979. Joined Glamorgan 1984. Tests: 2 for Pakistan v New Zealand 1969-70. 1,000 runs (12) – 1,760 runs (av. 47.56) in 1969 best. Shared in 4th wkt partnership record for Worcs, 281 with J.A. Ormrod v Notts (Nottingham) 1979. BH Gold Awards: 3 (1 for Surrey). HS: 221* Worcs v Notts (Nottingham) 1979. HSTC: 62 Pakistan v New Zealand (Karachi) 1969-70. HSGC/NW: 87 Surrey v Middlesex (Oval) 1970. HSJPL: 113 Surrey v Warwicks (Birmingham) 1976 and 113 Worcs v Middlesex (Lord's) 1979. HSBH: 115 Worcs v Yorks (Worcester) 1980. BB: 4-10 Surrey v Cambridge U (Cambridge) 1975. BBJPL: 3-26 v Surrey (Oval) 1979. BBBH: 4-37 Worcs v Northants (Northampton) 1980.

N.B. The following players whose figures appeared in the 1984 Annual have been omitted: W.W. Davis, D.A. Francis, E.W. Jones, B.J. Lloyd, E.A. Moseley, C.J.C. Rowe and M.W.W. Selvey.

County Averages

Britannic Assurance County Championship: Played 24, won 4, drawn 18, lost 2.
All first-class matches: Played 27, won 6, drawn 18, lost 3.

BATTING AND FIELDING

Cap		M	I	NO	RUNS	HS	Avge	100	50	Ct	St
1980	Javed Miandad	8	15	2	832	212*	64.00	2	3	4	—
—	Younis Ahmed	21	35	4	1369	158*	44.16	2	9	13	—
—	J. Derrick	10	15	7	351	69*	43.87	—	3	8	—
1983	A.L. Jones	27	51	2	1811	132	36.95	5	7	30	—
1979	R.C. Ontong	25	45	8	1320	204*	35.67	1	7	15	—
—	H. Morris	12	20	4	542	114*	33.87	1	4	2	—
1977	J.A. Hopkins	26	50	5	1500	128*	33.33	2	9	18	—
—	S.P. Henderson	10	17	1	487	108	30.43	1	3	4	—
—	G.C. Holmes	21	37	2	1039	90	29.68	—	6	10	—
1984	J.F. Steele	25	41	12	820	60*	28.27	—	1	33	—
—	W.W. Davis	17	20	6	278	50	19.85	—	1	7	—
1983	C.J.C. Rowe	6	11	2	155	60*	17.22	—	1	2	—
—	J.G. Thomas	20	26	5	314	36*	14.95	—	—	9	—
—	T. Davies	27	35	7	398	43	14.21	—	—	43	10
1983	M.W.W. Selvey	15	18	8	111	20	11.10	—	—	9	—
—	S.R. Barwick	20	19	9	105	25	10.50	—	—	6	—

Played in three matches: M.R. Price 1,7.
Played in two matches: D.A. Francis 20,7,0 (2 ct); R.C. Green 3* (1 ct).

BOWLING

	Type	O	M	R	W	Avge	Best	5 wI	10 wM
S.R. Barwick	RM	473.4	127	1299	50	25.98	7-38	2	—
J.F. Steele	SLA	674	175	1867	68	27.45	5-42	4	—
R.C. Ontong	RM	837.4	231	2155	74	29.12	7-96	4	—
C.J.C. Rowe	OB	135	41	356	12	29.66	3-20	—	—
Javed Miandad	LBG	51.2	9	187	6	31.16	2-26	—	—
W.W. Davis	RFM	481.5	105	1526	48	31.79	5-57	2	—
J.G. Thomas	RM	435.2	95	1575	47	33.51	5-56	2	1
M.W.W. Selvey	RFM	311.3	69	997	25	39.88	6-31	1	—
J. Derrick	RM	133.5	31	441	8	55.12	3-42	—	—

Also bowled: R.C. Green 31.5-9-92-2; G.C. Holmes 77-10-271-3; J.A. Hopkins 2.2-0-18-0; A.L. Jones 10-0-86-1; H. Morris 9-1-45-1; M.R. Price 31-4-109-2; Younis Ahmed 12-3-34-0.

County Records

First-class cricket

Highest innings	For	587-8d v Derby (Cardiff)	1951
totals:	Agst	653-6d by Glos (Bristol)	1928
Lowest innings	For	22 v Lancs (Liverpool)	1924
totals:	Agst	33 by Leics (Ebbw Vale)	1965
Highest indi-	For	287* D.E. Davies v Glos (Newport)	1939
vidual innings:	Agst	302* W.R. Hammond for Glos (Bristol)	1934
		302 W.R. Hammond for Glos (Newport)	1939
Best bowling	For	10-51 J. Mercer v Worcs (Worcester)	1936
in an innings	Agst	10-18 G. Geary for Leics (Pontypridd)	1929
Best bowling	For	17-212 J.C. Clay v Worcs (Swansea)	1937
in a match:	Agst	16-96 G. Geary for Leics (Pontypridd)	1929
Most runs in a season:		2,083 (av. 69.43) Javed Miandad	1981
runs in a career:		34,056 (av. 32.89) A. Jones	1957-1983
100s in a season:		8 by Javed Miandad	1981
100s in a career:		52 by A. Jones	1957-1983
wickets in a season:		176 (av. 17.34) J.C. Clay	1937
wickets in a career:		2,174 (av. 20.95) D.J. Shepherd	1950-1972

RECORD WICKET STANDS

1st	330	A. Jones & R.C. Fredericks v Northants (Swansea)	1972
2nd	238	A. Jones & A.R. Lewis v Sussex (Hastings)	1962
3rd	313	D.E. Davies & W.E. Jones v Essex (Brentwood)	1948
4th	263	G. Lavis & C. Smart v Worcs (Cardiff)	1934
5th	264	M. Robinson & S.W. Montgomery v Hants (Bournemouth)	1949
6th	230	W.E. Jones & B.L. Muncer v Worcs (Worcester)	1953
7th	195*	W. Wooller & W.E. Jones v Lancs (Liverpool)	1947
8th	202	D. Davies & J.J. Hills v Sussex (Eastbourne)	1928
9th	203*	J.J. Hills & J.C. Clay v Worcs (Swansea)	1929
10th	143	T. Davies & S.A.B. Daniels v Glos (Swansea)	1982

One-day cricket

Highest innings	Gillette Cup/	283-3 v Warwicks	
totals:	NatWest Trophy	(Birmingham)	1976
	John Player League	277-6 v Derby (Ebbw Vale)	1984
	Benson & Hedges Cup	245-7 v Hants (Swansea)	1982
Lowest innings	Gillette Cup/	76 v Northants	
totals:	NatWest Trophy	(Northampton)	1968
	John Player League	42 v Derby (Swansea)	1979
	Benson & Hedges Cup	68 v Lancs (Manchester)	1973
Highest indi-	Gillette Cup/	124* A. Jones v	
vidual innings:	NatWest Trophy	Warwicks (Birmingham)	1976
	John Player League	130* J.A. Hopkins v Somerset	1983
	Benson & Hedges Cup	103* M.A. Nash v Hants	
		(Swansea)	1976
		103* J.A. Hopkins v Minor	
		Counties (Swansea)	1980
Best bowling	Gillette Cup/	5-21 P.M. Walker v	
figures:	NatWest Trophy	Cornwall (Truro)	1970
	John Player League	6-29 M.A. Nash v Worcs	
		(Worcester)	1975
	Benson & Hedges Cup	5-17 A.H. Wilkins v	
		Worcs (Worcester)	1978

GLOUCESTERSHIRE

Formation of present club: 1871.
Colours: Blue, gold, brown, silver, green and red.
Badge: Coat of Arms of the City and County of Bristol.
County Champions (3): 1874, 1876 and 1877.
Joint Champions: 1873.
Gillette Cup Winners: 1973.
NatWest Trophy Quarter-finals (2): 1982 and 1983.
Best position in John Player League: 6th in 1969, 1973 and 1977.
Benson & Hedges Cup Winners: 1977.
Gillette Man of the Match Awards: 17.
NatWest Man of the Match Awards: 6.
Benson & Hedges Gold Awards: 26.

Secretary: D.G. Collier, County Ground, Nevil Road, Bristol BS7 9EJ.
Captain: D.A. Graveney.
Prospects of Play Telephone Nos: Bristol (0272) 48461
Prospects of Play Telephone Nos: Cheltenham (0242) 22000
Gloucester (0452) 24621

Charles William Jeffrey ATHEY (Stainsby Secondary, Acklam Hall HS) B Middlesbrough 27/9/1957. RHB, RM. Debut for Yorks 1976. Cap 1980. Joined Glos 1984. Tests: 3 in 1980 and 1980-81. One-day Internationals: 2. Tours: West Indies 1980-81, D.H. Robins' Under-23 to New Zealand 1979-80. 1,000 runs (3) – 1,812 (av. 37.75) in 1984 best. GC Man of the Match: 2 (for Yorks). BH Gold Awards: 3. HS: 134 Yorks v Derby (Derby) 1982. HSGC/NW: 115 Yorks v Kent (Leeds) 1980. HSJPL: 118 Yorks v Leics (Leicester) 1978. HSBH: 94* Yorks v Warwicks (Leeds) 1981. BB: 3-38 Yorks v Surrey (Oval) 1978. BBJPL: 5-35 Yorks v Derby (Chesterfield) 1981. BBBH: 4-48 v Combined Universities (Bristol) 1984.

Philip BAINBRIDGE (Hanley HS, Stoke-on-Trent SFC, Borough Road CE) B Stoke-on-Trent, Staffordshire 16/4/1958. RHB, RM. Debut 1977. Cap 1981. NW Man of the Match: 1. 1,000 runs (4) 1,217 (av. 29.68) in 1983 best. HS: 146 v New Zealanders (Bristol) 1983. HSNW: 75 v Scotland (Bristol) 1983. HSJPL: 55 v Essex (Colchester) 1983. HSBH: 80 v Somerset (Taunton) 1982. BB: 6-59 v Glamorgan (Swansea) 1982. BBNW: 3-49 v Scotland (Bristol) 1983. BBJPL: 4-27 v Middlesex (Cheltenham) 1980. BBBH: 3-21 v Notts (Gloucester) 1981.

Andrew James BRASSINGTON B Bagnall, Staffordshire 9/8/1954. RHB, WK. Debut 1974. Cap 1978. HS: 35 v Sussex (Hastings) 1982. HSGC/NW: 20 v Hants (Bristol) 1979. HSJPL: 14* v Northants (Bristol) 1982.

Dean Andrew BURROWS B Peterlee, Co. Durham 20/6/1966. RHB, RFM. Debut 1984.

John Henry CHILDS (Audley Park SMS, Torquay) B Plymouth, Devon 15/8/1951. LHB, SLA. Debut 1975. Cap 1977. BH Gold Award: 1. HS: 34* v Notts (Cheltenham) 1982. HSNW: 14* v Hants (Bristol) 1983. HSJPL: 16* v Warwicks (Bristol) 1981. HSBH: 10 v Somerset (Bristol) 1979. BB: 9-56 v Somerset (Bristol) 1981. BBJPL: 4-15 v Northants (Northampton) 1976. BBBH: 3-36 v Glamorgan (Bristol) 1982.

Edward James CUNNINGHAM (Marlborough) B Oxford 16/5/1962. LHB. Debut 1982. HS: 61* v Sri Lankans (Cheltenham) 1984. HSNW: 18 v Lancs (Bristol) 1984. HSJPL: 56 v Leics (Leicester) 1984.

David Anthony GRAVENEY (Millfield School) B Bristol 2/1/1953. Son of J.K. Graveney (Glos 1947-64). RHB, SLA. Debut 1972. Cap 1976. Captain 1981. HS: 119 v Oxford University (Oxford) 1980. HSGC/NW: 44 v Surrey (Bristol) 1973. HSJPL: 49 v Notts (Nottingham) 1981. HSBH: 49* v Somerset (Taunton) 1982. BB: 8-85 v Notts (Cheltenham) 1974. BBNW: 5-11 v Ireland (Dublin) 1981. BBJPL: 4-22 v Hants (Lydney) 1974. BBBH: 3-13 v Scotland (Glasgow) 1983.

David Valentine LAWRENCE (Linden School) B Gloucester 28/1/1964. RHB, RFM. Debut 1981. HS: 17 v Notts (Nottingham) 1984. HSJPL: 17 v Hants (Bristol) 1984. BB: 5-58 v Somerset (Bristol) 1984. BBJPL: 4-32 v Lancs (Moreton-in-Marsh) 1984. BBBH: 5-48 v Hants (Bristol) 1984.

Jeremy William LLOYDS (Blundell's School) B Penang, Malaya 17/11/1954. LHB, OB. Debut for Somerset 1979. Cap 1982. Scored 132* and 102* Somerset v Northants (Northampton) 1982. Played for Orange Free State 1983-84. Joined Glos for 1985. HS: 132* Somerset v Northants (Northampton) 1982. HSNW: 28* Somerset v Leics (Taunton) 1982 and v Sussex (Hove) 1983. HSJPL: 33 Somerset v Surrey (Oval) 1981. HSBH: 51 Somerset v Sussex (Taunton) 1983. BB: 7-88 Somerset v Essex (Chelmsford) 1982.

Paul Gerrard Peter ROEBUCK (Millfield and Cambridge U) B Bath, Somerset 13/10/1963. Brother of P.M. Roebuck (CU and Somerset). LHB, RFM. Debut for Cambridge U 1983. Blue 1984. Debut for Glos 1984. HS: 62 Cambridge U v Notts (Nottingham) 1984. HSC: 20 v Middlesex (Bristol) 1984. HSBH: 13 Combined Universities v Hants (Southampton) 1984.

Lawson Macgregor ROLLS B Bristol 8/3/1965. RHB, OB. Debut 1984.

Paul William ROMAINES (Leeholme School, Bishop Auckland) B Bishop Auckland, Co. Durham 25/12/1955. RHB. Played for Northants 1975-76. Debut for Glos 1982. Cap 1983. BH Gold Award: 1. 1,000 runs (2) – 1,844 (av. 35.46) best. HS: 186 v Warwicks (Nuneaton) 1982. HSNW: 82 v Hants (Bristol) 1983. HSJPL: 82 v Surrey (Cheltenham) 1984. HSBH: 98* v Hants (Bristol) 1984.

Robert Charles (Jack) RUSSELL (Archway Comprehensive) B Stroud 15/8/1963. LHB, WK. Debut 1981. HS: 64* v Worcs (Bristol) 1983. HSNW: 16 v Lancs (Bristol) 1984. HSJPL: 43 v Glamorgan (Swansea) 1984. HSBH: 36* v Scotland (Glasgow) 1983.

Gary Edward SAINBURY (Beal GS, Bath U) B Wanstead 17/1/1958. RHB, LM. Played for Essex 1979 and 1980. Joined Glos 1983. HS: 13 v Glamorgan (Cheltenham) 1983. BB: 6-66 v Worcs (Worcester) 1983. BBNW: 3-58 v Lancs (Bristol) 1984. BBJPL: 3-19 v Notts (Nottingham) 1984. BBBH: 4-28 v Northants (Northampton) 1983.

John Neil SHEPHERD (Alleyn's School, Barbados) B St Andrew, Barbados 9/11/1943. RHB, RM. Debut 1964-65 for Barbados v Cavaliers and played for Barbados in 1967-68, 1968-69 and 1970-71. Debut for Kent 1966. Cap 1967. Played for Rhodesia 1975-76. *Wisden* 1978. Benefit 1979 (£58,537). Debut for

GLOUCESTERSHIRE

Glos 1982. Cap 1983. Tests: 5 for West Indies in 1969 and 1970-71. Tours: West Indies to England 1969, D.H. Robins to South Africa 1973-74 and 1974-75, International Wanderers to South Africa 1974-75. 1,000 runs (2): 1,157 (av. 29.66) in 1968 best. GC Man of the Match: 1 (for Kent). NW Man of the Match: 1. BH Gold Awards: 3 (2 for Kent). HS: 170 Kent v Northants (Folkestone) 1968. HSC: 168 v Warwicks (Birmingham) 1983. HSTC: 32 West Indies v England (Lord's) 1969. HSGC/NW: 101 Kent v Middlesex (Canterbury) 1977. HSJPL: 94 Kent v Hants (Southampton) 1978. HSBH: 96 Kent v Middlesex (Lord's) 1975. BB: 8-40 West Indies v Glos (Bristol) 1969. BBC: 7-50 v Warwicks (Birmingham) 1983, BBTC: 5-104 West Indies v England (Manchester) 1969. BBNW: 4-20 v Staffs (Stone) 1984. BBJPL: 6-52 v Kent (Bristol) 1983. BBBH: 4-25 Kent v Derby (Lord's) 1978.

Andrew Willis STOVOLD (Filton HS; Loughborough CE) B Bristol 19/3/1953. RHB, WK. Debut 1973. Cap 1976. Played for Orange Free State in 1974-75 and 1975-76. 1,000 runs (6) 1,671 (av. 42.84) in 1983 best. NW Man of the Match: 2. BH Gold Awards: 6. HS: 212* v Northants (Northampton) 1982. NSNW: 82 v Scotland (Bristol) 1983. HSJPL: 98* v Kent (Cheltenham) 1977. HSBH: 123 v Combined Universities (Oxford) 1982.

Christopher Richard TREMBATH B London 27/9/1961. RHB, RM. Debut 1982. HS: 17* v Middlesex (Uxbridge) 1984. BB: 5-91 v Oxford U (Oxford) 1982.

Courtenay Andrew WALSH B Kingston, Jamaica 30/10/1962. RHB, RFM. Debut for Jamaica 1981-82. Debut for Glos 1984. Tours: Young West Indies to Zimbabwe 1983-84. West Indies to England 1984. HS: 30 v Lancs (Bristol) 1984. HSJPL: 14 v Worcs (Worcester) 1984. BB: 6-35 Jamaica v Guyana (Kingston) 1983-84. BBJPL: 6-70 v Middlesex (Bristol) 1984.

Simon Howard WOOTTON (Arthur Terry School) B Perivale, Middlesex 24/2/1959. LHB, SLA. Debut for Warwicks 1981. Debut for Glos 1984. HS: 104 Warwicks v Cambridge U (Cambridge) 1983. HSC: 97 v Sri Lankans (Cheltenham) 1984. HSJPL: 28* v Lancs (Manchester) 1982. HSBH: 33 v Kent (Oval) 1981.

Anthony John WRIGHT (Alleyn's GS, Stevenage) B Stevenage, Hertfordshire 27/6/1962. RHB, RM. Debut 1982. HS: 139 v Surrey (Cheltenham) 1984. HSNW: 14 v Middlesex (Bristol) 1982. HSJPL: 52 v Essex (Cheltenham) 1982.

Syed ZAHEER ABBAS (Jehangir Road HS, Islamia College, Karachi) B Sailkot, Pakistan 24/7/1947. RHB, OB. Wears glasses. Debut for Karachi Whites 1965-66 and has also played for Pakistan International Airways. *Wisden* 1971. Debut for Glos 1972. Cap 1975. Tests: 69 for Pakistan between 1969-70 and 1983-84. Captain in 9 Tests. 5 matches for Rest of the World v Australia 1971-72. One-day Internationals: 49 for Pakistan. Tours: Pakistan to England 1971, 1974 and 1982, Australia and New Zealand 1972-73, Sri Lanka 1975-76, Australia and West Indies 1976-77, New Zealand and Australia 1978-79, India 1979-80 and 1983-84, Australia 1981-82 and 1983-84, Rest of the World to Australia 1971-72. 1,000 runs (11) — 2,554 (av. 75.11) in 1976 best. Scored 1,597 runs (av. 84.05) in Pakistan in 1973-74 and 1,000 runs overseas 6 times in all. 4 centuries in consecutive innings in 1970-71. Centuries in each innings of a match on 8 occasions (world record and including world record of a double century and century 4 times). Scored 100th century in 1982-83. Benefit 1983. GC Man of the Match: 4. NW Man of the Match: 1. BH Gold Award: 1. HS: 274 Pakistan v England (Birmingham) 1971. HSC: 230* v Kent (Canterbury) 1976. HSNW: 158 v Leics (Leicester) 1983. HSJPL: 129* v Middlesex (Lord's) 1981. HSBH: 98 v Surrey (Oval) 1975. BB: 5-15 Dawood Club v Railways (Lahore) 1975-76. BBUK: 3-32 v Warwicks (Gloucester) 1981.

County Averages

Britannic Assurance County Championship; Played 24, won 1, drawn 13, lost 10.
All first-class matches; Played 26, won 1, drawn 15, lost 10.

BATTING AND FIELDING

Cap		M	I	NO	RUNS	HS	Avge	100	50	Ct	St
—	C.W.J. Athey	26	52	4	1812	114*	37.75	4	11	26	—
1983	P.W. Romaines	26	52	0	1844	141	35.46	4	10	12	—
1981	P. Bainbridge	22	42	7	1133	134*	32.37	2	6	9	—
1976	A.W. Stovold	25	50	2	1524	139*	31.75	2	11	18	2
1975	Zaheer Abbas	14	28	4	738	157*	30.75	1	4	2	—
—	S.H. Wootton	4	8	1	194	97	27.71	—	1	4	—
1983	J.N. Shepherd	24	39	7	885	87	27.65	—	6	13	—
—	A.J. Wright	22	39	3	971	139	26.97	1	6	11	—
—	R.C. Russell	21	27	6	513	63	24.42	—	1	26	9
1976	D.A. Graveney	26	40	13	430	33	15.92	—	—	18	—
—	C.S. Dale	8	8	2	100	49	16.66	—	—	1	—
—	E.J. Cunningham	6	11	3	162	61*	20.25	—	1	—	—
—	C.A. Walsh	6	10	1	96	30	10.66	—	—	—	—
—	G.E. Sainsbury	22	20	15	40	10*	8.00	—	—	8	—
—	D.V. Lawrence	19	25	4	135	17	6.42	—	—	2	—
1977	J.H. Childs	7	6	2	12	4*	3.00	—	—	2	—

Played in two matches: A.J. Brassington 22, 0*, 0 (2 ct 1 st); C.R. Trembath 17*,0*,8.

Played in one match; D.A. Burrows 0; R.J. Doughty 4; P.G.P. Roebuck 5,20; L.H. Rolls did not bat.

BOWLING

	Type	O	M	R	W	Avge	Best	5 wI	10 wM
D.A. Graveney	SLA	667.4	202	1584	54	29.33	6-73	2	—
J.N. Shepherd	RM	800.3	209	2225	72	30.90	5-30	2	—
G.E. Sainsbury	LM	566.2	141	1596	48	33.25	5-19	2	—
C.A. Walsh	RFM	185.2	48	622	18	34.55	6-70	1	—
D.V. Lawrence	RFM	455.1	80	1531	41	37.34	5-58	3	—
J.H. Childs	SLA	289	83	740	15	49.33	3-72	—	—
P. Bainbridge	RM	303.2	73	959	18	53.27	4-76	—	—
C.S. Dale	OB	125.1	22	467	7	66.71	3-10	—	—

Also bowled: C.W.J. Athey 13-1-54-0; D.A. Burrows 15-0-76-0; E.J. Cunningham 21-3-70-0; L.H. Rolls 15-1-49-0; P.W. Romaines 0.3-0-8-0; C.R. Trembath 46.5-5-225-5; Zaheer Abbas 5.4-4-1-0.

County Records

First-class cricket

Highest innings	For	653-6d v Glamorgan (Bristol)	1928
totals:	Agst	774-7d by Australians (Bristol)	1948
Lowest innings	For	17 v Australians (Cheltenham)	1896
totals:	Agst	12 by Northants (Gloucester)	1907

GLOUCESTERSHIRE

Highest indi-	For	318* W.G. Grace v Yorks (Cheltenham)	1876
vidual innings	Agst	296 A.O. Jones for Notts (Nottingham)	1903
Best bowling	For	10-40 G.E. Dennett v Essex (Bristol)	1906
in an innings:	Agst	10-66 A.A. Mailey for Aust (Cheltenham)	1921
		and K. Smales for Notts (Stroud)	1956
Best bowling	For	17-56 C.W.L. Parker v Essex (Gloucester)	1925
in a match:	Agst	15-87 A.J. Conway for Worcs	
		(Moreton-in-Marsh)	1914
Most runs in a season:		2,860 (av. 69.75) W.R. Hammond	1933
runs in a career:		33,664 (av. 57.05) W.R. Hammond	1920-1951
100s in a season:		13 by W.R. Hammond	1938
100s in a career:		113 by W.R. Hammond	1920-1951
wickets in a season:		222 (av. 16.80 & 16.37)	
		T.W.J. Goddard	1937 & 1947
wickets in a career:		3,170 (av. 19.44) C.W.L. Parker	1903-1935

RECORD WICKET STANDS

1st	395	D.M. Young & R.B. Nicholls v Oxford U (Oxford)	1962
2nd	256	C.T.M. Pugh & T.W. Graveney v Derby (Chesterfield)	1960
3rd	336	W.R. Hammond & B.H. Lyon v Leics (Leicester)	1933
4th	321	W.R. Hammond & W.L. Neale v Leics (Gloucester)	1937
5th	261	W.G. Grace & W.O. Moberley v Yorks (Cheltenham)	1876
6th	320	G.L. Jessop & J.H. Board v Sussex (Hove)	1903
7th	248	W.G. Grace & E.L. Thomas v Sussex (Hove)	1896
8th	239	W.R. Hammond & A.E. Wilson v Lancs (Bristol)	1938
9th	193	W.G. Grace & S.A.P. Kitcat v Sussex (Bristol)	1896
10th	131	W.R. Gouldsworthy & J.G. Bessant v Somerset (Bristol)	1923

One-day cricket

Highest innings totals:	Gillette Cup/NatWest Trophy	327-7 v Berkshire (Reading)	1966
	John Player League	272-4 v Middlesex (Lord's)	1983
	Benson & Hedges Cup	300-4 v Combined Universities (Oxford)	1982
Lowest innings totals:	NatWest Trophy	85 v Essex (Bristol)	1981
	John Player League	49 v Middlesex (Bristol)	1978
	Benson & Hedges Cup	62 v Hants (Bristol)	1975
Highest indi- vidual innings:	Gillette Cup/NatWest Trophy	158 Zaheer Abbas v Leics (Leicester)	1983
	John Player League	131 Sadiq Mohammad v Somerset (Imperial Ground, Bristol)	1975
	Benson & Hedges Cup	154* M.J. Procter v Somerset (Taunton)	1972
Best bowling figures:	NatWest Trophy	5-11 D.A. Graveney v Ireland (Dublin)	1981
	John Player League	6-52 v Kent (Bristol)	1983
	Benson & Hedges Cup	6-13 M.J. Procter v Hants (Southampton)	1977

HAMPSHIRE

Formation of present club: 1863.
Colours: Blue, gold and white.
Badge: Tudor rose and crown.
County Champions (2): 1961 and 1973.
Gillette Cup Semi-Finalists (2): 1966 and 1976.
NatWest Trophy Semi-finalists: 1983.
John Player League Champions (2): 1975 and 1978.
Benson & Hedges Cup Semi-Finalists (2): 1975 and 1977.
Fenner Trophy Winners (3): 1975, 1976 and 1977.
Gillette Man of the Match Awards: 25.
NatWest Man of the Match Awards: 5.
Benson & Hedges Gold Awards: 30.

Secretary: A.K. James, County Cricket Ground,
    Northlands Road, Southampton SO9 2TY.
Captain: M.C.J. Nicholas.

Stephen John Walter ANDREW (Milton Abbey School, Porchester Secondary School). B London 27/1/1966. RHB, RM. Debut 1984. BH Gold Award: 1. BB: 4-30 v Sussex (Hove) 1984. BBJPL: 3-38 v Northants (Southampton) 1984. BBBH: 3-12 v Surrey (Oval) 1984.

Cardigan Adolphus CONNOR (The Valley Secondary School; Langley College) B The Valley, Anguilla 24/3/1961. RHB, RFM. Debut 1984. HS: 13* v Kent (Bournemouth) 1984. BB: 7-37 v Kent (Bournemouth) 1984. BBJPL: 4-16 v Yorks (Bournemouth) 1984.

Nigel Geoffrey COWLEY (Mere Dutchy Manor) B Shaftesbury (Dorset) 1/3/1953. RHB, OB. Debut 1974. Cap 1978. Scored 1,042 runs (av. 30.64) in 1984. HS: 109* v Somerset (Taunton) 1977. HSGC/NW: 63* v Glos (Bristol 1979. HSJPL: 74 v Warwicks (Birmingham) 1981. HSBH: 59 v Glos (Southampton) 1977. BB: 6-48 v Leics (Southampton) 1982. BBNW: 5-24 v Norfolk (Norwich) 1984. BBJPL: 4-42 v Surrey (Portsmouth) 1983. BBBH: 3-39 v Sussex (Bournemouth) 1984.

Christopher Frederick Evelyn GOLDIE (St Paul's School and Cambridge) B Johannesburg, South Africa 2/11/1960. RHB, WK. Debut 1981 for Cambridge U. Blue 1981-82. Debut for county 1983. HS: 77 Cambridge U v Oxford U (Lord's) 1981.

Cuthbert Gordon GREENIDGE (Black Bess School; St. Peter's Boys' School; Sutton Secondary, Reading) B St. Peter, Barbados 1/5/1951. RHB, RM. Debut 1970. Cap 1972. Played for Barbados 1972-73 to date. *Wisden* 1976. Tests: 57 for West Indies between 1974-75 and 1984. One-day Internationals: 60 for West Indies. Tours: West Indies to India, Sri Lanka and Pakistan 1974-75, Australia 1975-76 and 1981-82, England 1976, 1980 and 1984, Australia and New Zealand 1979-80, Pakistan 1980-81, India 1983-84. 1,000 runs (13). 1,952 runs (av. 55.77) in 1976 best. Scored 1,168 runs (av. 58.40) in 1983-84. Scored two centuries in match (134 and 101) West Indies v England (Manchester) 1976 and (136 and 120) v Kent (Bournemouth) 1978. Benefit 1983. Gillette Man of the Match: 3. NW Man of the Match: 1. BH Gold Awards: 5. HS: 273* D.H. Robins' XI v Pakistanis (Eastbourne)

1974. HSC: 259 v Sussex (Southampton) 1975. HSTC: 223 West Indies v England (Manchester) 1984. HSGC/NW: 177 v Glamorgan (Southampton) 1975 – record for GC competition. HSJPL: 163* v Warwicks (Birmingham) 1979. HSBH: 173* v Minor Counties (South) (Amersham) 1973 and shared in partnership of 285* for second wicket with D.R. Turner – the record partnership for all one-day competition. BB: 5-49 v Surrey (Southampton) 1971. MBE 1985.

Jonathan James Ean HARDY (Canford School) B Nakaru, Kenya 2/10/1960. LHB. Debut 1984. HS: 95 v Warwicks (Birmingham) 1984. HSJPL: 58 v Northants (Southampton) 1984.

Kevan David JAMES (Edmonton County HS) B Lambeth 18/3/1961. LHB, LM. Debut for Middlesex 1980. Played for Wellington 1982-83. Joined Hants for 1985. HS: 34 Middlesex v Northants (Northampton) 1983. HSJPL: 25 v Notts (Cleethorpes) 1983. HSBH; 14 Middlesex v Glamorgan (Cardiff) 1984. BB: 5-28 Middlesex v Cambridge U (Cambridge) 1983.

Malcolm Denzil MARSHALL (Parkinson Comprehensive, Barbados) B St Michael, Barbados 18/4/1958. RHB, RF. Played for Barbados 1977-78 to 1982–83. Debut for county 1979. Cap 1981. *Wisden* 1982. Tests: 31 between 1978-79 and 1984. One-day Internationals: 44 for West Indies. Tours: West Indies to India and Sri Lanka 1978-79, Australia and New Zealand 1979-80, England 1980, Pakistan 1980-81, Zimbabwe 1981-82, Australia 1981-82, India 1983-84, England 1984. Hattrick in John Player League v Surrey (Southampton) 1981, 134 wkts (av. 15.73) in 1982. HS: 116* v Lancs (Southampton) 1982. HSTC: 92 West Indies v India (Kampur) 1983-84. HSGC/NW: 21* v Middlesex (Lord's) 1979. HSJPL: 46 v Leics (Leicester) 1982. HSBH: 21 v Kent (Canterbury) 1982. BB: 8-71 v Worcs (Southampton) 1982. BBTC: 7-53 West Indies v England (Leeds) 1984. BBNW: 4-15 v Kent (Canterbury) 1982. BBJPL: 5-13 v Glamorgan (Portsmouth) 1979. BBBH: 4-26 v Kent (Canterbury) 1983.

Rajesh Jaman MARU (Pinner SFC) B Nairobi, Kenya 28/10/1962. RHB, SLA. Debut for Middlesex 1980. For Hants 1984. Tour: Middlesex to Zimbabwe 1980-81. HS: 36 v Sussex (Bournemouth) 1984. BB: 7-79 v Middlesex (Bournemouth) 1984.

Tony Charles MIDDLETON (Montgomery of Alamein School and Peter Symonds SFC, Winchester) B Winchester 1/2/1964. RHB, SLA. Debut 1984. HS: 10 v Kent (Bournemouth) 1984.

Mark Charles Jefford NICHOLAS (Bradfield College) B London 29/9/1957. RHB, RM. Debut 1978. Cap 1982. Appointed Captain for 1985. 1,000 runs (3) – 1,559 (av. 33.89) in 1984 best. HS: 206* v Oxford U (Oxford) 1982. HSNW: 63 v Norfolk (Norwich) 1984. HSJPL: 108 v Glos (Bristol) 1984. HSBH: 49 v Surrey (Oval) 1984. BB;5-45 v Worcs (Southampton) 1983. BBJPL: 3-30 v Kent (Canterbury) 1983. BBBH: 3-29 v Surrey (Oval) 1980.

Robert James PARKS (Eastbourne GS) B Cuckfield, Sussex 15/6/1959. Son of J.M. Parks and grandson of J.H. Parks. RHB, WK. Debut 1980. Cap 1982. Dismissed 10 batsmen (all ct.) in match v Derby (Portsmouth) 1981. HS: 89 v Cambridge U (Cambridge) 1984. HSNW: 25 v Kent (Southampton) 1984. HSJPL: 36* v Leics (Leicester) 1982. HSBH: 11* v Essex (Southampton) 1984.

Christopher Lyall (Kippy) SMITH (Northlands HS, Durkan) B Durban, South

Africa 15/10/1958. Older brother of R.A. Smith. RHB, OB. Played for Natal B 1977-78 to 1982-83. Debut for Glamorgan 1979. Debut for Hants 1980. Cap 1981. *Wisden* 1983. Tests: 7 between 1983 and 1983-84. One-day Internationals: 4. 1,000 runs (3): 1,923 (av. 53.41) in 1983 best. NW Man of the Match: 1. BH Gold Awards: 2. HS: 193 v Derby (Derby) 1983. HSTC: 91 v New Zealand (Auckland) 1983-84. HSNW: 101* v Glos (Bristol) 1983. HSJPL: 95 v Leics (Basingstoke) 1984. HSBH: 82* v Combined Universities (Southampton) 1984. BB: 3-35 v Glamorgan (Southampton) 1983.

Robin Arnold SMITH (Northlands Boys HS, Durban) B Durban, South Africa 13/9/1963. Younger brother of C.L. Smith. RHB, LB. Played for Natal 1980-81 to date. Debut for Hants 1982. HS: 132 v Sri Lankans (Southampton) 1984. HSJPL: 104 v Glamorgan (Cardiff) 1984.

Vivian Paul TERRY (Millfield School) B Osnabruck, West Germany 14/1/1959. RHB, RM. Debut 1978. Cap 1983. Tests: 2 in 1984. 1,000 runs (2) – 1,208 (av. 48.32) in 1984 best. HS: 175* v Glos (Bristol) 1984. HSNW: 50 v Norfolk (Norwich) 1984. HSJPL: 110 v Notts (Southampton) 1984. HSBH: 72 v Kent (Canterbury) 1983 and 72 v Essex (Southampton) 1984.

Timothy Maurice TREMLETT (Bellemoor SM; Richard Taunton SFC) B Wellington, Somerset 26/7/1956. Son of M.E. Tremlett (Somerset and England). RHB, RM. Debut 1976. Cap 1983. HS: 88 v Lancs (Manchester) 1981. HSNW: 17 v Kent (Southampton) 1984. HSJPL: 35 v Worcs (Worcester) 1984. HSBH: 29 v Surrey (Bournemouth) 1981. BB: 6-82 v Derby (Portsmouth). BBNW: 4-38 v Kent (Canterbury) 1983. BBJPL: 4-22 v Lancs (Manchester) 1981. BBBH: 3-21 v Combined Universities (Cambridge) 1978.

David Roy TURNER (Chippenham Boys HS) B Chippenham, Wilts 5/2/1949. LHB, RM. Debut 1966. Cap 1970. Played for Western Province in 1977-78. Benefit in 1981. Tour: D.H. Robins to South Africa 1972-73. 1,000 runs (7) – 1,365 (av. 41.36) in 1984 best. Gillette Man of the Match: 1. BH Gold Awards: 4. HS: 181* v Surrey (Oval) 1969. HSGC/NW: 86 v Northants (Southampton) 1976. HSJPL: 114 v Essex (Colchester) 1984. HSBH: 123* v Minor Counties (South) (Amersham) 1973.

N.B. The following players whose particulars appeared in the 1984 Annual have been omitted: K.S.D. Emery, T.E. Jesty, S.J. Malone, N.E.J. Pocock and K. Stevenson.

County Averages

Britannic Assurance County Championship; Played 24, won 3, drawn 8, lost 13.
All first-class matches; Played 26, won 4, drawn 9, lost 13.

BATTING AND FIELDING

Cap		M	I	NO	RUNS	HS	Avge	100	50	Ct	St
1983	V.P. Terry	14	25	3	1192	175*	54.18	5	6	15	—
—	R.A. Smith	7	13	3	483	132	48.30	1	2	4	—
1970	D.R. Turner	20	37	4	1365	153	41.36	3	7	7	—
1971	T.E. Jesty	25	44	4	1625	248	40.62	5	4	16	—
—	J.J.E. Hardy	13	20	6	513	95	36.64	—	4	9	—
1982	M.C.J. Nicholas	25	46	1	1482	158	32.93	4	5	15	—
1978	N.G. Cowley	26	38	4	1042	80	30.64	—	6	9	—
1981	C.L. Smith	25	47	3	1244	125	28.27	4	3	13	—
—	E.L. Reifer	20	26	8	357	47	19.83	—	—	6	—
1980	N.E.J. Pocock	13	18	2	314	55	19.62	—	1	13	—
1983	T.M. Tremlett	23	31	7	438	74	18.25	—	2	4	—
1982	R.J. Parks	25	34	9	444	89	17.76	—	2	61	10
—	R.J. Maru	17	20	4	246	36	15.37	—	—	22	—
—	S.J.W. Andrew	7	6	4	12	6*	6.00	—	—	1	—
—	C.A. Connor	21	23	9	65	13*	4.64	—	—	7	—

Played in three matches: S.J. Malone 0,4 (2 ct).
Played in one match: T.C. Middleton 10,5; C.F.E. Goldie did not bat (2 ct 1 st).

BOWLING

	Type	O	M	R	W	Avge	Best	5 wI	10 wM
T.M. Tremlett	RM	669.5	210	1444	71	20.33	5-48	2	—
C.A. Connor	RFM	642.5	155	1949	62	31.43	7-37	1	—
N.G. Cowley	OB	588.1	133	1779	56	31.76	4-33	—	—
T.E. Jesty	RM	220.1	50	668	19	35.15	3-15	—	—
R.J. Maru	SLA	549.4	129	1664	47	35.40	7-79	2	—
E.L. Reifer	LFM	524.5	100	1761	49	35.93	4-43	—	—
S.J.W. Andrew	RM	162.2	43	530	11	48.18	4-30	—	—
M.C.J. Nicholas	RM	129	23	438	7	62.57	2-56	—	—

Also bowled: J.J.E. Hardy 1-0-3-0; S.J. Malone 65-17-204-6; N.E.J. Pocock 11-1-61-0; C.L. Smith 158-19-687-9; D.R. Turner 5-1-9-0.

County Records

First-class cricket

Highest innings totals:	For	672-7d v Somerset (Taunton)	1899
	Agst	742 by Surrey (Oval)	1909
Lowest innings totals:	For	15 v Warwicks (Birmingham)	1922
	Agst	23 by Yorks (Middlesbrough)	1965
Highest individual innings:	For	316 R.H. Moore v Warwicks (Bournemouth)	1937
	Agst	302* P. Holmes for Yorks (Portsmouth)	1920

Best bowling in an innings:	For	9-25 R.M.H. Cottam v Lancs (Manchester)	1965
	Agst	9-21 L.B. Richmond for Notts (Nottingham)	1922
Best bowling in a match:	For	16-88 J.A. Newman v Somerset (Weston-super-Mare)	1927
	Agst	17-119 W. Mead for Essex (Southampton)	1895
Most runs in a season:		2,854 (av. 79.27) C.P. Mead	1928
runs in a career:		48,892 (av. 48.84) C.P. Mead	1905-1936
100s in a season:		12 by C.P. Mead	1928
100s in a career:		138 by C.P. Mead	1905-1936
wickets in a season:		190 (av. 15.61) A.S. Kennedy	1922
wickets in a career:		2,669 (av. 18.22) D. Shackleton	1948-1969

RECORD WICKET STANDS

1st	249	R.E. Marshall & J.R. Gray v Middlesex (Portsmouth)	1960
2nd	321	G. Brown & E.I.M. Barrett v Glos (Southampton)	1920
3rd	344	C.P. Mead & G. Brown v Yorks (Portsmouth)	1927
4th	263	R.E. Marshall & D.A. Livingstone v Middlesex (Lord's)	1970
5th	235	G. Hill & D.F. Walker v Sussex (Portsmouth)	1937
6th	411	R.M. Poore & E.G. Wynyard v Somerset (Taunton)	1899
7th	325	G. Brown & C.H. Abercrombie v Essex (Leyton)	1913
8th	178	C.P. Mead & C.P. Brutton v Worcs (Bournemouth)	1925
9th	230	D.A. Livingstone & A.T. Castell v Surrey (Southampton)	1962
10th	192	A. Bowell & W.H. Livsey v Worcs (Bournemouth)	1921

NB. A partnership of 334 for the first wicket by B.A. Richards, C.G. Greenidge and D.R. Turner occurred against Kent at Southampton in 1973. Richards retired hurt after 241 runs had been scored.

One-day cricket

Highest innings totals:	Gillette Cup/ NatWest Trophy	371-4 v Glamorgan (Southampton)	1975
	John Player League	292-1 v Surrey (Portsmouth)	1983
	Benson & Hedges Cup	321-1 v Minor Counties (South) (Amersham)	1973
Lowest innings totals:	Gillette Cup/ NatWest Trophy	98 v Lancs (Manchester)	1975
	John Player League	43 v Essex (Basingstoke)	1972
	Benson & Hedges Cup	94 v Glamorgan (Swansea)	1973
Highest individual innings:	Gillette Cup/ NatWest Trophy	177 C.G. Greenidge v Glamorgan (Southampton)	1975
	John Player League	166* T.E. Jesty v Surrey (Portsmouth)	1983
	Benson & Hedges Cup	173* C.G. Greenidge v Minor Counties (South) (Amersham)	1973
Best bowling figures:	Gillette Cup/ NatWest Trophy	7-30 P.J. Sainsbury v Norfolk (Southampton)	1965
	John Player League	6-20 T.E. Jesty v Glamorgan (Cardiff)	1975
	Benson & Hedges Cup	5-24 R.S. Herman v Glos (Bristol)	1975
		5-24 K.S.D. Emery v Essex (Chelmsford)	1982

KENT

Formation of present club: 1859, re-organised 1870.
Colours: Maroon and white.
Badge: White horse.
County Champions (6): 1906, 1909, 1910, 1913, 1970 and 1978.
Joint Champions: 1977.
Gillette Cup Winners (2): 1967 and 1974.
Gillette Cup Finalists: 1971.
NatWest Trophy Finalists: 1983 and 1984.
John Player League Champions (3): 1972, 1973 and 1976.
Benson & Hedges Cup Winners (3): 1973, 1976 and 1978.
Benson & Hedges Cup Finalists: 1977.
Fenner Trophy Winners (2): 1971 and 1973.
Gillette Man of the Match Awards: 23.
NatWest Trophy Man of the Match Awards: 9.
Benson & Hedges Gold Awards: 37.

Secretary: D. Dalby, St. Lawrence Ground, Canterbury CT1 3NZ.
Cricket Manager: B.W. Luckhurst.
Captain: C.S. Cowdrey.
Prospects of Play Telephone No: Canterbury matches only, Canterbury (0227) 57323.

Derek George ASLETT (Dover GS, Leicester U) B Dover 12/2/1958. RHB, LB. Debut 1981 scoring 146* in first innings. Scored 168 & 119 v Derby (Chesterfield) 1983. Cap 1983. 1,000 runs (2) – 1,491 (av. 35.50) in 1984 best. HS: 221* v Sri Lankans (Canterbury) 1984. HSNW: 67 v Hants (Southampton) 1984. HSJPL: 100 v Somerset (Taunton) 1983. HSBH: 46 v Somerset (Canterbury) 1984. BB: 4-119 v Sussex (Hove) 1982.

Eldine Ashworth Elderfield BAPTISTE (All Saints Secondary) B St. John's, Antigua 12/3/1960. RHB, RFM. Debut 1981. Cap 1983. Played for Leeward Islands 1981-82 to date. NW Man of the Match: 1. Tests: 9 for West Indies between 1983-84 and 1984. One-day Internationals: 23 for West Indies. Tours: West Indies to India 1983-84, England 1984. HS: 136* v Yorkshire (Sheffield) 1983. HSTC: 87* West Indies v England (Birmingham) 1984. HSNW: 22 v Warwicks (Canterbury) 1983. HSJPL: 47 v Essex (Chelmsford) 1983. BB: 5-37 v Lancs (Maidstone) 1981. BBTC: 3-31 West Indies v England (Manchester) 1984. BBNW: 5-20 v Hants (Canterbury) 1983. BBJPL: 4-29 v Worcs (Canterbury) 1983.

Mark Richard BENSON (Sutton Valence School) B Shoreham, Sussex 6/7/1958. LHB, OB. Debut 1980. Cap 1981. NW Man of the Match: 1. 1,000 runs (3) – 1,515 (av. 44.55) in 1983 best. HS: 152* v Warwicks (Birmingham) 1983. HSNW: 113* v Warwicks (Birmingham) 1984. HSJPL: 97 v Surrey (Oval) 1982. HSBH: 65 v Surrey (Canterbury) 1982.

Christopher Stuart COWDREY (Tonbridge School) B Farnborough, Kent, 20/10/1957. Eldest son of M.C. Cowdrey (Kent and England). RHB, RM. Played for 2nd XI at age of 13. Debut 1977. Cap 1979. Appointed captain for 1985. 1,000 runs (2) – 1,364 (av. 56.83) in 1983 best. Tours: D.H. Robins to Sri Lanka 1977-78 and New Zealand 1979-80. BH Gold Awards: 2. NW Man of the Match: 3. HS: 125* v Essex (Colchester) 1984. HSNW: 122* v Essex (Chelmsford) 1983. HSJPL: 95 v Worcs (Canterbury) 1983. HSBH: 114 v Sussex (Canterbury) 1977. BB: 3-17 v Hants (Bournemouth) 1980. BBNW: 4-36 v Hants (Canterbury) 1983. BBJPL: 5-28 v Leics (Canterbury) 1984.

Graham Robert COWDREY (Tonbridge School; Durham U) B Farnborough, Kent 27/6/1964. RHB, RM. Son of M.C. Cowdrey (Kent and England). Debut 1984.

Graham Roy DILLEY (Dartford West Secondary) B Dartford 18/5/1959. LHB, RFM. Debut 1977. Cap 1980. Did not play in 1984. Tests: 18 between 1979-80 and 1983-84. One-day Internationals: 18. Tours: Australia and India 1979-80, West Indies 1980-81, India and Sri Lanka 1981-82. BH Gold Award: 1. HS: 81 v Northants (Northampton) 1979. HSTC: 56 v Australia (Leeds) 1981. HSNW: 19 v Somerset (Lord's) 1983. HSJPL: 33 v Northants (Northampton) 1982. HSBH: 37* v Hants (Kent) 1983. BB: 6-66 v Middlesex (Lord's) 1979. BBTC: 4-24 v Australia (Nottingham) 1981. BBNW: 4-29 v Somerset (Lord's) 1983. BBJPL: 4-20 v Glos (Canterbury) 1980. BBBH: 4-14 v Combined Universities (Canterbury) 1981.

Richard Mark ELLISON (Tonbridge School) B Ashford (Kent) 21/9/1959. LHB, RM. Debut 1981. Cap 1983. BH Gold Awards: 3. Hat-trick in JPL v Hants (Canterbury) 1983. Tests: 2 in 1984. HS: 108 v Oxford U (Oxford) 1984. HSTC: 41 v Sri Lanka (Lord's) 1984. HSNW: 49* v Warwicks (Birmingham) 1984. HSJPL: 84 v Glos (Canterbury) 1984. HSBH: 72 v Middlesex (Lord's) 1984. BB: 5-27 v Essex (Canterbury) 1984. BBTC: 3-60 v West Indies (Oval) 1984. BBNW: 4-19 v Cheshire (Canterbury) 1983. BBJPL: 4-25 v Hants (Canterbury) 1983. BBBH: 4-28 v Glamorgan (Canterbury) 1984.

Simon Graham HINKS (St George's C. of E. School, Gravesend) B Northfleet 12/10/1960. LHB, RM, WK. Debut 1982. HS: 87 v Glamorgan (Cardiff) 1983. HSJPL: 52* v Hants (Bournemouth) 1984.

Kevin Bertram Sidney JARVIS (Springhead School, Northfleet; Thames Polytechnic) B Dartford 23/4/1953. RHB, RFM. Debut 1975. Cap 1977. NW Man of the Match: 1. Tours: D.H. Robins to Sri Lanka 1977-78. International XI to Jamaica 1982-83. BH Gold Award: 1. HS: 19 v Derby (Maidstone) 1984. BB: 8-97 v Worcs (Worcester) 1978. BBNW: 4-19 v Warwicks (Canterbury) 1983. BBJPL: 4-27 v Surrey (Maidstone) 1977. BBBH: 4-34 v Worcs (Lord's) 1976.

Graham William JOHNSON (Beckenham & Penge GS; Shooter's Hill GS; London School of Economics) B Beckenham 8/11/1946. RHB, OB. Debut 1965. Cap 1970. Played for Transvaal 1981-82. Benefit 1983. 1,000 runs (3) – 1,438 runs (av. 31.26) in 1973 and 1,438 runs (av. 35.95) in 1975 best. Gillette Man of the Match Award: 1. BH Gold Awards: 3. HS: 168 v Surrey (Oval) 1976. HSGC/NW: 120* v Bucks (Canterbury) 1974. HSJPL: 89 v Sussex (Hove) 1976. HSBH: 85* v Minor Counties (South) (Canterbury) 1975. BB: 7-76 v Northants (Canterbury) 1983. BBJPL: 5-26 v Surrey (Oval) 1974.

Alan Philip Eric KNOTT (Northumberland Heath SMS, Erith) B Belvedere 9/4/1946. RHB, WK, OB. Debut 1964. Cap 1965. Best Young Cricketer of the Year in 1965. *Wisden* 1969. Played for Tasmania 1969-70. Benefit (£27,037) in 1976. Tests: 95 between 1967 and 1981. Played in 5 matches against Rest of World in 1970. One-day Internationals: 20. Tours: Cavaliers to West Indies 1964-65, Pakistan 1966-67, West Indies 1967-68 and 1973-74, Ceylon and Pakistan 1968-69, Australia and New Zealand 1970-71, 1974-75, India, Sri Lanka and Pakistan 1972-73, India, Sri Lanka and Australia 1976-77, SAB to South Africa 1981-82. Banned for 3 years from Test cricket. 1,000 runs (2) – 1,209 runs (av. 41.68) in 1971 best. Scored two centuries in match (127* and 118*) v Surrey (Maidstone) 1972. Gillette Man of the Match Awards: 2. BH Gold Award: 1. HS: 156 MCC v South Zone (Bangalore) 1972-73. HSUK: 144 v Sussex (Canterbury) 1976. HSTC: 135 v Ausrtralia (Nottingham) 1977. HSGC/NW: 46 v Notts (Nottingham) 1975. HSJPL: 60 v Hants (Canterbury) 1969. HSBH: 65 v Combined Universities (Oxford) 1976. Dismissed 84 batsmen (74 ct 10 st) in 1965. 81 batsmen (73 ct 7 st) in 1966, and 98 batsmen (90 ct 8 st) in 1967. Dismissed 7 batsmen (7 ct) on debut in Test cricket v Pakistan (Nottingham) 1967.

Steven Andrew MARSH (Walderslade Secondary; Mid-Kent CFE) B Westminster 27/1/1961. RHB, WK. Debut 1982. HS: 48 v Notts (Folkestone) 1984.

Kevin David MASTERS B Chatham 19/5/1961. LHB, RFM. Debut 1983.

Christopher PENN (Dover GS) B Dover 19/6/1963. LHB, RFM. Debut 1982. HS: 115 v Lancs (Manchester) 1984. HSJPL: 40 v Sussex (Maidstone) 1982. HSBH: 17 v Somerset (Canterbury) 1984. BBJPL: 3-35 v Yorks (Canterbury) 1982. BBBH: 4-34 v Surrey (Canterbury) 1982.

Laurie POTTER (Kelmscott HS, Perth, Western Australia) B Bexleyheath 7/11/1962. RHB, LM. Emigrated to Australia with parents at age of four. Debut 1981. HS: 118 v Indians (Canterbury) 1982. HSNW: 45 v Essex (Chelmsford) 1982. HSJPL: 45 v Warwicks (Birmingham) 1982. HSBH: 49 v Sussex (Hove) 1982. BBJPL: 4-27 v Somerset (Bath) 1981.

Christopher James TAVARÉ (Sevenoaks School and Oxford) B Orpington 27/10/1954. RHB, RM. Debut 1974. Blue 1975-76-77. Cap 1978. Captain 1983-84. Tests: 30 between 1980 and 1984. One-day Internationals: 29. Tours: India and Sri Lanka 1981-82, Australia 1982-83, New Zealand 1983-84. 1,000 runs (8) – 1,770 runs (av. 53.63) in 1981 best. NatWest Man of the Match Awards: 3. BH Gold Awards: 5 (2 for Combined Universities). HS: 168* v Essex (Chelmsford) 1982. HSTC: 149 v India (Delhi) 1981-82. HSNW: 118* v Yorks (Canterbury) 1981. HSJPL: 136* v Glos (Canterbury) 1978. HSBH: 95 v Surrey (Oval) 1980.

Neil Royston TAYLOR (Cray Valley THS) B Orpington 21/7/1959. RHB, OB. Debut 1979 scoring 110 v Sri Lankans (Canterbury). 1,000 runs (3) – 1,340 runs (av. 34.35) in 1982 best. BH Gold Awards: 4. HS: 155* v Glamorgan (Cardiff) 1983. HSNW: 49 v Middlesex (Lord's) 1984. HSJPL: 74 v Glos (Folkestone) 1982. HSBH: 121 v Sussex (Hove) and v Somerset (Canterbury) 1982.

Derek Leslie UNDERWOOD (Beckenham & Penge GS) B Bromley 8/6/1945. RHB, LM. Debut 1963, taking 100 wkts and being the youngest player ever to do so in debut season. Cap 1964. *Wisden* 1968. Benefit (£24,114) in 1975. Awarded MBE in 1981 New Year's Honours List. Took 1,000th wkt in first-class cricket in New Zealand 1970-71 at age of 25 years 264 days – only W. Rhodes (in 1902) and G.A. Lohmann (in 1890) have achieved the feat at a younger age – and 2,000th wkt in 1981. Took 200th wkt in Test cricket against Australia in 1975. Tests: 86 between 1966 and 1981-82. Played in 3 matches against Rest of World in 1970. Tours: Pakistan 1966-67, International XI to Africa and Asia 1967-68, Ceylon and Pakistan 1968-69, Duke of Norfolk to West Indies 1969-70, Australia and New Zealand 1970-71, 1974-75, India, Sri Lanka and Pakistan 1972-73, West Indies 1973-74, International Wanderers to South Africa 1975-76, India, Sri Lanka and Australia 1976-77, Australia and India 1979-80, India and Sri Lanka 1981-82, SAB to South Africa 1981-82. Banned from Test cricket for 3 years. BH Gold Award: 1. 100 wkts (10) – 157 wkts (av. 13.80) in 1966 best. Hat-trick v Sussex (Hove) 1977. HS: 111 v Sussex

(Hastings) 1984. HSTC: 45* v Australia (Leeds) 1968. HSGC/NW: 28 v Sussex (Tunbridge Wells) 1963. HSJPL: 22 v Worcs (Dudley) 1969. HSBH: 27 v Surrey (Canterbury) 1983. BB: 9-28 v Sussex (Hastings) 1964 and 9-32 v Surrey (Oval) 1978. BBTC: 8-51 v Pakistan (Lord's) 1974. BBGC/NW: 4-57 v Leics (Canterbury) 1974. BBJPL: 6-12 v Sussex (Hastings) 1984. BBBH: 5-35 v Surrey (Oval) 1976.

Stuart Nicholas Varney WATERTON (Gravesend School, London School of Ecnomics) B Dartford 6/12/1960. RHB, WK. Debut 1980. HS: 50 v Lancs (Manchester) 1984. HSJPL: 15 v Glamorgan (Canterbury) 1984.

Lindsay Jonathan WOOD B Ruislip (Middlesex) 12/5/1961. LHB, SLA. Debut 1981. Did not play in 1983 or 1984. BB: 4-124 v Essex (Chelmsford) 1981.

NB. The following player whose particulars appeared in the 1984 Annual has been omitted: R.A. Woolmer.

County Averages

Britannic Assurance County Championship; Played 24, won 8, drawn 11 lost 3, tied 2.
All first-class matches; Played 26, won 9, drawn 12, lost 3, tied 2.

BATTING AND FIELDING

Cap		M	I	NO	RUNS	HS	Avge	100	50	Ct	St
1970	R.A. Woolmer	8	14	3	427	153	38.81	1	2	4	—
1981	M.R. Benson	14	26	2	914	127	38.08	3	4	7	—
1983	D.G. Aslett	26	45	3	1491	221*	35.50	5	5	15	—
1982	N.R. Taylor	21	39	5	1098	139	32.29	2	5	8	—
1979	C.S. Cowdrey	21	36	3	1025	125*	31.06	2	5	18	—
1978	C.J. Tavaré	22	38	0	1119	117	29.44	2	5	20	—
—	C. Penn	12	15	2	317	115	24.38	1	1	8	—
—	L. Potter	14	25	1	574	117	23.91	1	2	7	—
1983	R.M. Ellison	19	29	6	546	108	23.73	1	1	7	—
—	S.N.V. Waterton	7	10	1	193	50	21.44	—	1	11	4
1970	G.W. Johnson	25	39	5	726	84	21.35	—	3	26	—
1964	D.L. Underwood	24	33	9	498	111	20.75	1	—	11	—
—	S.A. Marsh	5	7	1	106	48	17.66	—	—	11	—
1984	T.M. Alderman	20	27	13	220	52*	15.71	—	1	29	—
1965	A.P.E. Knott	14	22	2	295	43	14.75	—	—	29	1
—	S.G. Hinks	8	14	0	162	39	11.57	—	1	3	—
1977	K.B.S. Jarvis	23	25	13	41	19	3.41	—	—	6	—

Played in two matches: K.D. Masters 0,0,0*.
Played in one match: G.R. Cowdrey 7 (1 ct).

BOWLING

	Type	O	M	R	W	Avge	Best	5 wI	10 wM
D.L. Underwood	LM	676.4	250	1511	77	19.62	8-87	2	1
R.M. Ellison	RM	456.5	126	1123	53	21.18	5-27	1	—
T.M. Alderman	RFM	559.4	149	1725	76	22.69	5-25	6	—
K.B.S. Jarvis	RFM	570.5	128	1788	72	24.83	5-30	2	—
G.W. Johnson	OB	462.2	117	1220	39	31.28	5-38	3	—
C.S. Cowdrey	RM	245.1	47	757	22	34.40	3-64	—	—

Also bowled: D.G. Aslett 18.4-1-92-0; S.G. Hinks 16-3-53-2; G.R. Cowdrey 7-0-22-1; K.D. Masters 41.5-6-173-4; C. Penn 157-26-491-8; L. Potter 63-18-196-5; C.J. Tavaré 2-0-18-0; N.R. Taylor 15-3-54-0; R.A. Woolmer 20-3-51-5.

County Records

First-class cricket

Highest innings totals:	For	803-4d v Essex (Brentwood)	1934
	Agst	676 by Australians (Canterbury)	1921
Lowest innings totals:	For	18 v Sussex (Gravesend)	1867
	Agst	16 by Warwicks (Tonbridge)	1913
Highest individual innings:	For	332 W.H. Ashdown v Essex (Brentwood)	1934
	Agst	344 W.G. Grace for MCC (Canterbury)	1876
Best bowling in an innings:	For	10-30 C. Blythe v Northants (Northampton)	1907
	Agst	10-48 C.H.G. Bland for Sussex (Tonbridge)	1899
Best bowling in a match:	For	17-47 C. Blythe v Northants (Northampton)	1907
	Agst	17-106 T.W.J. Goddard for Glos (Bristol)	1939
Most runs in a season:		2,894 (av. 59.06) F.E. Woolley	1928
runs in a career:		47,868 (av. 41.77) F.E. Woolley	1906-1938
100s in a season:		10 by F.E. Woolley	1928 & 1934
100s in a career:		122 by F.E. Woolley	1906-1938
wickets in a season:		262 (av. 14.74) A.P. Freeman	1933
wickets in a career:		3,340 (av. 17.64) A.P. Freeman	1914-1936

RECORD WICKET STANDS

1st	283	A.E. Fagg & P.R. Sunnucks v Essex (Colchester)	1938
2nd	352	W.H. Ashdown & F.E. Woolley v Essex (Brentwood)	1934
3rd	321*	A. Hearne & J.R. Mason v Notts (Nottingham)	1899
4th	297	H.T.W. Hardinge & A.P.F. Chapman v Hants (Southampton)	1926
5th	277	F.E. Woolley & L.E.G. Ames v New Zealanders (Canterbury)	1931
6th	284	A.P.F. Chapman & G.B. Legge v Lancs (Maidstone)	1927
7th	248	A.P. Day & E. Humphreys v Somerset (Taunton)	1908
8th	157	A.L. Hilder & C. Wright v Essex (Gravesend)	1924
9th	161	B.R. Edrich & F. Ridgway v Sussex (Tunbridge Wells)	1949
10th	235	F.E. Woolley & A. Fielder v Worcs (Stourbridge)	1909

One-day cricket

Highest innings totals:	Gillette Cup/ NatWest Trophy	297-3 v Worcs (Canterbury)	1970
	John Player League	281-5 v Warwicks (Folkestone)	1983
	Benson & Hedges Cup	280-3 v Surrey (Oval)	1976
Lowest innings totals:	Gillette Cup/ NatWest Trophy	60 v Somerset (Taunton)	1979
	John Player League	83 v Middx (Lord's)	1984
	Benson & Hedges Cup	73 v Middlesex (Canterbury)	1979
Highest individual innings:	Gillette Cup/ NatWest Trophy	129 B.W. Luckhurst v Durham (Canterbury)	1974
	John Player League	142 B.W. Luckhurst v Somerset (Weston-super-Mare)	1970
	Benson & Hedges Cup	121 N.R. Taylor v Sussex (Hove)	1982
		121 N.R. Taylor v Somerset (Canterbury)	1982
Best bowling figures:	Gillette Cup/ NatWest Trophy	7-15 A.L. Dixon v Surrey (Oval)	1967
	John Player League	6-9 R.A. Woolmer v Derby (Chesterfield)	1979
	Benson & Hedges Cup	5-21 B.D. Julien v Surrey (Oval)	1973

LANCASHIRE

Formation of present club: 1864.
Colours: Red, green and blue.
Badge: Red rose.
County Champions (8): 1881, 1897, 1904, 1926, 1927, 1928, 1930 and 1934.
Joint Champions (4): 1879, 1882, 1889 and 1950.
Gillette Cup Winners (4): 1970, 1971, 1972 and 1975.
Gillette Cup Finalists (2): 1974 and 1976.
NatWest Trophy Semi-Finalists: 1981.
John Player League Champions (2): 1969 and 1970.
Benson & Hedges Cup Winners: 1984.
Gillette Man of the Match Awards: 35.
NatWest Man of the Match Awards: 5.
Benson & Hedges Gold Awards: 36.

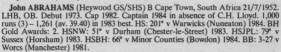

Secretary: C.D. Hassell, Old Trafford, Manchester MI6 0PX.
Cricket Manager: J.D. Bond.
Captain: C.H. Lloyd.
Prospects of Play Telephone No: 061-872 0261.

John ABRAHAMS (Heywood GS/SHS) B Cape Town, South Africa 21/7/1952. LHB, OB. Debut 1973. Cap 1982. Captain 1984 in absence of C.H. Lloyd. 1,000 runs (3) – 1,261 (av. 39.40) in 1983 best. HS: 201* v Warwicks (Nuneaton) 1984. BH Gold Awards: 2. HSNW: 51* v Durham (Chester-le-Street) 1983. HSJPL: 79* v Sussex (Horsham) 1983. HSBH: 66* v Minor Counties (Bowdon) 1984. BB: 3-27 v Worcs (Manchester) 1981.

Paul John Walter ALLOTT (Altrincham GS, Durham University) B Altrincham, Cheshire 14/9/1956. RHB, RFM. Debut 1978. Cap 1981. Tests: 9 between 1981 and 1984. One-day Internationals: 10. Tours: India and Sri Lanka 1981-82, International XI to Jamaica 1982-83. HS: 52* England v Australia (Manchester) 1981. HSC: 50* v Oxford U (Oxford) 1984. HSGC/NW: 19* v Worcs (Worcester) 1980. HSJPL: 32* v Yorks (Leeds) 1983. HSBH: 15* v Derby (Derby) 1984. BB: 8-48 v Northants (Northampton) 1981. BTBC: 6-61 v West Indies (Leeds) 1984. BBNW: 4-34 v Bucks (Manchester) 1984. BBJPL: 4-29 v Middlesex (Manchester) 1983. BBBH: 3-15 v Warwicks (Lord's) 1984.

Mark Robert CHADWICK (Roch Valley HS, Milnrow) B Rochdale 9/2/1963. RHB, RM. Debut 1983. BH Gold Award: 1. HS: 61 v Notts (Blackpool) 1984. HSBH: 87 v Notts (Nottingham) 1984. HSJPL: 10 v Glos (Bristol) 1983.

Neil Harvey FAIRBROTHER (Lymn GS) B Warrington 9/9/1963. LHB. Debut 1982. Scored 1,201 runs (av. 31.60) in 1984. HS: 102 v Derby (Buxton) 1984. HSNW: 36 v Glos (Bristol) 1984. HSJPL: 54* v Hants (Portsmouth) 1984. HSBH: 45* v Minor Counties (Bowdon) 1984.

Ian FOLLEY (Mansfield HS, Briersfield; Colne College) B Burnley 9/1/1963. RHB, SLA. Debut 1982. HS: 36 v Derby (Manchester) 1982. HSJPL: 11* v Somerset (Manchester) 1983. HSBH: 11* v Notts (Nottingham) 1982. BB: 5-65 v Glamorgan (Cardiff) 1984. BBBH: 4-18 v Middlesex (Lord's) 1982.

Graeme FOWLER (Accrington GS, Durham U) B Accrington 20/4/1957. LHB, WK. Debut 1979. Cap 1981. 16 Tests between 1982 and 1984. One-day Internationals: 13. Tours: International XI to Jamaica 1982-83, Australia and New

LANCASHIRE

Zealand 1982-83, New Zealand and Pakistan 1983-84. 1,000 runs (4) – 1,560 runs (av. 39.00) in 1981 best. Scored 126 and 128* v Warwicks (Southport) 1982. NW Man of the Match: 2. BH Gold Awards: 2. HS: 226 v Kent (Maidstone) 1984. HSTC: 106 v West Indies (Lord's) 1984. HSNW: 122 v Glos (Bristol) 1984. HSJPL: 75 v Sussex (Manchester) 1984. HSBH: 97 v Northants (Manchester) 1983.

Kevin Anthony HAYES (Queen Elizabeth's School, Blackburn; Oxford U) B Mexborough (Yorks) 26/9/1962. No relation to F.C. Hayes. RHB, RM. Debut 1980. Blue 1981-82-83-84. Secretary 1982. HS: 152 Oxford U v Warwicks (Oxford) 1982. HSC: 62 v Somerset (Taunton) 1982. HSJPL: 53 v Glos (Moreton-in-Marsh) 1984. HSBH: 67 Combined Universities v Hants (Southampton) 1984.

David Paul HUGHES (Newton-le-Willows GS) B Newton-le-Willows 13/5/1947. RHB, SLA. Debut 1967. Cap 1970. Played for Tasmania in 1975-76 and 1976-77. Testimonial in 1981. Tour: D.H. Robins to South Africa 1972-73. 1,000 runs (2) – 1,303 (av. 48.25) in 1982 best. Gillette Man of the Match: 1. BH Gold Awards: 1. HS: 153 v Glamorgan (Manchester) 1983. HSNW: 71 v Durham (Chester-le-Street) 1983. HSJPL: 92 v Kent (Maidstone) 1984. HSBH: 52 v Derby (Manchester) 1981. BB: 7-24 v Oxford U (Oxford) 1970. BBGC/NW: 4-61 v Somerset (Manchester) 1972. BBJPL: 6-29 v Somerset (Manchester) 1977. BBBH: 5-23 v Minor Counties (West) (Watford) 1978.

Stephen Thomas JEFFERIES (Plumstead HS) B Cape Town 8/12/1959. LHB, LFM. Played for Western Province 1978-79 to date. Derby 1982. Debut for Lancs 1983. Played for S. Africa v West Indies XI 1983-84. BH Gold Award: 1. HS: 75 v Essex (Manchester) 1983. HSNW: 23* v Glos (Bristol) 1984. HSJPL: 37* v Notts (Manchester) 1983. HSBH: 39 v Worcs (Manchester) 1984. BB: 8-46 v Notts (Nottingham) 1983. BBNW: 3-43 v Glos (Bristol) 1984. BBJPL: 4-20 v Worcs (Manchester) 1984. BBBH: 4-15 v Notts (Manchester) 1984.

Clive Hubert LLOYD (Chatham HS, Georgetown) B Georgetown, British Guiana 31/8/1944. 6ft 4½ins tall. Cousin of L.R. Gibbs. LHB, RM. Wears glasses. Debut 1963-64 for British Guiana. Played for Rest of World XI in 1967 and 1968. Debut for county 1968. Cap 1969. *Wisden* 1970. Testimonial (£27,199) in 1977. Appointed County Captain in 1981. Tests: 105 for West Indies between 1966-67 and 1983-84 captaining West Indies in 69 Tests, the record for all countries. Played in 5 matches for Rest of World 1970 and 2 in 1971-72. Scored 118 on debut v England (Port of Spain) 1967-68, 129 on debut v Australia (Brisbane) 1968-69. One-day Internationals: 73. Tours: West Indies to India and Ceylon 1966-67, Australia and New Zealand 1968-69, 1979-80 (captain), England 1969, 1973, 1976 (captain), 1980 (captain) and 1984 (captain), Rest of World to Australia 1971-72 (returning early owing to back injury), World XI to Pakistan 1973-74, India, Sri Lanka and Pakistan 1974-75 (captain), Australia 1975-76 (captain), 1981-82 (captain), Pakistan 1980-81 (captain), India 1983-84 (captain). 1,000 runs (10) – 1,603 (av. 47.14) in 1970 best. Also scored 1,000 runs in 1968-69, 1974-75, 1975-76 and 1980-81. Scored 201* in 120 minutes for West Indies v Glamorgan (Swansea) 1976 to equal record for fastest double-century in first-class cricket. Gillette Man of the Match: 6. NW Man of the Match: 1. BH Gold Award: 1. HS: 242* West Indies v India (Bombay) 1974-75. HSUK: 217* v Warwicks (Manchester) 1971. HSGC/NW: 126 v Warwicks (Lord's) 1972. HSJPL: 134* v Somerset (Manchester) 1970. HSBH: 124 v Warwicks (Manchester) 1981. BB: 4-48 v Leics (Manchester) 1970. BBGC/NW: 3-39 v Somerset (Taunton) 1970. BBJPL: 4-33 v Middlesex (Lord's) 1971. BBBH: 3-23 v Derby (Manchester) 1974.

David John MAKINSON (St Mary's HS, Leyland) B Eccleston 12/1/1961. RHB, LFM. Debut 1984. BBJPL: 3-20 v Sussex (Manchester) 1984.

108

Leslie Leopold McFARLANE B Portland, Jamaica 19/8/1952. RHB, RM. Played for Northants in 1979. Debut for Lancs 1982. HS: 15* v Northants (Southport) 1984. BB: 6-59 v Warwicks (Southport) 1982. BBJPL: 4-18 v Hants (Portsmouth) 1982.

Christopher MAYNARD (Bishop Vesey's GS, Sutton Coldfield) B Haslemere (Surrey) 8/4/1958. RHB, WK. Played for Warwicks 1978 to 1982. Specially registered for Lancs in middle of 1982 season. Tour: D.H. Robins to New Zealand 1979-80. 9 dismissals (8 ct 1 st) v Somerset (Taunton) 1982. HS: 85 Warwicks v Kent (Birmingham) 1979. HSNW: 16 v Somerset (Manchester) 1983. HSJPL: 46 v Notts (Manchester) 1983. HSBH: 60 v Notts (Nottingham) 1982.

Joseph Alan ORMROD (Kirkaldy HS) B Ramsbottom (Lancs) 22/12/1942. RHB, OB. Debut for Worcs 1962. Cap 1966. Debut for Lancs and cap 1984. Benefit (£19,000) in 1977. Tours: Worcs to Jamaica 1965-66, Pakistan 1966-67. 1,000 runs: (13) – 1,535 runs (av. 45.14) in 1978 best. Scored 101 and 131* v Somerset (Worcester) 1980. Shared in 4th wkt partnership record for Worcs, 281 with Younis Ahmed v Notts (Nottingham) 1979. BH Gold Awards: 4. HS: 204* Worcs v Kent (Dartford) 1973. HSGC/NW: 59 Worcs v Essex (Worcester) 1975. HSJPL: 110* Worcs v Kent (Canterbury) 1975. HSBH: 124* Worcs v Glos (Worcester) 1976. BB: 5-27 Worcs v Glos (Bristol) 1972. BBJPL: 3-51 Worcs v Hants (Worcester) 1972.

Steven Joseph O'SHAUGHNESSY (Harper Green Secondary, Farnworth) B Bury 9/9/1961. RHB, RM. Debut 1980. BH Gold Award: 1. Century in 35 minutes (equalling P.G.H. Fender's first-class record) v Leics (Manchester) 1983 but bowlers were bowling for a declaration. Scored 1,167 runs (av. 34.32) in 1984. HS: 159* v Somerset (Bath) 1984. HSNW: 49 v Somerset (Manchester) 1983. HSJPL: 101* v Leics (Leicester) 1984. HSBH: 51 v Worcs (Manchester) 1984. BB: 4-66 v Notts (Nottingham) 1982. BBJPL: 3-18 v Middlesex (Manchester) 1984. BBBH: 3-10 v Essex (Chelmsford) 1984.

Balfour Patrick PATTERSON B Portland, Jamaica 15/9/1961. RHB, RFM. Debut for Jamaica 1982-83. Debut for Lancs 1984. HS: 10 v Northants (Southport) 1984.

Jack SIMMONS (Accrington TS, Blackburn TC) B Clayton-le-Moors (Lancs) 28/3/1941. RHB, OB. Debut 1968. Cap 1971. Played for Tasmania from 1972-73 to 1978-79 whilst coaching there and for Overseas XI v Board President's XI (Calcutta) 1980-81. Benefit (£128,000) in 1980. Hat-trick v Notts (Liverpool) 1977. Gillette Man of the Match: 1. BH Gold Awards: 2. HS: 112 v Sussex (Hove) 1970. HSGC/NW: 54* v Essex (Manchester) 1979. HSJPL: 65 v Essex (Manchester) 1980. HSBH: 64 v Derby (Manchester) 1978. BB: 7-59 Tasmania v Queensland (Brisbane) 1978-79. BBUK: 7-64 v Hants (Southport) 1973. BBNW: 5-37 v Glos (Bristol) 1984. BBJPL: 5-17 v Worcs (Worcester) 1982. BBBH: 4-31 v Yorks (Manchester) 1975. Has played soccer in Lancs Combination.

Gary John SPEAK B Chorley 26/4/1962. RHB, RFM. Debut 1981. Did not play in 1983 or 1984. HS: 15* v Cambridge U (Cambridge) 1982.

John STANWORTH (Chadderton GS, N Cheshire College, Warrington) B Oldham 30/9/1960. RHB, WK. Debut 1983. HS: 31* v Essex (Manchester) 1983.

David William VAREY (Birkenhead School and Cambridge) B Darlington, Co Durham 15/10/1961. RHB. Debut for Cambridge U 1981. Blue 1982-83. Debut for Lancs 1984. Secretary 1983. HS: 156* Cambridge U v Northants (Cambridge) 1982. HSC: 61 v Hants (Portsmouth) 1984. HSBH: 27 v Worcs (Manchester) 1984. Twin brother of J.G. Varey (Oxford).

Michael WATKINSON (Rivington and Blackrod HS, Horwich) B Westhoughton

LANCASHIRE

1/8/1961. RHB, RM. Debut 1982. HS: 77 v Middlesex (Liverpool) 1984. HSJPL: 32* v Warwicks (Manchester) 1984. BB: 6-39 v Leics (Leicester) 1984. BBNW: 3-63 v Middlesex (Lord's) 1984. BBJPL: 3-25 v Essex (Manchester) 1984. BBBH: 4-39 v Notts (Manchester) 1983.

Roger Graeme WATSON (Fearns County Secondary, Bacup) B Rawtenstall 14/1/1964. LHB, OB. Debut 1982. Did not play in 1983 or 1984. HS: 11 v Somerset (Taunton) 1982.

NB. The following players whose figures appeared in the 1984 Annual have been omitted: F.C. Hayes, S.M. Nasir Zaidi, N.V. Radford, T.J. Taylor and M.A. Wallwork.

County Averages

Britannic Assurance County Championships: Played 24, won 1, drawn 14, lost 9.
All first-class matches: Played 25, won 2, drawn 14, lost 9.

BATTING AND FIELDING

Cap		M	I	NO	RUNS	HS	Avge	100	50	Ct	St
1981	G. Fowler	10	17	0	661	226	38.88	2	2	2	—
1982	J. Abrahams	23	39	6	1216	201*	36.84	3	4	19	—
—	S.J. O'Shaughnessy	21	38	4	1167	159*	34.32	3	3	11	—
—	S.M.N. Zaidi	6	6	3	98	36	32.66	—	—	6	—
1984	J.A. Ormrod	23	40	3	1199	139*	32.40	1	7	10	—
—	N.H. Fairbrother	23	39	1	1201	102*	31.60	1	10	19	—
—	M. Watkinson	16	29	6	668	77	29.04	—	4	7	—
1971	J. Simmons	21	34	5	748	72*	25.79	—	6	15	—
—	S.T. Jefferies	18	28	3	633	65	25.32	—	2	4	—
—	C. Maynard	15	21	5	402	50*	25.12	—	1	29	5
1970	D.P. Hughes	19	32	1	706	113	22.77	2	1	12	—
—	M.R. Chadwick	7	14	0	293	61	20.92	—	2	2	—
1981	P.J.W. Allott	15	18	4	259	50*	18.50	—	1	6	—
—	D.W. Varey	8	14	1	235	61	18.07	—	1	3	—
—	N.V. Radford	4	5	1	53	36	13.25	—	—	—	—
—	I. Folley	17	28	9	194	22*	10.21	—	—	2	—
—	D.J. Makinson	4	5	2	18	9	6.00	—	—	—	—
—	L.L. McFarlane	12	15	7	41	15*	5.12	—	—	2	—
—	J. Stanworth	10	10	3	18	6	2.57	—	—	16	1

Played in one match: F.C. Hayes 11; K.A. Hayes 2,13; B.P. Patterson 0,10.

BOWLING

	Type	O	M	R	W	Avge	Best	5 wI	10 wM
P.J.W. Allott	RFM	463	138	1123	64	17.54	7-72	5	—
J. Simmons	OB	619.4	177	1644	63	26.09	7-176	7	1
L.L. McFarlane	RFM	272.5	45	875	31	28.22	4-65	—	—
I. Folley	LFM	369	91	1015	34	29.85	5-65	2	—
S.T. Jefferies	RFM	450.5	86	1392	43	32.37	6-67	2	—
N.V. Radford	RFM	106.4	17	390	10	39.00	5-95	1	—
S.J. O'Shaughnessy	RM	214.3	40	753	19	39.63	3-76	—	—
M. Watkinson	RM	349.3	71	1202	29	41.44	6-39	1	—

Also Bowled: J. Abrahams 88-19-247-4; N.H. Fairbrother 4.1-1-20-1; G. Fowler 2.1-0-8-0; K.A. Hayes 4-0-25-0; D.P. Hughes 105-34-261-4; D.J. Makinson 93-17-313-7; C. Maynard 2-0-8-0; B.P. Patterson 21-3-51-0; S.M.N. Zaidi 80-12-297-3.

First-class cricket

Highest innings	For	801 v Somerset (Taunton)	1895
totals:	Agst	634 by Surrey (Oval)	1898
Lowest innings	For	25 v Derby (Manchester)	1871
totals:	Agst	22 by Glamorgan (Liverpool)	1924
Highest indi-	For	424 A.C. MacLaren v Somerset (Taunton)	1895
vidual innings:	Agst	315* T.W. Hayward for Surrey (Oval)	1898
Best bowling	For	10-55 J. Briggs v Worcs (Manchester)	1900
in innings:	Agst	10-40 G.O. Allen for Middlesex (Lord's)	1929
Best bowling	For	17-91 H. Dean v Yorks (Liverpool)	1913
in a match:	Agst	16-65 G. Giffen for Australians (Manchester)	1886
Most runs in a season:		2,633 (av. 56.02) J.T. Tyldesley	1901
runs in a career:		34,222 (av. 45.20) E. Tyldesley	1909-1936
100s in a season:		11 by C. Hallows	1928
100s in a career:		90 by E. Tyldesley	1909-1936
wickets in a season:		198 (av. 18.55) E.A. McDonald	1925
wickets in a career:		1,816 (av. 15.12) J.B. Statham	1950-1968

RECORD WICKET STANDS

1st	368	A.C. MacLaren & R.H. Spooner v Glos (Liverpool)	1903
2nd	371	F. Watson & E. Tyldesley v Surrey (Manchester)	1928
3rd	306	E. Paynter & N. Oldfield v Hants (Southampton)	1938
4th	324	A.C. MacLaren & J.T. Tyldesley v Notts (Nottingham)	1904
5th	249	B. Wood & A. Kennedy v Warwicks (Birmingham)	1975
6th	278	J. Iddon & H.R.W. Butterworth v Sussex (Manchester)	1932
7th	245	A.H. Hornby & J. Sharp v Leics (Manchester)	1912
8th	158	J. Lyon & R.M. Ratcliffe v Warwickshire (Manchester)	1979
9th	142	L.O.S. Poidevin & A. Kermode v Sussex (Eastbourne)	1907
10th	173	J. Briggs & R. Pilling v Surrey (Liverpool)	1885

One-day cricket

Highest innings totals:	Gillette Cup/ NatWest Trophy	349-6 v Glos (Bristol)	1984
	John Player League	255-5 v Somerset (Manchester)	1970
	Benson & Hedges Cup	290-5 v Northants (Manchester)	1983
Lowest innings totals:	Gillette Cup/ NatWest Trophy	59 v Worcs (Worcester)	1963
	John Player League	76 v Somerset (Manchester)	1972
	Benson & Hedges Cup	82 v Yorks (Bradford)	1972
Highest indi- vidual innings:	Gillette Cup/ NatWest Trophy	131 A. Kennedy v Middlesex (Manchester)	1978
	John Player League	134* C.H. Lloyd v Somerset (Manchester)	1970
	Benson & Hedges Cup	124 C.H. Lloyd v Warwicks (Manchester)	1981
Best bowling figures:	Gillette Cup/ NatWest Trophy	5-28 J.B. Statham v Leics (Manchester)	1963
	John Player League	6-29 D.P. Hughes v Somerset (Manchester)	1977
	Benson & Hedges Cup	6-10 C.E.H. Croft v Scotland (Manchester)	1982

LEICESTERSHIRE

Formation of present club: 1879.
Colours: Scarlet and dark green.
Badge: Running fox (gold) on green background.
County Champions: 1975.
Gillette Cup Semi-Finalists: 1977.
NatWest Trophy Quarter-Finalists (2): 1981 and 1984.
John Player League Champions (2): 1974 and 1977.
Benson & Hedges Cup Winners (2): 1972 and 1975.
Benson & Hedges Cup Finalists: 1974.
Fenner Trophy Winners: 1979.
Gillette Man of the Match Awards: 15
NatWest Man of the Match Awards: 5.
Benson & Hedges Gold Awards: 35.

Secretary/Manager: F.M. Turner, County Ground, Grace Road, Leicester LE2 8AD. Testimonial 1985.
Captain: D.I. Gower.
Prospects of Play Telephone No: Leicester (0533) 836236.

James Paul ADDISON (Blythe Bridge HS) B Leek, Staffs. 14/11/1965. RHB, SLA. Debut 1983. HS: 51 v New Zealanders (Leicester) 1983.

Jonathan Philip AGNEW (Uppingham School) B Macclesfield, Cheshire 4/4/1960. RHB, RF. Debut 1978. Cap 1984. Tour: Leics in Zimbabwe 1980-81. HS: 56 v Worcs (Worcester) 1982. HSBH: 23* v Warwicks (Leicester) 1984. BB: 8-47 v Cambridge U (Cambridge) 1984. BBJPL: 3-43 v Worcs (Worcester) 1984. BBBH: 5-43 v Warwicks (Leicester) 1984.

John Christopher BALDERSTONE (Paddock County School, Huddersfield) B Huddersfield 16/11/1940. RHB, SLA. Played for Yorks 1961 to 1970. Debut for Leics 1971. Cap 1973. Tests: 2 in 1976. Tour: Leics in Zimbabwe 1980-81. 1,000 runs (9) – 1,482 (av. 39.00) in 1982 best. Shared 2nd wkt partnership record for county (289*) with D.I. Gower v Essex (Leicester) 1981. Hat-trick v Sussex (Eastbourne) 1976. Testimonial 1984. GC Man of the Match: 2. BH Gold Awards: 8. HS: 181* v Glos (Leicester) 1984. HSTC: 35 v West Indies (Leeds) 1976. HSGC/NW: 119* v Somerset (Taunton) 1973. HSJPL: 96 v Northants (Leicester) 1984. HSBH: 113* v Glos (Leicester) 1977. BB: 6-25 v Hants (Southampton) 1978. BBGC/NW: 4-33 v Herts (Leicester) 1977. BBJPL: 3-29 v Worcs (Leicester) 1971. Soccer for Huddersfield Town, Carlisle United, Doncaster Rovers and Queen of the South.

Timothy James BOON (Edlington Comprehensive) B Doncaster, Yorks 1/11/1961. RHB, RM. Debut 1980. Scored 1,233 runs (av. 39.77) in 1984. Tour: Leics in Zimbabwe 1980-81. HS: 144 v Glos (Leicester) 1984. HSNW: 22* v Derby (Leicester) 1984. HSJPL: 48 v Notts (Leicester) 1984. HSBH: 36* v Northants (Leicester) 1984.

Nigel Edwin BRIERS (Lutterworth GS; Borough Road College) B Leicester 15/1/1955. RHB. Cousin of N. Briers who played once for county in 1967. Debut 1971 at age of 16 years 103 days. Youngest player ever to appear for county. Cap 1981. Tour: Leics to Zimbabwe 1980-81. 1,000 runs (3) – 1,289 (av. 40.28) in 1983 best. Shared in 5th wkt partnership record for county, 235 with R.W. Tolchard v

Somerset (Leicester) 1979. BH Gold Award: 1. HS: 201* v Warwicks (Birmingham) 1983. HSNW: 59 v Wilts (Swindon) 1984. HSJPL: 119* v Hants (Bournemouth) 1981. HSBH: 71* v Hants (Southampton) 1979. BB: 3-48 v Lancs (Leicester) 1984. BBJPL: 3-29 v Middlesex (Leicester) 1984.

Ian Paul BUTCHER (John Ruskin HS) B Farnborough, Kent 1/7/1962. RHB, WK. Brother of A.R. Butcher of Surrey. Debut 1980. Cap 1984. Scored 1,349 runs (av. 32.90) in 1984. HS: 139 v Notts (Leicester) 1983. HSNW: 81 v Northants (Northampton) 1984. HSJPL: 71 v Northants (Leicester) 1982. HSBH: 43 v Northants (Leicester) 1984.

Ian Robert CARMICHAEL B Hull, Yorks 17/12/1960. LHB, LFM. Debut for South Australia 1983-84. BB: 6-112 South Australia v Tasmania (Devonport) 1983-84. BBUK: 5-84 v Warwicks (Birmingham) 1984.

Patrick Bernard (Paddy) CLIFT (St George's College, Salisbury) B Salisbury, Rhodesia 14/7/1953. RHB, RM. Played for Rhodesia 1971-72 to 1979-80 and Natal 1980-81 to date. Debut for county 1975. Cap 1976. Hat-trick v Yorks (Leicester) 1976. HS: 100* v Sussex (Hove) 1983. HSGC/NW: 48* v Worcs (Leicester) 1979. HSJPL: 51* v Somerset (Leicester) 1979. HSBH: 91 v Notts (Leicester) 1980. BB: 8-17 v MCC (Lord's) 1976. BBGC/NW: 3-36 v Worcs (Leicester) 1979. BBJPL: 4-12 v Lancs (Leicester) 1978. BBBH: 4-13 v Minor Counties (East) (Amersham) 1978.

Russell Alan COBB (Trent College) B Leicester 18/5/1961. RHB, LM. Tours: D.H. Robins to New Zealand 1979-80, Leics to Zimbabwe 1980-81. Debut 1980. HS: 63 v Zimbabwe (Leicester) 1982. HSJPL: 24 v Worcs (Leicester) 1981.

Nicholas Grant Billson COOK (Lutterworth HS and Upper) B Leicester 17/6/1956. RHB, SLA. Debut 1978. Cap 1982. Tests: 9 between 1983 and 1984. One-day Internationals: 1. Tours: D.H. Robins to New Zealand 1979-80, Leics to Zimbabwe 1980-81, England to New Zealand and Pakistan 1983-84. HS: 75 v Somerset (Taunton) 1980. HSTC: 26 v New Zealand (Nottingham) 1983. HSJPL: 13* v Kent (Leicester) 1979 and 13* v Middlesex (Lord's) 1981. HSBH: 23 v Warwicks (Leicester) 1984. BB: 7-63 v Somerset (Taunton) 1982. BBTC: 6-65 v Pakistan (Karachi) 1983-84.

George John Fitzgerald FERRIS B Urlings Village, Antigua 18/10/1964. RHB, RF. Played for Leeward Islands 1982-83. Debut for county 1983. Tour: Young West Indies to Zimbabwe 1983-84. HS: 26 Leeward Islands v Guyana (Nevis) 1982-83. HSC: 11 v Sussex (Hove) 1984. BB: 7-42 v Glamorgan (Hinckley) 1983.

Michael Anthony GARNHAM (Camberwell GS, Melbourne; Scotch College, Perth; Park School, Barnstaple; N Devon College; University of East Anglia) B Johannesburg 20/8/1960. RHB, WK. Debut for Glos 1979. Debut for Leics 1980. BH Gold Award: 1. HS: 84 v Surrey (Oval) 1984. HSGC/NW: 25 v Essex (Leicester) 1980. HSJPL: 79* v Lancs (Leicester) 1982. HSBH: 55 v Derby (Leicester) 1982.

David Ivon GOWER (King's School, Canterbury) B Tunbridge Wells 1/4/1957. LHB, OB. Debut 1975. Cap 1977. *Wisden* 1978. Tests: 65 between 1978 and 1984. Captain in 7 tests. One-day Internationals: 66. Tours: D.H. Robins to Sri Lanka 1977-78, Australia 1978-79, Australia and India 1979-80, West Indies 1980-81, India and Sri Lanka 1981-82, Australia 1982-83, New Zealand and Pakistan 1983-84.

113

LEICESTERSHIRE

1,000 runs (5) – 1,530 (av. 46.36) in 1982 best. Shared in 2nd wkt partnership record for county, 289* with J.C. Balderstone v Essex (Leicester) 1981. Gillette Man of the Match: 1. NW Man of the Match: 2. BH Gold Awards: 1. HS: 200* England v India (Birmingham) 1979. HSC: 176* v Pakistanis (Leicester) 1982. HSNW: 156 v Derby (Leicester) 1984. HSJPL: 135* v Warwicks (Leicester) 1977. HSBH: 114* v Derby (Derby) 1980. BB: 3-47 v Essex (Leicester) 1977. County captain in 1984.

Gordon James PARSONS (Woodside County Secondary, Slough) B Slough (Bucks) 17/10/1959. LHB, RM. Debut 1978. Played for Boland 1983-84. Cap 1984. Tour: Leics to Zimbabwe 1980-81. HS: 63 v Yorks (Leicester) 1984. HSNW: 23 v Northants (Northampton) 1984. HSJPL: 23 v Somerset (Taunton) 1984. HSBH: 29* v Northants (Leicester) 1983. BB: 5-25 v Essex (Leicester) 1982. BBJPL: 4-19 v Essex (Harlow) 1982. BBBH: 4-33 v Worcs (Leicester) 1981.

Leslie Brian TAYLOR (Heathfield HS) B Earl Shilton 25/10/1953. RHB, RFM. Debut 1977. Cap 1981. Tour: Leics to Zimbabwe 1980-81. Played for Natal 1981-82 to date. Hat-trick v Middlesex (Leicester) 1979. HS: 47 v Derby (Derby) 1983. HSJPL: 15* v Somerset (Taunton) 1980. BB: 7-28 v Derby (Leicester) 1981. BBNW: 4-34 v Norfolk (Leicester) 1982. BBJPL: 5-23 v Notts (Nottingham) 1978. BBBH: 6-35 v Worcs (Worcester) 1982.

John James WHITAKER (Uppingham School) B Skipton, Yorks 5/5/1962. RHB, OB. Debut 1983. Scored 1,097 runs (av. 36.56) in 1984. NW Man of the Match: 1. HS: 160 v Somerset (Leicester) 1984. HSNW: 155 v Wilts (Swindon) 1984. HSJPL: 132 v Glamorgan (Swansea) 1984. HSBH: 46 v Northants (Leicester) 1984.

Philip WHITTICASE (Crestwood CS, Kingswinford) B Marston Green, Solihull 15/3/1965. RHB, WK. Debut 1984. HS: 14 v Lancs (Leicester) 1984.

Peter WILLEY (Seaham Secondary) B Sedgefield, County Durham 6/12/1949. RHB, OB. Debut 1966 for Northants aged 16 years 180 days scoring 78 in second innings of first match v Cambridge U (Cambridge). Cap 1971. Benefit (£31,400) in 1981. Debut for Leics and cap 1984. Tests: 20 between 1976 and 1981. One-day Internationals: 19. Tours: D.H. Robins to South Africa 1972-73 and to Sri Lanka 1977-78, Australia and India 1979-80, West Indies 1980-81, SAB to South Africa 1981-82. Banned from Test cricket for 3 years. Played for Eastern Province 1982-83 to date. 1,000 runs (5) – 1,783 (av. 50.94) in 1982 best. Shared in 4th wkt partnership record for Northants, 370 with R.T. Virgin v Somerset (Northampton) 1976. Gillette Man of Match: 4 (for Northants). NW Man of the Match: 1 (for Northants). BH Gold Awards: 3 (1 for Northants). HS: 227 Northants v Somerset (Northampton) 1976. HSTC: 102* v West Indies (St. John's) 1980-81. HSGC/NW: 89 Northants v Sussex (Hove) 1979. HSJPL: 107 Northants v Warwicks (Birmingham) 1975 and 107 Northants v Hants (Tring) 1976. HSBH: 88* v Northants (Leicester) 1984. BB: 7-37 Northants v Oxford U (Oxford) 1975. BBNW: 3-33 v Derby (Leicester) 1984. BBJPL: 4-38 Northants v Leics (Leicester) 1980. BBBH: 3-12 Northants v Minor Counties (East) (Horton) 1977.

NB. The following player whose figures appeared in the 1984 Annual has been omitted: K. Higgs.

County Averages

Britannic Assurance County Championship; Played 24, won 8, drawn 14, lost 2.
All first-class matches: Played 26, won 9, drawn 15, lost 2.

BATTING AND FIELDING

Cap		M	I	NO	RUNS	HS	Avge	100	50	Ct	St
1977	D.I. Gower	11	17	1	761	117*	47.56	2	4	10	—
—	T.J. Boon	21	37	6	1233	144	39.77	4	4	9	—
—	M.D. Haysman	5	10	4	230	102*	38.33	1	—	10	—
1973	J.C. Balderstone	20	36	2	1260	181*	37.05	3	5	14	—
—	J.J. Whitaker	19	32	2	1097	160	36.56	2	6	20	—
—	P. Willey	26	45	4	1472	167	35.90	6	2	17	—
1984	I.P. Butcher	24	42	1	1349	130	32.90	5	3	19	—
1984	G.J. Parsons	26	39	10	853	63	29.41	—	6	8	—
—	M.A. Garnham	18	29	6	666	84	28.95	—	6	45	5
—	R.A. Cobb	3	5	0	142	48	28.40	—	—	2	—
—	A.M.E. Roberts	8	12	4	188	89	23.50	—	1	2	—
1976	P.B. Clift	19	28	7	483	58	23.00	—	2	7	—
1981	N.E. Briers	22	37	3	616	73	18.11	—	1	9	—
1982	N.G.B. Cook	20	24	9	231	44	15.40	—	—	16	—
1984	J.P. Agnew	21	20	5	148	30	9.86	—	—	4	—
1981	L.B. Taylor	7	5	1	37	16*	9.25	—	—	1	—
—	P. Whitticase	8	9	2	35	14	5.00	—	—	18	—
—	I.R. Carmichael	7	6	3	6	4*	2.00	—	—	3	—

Played in one match: G.J.F. Ferris 0.

BOWLING

	Type	O	M	R	W	Avge	Best	5 wI	10 wM
N.E. Briers	RM	109	24	264	12	22.00	3-48	—	—
A.M.E. Roberts	RF	265	70	769	33	23.30	7-74	3	—
P.B. Clift	RM	620.1	165	1608	63	25.52	8-26	2	1
J.P. Agnew	RF	601.1	117	2139	80	26.73	8-47	5	1
P. Willey	OB	544.1	163	1291	43	30.02	6-78	2	—
G.J. Parsons	RM	662.1	140	2164	67	32.29	5-42	2	—
L.B. Taylor	RFM	142	42	369	10	36.90	2-22	—	—
I.R. Carmichael	LFM	208	40	661	17	38.88	5-84	1	—
N.G.B. Cook	SLA	659.4	193	1694	41	41.31	4-45	—	—

Also bowled: J.C. Balderstone 19-5-69-2; I.P. Butcher 2-1-13-0; G.J.F. Ferris 21-4-83-0.

County Records

First-class cricket

Highest innings totals:	For	701-4d v Worcs (Worcester)	1906
	Agst	739-7d by Notts (Nottingham)	1903
Lowest innings totals:	For	25 v Kent (Leicester)	1912
	Agst	24 by Glamorgan (Leicester)	1971

LEICESTERSHIRE

Highest indi-	For	252* S. Coe v Northants (Leicester)	1914
vidual innings:	Agst	341 G.H. Hirst for Yorks (Leicester)	1905
Best bowling	For	10-18 G. Geary v Glamorgan (Pontypridd)	1929
in an innings:	Agst	10-32 H. Pickett for Essex (Leyton)	1895
Best bowling	For	16-96 G. Geary v Glamorgan (Pontypridd)	1929
in a match:	Agst	16-102 C. Blythe for Kent (Leicester)	1909
Most runs in a season:		2,446 (av. 52.04) L.G. Berry	1937
runs in a career:		30,143 (av. 30.32) L.G. Berry	1924-1951
100s in a season:		7 by L.G. Berry, W. Watson	1937, 1959
		and B.F. Davison	and 1982
100s in a career:		45 by L.G. Berry	1924-1951
wickets in a season:		170 (av. 18.96) J.E. Walsh	1948
wickets in a career:		2,130 (av. 23.19) W.E. Astill	1906-1939

RECORD WICKET STANDS

1st	390	B. Dudleston & J.F. Steele v Derby (Leicester)	1979
2nd	239*	J.C. Balderstone & D.I. Gower v Essex (Leicester)	1981
3rd	316*	W. Watson & A. Wharton v Somerset (Taunton)	1961
4th	290*	P. Willey & T.J. Boon v Warwicks (Leicester)	1984
5th	233	N.E. Briers & R.W. Tolchard v Somerset (Leicester)	1979
6th	262	A.T. Sharpe & G.H.S. Fowke v Derby (Chesterfield)	1911
7th	206	B. Dudleston & J. Birkenshaw v Kent (Canterbury)	1969
8th	164	M.R. Hallam & C.T. Spencer v Essex (Leicester)	1964
9th	160	W.W. Odell & R.T. Crawford v Worcs (Leicester)	1902
10th	228	R. Illingworth & K. Higgs v Northants (Leicester)	1977

One-day cricket

Highest innings totals:	Gillette Cup/ NatWest Trophy	354-7 v Wilts (Swindon)	1984
	John Player League	291-5 v Glamorgan (Swansea)	1984
	Benson & Hedges Cup	327-4 v Warwicks (Coventry)	1972
Lowest innings totals:	Gillette Cup/ NatWest Trophy	56 v Northants (Leicester)	1964
	John Player League	36 v Sussex (Leicester)	1973
	Benson & Hedges Cup	56 v Minor Counties (Wellington)	1982
Highest indi- vidual innings:	Gillette Cup/ NatWest Trophy	156 D.I. Gower v Derby (Leicester)	1984
	John Player League	152 B. Dudleston v Lancs (Manchester)	1975
	Benson & Hedges Cup	158* B.F. Davison v Warwicks (Coventry)	1972
Best bowling figures:	Gillette Cup/ NatWest Trophy	6-20 K. Higgs v Staffs (Longton)	1975
	John Player League	6-17 K. Higgs v Glamorgan (Leicester)	1973
	Benson & Hedges Cup	6-35 L.B. Taylor v Worcs (Worcester)	1982

MIDDLESEX

Formation of present club: 1863.
Colours: Blue.
Badge: Three seaxes.
County Champions (8): 1866, 1903, 1920, 1921, 1947, 1976, 1980 and 1982.
Joint Champions (2): 1949 and 1977.
Gillette Cup Winners (2): 1977 and 1980.
Gillette Cup Finalists: 1975.
NatWest Trophy Winners: 1984.
Best position in John Player League: 2nd in 1982.
Benson & Hedges Cup Winners: 1983.
Gillette Man of the Match Awards: 27.
NatWest Man of the Match Awards: 7.
Benson & Hedges Gold Awards: 30

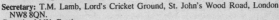

Secretary: T.M. Lamb, Lord's Cricket Ground, St. John's Wood Road, London NW8 8QN.
Captain: M.W. Gatting.
Prospects of Play Telephone No: 01-286 8011.

Graham Derek BARLOW (Ealing GS; Loughborough CE) B Folkestone 26/3/1950. LHB, RM. Debut 1969. Cap 1976. Tests: 3 in 1976-77 and 1977. One-day Internationals: 6. Tour: India, Sri Lanka and Australia 1976-77. 1,000 runs (6) – 1,545 (av. 48.28) in 1983 best. Shared 1st wkt partnership record for county (367*) with W.N. Slack v Kent (Lord's) 1981. GC man of the Match: 1. NW Man of the Match: 3. BH Gold Awards: 2. HS: 177 v Lancs (Southport) 1981. HSTC: 7* v India (Calcutta) 1976-77. HSNW: 158 v Lancs (Lord's) 1984. HSJPL: 114 v Warwicks (Lord's) 1979. HSBH: 129 v Northants (Northampton) 1977. Benefit 1984.

Keith Robert BROWN (Chase BS, Enfield) B Edmonton 18/3/1963. RHB, WK. Debut 1984.

Roland Orlando BUTCHER B East Point, St. Philip, Barbados 14/10/1953. RHB, RM. Debut 1974. Played for Barbados in 1974-75 and Tasmania 1982-83. Cap 1979. Tests: 3 v West Indies in 1980-81. One-day Internationals: 3. Tours: Middlesex to Zimbabwe 1980-81, West Indies 1980-81, International XI to Pakistan 1981-82 and to Jamaica 1982-83. BH Gold Award: 1. 1,000 runs (2) – 1,326 (av. 40.18) in 1984 best. HS: 197 v Yorks (Lord's) 1982. HSTC: 32 v West Indies (Kingston) 1980-81. HSGC/NW: 50* v Lancs (Lord's) 1980. HSJPL: 100 v Glos (Lord's) 1983. HSBH: 85 v Surrey (Oval) 1983.

John Donald CARR (Repton School and Oxford) B St. John's Wood, London 15/6/1963. RHB, OB. Son of D.B. Carr (Derbyshire and England). Debut for Oxford U and Middlesex 1983. Blue 1983-84. HS: 123 Oxford U v Lancs (Oxford) 1984. HSBH: 66 Combined Universities v Glos (Bristol) 1984. BB: 5-57 Oxford U v Glos (Oxford) 1984. BBBH: 3-22 Combined Universities v Glos (Bristol) 1984. HSC: 12* v Leics (Lord's) 1983.

Norman George COWANS (Park High Secondary, Stanmore) B Enfield St. Mary, Jamaica 17/4/1961. RHB, RFM. Debut 1980. Cap 1984. Tours: Middlesex to Zimbabwe 1980-81, Australia and New Zealand 1982-83, New Zealand and Pakistan 1983-84. Tests: 13 from 1982-83 to 1984. One-day Internationals: 13. NW Man of the Match: 1. HS: 66 v Surrey (Lord's) 1984. HSTC: 36 v Australia (Perth) 1982-83. HSNW: 12* v Lancs (Lord's) 1984. HSJPL: 14* v Sussex (Hove) 1982. BB: 6-64 v

117

MIDDLESEX

Warwicks (Lord's) 1984. BBTC: 6-77 v Australia (Melbourne) 1982-83. BBNW: 4-26 v Lancs (Lord's) 1982. BBJPL: 4-44 v Sussex (Hove) 1982. BBBH: 4-33 v Lancs (Lord's) 1983.

Wayne Wendell DANIEL B St. Philip, Barbados 16/1/1956. RHB, RF. Played for Barbados 1975-76 to date. Debut for county and cap 1977. Tests: 10 for West Indies between 1975-76 and 1983-84. One-day Internationals: 18. Tours: West Indies to England 1976. Young West Indies to Zimbabwe 1981-82, West Indies to India 1983-84. Hat-trick v Lancs (Southport) 1981. Gillette Man of the Match: 2. BH Gold Awards: 2. HS: 53* Barbados v Jamaica (Bridgetown) 1979-80 and 53* v Yorks (Lord's) 1981. HSTC: 11 West Indies v India (Kingston) 1975-76. HSGC/NW: 14 v Lancs (Manchester) 1978. HSJPL: 14 v Kent (Lord's) 1980. HSBH: 20* v Derby (Derby) 1980. BB: 9-61 v Glamorgan (Swansea) 1982. BBTC: 5-39 West Indies v India (Ahmedabad) 1983-84. BBGC/NW: 6-15 v Sussex (Hove) 1980. BBJPL: 5-27 v Lancs (Lord's) 1982. BBBH: 7-12 v Minor Counties (East) (Ipswich) 1978 – record for competition.

Paul Rupert DOWNTON (Sevenoaks School) B Farnborough (Kent) 4/4/1957. Son of G. Downton, former Kent player. RHB, WK. Debut for Kent 1977. Cap 1979. Debut for Middlesex in 1980. Cap 1981. Tests: 10 between 1980-81 and 1984. One-day Internationals: 1. Tours: Pakistan and New Zealand 1977-78, Middlesex to Zimbabwe 1980-81, West Indies 1980-81. HS: 90* v Derby (Uxbridge) 1980. HSTC: 56 v West Indies (Birmingham) 1984. HSNW: 62 v Notts (Nottingham) 1984. HSJPL: 58* v Worcs (Worcester) 1982. HSBH: 28 v Somerset (Taunton) 1984.

Phillipe Henri EDMONDS (Skinners School, Tunbridge Wells; Cranbrook School; Cambridge) B Lusaka, Northern Rhodesia (now Zambia) 8/3/1951. RHB, SLA. Debut for Cambridge U and county 1971. Blue 1971-73 (capt in 1973). Cap 1974. Played for Eastern Province in 1975-76. Tests: 23 between 1975 and 1984. One-day Internationals: 11. Tours: Pakistan and New Zealand 1977-78, Australia 1978-79. Hat-trick v Leics (Leicester) 1981. Benefit 1983. NW Man of the Match: 1. BH Gold Awards: 2. HS: 142 v Glamorgan (Swansea) 1984. HSTC: 64 v India (Lord's) 1982. HSGC/NW: 63* v Somerset (Lord's) 1979. HSJPL: 52 v Somerset (Taunton) 1980. HSBH: 44* v Notts (Newark) 1976. BB: 8-53 v Hants (Bournemouth) 1984. BBTC: 7-66 v Pakistan (Karachi) 1977-78. BBNW: 5-12 v Cheshire (Enfield) 1982. BBJPL: 3-19 v Leics (Leics) 1973. BBBH: 4-11 v Kent (Lord's) 1975. Also played rugby for University and narrowly missed Blue.

John Ernest EMBUREY (Peckham Manor Secondary) B Peckham 20/8/1952. RHB, OB. Debut 1973. Cap 1977. *Wisden* 1983. Tests: 22 between 1978 and 1982. One-day Internationals: 8. Tours: D.H. Robins to Sri Lanka 1977-78, Australia 1978-79, Australia and India 1979-80 (as replacement for G. Miller), Middlesex to Zimbabwe 1980-81, West Indies 1980-81, India and Sri Lanka 1981-82, SAB to South Africa 1981-82. Banned from Test cricket for 3 years. Played for Western Province 1982-83 to date. 103 wkts (av. 17.88) in 1983. NW Man of the Match: 1. BH Gold Award: 1. HS: 133 v Essex (Chelmsford) 1983. HSTC: 57 v Australia (Manchester) 1981. HSGC/NW: 36* v Lancs (Manchester) 1978. HSJPL: 40* v Leics (Lord's) 1983. HSBH: 50 v Kent (Lord's) 1984. BB: 7-36 v Cambridge U (Cambridge) 1977. BBTC: 6-33 v Sri Lanka (Colombo) 1981-82. BBNW: 3-20 v Northumberland (Jesmond) 1984. BBJPL: 5-36 v Warwicks (Lord's) 1983. BBBH: 3-35 v Kent (Lord's) 1980.

Angus Robert Charles FRASER (Gayton HS, Harrow) B Billinge, Lancs 8/8/1965. RHB, RFM. Debut 1984.

118

Michael William GATTING (John Kelly BHS) B Kingsbury 6/6/1957. RHB, RM. Debut 1975. Cap 1977. Captain 1983. *Wisden* 1983. Tests: 30 between 1977-78 and 1984. One-day Internationals: 31. Tours: Pakistan and New Zealand 1977-78, Middlesex to Zimbabwe 1980-81, West Indies 1980-81, India and Sri Lanka 1981-82, New Zealand and Pakistan 1983-84. 1,000 runs (6) – 2,257 (av. 68.39) in 1984 best. Gillette Man of the Match: 1. BH Gold Awards: 2. HS: 258 v Somerset (Bath) 1984. HSTC: 81 v New Zealand (Lord's) 1983. HSGC/NW: 95* v Notts (Nottingham) 1980. HSJPL: 109 v Leics (Leicester) 1984. HSBH: 95* v Somerset (Taunton) 1980. BB: 5-34 v Glamorgan (Swansea) 1982. BBJPL: 4-32 v Kent (Lord's) 1978. BBBH: 4-49 v Sussex (Lord's) 1984.

Simon Peter HUGHES (Latymer Upper, Hammersmith; Durham U) B Kingston-upon-Thames 20/12/1959. RHB, RFM. Debut 1980. Played for Northern Transvaal 1982-83. Cap 1981. Gillette Man of the Match: 1. Tours: Middlesex to Zimbabwe, Overseas XI to India 1980-81. HS: 41* v Glos (Uxbridge) 1984. BB: 6-32 v Glos (Bristol) 1983. BBGC/NW: 3-23 v Worcs (Worcester) 1980. BBJPL: 3-37 v Surrey (Oval) 1983.

Colin Peter METSON (Enfield GS; Stanborough School, Welwyn Garden City) B Cuffley, Herts 2/7/1963. RHB, WK. Debut 1981. HS: 96 v Glos (Uxbridge) 1984. HSJPL: 15* v Sussex (Hove) 1984.

Andrew John Trevor MILLER (Haileybury College and Oxford) B Chesham, Bucks 30/5/1963. LHB, RM. Debut for Oxford U 1982. Debut for county 1983. Blue 1983-84. 1,002 runs (av. 43.56) in 1983. HS: 128* Oxford U v Cambridge U (Lord's) 1984. HSC: 86 v Sussex (Hove) 1983.

Clive Thornton RADLEY (King Edward VI GS, Norwich) B Hertford 13/5/1944. RHB, LB. Debut 1964. Cap 1967. Benefit (£26,000) in 1977. *Wisden* 1978. Tests: 8 in 1977-78 and 1978. One-day Internationals: 4. Tours: D.H. Robins' to South Africa 1972-73 and 1974-75, Pakistan and New Zealand 1977-78 (as replacement for J.M. Brearley), Australia 1978-79, Middlesex to Zimbabwe 1980-81. 1,000 runs (15) – 1,491 runs (av. 57.34) in 1980 best. Shared in 6th wkt partnership record for county, 227 with F.J. Titmus v South Africans (Lord's) 1965. Gillette Man of the Match: 2. NW Man of the Match: 1. BH Gold Awards: 5. HS: 171 v Cambridge U (Cambridge) 1976. HSTC: 158 v New Zealand (Auckland) 1977-78. HSGC/NW: 105* v Worcs (Worcester) 1975. HSJPL: 133* v Glamorgan (Lord's) 1969. HSBH: 121* v Minor Counties (East) (Lord's) 1976.

Graham David ROSE (Northumberland Park School, Tottenham) B Tottenham 12/4/1964. RHB, RM. Played in two JPL matches in 1983 and one BH match in 1984. HSJPL: 33 v Notts (Cleethorpes) 1983.

Wilfred Norris SLACK (Wellesbourne Secondary, High Wycombe) B Troumaca, St. Vincent 12/12/1954. LHB, RM. Debut 1977. Cap 1981. Played for Windward Islands 1981-82 and 1982-83. 1,000 runs (4) – 1,631 (av. 42.92) in 1984 best. Tours: Middlesex to Zimbabwe 1980-81, International XI to Pakistan 1981-82. Shared 1st wicket partnership record for county, 367* with G.D. Barlow v Kent (Lord's) 1981. NW Man of the Match: 1. HS: 248* v Worcs (Lord's) 1981. HSNW: 79 v Northants (Lord's) 1984. HSJPL: 77 v Somerset (Weston-super-Mare) 1982. HSBH: 60* v Combined Universities (Cambridge) 1982. BB: 3-17 v Leics (Uxbridge) 1982. BBNW: 3-37 v Northants (Northampton) 1983. BBJPL: 5-32 v Leics (Lord's) 1984.

Keith Patrick TOMLINS (St. Benedict's, Ealing; Durham U) B Kingston-upon-Thames 23/10/1957. RHB, RM. Debut 1977. Cap 1983. Tour: Middlesex to Zimbabwe 1980-81. HS: 146 v Oxford U (Oxford) 1984. HSNW: 80 v Cambridgeshire (Wisbech) 1981. HSJPL: 59 v Somerset (Bath) 1984. HSBH: 40 v Somerset (Taunton) 1984. BBJPL: 4-24 v Notts (Lord's) 1978.

MIDDLESEX

Neil Fitzgerald WILLIAMS (Acland Burghley School) B Hope Well, St. Vincent 2/7/1962. RHB, RFM. Debut 1982. Played for Windward Islands 1982-83 and Tasmania 1983-84. Cap 1984. HS: 63 v Worcs (Worcester) 1983. HSNW: 10 v Northumberland (Jesmond) 1984. HSJPL: 31* v Notts (Cleethorpes) 1983. HSBH: 23 v Somerset (Taunton) 1984. BB: 5-77 v Yorks (Leeds) 1983. BBNW: 4-36 v Derby (Derby) 1983. BBJPL: 4-40 v Derby (Chesterfield) 1983. BBBH: 3-16 v Combined Universities (Cambridge) 1982.

NB. The following players whose particulars were included in the 1984 Annual have been omitted: C.R. Cook, R.G.P. Ellis, K.D. James, J.D. Monteith and J.F. Sykes.

County Averages

Britannic Assurance County Championships; Played 24, won 8, drawn 9 lost 7. All first-class matches; Played 26, won 8, drawn 11, lost 7.

BATTING AND FIELDING

Cap		M	I	NO	RUNS	HS	Avge	100	50	Ct	St
1977	M.W. Gatting	22	39	9	2150	258	71.66	8	9	21	—
1981	W.N. Slack	25	46	8	1631	145	42.92	4	6	23	—
1979	R.O. Butcher	23	40	7	1326	116	40.18	2	10	17	—
1967	C.T. Radley	24	38	7	1072	128*	34.58	2	7	21	—
1981	P.R. Downton	14	21	7	393	88	28.07	—	2	26	6
1976	G.D. Barlow	19	36	2	903	96	26.55	—	5	10	—
—	C.P. Metson	12	17	5	300	96	25.00	—	2	28	2
1983	K.P. Tomlins	10	18	1	363	103*	21.35	1	—	8	—
1974	P.H. Edmonds	25	33	4	600	142	20.68	1	2	20	—
1977	J.E. Emburey	26	35	2	579	57	17.54	—	3	18	—
1984	N.F. Williams	18	21	3	285	44	15.83	—	—	6	—
1981	S.P. Hughes	15	14	4	144	41*	14.40	—	—	5	—
1984	N.G. Cowans	19	23	1	255	66	11.59	—	1	8	—
—	A.J.T. Miller	3	5	0	57	29	11.40	—	—	1	—
1977	W.W. Daniel	21	24	14	87	16*	8.70	—	—	4	—

Played in two matches: J.D. Carr 0,0; C.R. Cook 47,16,43 (1 ct); R.G.P. Ellis 18, 33,3; K.D. James 2,28*.

Played in one match: K.R. Brown 6 (1 ct); A.R.C. Fraser did not bat.

BOWLING

	Type	O	M	R	W	Avge	Best	5 wI	10 wM
N.G. Cowans	RF	445.1	73	1386	71	19.52	6-64	2	—
M.W. Gatting	RM	87	20	205	8	25.62	3-16	—	—
W.W. Daniel	RF	462	86	1463	54	27.09	4-53	—	—
P.H. Edmonds	SLA	823.3	233	2096	77	27.22	8-53	2	1
J.E. Emburey	OB	865.3	255	1978	72	27.47	5-94	1	—
S.P. Hughes	RFM	314.2	53	1051	35	30.02	4-27	—	—
N.F. Williams	RFM	447.5	90	1568	42	37.33	4-19	—	—

Also bowled: J.D. Carr 30-5-73-4; A.R.C. Fraser 34-7-124-1; K.D. James 41-16-106-4; W.N. Slack 28-3-76-0; K.P. Tomlins 5-1-9-0.

County Records

First-class cricket

Highest innings totals:	For	642-3d v Hants (Southampton)	1923
	Agst	665 by West Indians (Lord's)	1939
Lowest innings totals:	For	20 v MCC (Lord's)	1864
	Agst	31 by Glos (Bristol)	1924
Highest individual innings:	For	331* J.D. Robertson v Worcs (Worcester)	1949
	Agst	316* J.B. Hobbs for Surrey (Lord's)	1926
Best bowling in an innings:	For	10-40 G.O. Allen v Lancs (Lord's)	1929
	Agst	9-38 R.C. Robertson-Glasgow for Somerset (Lord's)	1924
Best bowling in a match:	For	16-114 { G. Burton v Yorks (Sheffield)	1888
		{ J.T. Hearne v Lancs (Manchester)	1898
	Agst	16-109 C.W.L. Parker for Glos (Cheltenham)	1930
Most runs in a season:		2,650 (av. 85.48) W.J. Edrich	1947
runs in a career:		40,302 (av. 48.82) E.H. Hendren	1907-1937
100s in a season:		13 by D.C.S. Compton	1947
100s in a career:		119 by E.H. Hendren	1907-1937
wickets in a season:		158 (av. 14.63) F.J. Titmus	1955
wickets in a career:		2,361 (av. 21.27) F.J. Titmus	1949-1982

RECORD WICKET STANDS

1st	367*	G.D. Barlow & W.N. Slack v Kent (Lord's)	1981
2nd	380	F.A. Tarrant & J.W. Hearne v Lancs (Lord's)	1914
3rd	424*	W.J. Edrich & D.C.S. Compton v Somerset (Lord's)	1948
4th	325	J.W. Hearne & E.H. Hendren v Hants (Lord's)	1919
5th	338	R.S. Lucas & T.C. O'Brien v Sussex (Hove)	1895
6th	227	C.T. Radley & F.J. Titmus v South Africans (Lord's)	1965
7th	271*	E.H. Hendren & F.T. Mann v Notts (Nottingham)	1925
8th	182*	M.H.C. Doll & H.R. Murrell v Notts (Lord's)	1913
9th	160*	E.H. Hendren & T.J. Durston v Essex (Leyton)	1927
10th	230	R.W. Nicholls & W. Roche v Kent (Lord's)	1899

One-day cricket

Highest innings totals:	Gillette Cup/ NatWest Trophy	280-8 v Sussex (Lord's)	1965
	John Player League	270-5 v Glos. (Lord's)	1983
	Benson & Hedges Cup	303-7 v Northants (Northampton)	1977
Lowest innings totals:	Gillette Cup/ NatWest Trophy	41 v Essex (Westcliff)	1972
	John Player League	23 v Yorks (Leeds)	1974
	Benson & Hedges Cup	97 v Northants (Lord's)	1976
Highest individual innings:	Gillette Cup/ NatWest Trophy	158 G.D. Barlow v Lancs (Lord's)	1984
	John Player League	133* C.T. Radley v Glamorgan (Lord's)	1969
	Benson & Hedges Cup	129 G.D. Barlow v Northants (Northampton)	1977
Best bowling figures:	Gillette Cup/ NatWest Trophy	6-15 W.W. Daniel v Sussex (Hove)	1980
	John Player League	6-6 R.W. Hooker v Surrey (Lord's)	1969
	Benson & Hedges Cup	7-12 W.W. Daniel v Minor Counties (East) (Ipswich)	1978

NORTHAMPTONSHIRE

Formation of present club: 1878.
Colours: Maroon.
Badge: Tudor Rose.
County Championship Runners-up (4): 1912, 1957, 1965 and 1976.
Gillette Cup Winners: 1976.
Gillette Cup Finalists: 1979.
NatWest Trophy Finalists: 1981.
Best final position in John Player League: 4th in 1974.
Benson & Hedges Cup Winners: 1980.
Fenner Trophy Winners: 1978.
Gillette Cup Man of the Match Awards: 17.
NatWest Man of the Match Awards: 9.
Benson & Hedges Gold Awards: 23.

Secretary: County Ground, Wantage Rd, Northampton NN1 4TJ.
Captain: G. Cook.
Prospects of Play Telephone No: Northampton (0604) 37040.

Robert John BAILEY (Biddulph HS) B Biddulph, Staffordshire 28/10/1963. RHB, OB. Debut 1982. Scored 1,405 runs (av. 37.97) in 1984. HS: 114 v Somerset (Northampton) 1984. HSNW: 56* v Middlesex (Lord's) 1984. HSJPL: 77* v Glos (Bristol) 1984. HSBH: 77 v Scotland (Northampton) 1984. BB: 3-33 v Cambridge U (Cambridge) 1983.

Robin James BOYD-MOSS (Bedford School and Cambridge) B Hattoh, Ceylon 16/12/1959. RHB, SLA. Debut for Cambridge U and County in 1980. Blue 1980-83. Cap 1984. NW Man of the Match: 1. 1,000 runs (2) – 1,602 runs (av. 44.50) in 1982 best. 100 in each innings twice: 123 & 119 Cambridge U v Warwicks (Cambridge) 1982 and 139 & 124 for Cambridge U v Oxford University (Lord's) 1983 – the only instance in the University Match. HS: 139 as above. HSC: 105 v Lancs (Southport) 1984. HSNW: 88* v Leics (Northampton) 1984. HSJPL: 99 v Glos (Bristol) 1984. HSBH: 58 Combined Universities v Northants (Northampton) 1980. BB: 5-27 Cambridge U v Oxford U (Lord's) 1983. Rugby Blue.

David John CAPEL (Roade Comprehensive) B Northampton 6/2/1963. RHB, RM. Debut 1981. HS: 109* v Somerset (Northampton) 1983. HSNW: 27 v Middlesex (Northampton) 1983. HSJPL: 79 v Kent (Northampton) 1982. HSBH: 28 v Lancs (Manchester) 1983. BB: 5-28 v Surrey (Oval) 1984. BBJPL: 4-30 v Yorks (Middlesbrough) 1982. BBBH: 3-24 v Leics (Leicester) 1983.

Geoffrey COOK (Middlesbrough HS) B Middlesbrough 9/10/1951. RHB, SLA. Debut 1971. Cap 1975. Played for Eastern Province from 1978-79 to 1980-81. County Captain 1981. Benefit 1985. Tests: 7 between 1981-82 and 1982-83. One-day Internationals: 6. Tours: India and Sri Lanka 1981-82, Australia 1982-83. 1,000 runs (9) – 1,759 runs (av. 43.97) in 1981 best. Gillette Man of the Match: 2. NatWest Man of the Match: 2. BH Gold Awards: 2. HSUK: 155 v Derby (Northampton) 1978. HSTC: 66 v India (Manchester) 1982. HSGC/NW: 114* v Surrey (Northampton) 1979. HSJPL: 85 v Leics (Leicester) 1976. HSBH: 96 v Minor Counties (East) (Northampton) 1978.

122

Brian James GRIFFITHS (Irthlingborough Secondary) B Wellingborough 13/6/1949. RHB, RFM. Debut 1974. Cap 1978. NW Man of the Match: 1. HS: 16 v Glos (Bristol) 1982. HSJPL: 11* v Surrey (Tring) 1982. BB: 8-50 v Glamorgan (Northampton) 1981. BBNW: 5-33 v Yorks (Leeds) 1983. BBJPL: 4-22 v Somerset (Weston-super-Mare) 1977. BBBH: 5-43 v Sussex (Eastbourne) 1979.

Roger Andrew HARPER B Georgetown, British Guiana 17/3/1963. RHB, OB. Brother of L.S. and M.A. Harper (Guyana). Played for D.B. Close's XI 1983 and 1984. Debut for Demerara 1979-80. Played for Guyana 1979-80 to date. Joined Northants for 1985. Tests: 11 for West Indies between 1983-84 and 1984. One-day Internationals: 10 for West Indies. Tours: West Indies to India 1983-84, England 1984. HS: 86 Guyana v Australians (Georgetown) 1983-84. HSUK: 73 West Indians v Somerset (Taunton) 1984. HSTC: 39* West Indies v England (Manchester) 1984. BB: 6-57 West Indies v England (Manchester) 1984.

Ray Fitzpatrick JOSEPH B Guyana 12/2/1961. RHB, RFM. Debut for Berbice 1979-80. Played for Guyana 1979-80 to date. Joined Northants for 1985. HS: 17* Guyana v Barbados (Georgetown) 1979-80. BB: 6-114 Guyana v Jamaica (Kingston) 1983-84.

Allan Joseph LAMB (Wynberg BHS; Abbotts College) B Langebaanweg, Cape Province, South Africa 20/6/1954. RHB, RM. Played for Western Province 1972-73 to 1981-82. Debut for county and cap 1978. *Wisden* 1980. Tests: 27 between 1982 and 1984. One-day Internationals: 32. Tours: Australia 1982-83, New Zealand and Pakistan 1983-84. 1,000 runs (6) – 2,049 runs (av. 60.26) in 1981 best. NW Man of the Match: 1. BH Gold Awards: 5. HS: 178 v Leics (Leicester) 1979. HSTC: 137* v New Zealand (Nottingham) 1983. HSGC/NW: 101 v Sussex (Hove) 1979. HSJPL: 127* v Worcs (Worcester) 1981. HSBH: 106* v Leics (Leicester) 1983.

Wayne LARKINS (Bushmead, Eaton Socon) B Roxton (Beds) 22/11/1953. RHB, RM. Debut 1972. Cap 1976. Tests: 6 between 1979-80 and 1981. One-day Internationals: 6. Tours: Australia and India 19/9/1980. SAB to South Africa 1981-82. Banned from Test cricket for 3 years. Played for Overseas XI v Board President's XI (Calcutta) 1980-82, Western Province 1982-83 and Eastern Province 1983-84. 1,000 runs (7) – 1,863 runs (av. 45.43) in 1982 best. Shared in 2nd wkt partnership record for county, 342 with P. Willey v Lancs (Northampton) 1983. Hat-trick in Benson & Hedges Cup v Combined Universities (Northampton) 1980. NW Man of the Match: 1. BH Gold Awards: 4. HS: 252 v Glamorgan (Cardiff) 1983. HSTC: 34 v Australia (Oval) 1981. HSGC/NW: 92* v Leics (Northampton) 1979. HSJPL: 172* v Warwicks (Luton) 1983. HSBH: 132 v Warwicks (Birmingham) 1982. BB: 5-59 v Worcs (Worcester) 1984. BBJPL: 5-32 v Essex (Ilford) 1978. BBBH: 4-37 v Combined Universities (Northampton) 1980.

Neil Alan MALLENDER (Beverley GS) B Kirk Sandall (Yorks) 13/8/1961. RHB, RFM. Debut 1980. Played for Otago 1983-84. Cap 1984. HS: 71* v Oxford U (Oxford) 1982. HSNW: 11* v Yorks (Leeds) 1983. HSJPL: 22 v Warwicks (Northampton) 1981 and 22 v Somerset (Weston-super-Mare) 1983. BB: 7-41 v Derby (Northampton) 1982. BBNW: 7-37 v Worcs (Northampton) 1984. BBJPL: 5-34 v Middlesex (Tring) 1981. BBBH: 3-12 v Worcs (Worcester) 1983.

David RIPLEY (Royds Secondary, Leeds) B Leeds 13/9/1966. RHB, WK. Debut

NORTHAMPTONSHIRE

1984. HS: 61 v Surrey (Northampton) 1984. HSNW: 27* v Durham (Darlington) 1984. HSJPL: 24 v Derby (Northampton) 1984.

George SHARP (Elnick Road SM) B West Hartlepool 12/3/1949. RHB, WK, SLA. Debut 1968. Cap 1973. Benefit 1982. HS: 98 v Yorks (Northampton) 1983. HSNW: 41* v Yorks (Leeds) 1983. HSJPL: 51* v Glos (Northampton) 1983. HSBH: 43 v Surrey (Northampton) 1979.

Alan WALKER (Shelley High, Huddersfield) B Emsley, Yorks 7/7/1962. LHB, RFM. Debut 1983. HS: 19 v Sussex (Hove) 1984. HSJPL: 13 v Yorks (Tring) 1983. BB: 4-50 v Middlesex (Lord's) 1984. BBJPL: 3-12 v Sussex (Hove) 1984.

Duncan James WILD (Northampton BS) B Northampton 28/11/1962. Son of J. Wild, former Northants player. LHB, RM. Debut 1980. HS: 144 v Lancs (Southport) 1984. HSNW: 11 v Middlesex (Lord's) 1984. HSJPL: 51 v Lancs (Manchester) 1984. HSBH: 48 v Warwicks (Northampton) 1984. BB: 3-15 v Hants (Southampton) 1984. HSNW: 3-47 v Leics (Northampton) 1984. BBJPL: 3-29 v Derby (Northampton) 1984.

Richard Grenville WILLIAMS (Ellesmere Port GS) B Bangor, Caernarvonshire 10/8/1957. RHB, OB. Debut 1974 aged 16 years 313 days. Cap 1979. Tour: D.H. Robins' to New Zealand 1979-80. 1,000 runs (6) – 1,305 (av. 43.50) in 1983 best. Scored 109 and 151* v Warwicks (Northampton) 1979. Hat-trick v Glos (Northampton) 1980. Gillette Man of Match: 1. BH Gold Awards: 2. HS: 175* v Leics (Leicester) 1980. HSNW: 94 v Worcs (Northampton) 1984. HSJPL: 82 v Glos (Bristol) 1982. HSBH: 83 v Yorks (Bradford) 1980. BB: 7-73 v Cambridge U (Cambridge) 1980. BBGC/NW: 3-15 v Leics (Northampton) 1979. BBJPL: 5-30 v Warwicks (Luton) 1983.

N.B. The following players whose particulars were included in the 1984 Annual have been omitted: M.J. Bamber, R.W. Hanley and D.S. Steele.

County Averages

Britannic Assurance County Championship: Played 24, won 5, drawn 9, lost 9, tied 1.
All first-class matches: Played 25, won 5, drawn 10, lost 9, tied 1.

BATTING AND FIELDING

Cap		M	I	NO	RUNS	HS	Avge	100	50	Ct	St
1975	G. Cook	22	43	4	1539	102	39.46	2	9	15	—
—	R.J. Bailey	25	45	8	1405	114	37.97	3	8	14	—
1976	W. Larkins	25	49	3	1656	183*	36.00	3	7	11	—
1978	A.J. Lamb	12	23	3	716	133*	35.80	1	5	10	—
—	D.J. Capel	17	28	5	789	81	34.30	—	6	8	—
—	D.J. Wild	15	27	2	855	144	34.20	2	2	5	—
1979	R.G. Williams	19	36	4	1049	169	32.78	1	5	9	—
1984	R.J. Boyd-Moss	17	32	2	905	105	30.16	1	6	11	—
1965	D.S. Steele	25	39	13	639	78*	24.57	—	3	29	—
—	M.J. Bamber	5	10	1	220	51	24.44	—	1	1	—
—	D. Ripley	14	21	3	281	61	15.61	—	1	26	12
1973	G. Sharp	11	12	0	168	28	14.00	—	—	15	2
1984	N.A. Mallender	20	30	5	261	33*	10.44	—	—	7	—
—	R.W. Hanley	17	21	7	131	33*	9.35	—	—	3	—
—	A. Walker	13	15	4	64	19	5.81	—	—	4	—
1978	B.J. Griffiths	18	21	9	48	12	4.00	—	—	5	—

BOWLING

	Type	O	M	R	W	Avge	Best	5 wI	10 wM
B.J. Griffiths	RFM	474	114	1332	43	30.97	5-52	2	—
R.W. Hanley	RF	399.1	87	1182	37	31.94	6-21	3	—
N.A. Mallender	RFM	508	114	1533	47	32.61	4-45	—	—
D.J. Wild	RM	91.4	18	329	10	32.90	3-15	—	—
D.S. Steele	SLA	732	227	2100	61	34.42	5-86	2	—
A. Walker	RFM	308.5	52	1118	27	41.40	4-50	—	—
R.G. Williams	OB	442.2	104	1348	32	42.12	4-22	—	—
D.J. Capel	RM	155	20	679	16	42.43	5-28	1	—

Also bowled: R.J. Bailey 21-6-45-1; M.J. Bamber 2.3-1-3-0; R.J. Boyd-Moss 55-12-268-1; G. Cook 15.1-1-99-0; W. Larkins 68-19-175-6; G. Sharp 1-1-0-0.

County Records

First-class cricket

Highest innings totals:	For	557-6d v Sussex (Hove)	1914
	Agst	670-9d by Sussex (Hove)	1921
Lowest innings totals:	For	12 v Glos (Gloucester)	1907
	Agst	33 by Lancs (Northampton)	1977
Highest individual innings	For	300 R. Subba Row v Surrey (Oval)	1958
	Agst	333 K.S. Duleepsinhji for Sussex (Hove)	1930
Best bowling in an innings:	For	10-127 V.W.C. Jupp v Kent (Tunbridge Wells)	1932
	Agst	10-30 C. Blythe for Kent (Northampton)	1907
Best bowling in a match:	For	15-31 G.E. Tribe v Yorks (Northampton)	1958
	Agst	17-48 C. Blythe for Kent (Northampton)	1907
Most runs in a season:		2198 (av. 51.11) D. Brookes	1952
runs in a career:		28980 (av. 36.13) D. Brookes	1934-1959
100s in a season:		8 by R.A. Haywood	1921
100s in a career:		67 by D. Brookes	1934-1959
wickets in a season:		175 (av. 18.70) G.E. Tribe	1955
wickets in a career:		1097 (av. 21.31) E.W. Clark	1922-1947

RECORD WICKET STANDS

1st	361	N. Oldfield & V. Broderick v Scotland (Peterborough)	1953
2nd	342	W. Larkins & P. Willey v Lancs (Northampton)	1983
3rd	320	L. Livingston & F. Jakeman v South Africans (Northampton)	1951
4th	370	R.T. Virgin & P. Willey v Somerset (Northampton)	1976
5th	347	D. Brookes & D.W. Barrick v Essex (Northampton)	1952
6th	376	R. Subba Row & A. Lightfoot v Surrey (Oval)	1958
7th	229	W.W. Timms & F.A. Walden v Warwicks (Northampton)	1926
8th	155	F.R. Brown & A.E. Nutter v Glamorgan (Northampton)	1952
9th	156	R. Subba Row & S. Starkie v Lancs (Northampton)	1955
10th	148	B.W. Bellamy & J.V. Murdin v Glamorgan (Northampton)	1925

One-day cricket

Highest innings totals:	Gillette Cup/ NatWest Trophy	285-6 v Wilts (Swindon)	1983
	John Player League	298-2 v Warwicks (Luton)	1983
	Benson & Hedges Cup	259-5 v Scotland (Glasgow)	1982
Lowest innings totals:	Gillette Cup/ NatWest Trophy	62 v Leics (Leicester)	1974
	John Player League	41 v Middlesex (Northampton)	1972
	Benson & Hedges Cup	85 v Sussex (Northampton)	1978
Highest individual innings:	Gillette Cup/ NatWest Trophy	114* G. Cook v Surrey (Northampton)	1979
	John Player League	172* W. Larkins v Warwicks (Luton)	1983
	Benson & Hedges Cup	132 W. Larkins v Warwicks (Birmingham)	1982
Best bowling figures:	Gillette Cup/ NatWest Trophy	7-37 v Worcs (Northampton)	1984
	John Player League	7-39 A. Hodgson v Somerset (Northampton)	1976
	Benson & Hedges Cup	5-21 Sarfraz Nawaz v Middlesex (Lord's)	1980

NOTTINGHAMSHIRE

Formation of present club: 1841, reorganised 1866.
Colours: Green and gold.
Badge: Coat of Arms of the City of Nottingham.
County Champions (13): 1865, 1868, 1871, 1872, 1875, 1880, 1883, 1884, 1885, 1886, 1907, 1929 and 1981.
Joint Champions (5): 1869, 1873, 1879, 1882 and 1889.
Gillete Cup Semi-Finalists: 1969.
NatWest Trophy Third Round: 1981.
Best final position in John Player League: 2nd in 1984.
Benson & Hedges Finalists: 1982 and 1984.
Gillette Man of the Match Awards: 13.
NatWest Man of the Match Awards: 4.
Benson & Hedges Gold Awards: 34.

Secretary: B. Robson, County Cricket Ground, Trent Bridge, Nottingham NG2 6AG.
Cricket Manager: K. Taylor.
Captain: C.E.B. Rice.
Prospects of Play Telephone No: Nottingham (0602) 822753.

John Andrew AFFORD (Spalding GS) B Crowland, Lincs. 12/5/1964. RHB, SLA. Debut 1984.

John Dennis BIRCH (William Crane Bilateral School) B Nottingham 18/6/1955. RHB, RM. Debut 1973. Cap 1981. 1,000 runs (2) – 1,086 (av. 30.16) in 1983 best. BH Gold Award: 1. HS: 125 v Leics (Nottingham) 1982. HSGC/NW: 32 v Yorks (Bradford) 1978. HSJPL: 92 v Sussex (Nottingham) 1983. HSBH: 85 v Minor Counties (North) (Nottingham) 1979. BB: 6-64 v Hants (Bournemouth) 1975. BBJPL: 3-29 v Glamorgan (Swansea) 1976.

Michael Kenneth BORE (Maybury HS) B Hull 2/6/1947. RHB, LM. Played for Yorks 1969 to 1978. Debut for Notts 1979. Cap 1980. BH Gold Award: 1. HS: 37* Yorks v Notts (Bradford) 1973. HSC: 24* v Yorks (Nottingham) 1980. HSJPL: 28* v Northants (Northampton) 1979. BB: 8-89 v Kent (Folkestone) 1979. BBGC/NW: 3-35 Yorks v Kent (Canterbury) 1971. BBJPL: 4-21 Yorks v Sussex (Middlesbrough) 1971 and v Worcs (Worcester) 1970. BBBH: 6-22 v Leics (Leicester) 1980.

Brian Christopher BROAD (Colston's School, Bristol; St. Paul's College, Cheltenham) B Bristol 29/9/1957. LHB, RM. Debut for Glos 1979. Cap 1981. Debut for Notts and cap 1984. 1,000 runs (4) – 1,549 (av. 44.25) in 1984 best. NW Man of the Match: 1 (for Glos). BH Gold Award: 1. HS: 145 Glos v Notts (Bristol) 1983. HSNW: 98 v Middlesex (Bristol) 1982. HSJPL: 96 Glos v Yorks (Cheltenham) 1983. HSBH: 122 v Derby (Derby) 1984.

Kevin Edward COOPER B Hucknall (Notts) 27/12/1957. LHB, RFM. Debut 1976. Cap 1980. HS: 38* v Cambridge U (Cambridge) 1982. HSNW: 11 v Glos (Nottingham) 1982. HSJPL: 31 v Glos (Nottingham) 1984. HSBH: 25* v Lancs (Manchester) 1983. BB: 8-44 v Middlesex (Lord's) 1984. BBNW: 3-18 v Worcs (Worcester) 1983. BBJPL: 4-25 v Hants (Nottingham) 1976. BBBH: 4-23 v Kent (Canterbury) 1979.

NOTTINGHAMSHIRE

Kevin Paul EVANS (Colonel Frank Seeley School) B Calverton, 10/9/1963. RHB, RFM. Debut 1984. HS: 42 v Cambridge U (Nottingham) 1984. HSJPL: 27* v Warwicks (Nottingham) 1984.

Callum David FRASER-DARLING (The Edinburgh Academy) B Sheffield, Yorks 30/9/1963. RHB, RFM. Debut 1984.

Bruce Nicholas FRENCH (Meden School) B Warsop 13/8/1959. RHB, WK. Debut 1976 aged 16 years 287 days. Cap 1980. BH Gold Award: 1. HS: 98 v Lancs (Nottingham) 1984. HSNW: 33* v Kent (Canterbury) 1981. HSJPL: 25 v Northants (Nottingham) 1978. HSBH: 48* v Worcs (Nottingham) 1984.

Richard John HADLEE (Christchurch BHS) B Christchurch, New Zealand 3/7/1951. Youngest son of W.A. Hadlee, former New Zealand Test cricketer, and brother of D.R. and B.G. Hadlee. LHB, RFM. Played for Canterbury 1971-72 to date. Debut for county and cap 1978. Played for Tasmania in 1979-80. *Wisden* 1981. Tests: 50 for New Zealand between 1972-73 and 1983-84. One-day Internationals: 63. Tours: New Zealand to England 1973, 1978 and 1983. Australia 1972-73, 1973-74 and 1980-81, Pakistan and India 1976-77, Sri Lanka 1983-84. 1,000 runs (av. 51.26) and 117 wkts (av. 14.05) in 1984 – the first Double since 1967. Also took 100 wkts (av. 14.39) in 1981. NW Man of the Match awards: 1. BH Gold Awards: 6. HS: 210* v Middlesex (Lord's) 1984. HSTC: 103 New Zealand v West Indies (Christchurch) 1979-80. HSNW: 38* v Kent (Canterbury) 1981. HSJPL: 100* v Glos (Cheltenham) 1982. HSBH: 70 v Warwicks (Nottingham) 1982. BB: 7-23 New Zealand v India (Wellington) 1975-76 and 7-23 v Sussex (Nottingham) 1979. BBJPL: 6-12 v Lancs (Nottingham) 1980. BBBH: 4-13 v Derby (Nottingham) 1981.

Sheikh Basharat HASSAN (City HS, Nairobi) B Nairobi, Kenya 24/3/1944. RHB, RM, occasional WK. Debut for East African Invitation XI v MCC 1963-64. Played for Coast Invitation XI v Pakistan International Airways 1964. Debut for county 1966. Cap 1970. Benefit in 1978. BH Award: 1. 1,000 runs (5) – 1,395 runs (av. 32.44) in 1970 best. Scored century with aid of runner v Kent (Canterbury) 1977. HS: 182* v Glos (Nottingham) 1977. HSGC/NW: 79 v Hants (Southampton) 1977. HSJPL: 120* v Warwicks (Birmingham) 1981. HSBH: 99* v Warwicks (Nottingham) 1982. BB: 3-33 v Lancs (Manchester) 1976. BBGC/NW: 3-20 v Durham (Chester-le-Street) 1967.

Edward Ernest HEMMINGS (Campion School) B Leamington Spa 20/2/1949. RHB, OB. Played for Warwicks 1966 to 1978. Cap 1974. Debut for Notts 1979. Cap 1980. Hat-trick Warwicks v Worcs (Birmingham) 1977. Tours: D.H. Robins XI to South Africa 1974-75; International XIs to Pakistan 1981-82 and Jamaica 1982-83, Australia 1982-83. Tests: 5 in 1982 and 1982-83. One-day Internationals: 5. HS: 127 v Yorks (Worksop) 1982. HSTC: 95 v Australia (Sydney) 1982-83. HSNW: 22 v Glamorgan (Swansea) 1984. HSJPL: 44* v Warwicks v Kent (Birmingham) 1971. HSBH: 61* Warwicks v Leics (Birmingham) 1974. BB: 10-175 International XI v West Indies XI (Kingston) 1982-83. BBTC: 3-68 v Australia (Sydney) 1982-83. BBC: 7-23 v Lancs (Nottingham) 1983. BBJPL: 5-22 Warwicks v Notts (Birmingham) 1974. BBBH: 3-12 v Surrey (Nottingham) 1984.

Paul JOHNSON (Grove Comprehensive) B Newark 24/4/1965. RHB, RM. Debut 1982. HS: 133 v Kent (Folkestone) 1984. HSJPL: 44 v Warwicks (Birmingham) 1983.

Michael NEWELL (West Bridgford CS) B Blackburn, Lancs 25/2/1965. RHB, LB. Debut 1984. HS: 76 v Cambridge U (Nottingham) 1984.

Robert Andrew PICK (Alderman Derbyshire Comprehensive) B Nottingham 19/11/1963. LHB, RFM. Debut 1983. HS: 27* v Oxford U (Oxford) 1984. HSNW: 34* v Sussex (Hove) 1983. BB: 5-25 v Oxford U (Oxford) 1984. BBJPL: 4-36 v Leics (Leicester) 1984.

Derek William RANDALL (Sir Frederick Milner SM) B Retford 24/2/1951. RHB, RM. Debut 1972. Cap 1973. *Wisden* 1979. Tests: 47 between 1976-77 and 1984. One-day Internationals: 48. Tours: D.H. Robins to South Africa 1975-76, India, Sri Lanka and Australia 1976-77, Pakistan and New Zealand 1977-78, Australia 1978-79, Australia and India 1979-80, Australia 1982-83, New Zealand and Pakistan 1983–84. 1,000 runs (9) – 1,546 runs (av. 42.94) in 1976 best. Scored 209 and 146 v Middlesex (Nottingham) 1979. Gillette Man of Match: 1. NW Man of the Match: 1. BH Gold Awards: 3. HS: 209 v Middlesex (Nottingham) 1979. HSTC: 174 v Australia (Melbourne) 1976-77. HSNW: 71 v Glamorgan (Swansea) 1984. HSJPL: 107* v Middlesex (Lord's) 1976 and 107 v Essex (Nottingham) 1983. HSBH: 103* v Minor Counties (North) (Nottingham) 1979. BB: 3-15 v MCC (Lord's) 1982. Benefit 1983.

Clive Edward Butler RICE (St. John's College and Damelin College, Johannesburg; Natal U) B Johannesburg 23/7/1949. RHB, RFM. Played for Transvaal 1969-70 to date. Played for D.H. Robins XI v West Indians 1973 and Pakistanis 1974. Debut for county and cap 1975. Captain 1979. *Wisden* 1980. Benefit 1985. 1,000 runs (10) – 1,871 runs (av. 66.82) in 1978 best. Scored 131* and 114* v Somerset (Nottingham) 1980. Scored 105* out of innings total of 143 v Hants (Bournemouth) 1981 – lowest innings total in first-class cricket to contain a century. NW Man of the Match: 1. BH Gold Awards: 7. HS: 246 v Sussex (Hove) 1976. HSGC/NW: 71 v Yorks (Bradford) 1978. Scored 157 for Transvaal v Orange Free State (Bloemfontein) 1975-76 in South African Gillette Cup competition. HSJPL: 120* v Glamorgan (Swansea) 1978. HSBH: 130* v Scotland (Glasgow) 1982. BB: 7-62 Transvaal v Western Province (Johannesburg) 1975-76. BBUK: 6-16 v Worcs (Worcester) 1977. BBNW: 6-18 v Sussex (Hove) 1982. BBJPL: 4-15 v Hants (Nottingham) 1980. BBBH: 6-22 v Northants (Northampton) 1981.

Robert Timothy ROBINSON (Dunstable GS; High Pavement College, Nottingham; Sheffield U) B Sutton-in-Ashfield (Notts) 21/11/1958. RHB, RM. Debut 1978. Cap 1983. 1,000 runs (2) – 2,032 (av. 50.80) in 1984 best. BH Gold Awards: 1. HS: 207 v Warwicks (Nottingham) 1984. HSNW: 46 v Middlesex (Nottingham) 1984. HSJPL: 97* v Worcs (Worcester) 1984. HSBH: 77* v Worcs (Nottingham) 1981.

Kevin SAXELBY (Magnus GS, Newark) B Worksop 23/2/1959. RHB, RM. Debut 1978. Cap 1984. HS: 59* v Derby (Chesterfield) 1982. HSNW: 12 v Worcs (Worcester) 1984. HSJPL: 23* v Middlesex (Cleethorpes) 1983. HSBH: 13* v Lancs (Nottingham) 1982. BB: 5-43 v Middlesex (Lord's) 1984. BBNW: 4-28 v Middlesex (Nottingham) 1984. BBJPL: 4-29 v Warwicks (Birmingham) 1983. BBBH: 3-12 v Surrey (Nottingham) 1984.

Christopher William SCOTT (Robert Pattinson CS) B Thorpe-on-the-Hill (Lincs) 23/1/1964. RHB, WK. Debut 1981. HS: 78 v Cambridge U (Cambridge) 1983.

Continued on page 168.

County Averages

Britannic Assurance County Championship: Played 24, won 12, drawn 9, lost 3.
All first-class matches: Played 28, won 14, drawn 11, lost 3.

BATTING AND FIELDING

Cap		M	I	NO	RUNS	HS	Avge	100	50	Ct	St
1978	R.J. Hadlee	24	31	8	1179	210*	51.26	2	7	23	—
1983	R.T. Robinson	27	47	7	2032	171	50.80	5	11	16	—
—	P. Johnson	10	14	1	647	133	49.76	2	3	7	1
—	B.C. Broad	18	31	5	1268	108*	48.76	1	11	14	—
1975	C.E.B. Rice	24	39	7	1553	152*	48.53	3	6	21	—
1973	D.W. Randall	24	38	3	1527	136	43.62	3	12	25	—
1981	J.D. Birch	22	33	5	905	110*	32.32	1	5	20	—
1980	B.N. French	26	32	6	697	98	26.80	—	3	76	11
1970	S.B. Hassan	17	27	4	499	103*	21.69	1	1	23	—
—	R.A. Pick	12	10	5	96	27*	19.20	—	—	3	—
—	M. Newell	4	7	1	109	76	18.16	—	1	6	—
—	K. Saxelby	20	19	8	196	27	17.81	—	—	2	—
1980	E.E. Hemmings	24	24	7	248	35	14.58	—	—	7	—
1980	K.E. Cooper	24	19	6	117	19	9.00	—	—	10	—
—	P.M. Such	15	10	5	29	16	5.80	—	—	6	—

Played in four matches: M.K. Bore 1, 27 (1 ct).
Played in three matches: K.P. Evans 42, 1, 3, 2 (3 ct); J.A. Afford did not bat (1 ct); M. Hendrick did not bat (2 ct).
Played in two matches: C.W. Scott 15, 11* (6 ct).
Played in one match: C.D. Fraser-Darling did not bat (1 ct); S. Mee did not bat.

BOWLING

	Type	O	M	R	W	Avge	Best	5 wI	10 wM
R.J. Hadlee	RF	772.2	248	1645	117	14.05	7-35	6	1
P.M. Such	OB	386.5	122	937	42	22.30	5-34	2	—
E.E. Hemmings	OB	797.5	234	2220	94	23.61	7-47	7	1
K.E. Cooper	RFM	623.2	217	1364	51	26.74	8-44	1	—
C.E.B. Rice	RFM	206	54	569	19	29.94	4-61	—	—
R.A. Pick	RM	243.5	52	773	25	30.92	5-25	2	1
M.K. Bore	LM	151.2	40	413	13	31.76	5-30	1	—
K. Saxelby	RM	516.5	140	1592	47	33.87	5-43	1	—

Also bowled: J.A. Afford 88.3-32-256-7; J.D. Birch 3-0-20-0; B.C. Broad 31.2-6-131-2; K.P. Evans 48-8-173-2; C.D. Fraser-Darling 29-9-55-3; B.N. French 1-0-22-0; M. Hendrick 72.1-33-86-8; P. Johnson 4-0-23-2; S. Mee 23-4-63-2; M. Newell 4-0-14-0; D.W. Randall 9.4-0-43-3.

County Records

First-class cricket

Highest innings totals:	For	739-7d v Leics (Nottingham)	1903
	Agst	706-4d by Surrey (Nottingham)	1947
Lowest innings totals:	For	13 v Yorks (Nottingham)	1901
	Agst	16 by Derby (Nottingham) and Surrey (Oval)	1879 & 1880

Highest indi-	For	312* W.W. Keeton v Middlesex (Oval)	1939
vidual innings:	Agst	345 C.G. Macartney for Australians (Nottingham)	1921
Best bowling	For	10-66 K. Smales v Glos (Stroud)	1956
in an innings:	Agst	10-10 H. Verity for Yorks (Leeds)	1932
Best bowling	For	17-89 F.C.L. Matthews v Northants (Nottingham)	1923
in a match:	Agst	17-89 W.G. Grace for Glos (Cheltenham)	1877
Most runs in a season:		2,620 (av. 53.46) W.W. Whysall	1929
runs in a career:		31,592 (av. 35.70) G. Gunn	1902-1932
100s in a season:		9 by W.W. Whysall	1928
		and M.J. Harris	1971
100s in a career:		65 by J. Hardstaff	1930-1955
wickets in a season:		181 (av. 14.96) B. Dooland	1954
wickets in a career:		1,653 (av. 20.34) T. Wass	1896-1920

RECORD WICKET STANDS

1st	391	A.O. Jones & A. Shrewsbury v Glos (Bristol)	1899
2nd	398	W. Gunn & A. Shrewsbury v Sussex (Nottingham)	1890
3rd	369	J.R. Gunn & W. Gunn v Leics (Nottingham)	1903
4th	361	A.O. Jones & J.R. Gunn v Essex (Leyton)	1905
5th	266	A. Shrewsbury & W. Gunn v Sussex (Hove)	1884
6th	303*	F.H. Winrow & P.F. Harvey v Derby (Nottingham)	1947
7th	204	M.J. Smedley & R.A. White v Surrey (Oval)	1967
8th	220	G.F.H. Heane & R. Winrow v Somerset (Nottingham)	1935
9th	165	W. McIntyre & G. Wootton v Kent (Nottingham)	1869
10th	152	E. Alletson & W. Riley v Sussex (Hove)	1911

One-day cricket

Highest innings totals:	Gillette Cup/ NatWest Trophy	271 v Glos (Nottingham)	1968
	John Player League	260-5 v Warwicks (Birmingham)	1976
	Benson & Hedges Cup	269-5 v Derby (Nottingham)	1980
Lowest innings totals:	Gillette Cup/ NatWest Trophy	123 v Yorks (Scarborough)	1969
	John Player League	66 v Yorks (Bradford)	1969
	Benson & Hedges Cup	94 v Lancs (Nottingham)	1975
Highest indi- vidual innings:	Gillette Cup/ NatWest Trophy	107 M. Hill v Somerset (Taunton)	1964
	John Player League	120* C.E.B. Rice v Glamorgan (Swansea)	1978
		120* S.B. Hassan v Warwicks (Birmingham)	1981
	Benson & Hedges Cup	130* C.E.B. Rice v Scotland (Glasgow)	1982
Best bowling figures:	Gillette Cup/ NatWest Trophy	6-18 C.E.B. Rice v Sussex (Hove)	1982
	John Player League	6-12 R.J. Hadlee v Lancs (Nottingham)	1980
	Benson & Hedges Cup	6-22 M.K. Bore v Leics (Leicester)	1980
		6-22 C.E.B. Rice v Northants (Northampton)	1981

SOMERSET

Formation of present club: 1875, reorganised 1885.
Colours: Black, silver and maroon.
Badge: Wessex Wyvern.
Best final position in Championship: Third (5): 1892, 1958, 1963, 1966 and 1981.
Gillette Cup Winners: 1979.
Gillette Cup Finalists (2): 1967 and 1978.
NatWest Trophy Winners: 1983.
John Player League Champions: 1979.
Benson & Hedges Cup Winners (2): 1981 and 1982.
Gillette Man of the Match Awards: 26.
NatWest Man of the Match Awards: 6.
Benson & Hedges Gold Awards: 35.

Secretary and Chief Executive: A.S. Brown, County Cricket Ground, St. James's Street, Taunton TA1 1JT.
Captain: I.T. Botham.
Prospects of Play Telephone No: Taunton (0823) 70007.

Stephen Charles BOOTH (Boston Spa Comprehensive) B Leeds (Yorks) 30/10/1963. RHB, SLA. Debut 1983. HS: 42 v Derby (Taunton) 1984. BB: 4-26 v Middlesex (Lord's) 1983.

Ian Terrence BOTHAM (Buckler's Mead Secondary, Yeovil) B Haswell (Cheshire) 24/11/1955. RHB, REM. Debut 1974. Cap 1976. *Wisden* 1977. County Captain 1984. Testimonial 1984. Tests: 73 between 1977 and 1984 captaining England in 12 Tests. One-day Internationals: 72. Tours: Pakistan and New Zealand 1977-78, Australia 1978-79, Australia and India 1979-80, West Indies 1980-81 (Captain), India and Sri Lanka 1981-82, Australia 1982-83, New Zealand and Pakistan 1983-84. 1,000 runs (3) – 1,241 (av. 44.32) in 1982 best. Took 100 wkts (av. 16.40) in 1978. Became first player ever to score a century and take 8 wkts in innings in a Test match v Pakistan (Lord's) 1978, and to score a century and take 10 wkts in a Test, v India (Bombay) 1979-80. Took 100th wkt in Test cricket in 1979 in record time of 2 years 9 days. Achieved double of 1,000 runs and 100 wkts in Tests in 1979 to create record of fewest Tests (21). Too 200th wkt in 1981 in record time of 4 years 34 days and at youngest age of 25 years 280 days. Became third player in Test cricket to achieve double of 2,000 runs and 200 wkts in 1981-82 in fewest Tests (42), shortest time (4 years 126 days) and youngest age (26 years 7 days). Only player to have scored 4,000 runs and taken 300 wickets in Tests. Scored centuries against Australia in 1981 off 87 balls (Leeds) and 86 balls (Manchester). Hat-trick for MCC v Middlesex (Lord's) 1978. Gillette Man of the Match: 1. BH Gold Awards: 5. HS: 228 v Glos (Taunton) 1980 in 184 minutes with 10 6's and 27 4's, scoring 182 between lunch and tea, and sharing in 4th wkt partnership record for county, 310 with P.W. Denning. HSTC: 208 v India (Oval) 1982. HSNW: 96* v Middlesex (Lord's) 1983. HSJPL: 106 v Hants (Taunton) 1981. HSBH: 57* v Kent (Taunton) 1981. BB: 8-34 v Pakistan (Lord's) 1978. BBC: 7-61 v Glamorgan (Cardiff) 1979. BBNW: 4-20 v Sussex (Hove) 1983. BBJPL: 4-10 v Yorks (Scarborough) 1979. BBBH: 4-16 v Combined Universities (Taunton) 1978. Soccer for Scunthorpe United.

Martin David CROWE B Auckland 22/9/1962. RHB, RM. Debut for Auckland 1979-80. Played for D.B. Close's XI v Pakistanis (Scarborough) 1982. Played for

132

Central Districts 1983-84. Debut for Somerset and cap 1984. Son of D.W. Crowe
(Wellington). Tests: 13 for New Zealand between 1981-82 and 1983-4. One-day
Internationals: 18. Tours: New Zealand to Australia 1982-83, England 1983, Sri
Lanka 1983–84. Scored 1,870 runs (av. 53.42) in 1984. NW Man of the Match: 1.
BH Gold Award: 1. HS: 190 v Leics (Taunton) 1984. HSNW: 114 v Sussex (Hove)
1984. HSJPL: 78 v Kent (Bath) 1984. HSBH: 89 v Warwicks (Birmingham) 1984.
BB: 5-18 Central Districts v Auckland (Auckland) 1983-84. BBC: 5-66 v Leics
(Leicester) 1984. BBNW: 3-33 v Kent (Taunton) 1984. BBBH: 4-24 v Kent
(Canterbury) 1984.

Mark Richard DAVIS (West Somerset School; Bridgwater College) B Kilve
(Somerset) 26/2/1962. LHB, LFM. Debut 1982. HS: 60* v Glamorgan (Taunton)
1984. HSJPL: 11 v Middlesex (Weston-super-Mare) 1982. BB: 7-55 v Northants
(Northampton) 1984. BBJPL: 3-30 v Essex (Chelmsford) 1984.

Colin Herbert DREDGE (Oakfield School) B Frome 4/8/1954. LHB, RM. 6ft
5ins tall. Debut 1976. Cap 1978. Gillette Man of Match: 1. HS: 56* v Yorks
(Harrogate) 1977. HSJPL: 25* v Middlesex (Weston-super-Mare) 1982 and 25* v
Glamorgan (Bath) 1983. HSBH: 17* v Warwicks (Birmingham) 1984. BB: 6-37 v
Glos (Bristol) 1981. BBGC/NW: 4-23 v Kent (Canterbury) 1978. BBJPL: 5-35 v
Middlesex (Lord's) 1981. BBBH: 4-10 v Hants (Bournemouth) 1980.

Nigel Alfred FELTON (Millfield School; Loughborough U) B Guildford, Surrey
24/10/1960. LHB. Debut 1982. HS: 173* v Kent (Taunton) 1983. HSNW: 87 v Kent
(Taunton) 1984. HSJPL: 84* v Glamorgan (Cardiff) 1984.

Trevor GARD (Huish Episcopi Comprehensive) B West Lambrook, near South
Petherton 2/6/1957. RHB, WK. Debut 1976. Cap 1983. NW Man of the Match: 1.
BH Gold Award: 1. HS: 51* v Indians (Taunton) 1979. HSNW: 17 v Shropshire
(Wellington) 1983. HSJPL: 14* v Derbyshire (Heanor) 1983. HSBH: 19 v Warwicks
(Birmingham) 1984.

Joel GARNER (Boys' Foundation School, Christchurch, Barbados) B Barbados
16/12/1952. RHB, RF. 6ft 8ins tall. Played for Barbados 1975-76 to date. Debut for
county 1977. Cap 1979. *Wisden* 1979. Tests: 42 for West Indies between 1976-77 and
1984. One-day Internationals: 55 for West Indies. Tours: West Indies to Australia
and New Zealand 1979-80, England 1980, Pakistan 1980-81, Australia 1981-82,
England 1984. Gillette Man of Match: 1. BH Gold Awards: 2. HS: 104 West Indians
v Glos (Bristol) 1980 HSTC: 60 West Indies v Australia (Brisbane) 1979-80. HSC:
90 v Glos (Bath) 1981. HSGC/NW: 38* v Glamorgan (Cardiff) 1978. HSJPL: 59*
v Surrey (Bath) 1982. HSBH: 17 v Sussex (Hove) 1978. BB: 8-31 v Glamorgan
(Cardiff) 1977. BBTC: 6-56 West Indies v New Zealand (Auckland) 1979-80.
BBGC/NW: 6-29 v Northants (Lord's) 1979. BBJPL: 4-6 v Notts (Bath) 1982.
BBBH: 5-14 v Surrey (Lord's) 1981. MBE 1985.

Victor James MARKS (Blundell's School and Oxford) B Middle Chinnock
25/6/1955. RHB, OB. Debut for Oxford U and county 1975. Blue 1975-76-77-78
(Captain in 1976-77). Cap 1979. Tests: 6 between 1982 and 1983-84. One-day
Internationals: 25. Tours: Australia 1982-83, New Zealand and Pakistan 1983-84.
Scored 1,262 runs (av. 52.58) in 1984. NW Man of the Match: 2. BH Gold Awards:
3. HS: 134 v Worcs (Weston-super-Mare) 1984. HSTC: 83 v Pakistan (Faisalabad)
1983-84. HSNW: 55 v Warwicks (Taunton) 1982. HSJPL: 72 v Worcs (Taunton)
1982. HSBH: 81* v Hants (Bournemouth) 1980. BB: 8-141 v Kent (Taunton) 1984.

SOMERSET

BBTC: 3-78 v New Zealand (Oval) 1983. BBNW: 3-15 v Herts (St. Albans) 1984. BBJPL: 4-11 v Surrey (Weston-super-Mare) 1984. BBBH: 3-25 v Sussex (Taunton) 1982. Half-blue for Rugby Fives.

Richard Leslie OLLIS (Wellesway Comprehensive, Keynsham) B Clifton (Glos) 14/1/1961. LHB, RM. Debut 1981. HS: 99* v Glos (Bristol) 1983.

Gary Vincent PALMER (Queen's College) B Taunton 1/11/1965. RHB, RM. Debut 1982. HS: 78 v Glos (Bristol) 1983. HSJPL: 32* v Leics (Leicester) 1984. BB: 5-38 v Warwicks (Taunton) 1983.

Nigel Francis Mark POPPLEWELL (Radley College and Cambridge) B Chislehurst (Kent) 8/8/1957. Son of O.B. Popplewell, Q.C., former Cambridge Blue. RHB, RM. Debut for Cambridge U 1977. Blue 1977-78-79 (secretary). Debut for county 1979. Cap 1983. NW Man of the Match: 1. BH Gold Awards: 3. Scored 1,116 runs (av. 32.82) in 1984. HS: 143 v Glos (Bath) 1983 including 100 in 41 minutes. HSNW: 68* v Lancs (Manchester) 1983. HSJPL: 84 v Glamorgan (Bath) 1983. HSBH: 67 v Middlesex (Taunton) 1984. BB: 5-33 v Northants (Weston-super-Mare) 1981. BBNW: 3-34 v Middlesex (Lord's) 1983. BBJPL: 3-38 v Glos (Bath) 1983.

Isaac Vivian Alexander RICHARDS (Antigua GS) B St. John's, Antigua 7/3/1952. RHB, OB. Played for Leeward Islands and Combined Islands 1971-72 to date. *Wisden* 1976. Played for Queensland 1976-77. Benefit in 1982 (£56,440). Tests: 68 for West Indies between 1974-75 and 1984. Captain in 2 Tests. One-day Internationals: 76 for West Indies. Tours: West Indies to India, Sri Lanka and Pakistan 1974-75, Australia 1975-76, 1979-80, 1981-82, England 1976 and 1980, Pakistan 1980-81, India 1983-84. 1,000 runs (10) – 2,161 runs (av. 65.48) in 1977 best. Also scored 1,267 runs (av. 60.33) on 1974-75 tour and 1,107 runs (av. 58.26) on 1975-76 tour, and in 1980-81. Scored 1,710 in 11 Test matches in 1976 (including 829 runs in 4 Tests against England. Hat-trick in JPL v Essex (Chelmsford) 1982. Gillette Man of Match: 3. NW Man of the Match: 1. BH Gold Awards: 5. HS: 291 West Indies v England (Oval) 1976. HSC: 241* v Glos (Bristol) 1977. HSGC/NW: 139* v Warwicks (Taunton) 1978. HSJPL: 126* v Glos (Bristol, Imperial Ground) 1975. HSBH: 132* v Surrey (Lord's) 1981. BB: 5-88 West Indians v Queensland (Brisbane) 1981-82. BBUK: 4-55 v Glamorgan (Taunton) 1981. BBJPL: 6-24 v Lancs (Manchester) 1983.

Peter Michael ROEBUCK (Millfield School and Cambridge) B Oxford 6/3/1956. RHB, OB. Debut 1974. Blue 1975-76-77. Cap 1978. 1,000 runs (4) – 1,702 (av. 47.27) in 1984 best. BH Gold Awards: 1. HS: 159 v Northants (Northampton) 1984. HSNW: 98 v Sussex (Hove) 1984. HSJPL: 105 v Glos (Bath) 1983. HSBH: 53* v Notts (Lord's) 1982. BB: 6-50 Cambridge U v Kent (Canterbury) 1977.

Brian Charles ROSE (Weston-super-Mare GS; Isleworth TTC) B Dartford (Kent) 4/6/1950. LHB, LM. Wears spectacles. Debut 1969. Cap 1975. Captain 1978-1983. *Wisden* 1979. Tests: 9 between 1977-78 and 1980-81. One-day Internationals: 2. Tours: Pakistan and New Zealand 1977-78, West Indies 1980-81 (returned through eyesight problem). 1,000 runs (8) – 1,624 runs (av. 46.40) in 1976 best. Scored 124 and 150* v Worcs (Worcester) 1980. Gillette Man of Match: 2. BH Gold Awards: 2. HS: 205 v Northants (Weston-super-Mare) 1977. HSTC: 70 v West Indies (Manchester) 1980. HSGC/NW: 128 v Derby (Ilkeston) 1977. HSJPL: 112* v Essex (Ilford) 1980. HSBH: 137* v Kent (Canterbury) 1980. BB: 3-9 v Glos (Taunton) 1975. BBJPL: 3-25 v Lancs (Manchester) 1975. Benefit 1983.

Murray Stewart TURNER (Richard Huish GS, Taunton) B Shaftesbury, Dorset 27/1/1964. RHB, RFM. Debut 1984.

Simon Jonathan TURNER (Broadoak School) B Cuckfield, Sussex 28/4/1960. LHB, WK. Debut 1984. HS: 27* v Glamorgan (Taunton) 1984.

Julian George WYATT (Wells Cathedral School) B Paulton (19/6/1963. RHB, RM. Debut 1983. HS: 103 v Oxford U (Oxford) 1984. HSJPL: 21 v Worcs (Taunton) 1984.

N.B. The following players whose particulars appeared in the 1984 Annual have been omitted: P.W. Denning, J.W. Lloyds, H.R. Moseley, P.A. Slocombe and P.H.L. Wilson.

County Averages

Britannic Assurance County Championship: Played 24, won 6, drawn 11, lost 7.
All first-class matches: Played 26, won 7, drawn 11, lost 8.

BATTING AND FIELDING

Cap		M	I	NO	RUNS	HS	Avge	100	50	Ct	St
1973	P.W. Denning	5	8	3	338	90	67.60	—	3	2	—
1984	M.D. Crowe	25	41	6	1870	190	53.42	6	11	28	—
1979	V.J. Marks	24	34	10	1262	134	52.58	3	6	16	—
1978	P.M. Roebuck	24	37	1	1702	159	47.27	7	4	4	—
1982	J.W. Lloyds	20	30	10	812	113*	40.60	1	5	22	—
1983	N.F.M. Popplewell	22	36	2	1116	133	32.82	1	7	27	—
1976	I.T. Botham	11	15	1	444	90	31.71	—	4	2	—
1975	B.C. Rose	20	33	4	856	123	29.51	1	4	5	—
—	S.J. Turner	5	6	3	75	27*	25.00	—	—	12	3
—	J.G. Wyatt	16	28	0	666	103	23.78	1	3	8	—
—	M.R. Davis	19	14	6	178	60*	22.25	—	1	9	—
—	N.A. Felton	14	24	1	499	101	21.69	1	3	6	—
—	G.V. Palmer	16	20	2	299	73*	16.61	—	1	15	—
—	S.C. Booth	12	14	7	100	42	14.28	—	—	13	—
1978	C.H. Dredge	21	26	8	214	25*	11.88	—	—	12	—
1983	T. Gard	21	24	5	209	26	11.00	—	—	48	10
—	R.L. Ollis	7	12	1	112	22	10.18	—	—	8	—

Played in four matches: P.H.L. Wilson 0, 0 (1 ct).
Played in one match: M.S. Turner 0, 1.

BOWLING

	Type	O	M	R	W	Avge	Best	5 wI	10 wM
I.T. Botham	RFM	230.2	51	691	33	20.93	5-57	1	—
M.R. Davis	LFM	500.4	108	1569	66	23.77	7-55	4	1
V.J. Marks	OB	808	231	2233	86	25.96	7-83	5	1
C.H. Dredge	RM	533	125	1534	53	28.94	4-48	—	—
M.D. Crowe	RM	435	101	1353	44	30.75	5-66	1	—
S.C. Booth	SLA	408.4	117	1172	38	30.84	4-50	—	—
G.V. Palmer	RM	320.3	56	1231	30	41.03	4-58	—	—
N.F.M. Popplewell	RM	125.3	30	370	8	46.25	3-79	—	—
J.W. Lloyds	OB	240.2	69	697	14	49.78	3-62	—	—

Also bowled: N.A. Felton 0.1-0-4-0; P.M. Roebuck 10.2-5-18-0; M.S. Turner 29-8-85-0; P.H.L. Wilson 56-14-176-5; J.G. Wyatt 3-1-4-1.

County Records

First-class cricket

Highest innings totals:	For	675-9d v Hants (Bath)	1924
	Agst	811 by Surrey (Oval)	1899
Lowest innings totals:	For	25 v Glos (Bristol)	1947
	Agst	22 by Glos (Bristol)	1920
Highest individual innings:	For	310 H. Gimblett v Sussex (Eastbourne)	1948
	Agst	424 A.C. MacLaren for Lancs (Taunton)	1895
Best bowling:	For	10-49 E.J. Tyler v Surrey (Taunton)	1895
in an innings:	Agst	10-35 A. Drake for Yorks (Weston-s-Mare)	1914
Best bowling in a match:	For	16-83 J.C. White v Worcs (Bath)	1919
	Agst	17-137 W. Brearley for Lancs (Manchester)	1905
Most runs in a season:		2,761 (av. 58.74) W.E. Alley	1961
runs in a career:		21,142 (av. 36.96) H. Gimblett	1935-1954
100s in a season:		10 by W.E. Alley	1961
100s in a career:		49 by H. Gimblett	1935-1954
wickets in a season:		169 (av. 19.24) A.W. Wellard	1938
wickets in a career:		2,166 (av. 18.02) J.C. White	1909-1937

RECORD WICKET STANDS

1st	346	H.T. Hewett & L.C.H. Palairet v Yorks (Taunton)	1892
2nd	290	J.C.W. MacBryan & M.D. Lyon v Derby (Buxton)	1924
3rd	319	M.D. Crowe & P.M. Roebuck v Leics (Taunton)	1984
4th	310	P.W. Denning & I.T. Botham v Glos (Taunton)	1980
5th	235	J.C. White & C.C.C. Case v Glos (Taunton)	1927
6th	265	W.E. Alley & K.E. Palmer v Northants (Northampton)	1961
7th	240	S.M.J. Woods & V.T. Hill v Kent (Taunton)	1898
8th	172	I.V.A. Richards & I.T. Botham v Leics (Leicester)	1983
9th	183	C. Greetham & H.W. Stephenson v Leics (Weston-super-Mare)	1963
10th	143	J.J. Bridges & H. Gibbs v Essex (Weston-super-Mare)	1919

One-day cricket

Highest innings totals:	Gillette Cup/ NatWest Trophy	330-4 v Glamorgan (Cardiff)	1978
	John Player League	286-7 v Hants (Taunton)	1981
	Benson & Hedges Cup	307-6 v Glos (Taunton)	1982
Lowest innings totals:	Gillette Cup/ NatWest Trophy	59 v Middlesex (Lord's)	1977
	John Player League	58 v Essex (Chelmsford)	1977
	Benson & Hedges Cup	98 v Middlesex (Lord's)	1982
Highest individual innings:	Gillette Cup/ NatWest Trophy	145 P.W. Denning v Glamorgan (Cardiff)	1978
	John Player League	131 D.B. Close v Yorks (Bath)	1974
	Benson & Hedges Cup	137* B.C. Rose v Kent (Canterbury)	1980
Best bowling figures:	Gillette Cup/ NatWest Trophy	6-29 J. Garner v Northants (Lord's)	1979
	John Player League	6-24 I.V.A. Richards v Lancs (Manchester)	1983
	Benson & Hedges Cup	5-14 J. Garner v Surrey (Lord's)	1981

SURREY

Formation of present club: 1845.
Colours: Chocolate and Silver.
Badge: Prince of Wales' Feathers.
County Champions (18): 1864, 1887, 1888, 1890, 1891, 1892, 1894, 1895, 1899, 1914, 1952, 1953, 1954, 1955, 1956, 1957, 1958 and 1971.
Joint Champions (2): 1889 and 1950.
Gillette Cup Finalists (2): 1965 and 1980.
NatWest Trophy Winners: 1982.
Best final position in John Player League: 5th in 1969 and 1980.
Benson & Hedges Cup Winners: 1974.
Benson & Hedges Cup Finalists: (2): 1979 and 1981.
Gillette Man of the Match Awards: 18.
NatWest Trophy Man of the Match Awards: 6.
Benson & Hedges Gold Awards: 32.

Secretary: I.F.B. Scott-Browne, Kennington Oval, London, SE11 5SS.
Cricket manager: M.J. Stewart.
Captain: G.P. Howarth.
Prospects of Play Telephone No: (01) 735 4911.

Christopher Keith BULLEN (Chaucer Middle School) B Clapham 5/11/1962. RHB, OB. Debut 1982. Did not play in 1983 or 1984.

Alan Raymond BUTCHER (Heath Clark GS) B Croydon 7/1/1954. LHB, SLA. Debut 1972. Cap 1975. Played for Overseas XI v Board Presidents XI (Calcutta) 1980-81. Benefit 1985. Tour: International XI to Jamaica 1982-83. Tests: 1 in 1979. One-day Internationals: 1. 1,000 runs (6) – 1,713 runs (av. 46.29) in 1980 best. BH Gold Awards: 4. HS: 216 v Cambridge U (Cambridge) 1980. HSTC: 20 v India (Oval) 1979. HSNW: 86* v Warwicks (Lord's) 1982. HSJPL: 113* v Warwicks (Birmingham) 1978. HSBH: 80 v Sussex (Oval) 1980. BB: 6-48 v Hants (Guildford) 1972. BBJPL: 5-19 v Glos (Bristol) 1975. BBBH: 3-11 v Lancs (Manchester) 1974.

Sylvester Theophilus CLARKE (St. Bartholomew BS) B Christ Church, Barbados 11/12/1954. RHB, RF. Played for Barbados 1977-78 to 1981-82 and for West Indies XI v International XI (Kingston) 1982-83. Debut for county 1979. Cap 1980. Played for Transvaal 1983–84. Tests: 11 for West Indies between 1977-78 and 1981-82. One-day Internationals: 10. Tours: West Indies to India and Sri Lanka 1978-79, Pakistan 1980-81, Australia 1981-82, West Indian "rebels" to South Africa 1982-83 and 1983-84. Hat-tricks (2): Barbados v Trinidad (Bridgetown) 1977-78; v Notts (Oval) 1980. NW Man of the Match: 1. BH Gold Awards: 2. HS: 100* (in 62 minutes) v Glamorgan (Swansea) 1981. HSTC: 35* West Indies v Pakistan (Faialabad) 1980-81. HSNW: 45* v Leics (Oval) 1981. HSJPL: 34* v Hants (Oval) 1980. HSBH: 39 v Hants (Southampton) 1982. BB: 7-34 West Indian XI v South Africa (Johannesburg) 1982-83. BBUK: 7-53 v Warwicks (Oval) 1983. BBTC: 5-126 West Indies v India (Bangalore) 1978-79. BBGC/NW: 4-38 v Yorks (Oval) 1980. BBJPL: 3-18 v Somerset (Weston-super-Mare) 1984. BBBH: 5-23 v Kent (Oval) 1980.

Grahame Selvey CLINTON (Chislehurst & Sidcup GS) B Sidcup 5/5/1953. LHB,

SURREY

RM. Debut for Kent 1974. Debut for Surrey 1979. Played for Zimbabwe/Rhodesia in 1979-80. Cap 1980. 1,000 runs (3) – 1,240 runs (av. 37.57) in 1980 best. BH Gold Awards: 3 (1 for Kent). HS: 192 v Yorks (Oval) 1984. HSNW: 79 v Ireland (Oval) 1984. HSJPL: 105* v Yorks (Scarborough) 1981. HSBH: 94 v Glos (Oval) 1984.

Nicholas James FALKNER (Reigate GS) B Redhill, Surrey 30/9/1962. RHB, RM. Debut 1984 scoring 101* v Cambridge U (Banbury). HS: 101* as above. HSJPL: 24 v Glamorgan (Oval) 1984.

Mark Andrew FELTHAM (Tiffin BS) B Wandsworth 26/6/1963. RHB, RFM. Debut 1983. HS: 44 v Derby (Oval) 1984. HSBH: 22* v Hants (Oval) 1984. BB: 5-62 v Warwicks (Birmingham) 1984. BBJPL: 3-41 v Warwicks (Birmingham) 1984. BBBH: 3-25 v Glos (Oval) 1984.

Geoffrey Philip HOWARTH (Auckland GS) B Auckland 29/3/1951. Younger brother of H.J. Howarth, New Zealand Test cricketer. RHB, OB. Debut for New Zealand under-23 XI v Auckland (Auckland) 1968-69 and has played for Auckland 1972-73 and 1973-74 and Northern Districts 1974-75 to date. Debut for Surrey 1971. Cap 1974. Awarded M.B.E. in 1981 Birthday Honours List. County captain 1984. Tests 40 for New Zealand between 1974-75 and 1983-84 captain in 26 tests. One-day Internationals: 57 for New Zealand. Tours: D.H. Robins to South Africa 1975-76 and to India 1977-78. New Zealand to Pakistan and India 1976-77, England 1978 and 1983 (captain), Australia 1980-81 (captain) and 1982-83 (captain), Sri Lanka 1983-84 (captain). 1,000 runs (4) – 1,554 runs (av. 37.90) in 1976 best. Scored 122 and 102 New Zealand v England (Auckland) 1977-78. BH Gold Awards: 1. HS: 183 v Hants (Oval) 1979. HSTC: 147 New Zealand v West Indies (Christchurch) 1979-80. HSGC/NW: 34 v Lancs (Manchester) 1977 and 34 v Northants (Northampton) 1979. HSJPL: 122 v Glos (Oval) 1976. HSBH: 80 v Yorks (Oval) 1984. BB: 5-32 Auckland v Central Districts (Auckland) 1973-74. BBUK: 3-20 v Northants (Northampton) 1976. BBJPL: 4-16 v Warwicks (Byfleet) 1979. Benefit 1983.

Monte Alan LYNCH (Ryden's School, Walton-on-Thames) B Georgetown, British Guiana 21/5/1958. RHB, RM/OB. Debut 1977. Cap 1982. Played for Guyana 1982-83. 1,000 runs (3) – 1,558 (av. 53.72) in 1983 best. Tours International XI to Pakistan 1981-82. West Indies "rebels" to South Africa 1983-84. NW Man of the Match: 1. HS: 144 v Leics (Oval) 1984. HSNW: 129 v Durham (Oval) 1982. HSJPL: 103 v Northants (Northampton) 1984. HSBH: 85 v Combined Universities (Oxford) 1984. BB: 3-6 v Glamorgan (Swansea) 1981.

Kevin Scott MACKINTOSH (Kingston-upon-Thames GS) B Surbiton (Surrey) 30/8/1957. RHB, RM. Debut for Notts in 1978. Rejoined Surrey in 1981. Did not play in 1984. HS: 31 v Somerset (Oval) 1982. HSJPL: 12* Notts v Lancs (Nottingham) 1978. BB: 6-61 v Middlesex (Lord's) 1982. BBNW: 3-27 v Durham (Oval) 1982. BBJPL: 4-26 Notts v Glos (Nottingham) 1979.

Keith Thomas MEDLYCOTT (Parmiters GS, Wandsworth) B Whitechapel, London 12/5/1965. RHB, SLA. Debut 1984 scoring 117* v Cambridge U (Banstead). HS: 117* as above.

Graham MONKHOUSE (Penrith QE GS; Notts College of Agriculture) B Carlisle 26/4/1955. RHB, RM. Debut 1981. HS: 100* v Kent (Oval) 1984. HSJPL: 27 v Sussex (Hove) 1983. BB: 7-51 v Notts (Oval) 1983. BBNW: 3-26 v

138

Lincolnshire (Sleaford) 1983. BBJPL: 3-22 v Hants (Oval) 1982. BBBH: 3-43 v Combined Universities (Oxford) 1984. Has played soccer for Carlisle United and Workington.

Andrew NEEDHAM (Paisley GS; Watford GS) B Calow (Derbyshire) 23/3/1957. RHB, OB. Debut 1977. HS: 134* v Lancs (Manchester) 1982. HSJPL: 55 v Essex (Southend) 1982. HSBH: 30 v Glos (Oval) 1984. BB: 6-30 v Oxford U (Oval) 1983. BBJPL: 3-41 v Lancs (Manchester) 1982.

Duncan Brian PAULINE (Bishop Fox, East Molesey) B Aberdeen 15/12/1960. RHB, RM. Debut 1979. HS: 115 v Sussex (Oval) 1983. HSNW: 10 v Durham (Oval) 1982. HSJPL: 92 v Worcs (Oval) 1981. HSBH: 19 v Essex (Chelmsford) 1984.

Patrick Ian POCOCK B Bangor, Caernarvonshire 24/9/1946. RHB, OB. Debut 1964. Cap 1967. Benefit (£18,500) in 1977. Played for Northern Transvaal in 1971-72. Tests: 20 between 1967-68 and 1984. Tours: Pakistan 1966-67, West Indies 1967-68 and 1973-74, Ceylon and Pakistan 1968-69, Ceylon 1969-70, India, Pakistan and Sri Lanka 1972-73. Played for Rest of the World XI v Pakistan (Karachi) 1970-71. Took 112 wkts (av. 18.22) in 1967. Took 4 wkts in 4 balls, 5 in 6, 6 in 9, and 7 in 11 (the last two being first-class records) v Sussex (Eastbourne) 1972. Hat-tricks (2): as above and v Worcs (Guildford) 1971. BH Gold Awards: 2. HS: 75* v Notts (Oval) 1968. HSTC: 33 v Pakistan (Hyderabad) 1972-73. HSGC/NW: 14 v Essex (Colchester) 1978. HSJPL: 22 v Notts (Nottingham) 1971. HSBH: 19 v Middlesex (Oval) 1972. BB: 9-57 v Glamorgan (Cardiff) 1979. BBTC: 6-79 v Australia (Manchester) 1968. BBGC/NW: 3-34 v Somerset (Oval) 1975. BBJPL: 4-27 v Essex (Chelmsford) 1974. BBBH: 4-11 v Yorks (Barnsley) 1978.

Clifton James RICHARDS (Humphrey Davy GS) B Penzance 10/8/1958. RHB, WK. Debut 1976. Cap 1978. Played for Orange Free State 1983-84. One-day Internationals: 3. Tours: D.H. Robins to New Zealand 1979-80, India and Sri Lanka 1981-82. International XI to Jamaica 1982-83. NW Man of the Match: 1. HS: 117* v Notts (Oval) 1982. HSNW: 105* v Lincolnshire (Sleaford) 1983. HSJPL: 52 v Lancs (Manchester) 1982. HSBH: 32 v Leics (Oval) 1981.

Alec James STEWART (Tiffin School) B Merton 8/4/1963. Son of M.J. Stewart, (Surrey). RHB, WK. Debut 1981. HS: 118* v Oxford U (Oval) 1983. HSJPL: 53* v Notts (Nottingham) 1984. HSBH: 10 v Hants (Oval) 1984.

Nicholas Simon TAYLOR (Gresham's School, Holt) B Holmfirth 2/6/1963. RHB, RFM. Son of K. Taylor (England, Yorks and Auckland). Debut for Yorks 1982. Debut for Surrey 1984. BB: 5-49 v Sussex (Leeds) 1983.

David James THOMAS (Licensed Victuallers' School, Slough) B Solihull (Warwicks) 30/6/1959. LHB, LM. Debut 1977. Cap 1982. Played for Northern Transvaal in 1980-81, Natal 1983-84. HS: 119 v Notts (Oval) 1983. HSNW: 53 v Warwicks (Birmingham) 1984. HSJPL: 72 v Glamorgan (Swansea) 1983. HSBH: 19 v Notts (Nottingham) 1984. BB: 6-36 v Somerset (Oval) 1984. BBNW: 3-16 v Durham (Oval) 1982. BBJPL: 4-13 v Sussex (Oval) 1978. BBBH: 3-30 v Leics (Oval) 1981.

David Mark WARD (Haling Manor HS) B Croydon 10/2/1961. RHB, OB. Played in two JPL matches in 1984. HSJPL: 59* v Worcs (Oval) 1984.

SURREY

Peter Andrew WATERMAN (Rooks Heath HS, Pinner SFC) B Hendon, Middlesex 26/3/1961. RHB, RFM. Debut 1983.

NB. The following players whose particulars appeared in the 1984 Annual have been omitted: I.J. Curtis, R.D.V. Knight and I.R. Payne.

County Averages

Britannic Assurance County Championship: Played 24, won 6, drawn 12, lost 6.
All first-class matches: Played 26, won 7, drawn 13, lost 6.

BATTING AND FIELDING

Cap		M	I	NO	RUNS	HS	Avge	100	50	Ct	St
—	K.T. Medlycott	6	6	5	128	117*	128.00	1	—	—	—
1980	G.S. Clinton	19	28	6	948	192	43.09	2	5	6	—
1978	R.D.V. Knight	21	35	3	1254	142	39.18	3	8	19	—
1982	M.A. Lynch	25	41	1	1546	144	38.65	4	8	32	—
1975	A.R. Butcher	24	41	4	1415	135*	38.24	4	5	11	—
—	A.J. Stewart	15	21	3	570	73	31.66	—	4	26	—
1978	C.J. Richards	25	38	8	908	109	30.26	2	4	46	6
1974	G.P. Howarth	22	37	3	833	113	24.50	2	4	17	—
—	D.P. Pauline	10	16	1	367	88	24.46	—	3	9	—
—	A. Needham	19	30	1	644	70	22.20	—	4	10	—
—	M.A. Feltham	12	15	5	206	44	20.60	—	—	5	—
1982	D.J. Thomas	20	28	5	425	48	18.47	—	—	10	—
—	G. Monkhouse	18	25	7	328	100*	18.22	1	1	8	—
1980	S.T. Clarke	23	25	3	329	35	14.95	—	—	23	—
1967	P.I. Pocock	17	16	6	110	29*	11.00	—	—	8	—

Played in three matches: N.S. Taylor 6* (2 ct); P.A. Waterman 0,0* (2 ct).
Played in two matches: I.R. Payne 0, 17, 13 (4 ct).
Played in one match: I.J. Curtis 1*; N.J. Falkner 101*.

BOWLING

	Type	O	M	R	W	Avge	Best	5 wI	10 wM
S.T. Clarke	RF	651	165	1687	78	21.62	6-62	2	—
P.I. Pocock	OB	515.2	123	1323	56	23.62	7-74	3	1
G. Monkhouse	RM	460.5	120	1273	50	25.46	4-41	—	—
D.J. Thomas	LFM	505.4	114	1654	60	27.56	6-36	2	1
M.A. Feltham	RM	291.2	53	1012	32	31.62	5-62	1	—
R.D.V. Knight	RM	349.4	99	925	27	34.25	4-7	—	—
A. Needham	OB	328.5	79	1047	29	36.10	5-82	1	—

Also bowled: A.R. Butcher 38-9-134-4; G.S. Clinton 6-1-30-0; I.J. Curtis 11.3-3-36-1; G.P. Howarth 0.4-0-2-0; M.A. Lynch 22.3-3-89-4; K.T. Medlycott 98-34-186-7; D.B. Pauline 6-4-6-0; I.R. Payne 42.5-18-102-3; C.J. Richards 4-0-20-0; N.S. Taylor 80-20-254-10; P.A. Waterman 58.2-7-194-5.

County Records

First-class cricket

Highest innings	For	811 v Somerset (Oval)	1899
totals:	Agst	705-8d by Sussex (Hastings)	1902
Lowest innings	For	14 v Essex (Chelmsford)	1983
totals:	Agst	16 by MCC (Lord's)	1872
Highest Indi-	For	357* R. Abel v Somerset (Oval)	1899
vidual innings:	Agst	300* F. Watson for Lancs (Manchester)	1928
		300 R. Subba Row for Northants (Oval)	1958
Best bowling	For	10-43 T. Rushby v Somerset (Taunton)	1921
in an innings:	Agst	10-28 W. P. Howell for Australians (Oval)	1899
Best bowling	For	16-83 G. A. R. Lock v Kent (Blackheath)	1956
in a match:	Agst	15-57 W. P. Howell for Australians (Oval)	1899
Most runs in a season:		3,246 (av. 72.13) T. W. Hayward	1906
runs in a career:		43,554 (av. 49.72) J. B. Hobbs	1905-1934
100s in a season:		13 by T. W. Hayward and	1906
		J. B. Hobbs	1925
100s in a career:		144 by J. B. Hobbs	1905-1934
wickets in a season:		252 (av. 17.87) T. Richardson	1895
wickets in a career:		1,775 (av. 17.88) T. Richardson	1892-1904

RECORD WICKET STANDS

1st	428	J. B. Hobbs & A. Sandham v Oxford U (Oval)	1926
2nd	371	J. B. Hobbs & E. G. Hayes v Hants (Oval)	1909
3rd	353	A. Ducat & E. G. Hayes v Hants (Southampton)	1919
4th	448	R. Abel & T. W. Hayward v Yorks (Oval)	1899
5th	308	J. N. Crawford & F. C. Holland v Somerset (Oval)	1908
6th	298	A. Sandham & H. S. Harrison v Sussex (Oval)	1913
7th	200	T. F. Shepherd & J. W. Hitch v Kent (Blackheath)	1921
8th	204	T. W. Hayward & L. C. Braund v Lancs (Oval)	1898
9th	168	E. R. T. Holmes & E. W. J. Brooks v Hants (Oval)	1936
10th	173	A. Ducat & A. Sandham v Essex (Leyton)	1921

One-day cricket

Highest innings	GC/Natwest Trophy	297-6 v Lincoln (Sleaford)	1983
totals:	John Player League	270-6 v Worcs (Guildford)	1983
	Benson & Hedges Cup	276-6 v Essex (Oval)	1982
Lowest innings	GC/NatWest Trophy	74 v Kent (Oval)	1967
totals:	John Player League	64 v Worcs (Worcester)	1978
	Benson & Hedges Cup	89 v Notts (Nottingham)	1984
Highest indi-	Gillette Cup/	129 M.A. Lynch v Durham	
vidual innings:	NatWest Trophy	(Oval)	1982
	John Player League	122 G.P. Howarth v	
		Glos (Oval)	1976
	Benson & Hedges Cup	115 G.R.J. Roope v Essex	
		(Chelmsford)	1973
Best bowling	Gillette Cup/	7-33 R.D. Jackman v	
figures:	NatWest Trophy	Yorks (Harrogate)	1970
	John Player League	6-25 Intikhab Alam v	
		Derby (Oval)	1974
	Benson & Hedges Cup	5-21 P.H.L. Wilson v	
		Combined U. (Oval)	1979

SUSSEX

Formation of present club: 1839, reorganised 1857.
Colours: Dark blue, light blue, and gold.
Badge: County Arms of six martlets (in shape of inverted pyramid).
County Championship Runners-up (7): 1902, 1903, 1932, 1933, 1934, 1953 and 1981.
Gillette Cup Winners (3): 1963, 1964 and 1978.
Gillette Cup Finalists (3): 1968, 1970 and 1973.
NatWest Trophy third round (2): 1981 and 1983.
John Player League Winners: 1982.
Benson & Hedges Cup Semi-finalists: 1982.
Gillette Man of the Match Awards: 30.
NatWest Man of the Match Awards: 3.
Benson & Hedges Gold Awards: 32.

Secretary: R. Renold, County Ground, Eaton Road, Hove BN3 3AN.
Captain: J.R.T. Barclay.
Prospects of Play Telephone No: Brighton (0273) 772766.

John Robert Troutbeck BARCLAY (Eton College) B Bonn, West Germany 22/1/1954. RHB, OB. Debut 1970 aged 16 years 205 days. Cap 1976. Captain 1981. Played for Orange Free State in 1978-79. 1,000 runs (4) – 1,093 (av. 32.14) in 1979 best. Gillette Man of the Match: 1. BH Gold Awards: 3. HS: 119 v Leics (Hove) 1980. HSNW: 48 v Ireland (Dublin) 1983. HSJPL: 48 v Derby (Derby) 1974. HSBH: 93* v Surrey (Oval) 1976. BB: 6-61 v Sri Lankans (Hove) 1979. BBNW: 5-53 v Devon (Hove) 1984. BBJPL: 3-11 v Worcs (Eastbourne) 1978. BBBH: 5-43 v Combined Universities (Oxford) 1979.

Ian James GOULD (Westgate School) B Slough (Bucks) 19/8/1957. LHB, WK. Debut for Middlesex 1975. Cap 1977. Played for Auckland in 1979-80. Debut for Sussex in 1981. Cap 1981. One-day Internationals: 18. Tour: Australia 1982-83. BH Gold Award: 1. HS: 128 Middlesex v Worcs (Worcester) 1978. HSC: 94 v Somerset (Hove) 1982. HSGC/NW: 58 Middlesex v Derby (Derby) 1978. HSJPL: 69* v Hants (Basingstoke) 1981. HSBH: 72 v Kent (Hove) 1982.

Allan Michael GREEN (Knoll School, Hove; Brighton SFC) B Pulborough 28/5/1960. RHB, RM. Debut 1980. Scored 1,006 runs (av. 26.47) in 1984. HS: 99 v Middlesex (Hove) 1982. HSNW: 74 v Devon (Hove) 1984. HSJPL: 83 v Derby (Heanor) 1984. HSBH: 30 v Somerset (Taunton) 1983.

Ian Alexander GREIG (Queen's College, Queenstown and Cambridge) B Queenstown, South Africa 8/12/1955. RHB, RM. Younger brother of A.W. Greig. Played for Border in 1974-75 and 1979-80 and for Griqualand West in 1975-76. Debut for Cambridge U 1977. Blue 1977-78-79 (captain). Debut for county 1980. Cap 1981. Tests: 2 in 1982. Had maiden double of 100 runs and 10 wkts (118*, 6-75, 4-57) v Hants (Hove) 1981. NW Man of the Match: 1. BH Gold Award: 1. HS: 147* v Oxford U (Oxford) 1983. HSTC: 14 v Pakistan (Birmingham) 1982. HSNW: 82 v Warwicks (Birmingham) 1981. HSJPL: 48 v Notts (Nottingham) 1981. HSBH: 51 v Hants (Hove) 1981. BB: 7-43 v Cambridge U (Cambridge) 1981. BBTC: 4-53 v Pakistan (Birmingham) 1982. BBNW: 4-31 v Warwicks (Birmingham) 1981. BBJPL:

142

5-42 v Leics (Hove) 1982. BBBH: 5-35 v Hants (Hove) 1981. Blues for rugby 1977-78.

IMRAN KHAN NIAZI (Aitchison College, Lahore and Oxford) B Lahore, Pakistan 25/11/1952. RHB, RF. Cousin of Majid Jahangir Khan. Debut for Lahore A 1969-70 and has played subsequently for various Lahore teams and Pakistan International Airways. Debut for Worcs 1971. Blue 1973-74-75 (capt in 1974). Cap 1976. Debut for Sussex by special registration 1977. Cap 1978. Tests: 51 for Pakistan between 1971 and 1983-84. Captain in 14 Tests. One-day Internationals: 48 for Pakistan. Tours: Pakistan to England 1971, 1974 and 1982, Pakistan to Sri Lanka 1975-76, Australia and West Indies 1976-77, New Zealand and Australia 1978-79, India 1979-80, Australia 1981-82, 1983-84. 1,000 runs (4) – 1,339 runs (av. 41.84) in 1978 best. Scored 117* and 106 Oxford U v Notts (Oxford) 1974. Had match double of 111* and 13-99 (7-53 and 6-46) v Lancs (Worcester) 1976. Gillette Man of the Match Awards: 4. (1 for Worcs). NW Man of the Match: 1. BH Gold Awards: 6, (1 for Oxford and Cambridge Universities, 1 for Worcs). HS: 170 Oxford U v Northants (Oxford) 1974. HSC: 167 v Glos (Hove) 1978. HSTC: 123 Pakistan v West Indies (Lahore) 1980-81. HSNW: 114* v Notts (Hove) 1983. HSJPL: 90 v Hants (Southampton) 1983. HSBH: 72 Worcs v Warwicks (Birmingham) 1976. BB: 8-58 Pakistan v Sri Lanka (Faisalabad) 1981-82. BBUK: 7-52 v Glos (Bristol) 1978 and for Pakistan v England (Birmingham) 1982. BBGC/NW: 4-27 v Staffs (Stone) 1978. BBJPL: 5-29 Worcs v Leics (Leicester) 1973. BBBH: 5-8 v Northants (Northampton) 1978. *Wisden* 1982.

Adrian Nicholas JONES (Seaford College) B Woking (Surrey) 22/7/1961. LHB, RFM. Debut 1981. Played for Border 1981-82. HS: 35 v Middlesex (Hove) 1984. BB: 5-29 v Glos (Hove) 1984. BBJPL: 5-28 v Essex (Eastbourne) 1984.

Garth Stirling LE ROUX (Wynberg BHS; Stellenbosch U) B Cape Town 4/9/1955. RHB, RF. Played for Western Province 1975-76 to date. Debut for county 1978. Cap 1981. Hat-trick v Warwicks (Hove) 1981. HS: 83 v Surrey (Hove) 1982. HSNW: 22 v Ireland (Dublin) 1983 and v Devon (Hove) 1984. HSJPL: 88 v Glamorgan (Hastings) 1982. HSBH: 50 v Yorks (Hove) 1984. BB: 8-107 v Somerset (Taunton) 1981. BBNW: 5-35 v Essex (Hove) 1981. BBJPL: 4-18 v Notts (Hove) 1982. BBBH: 4-22 v Hants (Hove) 1983.

Neil John LENHAM (Brighton College) B Worthing 17/12/1965. RHB, RFM. Son of L.J. Lenham (Sussex). Debut 1984. HS: 31 v Sri Lankans (Hove) 1984.

Gehan Dixon MENDIS (St Thomas College, Colombo) B Colombo, Ceylon 20/4/1955. RHB, occasional WK. Debut 1974. Cap 1980. Tours: International teams to Pakistan 1981-82 and Jamaica 1982-83. 1,000 runs (5) – 1,624 (av. 40.60) in 1983 best. Gillette Man of Match: 2. BH Gold Awards: 3. HS: 209* v Somerset (Hove) 1984. HSGC/NW: 141* v Warwicks (Hove) 1980. HSJPL: 125* v Glos (Hove) 1981. HSBH: 109 v Glos (Hove) 1980.

Paul William Giles PARKER (Collyers GS; Cambridge U) B Bulawayo, Rhodesia 15/1/1956. RHB, RM. Debut for Cambridge U and county 1976. Blue 1976-77-78. Cap 1979. Tests: 1 in 1981. 1,000 runs (6) – 1,692 (av. 47.00) in 1984 best. Gillette Man of Match: 2. BH Gold Awards: 3. HS: 215 Cambridge U v Essex (Cambridge) 1976. HSC: 181 v Sri Lankans (Hove) 1984. HSGC/NW: 69 v Lancs (Hove) 1978. HSJPL: 121* v Northants (Hastings) 1983. HSBH: 77 v Hants (Bournemouth) 1982. Selected for University rugby match in 1977, but had to withdraw through injury.

SUSSEX

Christopher Paul PHILLIPSON (Ardingly College) B Vrindaban, India 10/2/1952. RHB, RM. Debut 1970. Cap 1980. Benefit 1985. BH Gold Awards: 2. HS: 87 v Hants (Hove) 1980. HSGC/NW: 70* v Suffolk (Hove) 1980. HSJPL: 71 v Lancs (Hastings) 1979. HSBH: 66* v Surrey (Oval) 1982. BB: 6-56 v Notts (Hove) 1972. BBJPL: 4-25 v Middlesex (Eastbourne) 1972. BBBH: 5-32 v Combined Universities (Oxford) 1977.

Anthony Charles Shackleton PIGOTT (Harrow School) B London 4/6/1958. RHB, RFM. Debut 1978. Cap 1982. Tour: D.H. Robins to New Zealand 1979-80. Played for Wellington 1982-83 and 1983-84. Tests: 1 in 1983-84. Hat-trick v Surrey (Hove) 1978. HS: 63 v Hants (Eastbourne) 1983. HSGC/NW: 30 v Northants (Hove) 1979. HSJPL: 49 v Warwicks (Hove) 1979. BB: 7-74 v Northants (Eastbourne) 1982. BBGC/NW: 3-43 v Notts (Hove) 1979. BBJPL: 5-28 v Surrey (Guildford) 1982. BBBH: 3-33 v Hants (Bournemouth) 1982.

Dermot Alexander REEVE (King George V School, Kowloon) B Hong Kong 2/4/1963. RHB, RFM. Debut 1983. HS: 119 v Surrey (Guildford) 1984. HSNW: 16* v Ireland (Dublin) 1983. HSJPL: 15 v Notts (Nottingham) 1984. HSBH: 16 v Middlesex (Lord's) 1984. BB: 5-22 v Cambridge U (Cambridge) 1984. BBNW: 3-26 v Ireland (Dublin) 1983. BBJPL: 4-31 v Somerset (Hove) 1984. BBBH: 3-34 v Glamorgan (Hove) 1984.

Mark Stephen SCOTT B Muswell Hill (Middlesex) 10/3/1959. RHB. Debut for Worcs 1981. Joined Sussex for 1985. HS: 109 v Glos (Bristol) 1981. HSNW: 23 Worcs v Notts (Worcester) 1983. HSJPL: 42 Worcs v Glos (Worcester) 1981.

David James SMITH (Hove GS) B Brighton 28/4/1962. LHB, WK. Debut 1981. HS: 13 v Somerset (Hove) 1983.

David Kevin STANDING (Tideway School, Newhaven; Brighton and Hove SFC) B Brighton 21/10/1963. RHB, OB. Debut 1983. HS: 60 v Worcs (Worcester) 1983.

Christopher Edward WALLER (St. Bede's C of E Secondary, Send) B Guildford 3/10/1948. RHB, SLA. Debut for Surrey 1967. Cap 1972. Debut for Sussex 1974. Cap 1976. Benefit 1984. HS: 51* v Cambridge U (Cambridge) 1981. HSGC/NW: 14* v Notts (Nottingham) 1975. HSJPL: 18* v Glamorgan (Hove) 1975. HSBH: 11* v Essex (Chelmsford) 1975. BB: 7-64 Surrey v Sussex (Oval) 1971. BBC: 6-40 v Surrey (Hove) 1975. BBJPL: 4-28 v Essex (Hove) 1976. BBBH: 4-25 v Minor Counties (South) (Hove) 1975.

Alan Peter WELLS (Tideway Comprehensive, Newhaven) B Newhaven 2/10/1961. Younger brother of C.M. Wells. RHB, RM. Debut 1981. Played for Border 1981-82. Scored 1,045 runs (av. 32.65) in 1984. HS: 127 v Northants (Northampton) 1984. HSNW: 24 v Somerset (Hove) 1984. HSJPL: 71* v Hants (Southampton) 1984. HSBH: 51 v Yorks (Hove) 1984.

Colin Mark WELLS (Tideway Comprehensive, Newhaven) B Newhaven 3/3/1960. Older brother of A.P. Wells. Debut 1979. Cap 1982. RHB, RM. BH Gold Award: 1. 1,000 runs (3) – 1,389 (av. 43.40) in 1984 best. HS: 203 v Hants (Hove) 1984. HSNW: 28 v Warwicks (Birmingham) 1981 and v Notts (Hove) 1983. HSJPL: 104* v Warwicks (Hove) 1983. HSBH: 80 v Kent (Hove) 1982. BB: 5-25 v Kent

144

(Hastings) 1984. BBJPL: 4-15 v Worcs (Worcester) 1983. BBBH: 4-21 v Middlesex (Lord's) 1980.

NB. The following players whose particulars appeared in the 1984 Annual have been omitted: J.R.P. Heath and A. Willows.

County Averages

Britannic Assurance County Championship; Played 24, won 7, drawn 10, lost 6, tied 1.
All first-class matches: Played 26, won 7, drawn 12, lost 6, tied 1.

BATTING AND FIELDING

Cap		M	I	NO	RUNS	HS	Avge	100	50	Ct	St
1979	P.W.G. Parker	26	40	4	1692	181	47.00	6	6	23	—
1982	C.M. Wells	26	39	7	1389	203	43.40	5	4	4	—
1980	G.D. Mendis	23	36	2	1141	209*	33.55	3	4	9	—
—	A.P. Wells	25	39	7	1045	127	32.65	2	7	10	—
1981	I.A. Greig	26	35	5	813	106*	27.10	1	2	17	—
—	D.A. Reeve	21	22	4	486	119	27.00	1	3	14	—
—	A.M. Green	24	40	2	1006	81	26.47	—	4	12	—
—	A.N. Jones	10	7	4	73	35	24.33	—	—	3	—
1976	J.R.T. Barclay	26	35	3	761	82	23.78	—	4	21	—
1981	I.J. Gould	23	27	4	529	84	23.00	—	2	62	6
1981	G.S. Le Roux	24	24	6	321	68*	17.83	—	2	4	—
1976	C.E. Waller	22	21	14	56	16*	8.00	—	—	13	—

Played in three matches: D.J. Smith 2,1, (9 ct).
Played in two matches: D.K. Standing 5*, 7 (1 ct); D.J. Wood 15, 12, 5; A.C.S. Pigott did not bat.
Played in one match: N.J. Lenham 31 (1 ct).

BOWLING

	Type	O	M	R	W	Avge	Best	5 wI	10 wM
G.S. Le Roux	RF	604.2	154	1647	78	21.11	6-57	2	—
C.M. Wells	RM	497.2	146	1396	59	23.66	5-25	2	—
A.N. Jones	RFM	208.1	44	636	25	25.44	5-29	1	—
C.E. Waller	SLA	610.3	221	1349	53	25.45	6-75	1	—
D.A. Reeve	RM	572.4	175	1420	55	25.81	5-22	1	—
J.R.T. Barclay	OB	417	117	1023	36	28.41	4-32	—	—
I.A. Greig	RM	648	153	1913	62	30.85	4-39	—	—

Also bowled: A.M. Green 18-2-41-1; P.W.G. Parker 11.1-2-40-2; A.C.S. Pigott 32-5-96-2.

County Records

First-class cricket

Highest innings totals:	For	705-8d v Surrey (Hastings)	1902
	Agst	726 by Notts (Nottingham)	1895
Lowest innings totals:	For	19 v Surrey (Godalming)	1830
		19 v Notts (Hove)	1873
	Agst	18 by Kent (Gravesend)	1867
Highest individual innings:	For	333 by K.S. Duleepsinhji v Northants (Hove)	1930
	Agst	322 E. Paynter for Lancs (Hove)	1937
Best bowling in an innings:	For	10-48 C.H.G. Bland v Kent (Tonbridge)	1899
	Agst	9-11 A.P. Freeman for Kent (Hove)	1922
Best bowling in a match:	For	17-106 G.R. Cox v Warwicks (Horsham)	1926
	Agst	17-67 A.P. Freeman for Kent (Hove)	1922
Most runs in a season:		2850 (av. 64.77) John Langridge	1949
runs in a career:		34152 (av. 37.69) John Langridge	1928-1955
100s in a season:		12 by John Langridge	1949
100s in a career:		76 by John Langridge	1928-1955
wickets in a season:		198 (av. 13.45) M.W. Tate	1925
wickets in a career:		2223 (av. 16.34) M.W. Tate	1912-1937

RECORD WICKET STANDS

1st	490	E.H. Bowley & John Langridge v Middlesex (Hove)	1933
2nd	385	E.H. Bowley & M.W. Tate v Northants (Hove)	1921
3rd	298	K.S. Ranjitsinhji & E.H. Killick v Lancs (Hove)	1901
4th	326*	G. Cox & James Langridge v Yorks (Leeds)	1949
5th	297	J.H. Parks & H.W. Parks v Hants (Portsmouth)	1937
6th	255	K.S. Duleepsinhji & M.W. Tate v Northants (Hove)	1930
7th	344	K.S. Ranjitsinhji & W. Newham v Essex (Leyton)	1902
8th	229*	C.L.A. Smith & G. Brann v Kent (Hove)	1902
9th	178	H.W. Parks & A.F. Wensley v Derby (Horsham)	1930
10th	156	G.R. Cox & H.R. Butt v Cambridge U (Cambridge)	1908

One-day cricket

Highest innings totals:	Gillette Cup/ NatWest Trophy	314-7 v Kent (Tunbridge Wells)	1963
	John Player League	293-4 v Worcs (Horsham)	1980
	Benson & Hedges Cup	305-6 v Kent (Hove)	1982
Lowest innings totals:	Gillette Cup/ NatWest Trophy	49 v Derby (Chesterfield)	1969
	John Player League	61 v Derby (Derby)	1978
	Benson & Hedges Cup	61 v Middlesex (Hove)	1978
Highest individual innings:	Gillette Cup/ NatWest Trophy	141* G.D. Mendis v Warwicks (Hove)	1980
	John Player League	129 A.W. Greig v Yorks (Scarborough)	1976
	Benson & Hedges Cup	117 R.D.V. Knight v Surrey (Oval)	1977
Best bowling figures:	Gillette Cup/ NatWest Trophy	6-30 D.L. Bates v Glos (Hove)	1968
	John Player League	6-14 M.A. Buss v Lancs (Hove)	1973
	Benson & Hedges Cup	5-8 Imran Khan v Northants (Northampton)	1978

WARWICKSHIRE

Formation of club: 1882.
Colours: Blue, gold and silver.
Badge: Bear and ragged staff.
County Champions (3): 1911, 1951 and 1972.
Gillette Cup Winners (2): 1966 and 1968.
Gillette Cup Finalists (2): 1964 and 1972.
NatWest Trophy Finalists: 1982.
John Player League Champions: 1980.
Benson & Hedges Cup Finalists: 1984.
Gillette Man of the Match Awards: 24.
NatWest Man of the Match Awards: 8.
Benson & Hedges Gold Awards: 32.

Secretary: A.C. Smith, County Ground, Edgbaston, Birmingham B5 7QU.
Cricket Manager: D.J. Brown.
Captain: N. Gifford, MBE.
Prospects of Play Telephone No: (021) 440 3624.

Dennis Leslie AMISS (Oldknow SM, Small Heath) B Birmingham 7/4/1943. RHB, SLC. Debut 1960. Cap 1965. Benefit 1975 (£34,947). Testimonial 1985. Tests: 50 between 1966 and 1977 and 1 match v Rest of the World in 1970. One-day Internationals: 18. Tours: Pakistan 1966-67, India, Pakistan and Sri Lanka 1972-73, West Indies 1973-74, Australia and New Zealand 1974-75, India, Sri Lanka and Australia 1976-77, International XI in India and Pakistan 1967-68, SAB XI in South Africa 1981-82. Banned for 3 years from Test cricket. Also played for Rest of the World XI v Pakistan XI in Pakistan 1970-71. 1,000 runs (20) – 2,239 (av. 55.97) in 1984 best. Scored 1,120 runs (av. 74.66) in West Indies in 1973-74. Two centuries in a match twice: 165* and 112 v Worcs (Birmingham) 1978 and 109 and 127 v Derby (Derby) 1981. Gillette Man of the Match: 3. NW Man of the Match: 1. BH Gold Awards: 4. HS: 262* England v West Indies (Kingston) 1973-74. HSUK: 232* v Glos (Bristol) 1979. HSNW: 135 v Cambs U (Birmingham) 1982. HSJPL: 117* v Sussex (Horsham) 1981. HSBH: 115 v Leics (Leicester) 1984. BB: 3-21 v Middlesex (Lord's) 1970.

Mohamed ASIF DIN (Ladywood Comprehensive, Birmingham) B Kampala, Uganda 21/9/1960. RHB, LB. Debut 1981. HS: 102 v Middlesex (Coventry) 1982. HSNW: 45 v Surrey (Lord's) 1982. HSJPL: 56* v Hants (Bournemouth) 1982. HSBH: 61 v Notts (Nottingham) 1982. BB: 5-100 v Glamorgan (Birmingham) 1982.

Robin Ian Henry Benbow DYER (Wellington College) B Hertford 22/12/1958. 6ft 4ins tall. RHB, RM. Debut 1981. NW Man of the Match: 1. Scored 1,187 runs (av. 34.91) in 1984. HS: 106* v Glamorgan (Cardiff) 1984. HSNW: 119 v Shropshire (Birmingham) 1984. HSJPL: 44 v Glos (Birmingham) 1984. HSBH: 54 v Yorks (Leeds) 1984.

Anthonie Michal (Yogi) FERREIRA (Hillview High School, Pretoria) B Pretoria, South Africa 13/4/1955. RHB, RM. Played for Northern Transvaal 1974-75 to date. Played for D.H. Robins XI v both Oxford and Cambridge Universities at Eastbourne in 1978. Debut for county 1979. Cap 1983. HS: 112* v Indians (Birmingham) 1982. HSNW: 21 v Shropshire (Birmingham) 1984. HSJPL: 52 v Hants (Birmingham) 1983. HSBH: 71 v Yorks (Birmingham) 1984. BB: 8-38 Northern Transvaal v

147

WARWICKSHIRE

Transvaal B (Pretoria) 1977-78. BBUK: 6-70 v Leics (Birmingham) 1984. BBGC/NW: 4-50 v Notts (Birmingham) 1979. BBJPL: 4-26 v Sussex (Horsham) 1981. BBBH: 4-42 v Scotland (Birmingham) 1982.

Norman GIFFORD B Ulverston (Lancs) 30/3/1940. LHB, SLA. Played for Worcs 1960-82. Cap 1961. County captain 1971 to 1980. Benefit (£11,047) in 1974. *Wisden* 1974. Awarded MBE in 1978. Second benefit in 1981. Debut for Warwicks and cap 1983. England selector. Tests: 15 between 1964 and 1973. Played in one match for Rest of World v Australia 1971-72. Tours: International team to South Africa and Pakistan 1961-62. Worcs to South Africa 1964-65. Commonwealth to Pakistan 1970-71. Rest of World to Australia 1971-72. International Wanderers to South Africa 1972-73, India, Pakistan and Sri Lanka 1972-73. 100 wkts: (4) – 133 wkts (av. 19.66) in 1961 best. Hat-trick v Derby (Chesterfield) 1965. Took 4 wkts in 6 balls v Cambridge U (Cambridge) 1972. Gillette Man of Match Awards: 1. BH Gold Awards: 2. HS: 89 Worcs v Oxford U (Oxford) 1963. HSGC/NW: 38 Worcs v Warwicks (Lord's) 1966. HSJPL: 32* v Northants (Luton) 1983. HSBH: 33 Worcs v Kent (Lord's) 1973. BB: 8-28 Worcs v Yorks (Sheffield) 1968. BBTC: 5-55 v Pakistan (Karachi) 1972-73. BBGC/NW: 4-7 Worcs v Surrey (Worcester) 1972. BBJPL: 5-28 Worcs v Northants (Worcester) 1979. BBBH: 6-8 Worcs v Minor Counties (South) (High Wycombe) 1979. Appointed captain for 1985.

William HOGG B Ulverston (Lancs) 12/7/1955. RHB, RFM. Debut for Lancs 1976. Debut for Warwicks 1981. Did not play in 1984. HS: 31 v Hants (Birmingham) 1981. BB: 7-84 Lancs v Warwicks (Manchester) 1978. BBC: 4-46 v Northants (Northampton) 1981. BBJPL: 4-23 Lancs v Essex (Ilford) 1981. BBBH: 4-35 Lancs v Hants (Manchester) 1979.

Geoffrey William HUMPAGE (Golden Hillock CS, Birmingham) B Birmingham 24/4/1954. RHB, WK, RM. Debut 1974. Cap 1976. One-day Internationals: 3. 1,000 runs (7) – 1,891 (av. 48.48) in 1984 best. Scored 146 and 110 v Glos (Gloucester) 1981. BH Gold Awards: 2. HS: 254 v Lancs (Southport) 1982 sharing in English record 4th wkt partnership of 470 with A.I. Kallicharran. HSNW: 77 v Shropshire (Birmingham) 1984. HSJPL: 109* v Glos (Birmingham) 1984. HSBH: 100* v Scotland (Birmingham) 1984. BBJPL: 4-53 v Glos (Moreton-in-Marsh) 1979.

Alvin Isaac KALLICHARRAN (Port Mourant Comp Inst) B Port Mourant, Berbice, British Guiana 21/3/1949. LHB, OB. 5ft 4ins tall. Played for Guyana 1966-67 to 1980-81. Debut for county 1971. Cap 1972. Played for Queensland in 1977-78 and for Transvaal in 1981-82 to date. *Wisden* 1982. Benefit 1983. Tests: 66 for West Indies between 1971-72 and 1980-81 scoring 100* and 101 in first two innings in Tests v New Zealand and captaining country in 9 Tests. One-day Internationals: 31 for West Indies. Tours: West Indies to England 1973, 1976 and 1980, World XI in Pakistan 1973-74, India, Sri Lanka and Pakistan 1974-75, Australia 1975-76, India and Sri Lanka 1978-79 (captain), Australia and New Zealand 1979-80, Pakistan 1980-81, West Indies XI in South Africa 1982-83. 1,000 runs (10) – 2,301 (av. 52.29) in 1984 best. Also scored 1,249 runs (av. 56.77) on 1974-75 tour. NW Man of the Match: 3. BH Gold Awards: 3. HS: 243* v Glamorgan (Birmingham) 1983. HSTC: 187 West Indies v India (Bombay) 1978-79. HSNW: 206 v Oxfordshire (Birmingham) 1984 (Competition record). HSJPL: 102* v Notts (Birmingham) 1981. HSBH: 122* v Northants (Northampton) 1984. BB: 4-48 v Derby (Birmingham) 1978. BBNW: 6-32 v Oxfordshire (Birmingham) 1984.

Christopher LETHBRIDGE (Normanton County Secondary) B Castleford (Yorks) 23/6/1961. RHB, RM. Debut 1981 taking wicket of G. Boycott with his first ball in first-class cricket. HS: 87* v Somerset (Taunton) 1982. HSNW: 19 v Kent (Birmingham) 1984. HSJPL: 57* v Somerset (Birmingham) 1982. HSBH: 13* v Lancs (Manchester) 1982. BB: 5-68 v Glamorgan (Cardiff) 1982. BBJPL: 5-47 v Northants (Birmingham) 1982. BBBH: 3-49 v Northants (Birmingham) 1982.

Timothy Andrew LLOYD (Oswestry BHS; Dorset CHE) B Oswestry (Shropshire) 5/11/1956. LHB, RM. Debut 1977. Played for Orange Free State in 1978-79 and 1979-80. Cap 1980. One-day Internationals: 3. NW Man of the Match: 2. BH Gold Awards: 2. 1,000 runs (4) – 1,673 (av. 45.21) in 1983 best. HS: 208* v Glos (Birmingham) 1983. HSGC/NW: 81 v Devon (Birmingham) 1980. HSJPL: 90 v Kent (Birmingham) 1980. HSBH: 77 v Somerset (Birmingham) 1984.

Gordon John LORD (Warwick School) B Birmingham 25/4/1961. LHB, SLA. Debut 1983. HS: 61 v Notts (Nottingham) 1983. HSJPL: 40 v Notts (Birmingham) 1983.

William MORTON B Stirling, Scotland 21/4/1961. LHB, SLA. Debut for Scotland 1982. Debut for Warwicks 1984. HS: 13* v Surrey (Birmingham) 1984. HSJPL: 10 v Kent (Birmingham) 1984. HSBH: 11* Scotland v Glos (Glasgow) 1983. BB: 4-40 Scotland v Ireland (Downpatrick) 1983. BBC: 4-85 v Glamorgan (Birmingham) 1984. BBBH: 3-17 Scotland v Glos (Glasgow) 1983.

Christopher Middleton OLD (Acklam Hall SGS, Middlesbrough) B Middlesbrough 22/12/1948. LHB, RFM. Debut for Yorks 1966. Brother of A.G.B. Old (Warwicks). Cap 1969. *Wisden* 1978. Benefit (£32,916) in 1979. County Captain 1981. Replaced in 1982 and joined Warwicks 1983. Cap 1984. Played for Northern Transvaal in 1981-82 and 1982-83. Tests: 46 between 1972-73 and 1981. Played in 2 matches against Rest of World 1970. One-day Internationals: 32. Tours: Duke of Norfolk to West Indies 1969-70, India, Pakistan and Sri Lanka 1972-73, West Indies 1973-74 and 1980-81, Australia and New Zealand 1974-75, International Wanderers to South Africa 1975-76, India, Sri Lanka and Australia 1976-77, Pakistan and New Zealand 1977-78, Australia 1978-79, SAB XI to South Africa 1981-82. Banned from Test cricket for 3 years. Scored century in 37 minutes v Warwicks (Birmingham) 1977 – third fastest ever in first-class cricket. Took 4 wickets in 5 balls, England v Pakistan (Birmingham) 1978. BH Gold Awards: 4 (3 for Yorks). HS: 116 Yorks v Indians (Bradford) 1974. HSTC: 65 v Pakistan (Oval) 1974. HSNW: 55* Yorks v Worcs (Leeds) 1982. HSJPL: 82 Yorks v Somerset (Bath) 1974 and 82* v Somerset (Glastonbury) 1976. HSBH: 78* Yorks v Scotland (Bradford) 1981. BB: 7-20 Yorks v Glos (Middlesbrough) 1969. BBTC: 7-50 v Pakistan (Birmingham) 1978. BBGC/NW: 4-9 Yorks v Durham (Middlesbrough) 1978. BBJPL: 5-33 Yorks v Sussex (Hove) 1971. BBBH: 5-19 v Scotland (Birmingham) 1984.

Gladstone Cleophas SMALL (Moseley School, Birmingham) B St. George, Barbados 18/10/1961. RHB, RFM. Toured New Zealand with D.H. Robins' XI in 1979-80 and made debut v Northern Districts (Hamilton). Debut for county 1980. Toured Pakistan with International XI 1981-82. Cap 1982. HS: 57* v Oxford U (Oxford) 1982. HSNW: 33 v Surrey (Lord's) 1982. HSJPL: 40* v Essex (Ilford) 1984. HSBH: 19* v Yorks (Birmingham) 1981. BB: 7-68 v Yorks (Birmingham) 1982. BBNW: 3-22 v Glamorgan (Cardiff) 1982. BBJPL: 5-29 v Surrey (Birmingham) 1980. BBBH: 3-41 v Leics (Leicester) 1984.

Continued on page 242.

149

County Averages

Britannic Assurance County Championship: Played 24, won 6, drawn 11, lost 7.
All first-class matches: Played 26, won 7, drawn 12, lost 7.

BATTING AND FIELDING

Cap		M	I	NO	RUNS	HS	Avge	100	50	Ct	St
1965	D.L. Amiss	26	50	10	2239	122	55.97	6	14	16	—
1972	A.I. Kallicharran	26	50	6	2304	200*	52.29	9	7	17	—
1976	G.W. Humpage	26	47	8	1891	205	48.48	5	9	55	11
1980	T.A. Lloyd	6	11	0	418	110	38.00	1	3	3	—
—	R.I.H.B. Dyer	18	36	2	1187	106*	34.91	1	9	7	—
1983	A.M. Ferreira	26	39	13	777	76*	29.88	—	4	12	—
—	P.A. Smith	23	41	4	1040	89	28.10	—	8	10	—
—	C. Lethbridge	15	17	3	324	46	23.14	—	—	6	—
—	C.M. Old	18	21	4	393	70	23.11	—	2	8	—
1982	G.C. Small	24	30	8	400	41*	18.18	—	—	6	—
1978	K.D. Smith	21	40	1	692	93	17.74	—	3	3	—
—	M. Asif Din	6	9	2	99	35*	14.14	—	—	2	—
—	G.J. Lord	4	6	0	83	55	13.83	—	1	3	—
1972	R.G.D. Willis	5	3	2	13	5	13.00	—	—	2	—
—	N. Gifford	25	24	10	146	28*	10.42	—	—	10	—
—	S. Wall	7	9	4	47	19	9.40	—	—	1	—
—	W. Morton	8	8	2	39	13*	6.50	—	—	3	—

Played in one match: G.A. Tedstone 0* (1 ct, 1 st); D.A. Thorne 49, 20* (1 ct).

BOWLING

	Type	O	M	R	W	Avge	Best	5 wI	10 wM
A.M. Ferreira	RM	772.1	156	2208	79	27.94	6-70	1	—
G.C. Small	RFM	643.4	127	2027	71	28.54	5-41	2	—
C.M. Old	RFM	496	134	1306	45	29.02	6-46	3	1
N. Gifford	SLA	812.4	238	1919	65	29.52	6-83	2	—
C. Lethbridge	RM	279.5	42	987	30	32.90	4-35	—	—
W. Morton	SLA	189.5	45	549	14	39.21	4-85	—	—
P.A. Smith	RFM	194.4	23	839	20	41.95	4-41	—	—
R.G.D. Willis	RF	128	27	380	9	42.22	2-19	—	—
S. Wall	RFM	140.4	28	545	9	60.55	2-65	—	—

Also bowled: M. Asif Din 11.3-1-55-5; R.L.H.B. Dyer 5-0-39-0; G.W. Humpage 14-0-57-2; A.I. Kallicharran 10-5-12-0; T.A. Lloyd 8-2-41-1; D.A. Thorne 3-1-9-0.

County Records

First-class cricket

Highest innings	For	657-6d v Hants (Birmingham)	1899
totals:	Agst	887 by Yorks (Birmingham)	1896
Lowest innings	For	16 v Kent (Tonbridge)	1913

totals:	Agst	15 by Hants (Birmingham)	1922
Highest individual innings:	For	305* F.R. Foster v Worcs (Dudley)	1914
	Agst	316 R.H. Moore for Hants (Bournemouth)	1937
Best bowling in an innings:	For	10-41 J.D. Bannister v Combined Services (Birmingham)	1959
	Agst	10-36 H. Verity for Yorks (Leeds)	1931
Best bowling in a match:	For	15-76 S. Hargreave v Surrey (Oval)	1903
	Agst	17-92 A.P. Freeman for Kent (Folkestone)	1932
Most runs in a season:		2,417 (av. 60.42) M.J.K. Smith	1959
runs in a career:		33,862 (av. 36.18) W.G. Quaife	1894-1928
100s in a season:		9 by A.I. Kallicharran	1984
100s in a career:		71 by W.G. Quaife	1894-1928
wickets in a season:		180 (av. 15.13) W.E. Hollies	1946
wickets in a career:		2,201 (av 20.45) W.E. Hollies	1932-1957

RECORD WICKET STANDS

1st	377*	N.F. Horner & K. Ibadulla v Surrey (Oval)	1960
2nd	465*	J.A. Jameson & R.B. Kanhai v Glos (Birmingham)	1974
3rd	327	S. P. Kinneir & W.G. Quaife v Lancs (Birmingham)	1901
4th	470	A.I. Kallicharran & G.W. Humpage v Lancs (Southport)	1982
5th	268	Walter Quaife & W.G. Quaife v Essex (Leyton)	1900
6th	220	H.E. Dollery & J. Buckingham v Derby (Derby)	1938
7th	250	H.E. Dollery & J.S. Ord v Kent (Maidstone)	1953
8th	228	A.J.W. Croom & R.E.S. Wyatt v Worcs (Dudley)	1925
9th	154	G.W. Stephens & A.J.W. Croom v Derby (Birmingham)	1925
10th	128	F.R. Santall & W. Sanders v Yorks (Birmingham)	1930

One-day cricket

Highest innings totals:	Gillette Cup/ NatWest Trophy	392-5 v Oxfordshire (Birmingham)	1984
	John Player League	301-6 v Essex (Colchester)	1982
	Benson & Hedges Cup	291-5 v Lancs (Manchester)	1981
Lowest innings totals:	Gillette Cup/ NatWest Trophy	109 v Kent (Canterbury)	1971
	John Player League	65 v Kent (Maidstone)	1979
	Benson & Hedges Cup	96 v Leics (Leicester)	1972
Highest individual innings:	Gillette Cup/ NatWest Trophy	206 A.I. Kallicharran v Oxfordshire (Birmingham)	1984
	John Player League	123* J.A. Jameson v Notts (Nottingham)	1973
	Benson & Hedges Cup	122* A.I. Kallicharran v Northants (Northampton)	1984
Best bowling figures	Gillette Cup/ NatWest Trophy	6-32 K. Ibadulla v Hants (Birmingham)	1965
		6-32 A.I. Kallicharran v Oxfordshire (Birmingham)	1984
	John Player League	5-13 D.J. Brown v Worcs (Birmingham)	1970
	Benson & Hedges Cup	7-32 R.G.D. Willis v Yorks (Birmingham)	1981

WORCESTERSHIRE

Formation of present club: 1865.
Colours: Dark Green and Black.
Badge: Shield, *Argent*, bearing *Fess* between three *Pears Sable*.
County Champions (3): 1964, 1965 and 1974.
Gillette Cup Finalists (2): 1963 and 1966.
NatWest Trophy Second Round: 1981, 1982 and 1984.
John Player League Champions: 1971.
Benson & Hedges Cup Finalists (2): 1973 and 1976.
Gillette Man of the Match Awards: 18.
NatWest Man of the Match Awards: 2.
Benson & Hedges Gold Awards: 28.

Secretary: M.D. Vockins, County Ground, New Road, Worcester WR2 4QQ.
Captain: P.A. Neale.
Prospects of Play Telephone No: (0905) 422011.

David Andrew BANKS (Pensnett SM; Dudley TC) B Brierley Hill, Staffordshire 11/1/1965. RHB, RM. Debut 1983 scoring 100 v Oxford University (Oxford). HS: 100 (see before). HSJPL: 23 v Essex (Chelmsford) 1984.

Timothy Stephen CURTIS (Royal GS, Worcester; Durham U, Cambridge U) B Chislehurst (Kent) 15/1/1960. RHB, LB, Debut 1979. Cambridge Blue 1983. Cap 1984. Scored 1,405 runs (av. 42.57) in 1984. NW Man of the Match: 1. HS: 129 v Cambridge U (Worcester) 1984. HSNW: 54* v Suffolk (Worcester) 1984. HSJPL: 75* v Kent (Worcester) 1984. HSBH: 44 v Derby (Worcester) 1984.

Damian Basil D'OLIVEIRA (Blessed Edward Oldcome Secondary) B Cape Town, South Africa 19/10/1960. RHB, RM/OB. Son of Basil D'Oliveira (England and Worcs). Debut 1982. NW Man of the Match: 1. BH Gold Award: 1. HS: 102 v Middlesex (Worcester) 1983. HSNW: 48 v Notts (Worcester) 1983. HSJPL: 51* v Lancs (Manchester) 1983. HSBH: 57 v Derby (Worcester) 1984. BBJPL: 3-23 v Derby (Derby) 1983.

Ricardo McDonald ELLCOCK (Malvern College) B Bridgetown, Barbados 17/6/1965. RHB, RFM. Debut 1982 aged 17 years 86 days. Played for Barbados 1983-84. HS: 45* v Essex (Worcester) 1984. HSBH: 12 v Notts (Nottingham) 1984. BB: 4-34 v Glamorgan (Worcester) 1984. BBNW: 3-49 v Notts (Worcester) 1983. BBJPL: 4-43 v Kent (Canterbury) 1983.

Graeme Ashley HICK B Salisbury, Rhodesia 23/5/1966. RHB, OB. Debut for Zimbabwe 1983-84. Debut for Worcs 1984. Tour: Zimbabwe to Sri Lanka 1983-84. HS: 82* v Surrey (Oval) 1984. BB: 3-39 Zimbabwe v Sri Lanka Board Presidents XI (Moratuwa) 1983-84.

David John HUMPHRIES (Bridgnorth SM; Wulfrun College, Wolverhampton) B Alveley (Shropshire) 6/8/1953. LHB, WK. Debut for Leics 1974. Debut for Worcs 1977. Cap 1978. Gillette Man of Match: 1. HS: 133* v Derby (Worcester) 1984. HSGC/NW: 58 v Glamorgan (Worcester) 1977. HSJPL: 62 v Notts (Dudley) 1977. HSBH: 41 v Yorks (Leeds) 1982.

Richard Keith ILLINGWORTH (Salts GS) B Bradford, Yorks 23/8/1963. RHB, SLA. Debut 1982. HS: 55 v Leics (Hereford) 1983. HSNW: 22 v Northants (Northampton) 1984. HSJPL: 21 v Middlesex (Worcester) 1982. HSBH: 11* v Leics (Worcester) 1983. BB: 5-26 v Glos (Worcester) 1983. BBJPL: 5-24 v Somerset (Worcester) 1983. BBBH: 3-24 v Leics (Worcester) 1983.

John Darling INCHMORE (Ashington GS; St. Peters CE, Birmingham) B Ashington (Northumberland) 22/2/1949. RHB, RFM. Debut 1973. Cap 1976. Played for Northern Transvaal in 1976-77. Benefit 1985. BH Gold Awards: 2. HS: 113 v Essex (Worcester) 1974. HSNW: 32* v Yorks (Leeds) 1982. HSJPL: 45 v Northants (Worcester) 1981 and 45 v Derby (Chesterfield) 1981. HSBH: 49* v Somerset (Taunton) 1976. BB: 8-58 v Yorks (Worcester) 1977. BBNW: 4-47 v Yorks (Leeds) 1982. BBJPL: 4-9 v Northants (Dudley) 1975. BBBH: 6-29 v Lancs (Manchester) 1984.

KAPIL DEV NIKHANJ (Punjab U) B Chandigarh, India 6/1/1959. RHB, RFM. Debut for Haryana in Ranji Trophy 1975-76 aged 16 years 10 months taking 6-39 in debut match v Punjab (Rohtak). Debut for Northants 1981. Joined Worcs 1984. *Wisden* 1982. Tests: 62 for India between 1978-79 and 1983-84. Captain in 8 Tests. One-day Internationals: 47 for India. Tours: India to England 1979, Australia and New Zealand 1980-81, West Indies 1982-83. Is youngest player to take 100 wkts in Test cricket (21 years 25 days) and score 1,000 runs (21 years 27 days). Took 100 wkts in 1 year 107 days to beat record held previously by I.T. Botham. Hat-trick North Zone v West Zone (Delhi) 1978-79. HS: 193 Haryana v Punjab (Chandigarh) 1979-80. HSTC: 126* India v West Indies (Delhi) 1978-79. HSUK: 120 v Somerset (Weston-super-Mare) 1983. HSC: 95 v Hants (Worcester) 1984. HSJPL: 75 v Derby (Milton Keynes) 1982. HSBH: 49 Northants v Lancs (Manchester) 1983. BB: 9-83 India v West Indies (Ahmedabad) 1983–84. BBUK: 5-30 v Somerset (Worcester) 1984. BBJPL: 3-20 v Middlesex (Lord's) 1984.

Collis Llewellyn KING B Barbados 11/6/1951. RHB, RM. Played for Barbados 1972-73 to 1981-82, Glamorgan 1977, D.B. Close's XI 1982. Debut for Worcs 1983. Tests: 9 for West Indies between 1976 and 1980. One-day Internationals: 18. Tours: West Indies to England 1976 and 1980; Australia and New Zealand 1979-80, International XI to Pakistan 1981-82; West Indians in South Africa 1982-83. Scored 1,320 runs (av. 55.00) in 1976. HS: 163 West Indians v Northants (Northampton) 1976. HSTC: 100* West Indians v New Zealand (Christchurch) 1979-80. HSC: 123 v Somerset (Worcester) 1983. HSJPL: 127 v Surrey (Guildford) 1983. HSBH: 61 v Minor Counties (Worcester) 1984. BB: 5-91 Barbados v Jamaica (Bridgetown) 1975-76.

Philip Anthony NEALE (Frederick Gough GS; John Leggot SFC; Leeds U) B Scunthorpe (Lincs) 5/6/1954. RHB, RM. Debut 1975. Cap 1978. Captain 1983. 1,000 runs (6) – 1,706 (av. 47.38) in 1984 best. HS: 183* v Notts (Worcester) 1979. HSGC/NW: 68 v Glos (Bristol) 1976. HSJPL: 102 v Northants (Luton) 1982. HSBH: 128 v Lancs (Manchester) 1980. Soccer for Lincoln City.

Philip John NEWPORT (Royal GS, High Wycombe; Portsmouth Polytechnic) B High Wycombe, Buckinghamshire 11/10/1962. RHB, RFM. Debut 1982. HS: 41* v Warwicks (Birmingham) 1983. HSNW: 25 v Northants (Northampton) 1984. HSJPL: 24 v Northants (Wellingborough) 1984. BB: 5-51 v Warwicks (Worcester) 1984. BBJPL: 3-20 v Somerset (Taunton) 1984.

WORCESTERSHIRE

Dipak Narshibhai PATEL (George Salter Comprehensive, West Bromwich) B Nairobi, Kenya 25/10/1958. Has lived in UK since 1967. RHB, OB. Debut 1976. Cap 1979. Tour: D.H. Robins to New Zealand 1979-80. 1,000 runs (4) – 1,615 (av. 38.45) in 1983 best. Shared in 6th wkt partnership record for county, 227 with E.J.O. Hemsley v Oxford U (Oxford) 1976. BH Gold Awards: 2. HS: 197 v Cambridge U (Worcester) 1984. HSNW: 42 v Derby (Derby) 1981. HSJPL: 125 v Hants (Southampton) 1982. HSBH: 90* v Lancs (Manchester) 1984. BB: 7-46 v Lancs (Worcester) 1982. BBNW: 4-22 v Suffolk (Worcester) 1984. BBJPL: 5-27 v Northants (Worcester) 1983. BBBH: 3-42 v Yorks (Worcester) 1980.

Alan Paul PRIDGEON (Summerhill Secondary, Kingswinford) B Wall Heath (Staffs) 22/2/1954. RHB, RM. Debut 1972. Cap 1980. HS: 67 v Warwicks (Worcester) 1984. HSGC/NW: 13* v Somerset (Taunton) 1980. HSJPL: 17 v Kent (Worcester) 1982. HSBH: 13* v Leics (Worcester) 1982. BB: 7-35 v Oxford U (Oxford) 1976. BBGC/NW: 3-25 v Somerset (Taunton) 1980. BBJPL: 6-26 v Surrey (Worcester) 1978. BBBH: 3-57 v Warwicks (Birmingham) 1976. Soccer for Ledbury Town in West Midland League.

Neal Victor RADFORD (Athlone Boys HS, Johannesburg) B Luanshya, Northern Rhodesia (now Zambia) 7/6/1957. RHB, RFM. Played for Transvaal 1978-79 to 1983-84. Debut for Lancs 1980. Joined Worcs for 1985. HS: 76* Lancs v Derbyshire (Blackpool) 1981. HSNW: 14 v Durham (Chester-le-Street) 1983. HSJPL: 48* v Glamorgan (Cardiff) 1981. HSBH: 14 Lancs v Middlesex (Lord's) 1983. BB: 6-41 Transvaal B v Griqualand West (Kimberley) 1980-81. BBUK: 5-107 Lancs v Notts (Nottingham) 1981. BBNW: 3-20 v Middlesex (Manchester) 1981. BBJPL: 3-16 Lancs v Hants (Manchester) 1981.

David Mark SMITH (Battersea GS) B Balham 9/1/1956. LHB, RM. Debut for Surrey 1973 aged 17 years 4 months whilst still at school. Cap 1980. Debut for Worcs and cap 1984. 1,000 runs (2) – 1,093 (av. 42.03) in 1984 best. NW Man of the Match: 1. BH Gold Award: 1. HS: 189* v Kent (Worcester) 1984. HSNW: 103* v Northants (Oval) 1984. HSJPL: 87* v Hants (Oval) 1980. HSBH: 45* Surrey v Northants (Northampton) 1979 and 45* v Hants (Oval) 1980. BB: 3-40 v Sussex (Oval) 1976. BBGC/NW: 3-39 v Derby (Ilkeston) 1976. BBBH: 4-29 Surrey v Kent (Oval) 1980.

Martin John WESTON (Samuel Southall SM) B Worcester 8/4/1959. RHB, RM. Debut 1979. Scored 1,061 runs (av. 27.92) in 1984. HS: 145* v Northants (Worcester) 1984. HSNW: 23 v Yorks (Leeds) 1982. HSJPL: 109 v Somerset (Taunton) 1982. HSBH: 56 v Scotland (Aberdeen) 1983. BB: 4-44 v Northants (Wellingborough) 1984. BBNW: 4-30 v Suffolk (Worcester) 1984. BBJPL: 4-24 v Kent (Worcester) 1984.

N.B. The following players whose particulars were included in the 1984 Annual have been omitted: M.S.A. McEvoy, P. Moores, J.A. Ormrod, A.E. Warner and S.G. Watkins.

County Averages

Britannic Assurance County Championship: Played 24, won 5, drawn 14, lost 5.
All first-class matches: Played 26, won 6, drawn 15, lost 5.

BATTING AND FIELDING

Cap		M	I	NO	RUNS	HS	Avge	100	50	Ct	St
1978	P.A. Neale	25	43	7	1706	143	47.38	2	11	9	—
—	Kapil Dev	12	19	4	640	95	42.66	—	6	10	—
1984	T.S. Curtis	22	36	3	1405	129	42.57	3	8	13	—
—	D.M. Smith	17	31	5	1093	189*	42.03	2	6	12	—
1979	D.N. Patel	25	41	1	1348	197	33.70	2	7	11	—
—	P.J. Newport	10	11	5	187	40*	31.16	—	—	2	—
—	P. Moores	4	4	2	61	44	30.50	—	—	7	4
1978	D.J. Humphries	22	32	9	644	133*	28.00	2	2	37	7
—	M.J. Weston	24	41	3	1061	145*	27.92	1	7	15	—
—	R.M. Ellcock	9	8	3	134	45*	26.80	—	—	1	—
—	R.K. Illingworth	21	20	7	346	43*	26.61	—	—	9	—
—	D.B. D'Oliveira	23	34	3	796	74	25.67	—	5	17	—
1976	J.D. Inchmore	23	24	8	295	34	18.43	—	—	10	—
—	D.A. Banks	6	9	0	132	43	14.66	—	—	3	—
—	M.S.A. McEvoy	10	13	0	188	46	14.46	—	—	11	—
1980	A.P. Pridgeon	24	23	7	211	67	13.18	—	1	14	—
—	A.E. Warner	8	7	2	62	27	12.40	—	—	5	—

Played in one match: G.A. Hick 82* (1 ct).

BOWLING

	Type	O	M	R	W	Avge	Best	5 wI	10 wM
M.J. Weston	RM	123.4	29	315	14	22.50	4-44	—	—
Kapil Dev	RFM	296.3	75	819	35	23.40	5-30	2	—
R.M. Elcock	RF	221.2	32	714	29	24.62	4-34	—	—
A.P. Pridgeon	RM	719.5	168	1949	66	29.53	5-50	2	—
P.J. Newport	RFM	204.4	36	689	21	32.80	5-51	1	—
J.D. Inchmore	RFM	497	110	1364	44	31.00	4-37	—	—
R.K. Illingworth	SLA	744	220	1872	57	32.84	5-32	2	—
D.N. Patel	OB	770	219	2063	61	33.81	5-28	2	—
D.B. D'Oliveira	RM/OB	113	24	341	10	34.10	2-50	—	—
A.E. Warner	RFM	186	33	632	15	42.13	5-27	1	—

Also bowled: D.A. Banks 4-0-17-0; T.S. Curtis 3.3-0-22-0; G.A. Hick 6-0-27-0;
P.A. Neale 1.3-0-11-0; D.M. Smith 6-0-22-1.

County Records
First-class Cricket

Highest innings	For	633 v Warwicks (Worcester)	1906
totals:	Agst	701-4d by Leics (Worcester)	1906
Lowest innings	For	24 v Yorks (Huddersfield)	1903
totals:	Agst	30 by Hants (Worcester)	1903
Highest indi-	For	311* by G.M. Turner v Warwicks (Worcester)	1982
vidual innings:	Agst	311* J.D. Robertson for Middlesex (Worcester)	1949
Best bowling	For	9-23 C.F. Root v Lancs (Worcester)	1931
in an innings:	Agst	10-51 J. Mercer for Glamorgan (Worcester)	1936
Best bowling	For	15-87 A.J. Conway v Glos (Moreton-in-Marsh)	1914
in a match:	Agst	17-212 J.C. Clay for Glamorgan (Swansea)	1937
Most runs in a season:		2654 (av. 52.03) H.H.I. Gibbons	1934
runs in a career:		34490 (av. 34.04) D. Kenyon	1946-1967
100s in a season:		10 by G.M. Turner	1970
100s in a career:		72 by G.M. Turner	1967-1982
wickets in a season:		207 (av. 17.52) C.F. Root	1925
wickets in a career:		2143 (av. 23.73) R.T.D. Perks	1930-1955

RECORD WICKET STANDS

1st	309	F.L. Bowley & H.K. Foster v Derby (Derby)	1901
2nd	274	H.H.I Gibbons & Nawab of Pataudi v Kent (Worcester)	1933
		H.H.I Gibbons & Nawab of Pataudi v Glam (Worcester)	1934
3rd	314	M.J. Horton & T.W. Graveney v Somerset (Worcester)	1962
4th	281	J.A. Ormrod & Younis Ahmed v Notts (Nottingham)	1979
5th	393	E.G. Arnold & W.B. Burns v Warwicks (Birmingham)	1909
6th	227	E.J.O. Hemsley & D.N. Patel v Oxford U (Oxford)	1976
7th	197	H.H.I. Gibbons & R. Howorth v Surrey (Oval)	1938
8th	145*	F. Chester & W.H. Taylor v Essex (Worcester)	1914
9th	181	J.A. Cuffe & R.D. Burrows v Glos (Worcester)	1907
10th	119	W.B. Burns & G.A. Wilson v Somerset (Worcester)	1906

One-day Cricket

Highest innings:	GC/NatWest Trophy	286-5 v Yorks (Leeds)	1982
	John Player League	307-4 v Derby (Worcester)	1975
	Benson & Hedges Cup	314-5 v Lancs (Manchester)	1980
Lowest innings	Gillette Cup	98 v Durham	
totals:	NatWest Trophy	(Chester-le-Street)	1968
	John Player League	86 v Yorks (Leeds)	1969
	Benson & Hedges Cup	92 v Oxford & Cambridge	
		Universities (Cambridge)	1975
Highest indi-	Gillette Cup/	117* G.M. Turner v	
vidual innings:	NatWest Trophy	Lancs (Worcester)	1971
	John Player League	147 G.M. Turner v Sussex	
		(Horsham)	1980
	Benson & Hedges Cup	143* G.M. Turner v	
		Warwicks (Birmingham)	1976
Best bowling	Gillette Cup/	6-14 J.A. Flavell v Lancs	
figures:	NatWest Trophy	(Worcester)	1963
	John Player League	6-26 A.P. Pridgeon v Surrey	
		(Worcester)	1978
	Benson & Hedges Cup	6-8 N. Gifford v Minor Cos.	
		(South) (High Wycombe)	1979

YORKSHIRE

Formation of present club: 1863, reorganised 1891.
Colours: Oxford blue, Cambridge blue, and gold.
Badge: White rose.
County Champions (31): 1867, 1870, 1893, 1896, 1898, 1900, 1901, 1902, 1905, 1908, 1912, 1919, 1922, 1923, 1924, 1925, 1931, 1932, 1933, 1935, 1937, 1938, 1939, 1946, 1959, 1960, 1962, 1963, 1966, 1967, and 1968.
Joint Champions (2): 1869 and 1949.
Gillette Cup Winners (2): 1965 and 1969.
NatWest Trophy Semi-Finalists: 1982.
John Player League Winners: 1983.
Benson & Hedges Cup Finalists: 1972.
Fenner Trophy Winners: 1972, 1974 and 1981.
Gillette Man of the Match Awards: 14.
NatWest Man of the Match Awards: 3.
Benson & Hedges Gold Awards: 33.

Secretary: J. Lister, Headingley Cricket Ground, Leeds LS6 3BU.
Captain: D.L. Bairstow.

David Leslie BAIRSTOW (Hanson GS, Bradford) B Bradford 1/9/1951. RHB, WK, RM. Debut 1970. Cap 1973. Played for Griqualand West 1976-77 and 1977-78 (captain). Benefit 1982. County captain 1984. Tests: 4 between 1979 and 1980-81. One-day Internationals: 21. Tours: Australia 1979-80, West Indies 1980-81. 1,000 runs (2) – 1,102 (av. 38.00) in 1983 best. Dismissed 11 batsmen (all ct) for Yorks v Derby (Scarborough) 1982 equalling world record for most catches in a match. NW Man of the Match: 1. BH Gold Awards: 5. HS: 145 v Middlesex (Scarborough) 1980. HSTC: 59 v India (Oval) 1979. HSNW: 92 v Worcs (Leeds) 1982. HSJPL: 78 v Surrey (Scarborough) 1981. HSBH: 103* v Derby (Derby) 1981. BB: 3-82 Griqualand West v Transvaal B (Johannesburg) 1976-77. Soccer for Bradford City.

Paul Anthony BOOTH (Hanley HS) B Huddersfield 5/9/1965. LHB, SLA. Debut 1982 aged 17 years 3 days. HS: 26 v Worcs (Scarborough) 1984. BB: 3-22 v Northants (Northampton) 1984.

Geoffrey BOYCOTT (Hemsworth GS) B Fitzwilliam (Yorks) 21/10/1940. RHB, RM. Plays in contact lenses. Debut for Yorks 1962. Cap 1963. *Wisden* 1964. County captain 1971 to 1978. Played for Northern Transvaal in 1971-72. Benefit (£20,639) in 1974. Awarded OBE in 1980. Tests: 108 between 1964 and 1981-82 captaining England in 4 Tests in 1977-78. Played in 2 matches against Rest of World in 1970. One-day Internationals: 36. Tours: South Africa 1964-65, Australia and New Zealand 1965-66 and 1970-71 (returned home early through broken arm injury), West Indies 1967-68, 1973-74 and 1980-81, Ceylon 1969-70, Pakistan and New Zealand 1977-78 (vice-captain), Australia 1978-79, Australia and India 1979-80, India and Sri Lanka 1981-82, SAB to South Africa 1981-82. Banned for 3 years from Test cricket. 1,000 runs (22) – 2,503 runs (av. 100.12 in 1971 best. Only English batsmen ever to have an average of 100 for season and repeated the feat in 1979 with, 1,538 runs (av. 102.53). Also scored 1,000 runs in South Africa 1964-65 (1,135 runs, av. 56.75), West Indies 1967-68 (1,154, av. 82.42), Australia 1970-71 (1,535 runs, av. 95.93). Scored 103 and 105 v Notts (Sheffield) 1966 and 160* and 116

YORKSHIRE

England v The Rest (Worcester) 1974. Completed 40,000 runs in 1981-82 and scored his 100th century in Leeds Test of that year – only player to have done so in a Test match. Scored 155 v India (Birmingham) 1979 to become the second batsman to have scored a century in a Test on all six grounds in this country. Gillette Man of Match: 2. BH Gold Awards: 9. HS: 261* MCC v President's XI (Bridgetown) 1973-74. HSUK: 260* v Essex (Colchester) 1970. HSTC: 246* v India (Leeds) 1967. HSGC/NW: 146 v Surrey (Lord's) 1965. HSJPL: 108* v Northants (Huddersfield) 1974. HSBH: 142 v Worcs (Worcester) 1980. BB: 4-14 v Lancs (Leeds) 1979. BBTC: 3-47 England v South Africa (Cape Town) 1964-65. BBJPL: 3-15 v Middlesex (Hull) 1983. Testimonial 1984.

Philip CARRICK (Bramley CS; Intake CS; Park Lane CPE) B Armley, Leeds 16/7/1952. RHB, SLA. Debut 1970. Cap 1976. Played for Eastern Province in 1976-77 and for Northern Transvaal in 1982-83. Benefit 1985. Tours: D.H. Robins to South Africa 1975-76 and Sri Lanka 1977-78. HS: 131* v Northants (Northampton) 1980. HSNW: 37 v Shropshire (Telford) 1984. HSJPL: 43* v Surrey (Oval) 1984. HSBH: 24 v Warwicks (Birmingham) 1984. BB: 8-33 v Cambridge U (Cambridge) 1973. BBNW: 3-27 v Northants (Leeds) 1983. BBJPL: 4-13 v Derby (Bradford) 1983. BBBH: 3-40 v Warwicks (Birmingham) 1984.

Simon John DENNIS (Scarborough College) B Scarborough 18/10/1960. Nephew of Sir Leonard Hutton and F. Dennis, former Yorkshire player. RHB, LFM. Debut 1980. Played for Orange Free State 1982-83. Cap 1983. HS: 53* v Notts (Nottingham) 1984. HSNW: 14 v Shropshire (Telford) 1984. HSJPL: 16* v Glamorgan (Cardiff) and Derby (Bradford) 1983. HSBH: 10 v Warwicks (Birmingham) 1984. BB: 5-35 v Somerset (Sheffield) 1981. BBJPL: 3-19 v Hants (Middlesbrough) 1981. BBBH: 3-41 v Northants (Bradford) 1984.

Stuart David FLETCHER (Reins Wood Secondary) B Keighley 8/6/1964. RHB, RFM. Debut 1983. HS: 28* v Kent (Tunbridge Wells) 1984. BB: 4-24 v Somerset (Maidstone) 1984.

Stuart Neil HARTLEY (Beekfoot GS, Bingley; Cannington High, Perth, WA) B Shipley (Yorks) 18/3/1956. RHB, RM. Debut 1978. Acted as captain in a number of matches in 1981. Cap 1981. Played for Orange Free State in 1981-82 and 1982-83. BH Gold Award: 1. HS: 114 v Glos (Bradford) 1982. HSNW: 58 v Worcs (Leeds) 1982. HSJPL: 73 v Warwicks (Scarborough) 1984. HSBH: 65* v Warwicks (Birmingham) 1984. BB: 3-40 v Glos (Sheffield) 1980. BBJPL: 3-31 v Notts (Scarborough) 1980. BBBH: 4-39 v Scotland (Perth) 1984.

Paul William JARVIS (Bydales CS, Marske) B Redcar 29/6/1965. RHB, RFM. Debut 1981 aged 16 years 75 days. Hat-trick in JPL v Derby (Derby) 1982. HS: 37 v Surrey (Oval) 1984. BB: 6-61 v Lancs (Manchester) 1984. BBJPL: 4-28 v Glamorgan (Leeds) 1984.

James Derek LOVE (Brudenell County Secondary, Leeds) B Leeds 22/4/1955. RHB, RM. Debut 1975. Cap 1980. One-day Internationals: 3. 1,000 runs (2) – 1,203 (av. 33.41) in 1981 best. BH Gold Awards: 2. HS: 170* v Worcs (Worcester) 1979. HSGC/NW: 61* v Hants (Southampton) 1980. HSJPL: 90 v Derby (Chesterfield) 1979. HSBH: 118* v Scotland (Bradford) 1981.

Ashley Anthony METCALFE (Bradford GS; University College, London) B

Horsforth 25/12/1963. RHB, OB. Debut 1983 scoring 122 v Notts (Bradford). HS: 122 as before. HSJPL: 115* v Glos (Scarborough) 1984.

Martyn Douglas MOXON (Holgate GS, Barnsley) B Barnsley 4/5/1960. RHB, RM. Debut 1981 scoring 116 in second innings of debut match. Played for Griqualand West in 1982-83 and 1983-84. Cap 1984. NW Man of the Match: 1. BH Gold Award: 1. Scored 1,034 runs (av. 35.65) in 1984. HS: 153 v Lancs (Leeds) 1983. HSNW: 78* v Essex (Leeds) 1982. HSJPL: 77 v Kent (Canterbury) 1984. HSBH: 79 v Sussex (Hove) 1984.

Stephen OLDHAM (High Green SM) B High Green, Sheffield, Yorks 26/7/1948. RHB, RFM. Played for Yorkshire 1974-79. Debut and cap for Derby 1980. Rejoined Yorks 1984. BH Gold Award: 1 (for Yorks). HS: 50 v Sussex (Hove) 1979. HSNW: 19 v Shropshire (Telford) 1984. HSJPL: 38* v Glamorgan (Cardiff) 1977. BB: 7-78 Derby v Warwicks (Birmingham) 1982. BBC: 5-40 v Surrey (Oval) 1978. BBNW: 3-29 Derby v Notts (Derby) 1981. BBJPL: 5-37 Derby v Lancs (Derby) 1982. BBBH: 5-32 v Minor Counties (North) (Scunthorpe) 1975.

Steven John RHODES (Carlton-Bolling School, Bradford) B Bradford 17/6/1964. Son of W.E. Rhodes (Notts 1961 to 1964). RHB, WK. Debut 1981 aged 17 years 35 days. HS: 35 v Somerset (Maidstone) 1984.

Phillip Edward ROBINSON (Greenhead GS, Keighley) B Keighley, Yorks. RHB, LM. Debut 1984. HS: 92 v Glamorgan (Bradford) 1984. HSJPL: 39 v Derby (Chesterfield) 1984.

Kevin SHARP (Abbey Grange CEHS, Leeds) B Leeds 6/4/1959. LHB, OB. Debut 1976. Played for Griqualand West in 1981-82 to date. Cap 1982. Scored 1,445 runs (av. 39.05) in 1984. Tour: D.H. Robins to New Zealand 1979-80. HS: 173 v Derby (Chesterfield) 1984: HSGC/NW: 25 v Middlesex (Lord's) 1979. HSJPL: 74 v Hants (Bournemouth) 1984. HSBH: 87* v Northants (Bradford) 1984.

Christopher SHAW (Crofton HS) B Hemsworth, Yorks 17/2/1964. RHB, RFM. Debut 1984. HS: 17 v Worcs (Scarborough) 1984. HSJPL: 26 v Glamorgan (Leeds) 1984. BB: 4-68 v Middlesex (Lord's) 1984. BBJPL: 5-41 v Hants (Bournemouth) 1984.

Arnold SIDEBOTTOM (Broadway GS, Barnsley) B Barnsley 1/4/1954. RHB, RFM. Debut 1973. Cap 1980. Played for Orange Free State 1981-82 and 1983-84. HS: 124 v Glamorgan (Cardiff) 1977. HSGC/NW: 45 v Hants (Bournemouth) 1977. HSJPL: 52* v Northants (Middlesbrough) 1982. HSBH: 32 v Notts (Leeds) 1983. BB: 7-18 v Oxford U (Oxford) 1980. BBGC/NW: 4-35 v Kent (Leeds) 1980. BBJPL: 4-24 v Surrey (Scarborough) 1975. BBBH: 3-21 v Minor Counties (North) (Jesmond) 1979. Soccer for Manchester United, Huddersfield Town and Halifax Town.

Graham Barry STEVENSON (Minsthorpe HS) B Ackworth 16/12/1955. RHB, RM. Debut 1973. Cap 1978. Tests: 2 in 1979-80 and 1980-81. One-day Internationals: 4. NW Man of the Match: 1. BH Gold Award: 1. Tours: Australia and India 1979-80 (flown out as a replacement for M. Hendrick), West Indies 1980-81. HS: 115* v Warwicks (Birmingham) 1982. HSTC: 27* v India (Bombay) 1979-80. HSNW: 34 v Northants (Leeds) 1983. HSJPL: 81* v Somerset (Middlesbrough) 1984. HSBH: 36 v Warwicks (Leeds) 1984. BB: 8-57 v Northants (Leeds) 1980. BBTC: 3-111 v

YORKSHIRE

West Indies (St. John's) 1980-81. BBNW: 5-27 v Berkshire (Reading) 1983. BBJPL: 5-41 v Leics (Leicester) 1976. BBBH: 5-28 v Kent (Canterbury) 1978.

Ian Geoffrey SWALLOW (Hayford Kirk Comprehensive, Balk; Barnsley TC) B Barnsley 18/12/1962. RHB, OB. Debut 1983. HS: 34* v Somerset (Maidstone) 1984. BB: 4-52 v Kent (Tunbridge Wells) 1984.

NB. The following player whose figures appeared in the 1984 Annual has been omitted: R.G. Lumb.

County Averages

Britannic Assurance County Championship: Played 24, won 5, drawn 15, lost 4.

BATTING AND FIELDING

Cap		M	I	NO	RUNS	HS	Avge	100	50	Ct	St
1963	G. Boycott	20	35	10	1567	153*	62.68	4	9	13	—
—	P.E. Robinson	15	24	5	756	92	39.78	—	6	7	—
1982	K. Sharp	24	39	2	1445	173	39.05	3	8	17	—
1973	D.L. Bairstow	22	26	5	787	94	37.47	—	7	39	7
1984	M.D. Moxon	18	31	3	1016	126*	36.28	2	6	19	—
1974	R.G. Lumb	10	17	2	534	165*	35.60	2	1	6	—
1980	A. Sidebottom	19	22	6	511	54*	31.93	—	2	1	—
—	S. Oldham	8	6	3	85	22	28.33	—	—	2	—
1980	J.D. Love	15	23	2	568	112	27.04	1	3	7	—
1981	S.N. Hartley	13	21	4	437	104*	25.70	1	1	2	—
—	I.G. Swallow	11	9	3	136	34*	22.66	—	—	9	—
1983	S.J. Dennis	9	9	4	104	53*	20.80	—	1	1	—
1976	P. Carrick	22	28	5	400	47*	17.39	—	—	13	—
—	A.A. Metcalfe	9	13	0	216	60	16.61	—	2	5	—
—	P.W. Jarvis	12	14	4	157	37	15.70	—	—	2	—
1978	G.B. Stevenson	14	16	1	180	27	12.00	—	—	5	—
—	C. Shaw	3	5	2	32	17	10.66	—	—	—	—
—	S.D. Fletcher	8	5	1	35	28*	8.75	—	—	—	—
—	P.A. Booth	10	13	3	78	26	7.80	—	—	2	—

Played in two matches: S.J. Rhodes 6*, 35 (3 ct).

BOWLING

	Type	O	M	R	W	Avge	Best	5 wI	10 wM
A. Sidebottom	RFM	479.1	103	1265	63	20.07	6-41	3	—
S.D. Fletcher	RFM	162	35	471	14	33.64	4-24	—	—
P.W. Jarvis	RFM	304	53	1115	32	34.84	6-61	2	—
P. Carrick	SLA	665.5	219	1606	44	36.50	6-32	3	1
S.J. Dennis	LFM	277.2	48	953	25	38.12	5-124	1	—
S. Oldham	RFM	244.5	57	703	18	39.05	4-59	—	—
I.G. Swallow	OB	229.1	62	620	15	41.33	4-52	—	—
P.A. Booth	SLA	347	124	749	17	44.05	3-22	—	—
G.B. Stevenson	RM	262.3	44	892	19	46.94	4-35	—	—

Also bowled: D.L. Bairstow 11-1-39-0; G. Boycott 11-0-25-0; S.N. Hartley 93-13-359-6; R.G. Lumb 1-0-5-0; M.D. Moxon 98-19-327-4; P.E. Robinson 2-0-12-0; K. Sharp 71-18-229-7; C. Shaw 53.4-5-177-5.

County Records

First-class cricket

Highest innings totals:	For	887 v Warwicks (Birmingham)	1896
	Agst	630 by Somerset (Leeds)	1901
Lowest innings totals:	For	23 v Hants (Middlesbrough)	1965
	Agst	13 by Notts (Nottingham)	1901
Highest individual innings:	For	341 G.H. Hirst v Leics (Leicester)	1905
	Agst	318* W.G. Grace for Glos (Cheltenham)	1876
Best bowling in an innings:	For	10-10 H. Verity v Notts (Leeds)	1932
	Agst	10-37 C.V. Grimmett for Australians (Sheffield)	1930
Best bowling in a match:	For	17-91 H. Verity v Essex (Leyton)	1933
	Agst	17-91 H. Dean for Lancs (Liverpool)	1913
Most runs in a season:		2883 (av. 80.08) H. Sutcliffe	1932
Most runs in a career:		38561 (av. 50.21) H. Sutcliffe	1919-1945
100s in a season:		12 by H. Sutcliffe	1932
100s in a career:		112 by H. Sutcliffe	1919-1945
wickets in a season:		240 (av. 12.72) W. Rhodes	1900
wickets in a career:		3608 (av. 16.00) W. Rhodes	1898-1930

RECORD WICKET STANDS

1st	555	P. Holmes & H. Sutcliffe v Essex (Leyton)	1932
2nd	346	W. Barber & M. Leyland v Middlesex (Sheffield)	1932
3rd	323*	H. Sutcliffe & M. Leyland v Glamorgan (Huddersfield)	1928
4th	312	G.H. Hirst & D. Denton v Hants (Southampton)	1914
5th	340	E. Wainwright & G.H. Hirst v Surrey (Oval)	1899
6th	276	M. Leyland & E. Robinson v Glamorgan (Swansea)	1926
7th	254	D.C.F. Burton & W. Rhodes v Hants (Dewsbury)	1919
8th	292	Lord Hawke & R. Peel v Warwicks (Birmingham)	1896
9th	192	G.H. Hirst & S. Haigh v Surrey (Bradford)	1898
10th	149	G. Boycott & G.B. Stevenson v Warwicks (Birmingham)	1982

One-day cricket

Highest innings totals:	Gillette Cup/ NatWest Trophy	317-4 v Surrey (Lord's)	1965
	John Player League	257-4 v Hants (Middlesbrough)	1983
	Benson & Hedges Cup	273-8 v Warwicks (Leeds)	1984
Lowest innings totals:	Gillette Cup/ NatWest Trophy	76 v Surrey (Harrogate)	1970
	John Player League	74 v Warwicks (Birmingham)	1972
	Benson & Hedges Cup	114 v Kent (Canterbury)	1978
Highest individual innings:	Gillette Cup/ NatWest Trophy	146 G. Boycott v Surrey (Lord's)	1965
	John Player League	119 J.H. Hampshire v Leicestershire (Hull)	1971
	Benson & Hedges Cup	142 G. Boycott v Worcs (Worcester)	1980
Best bowling figures:	Gillette Cup/ NatWest Trophy	6-15 F.S. Trueman v Somerset (Taunton)	1965
	John Player League	7-15 R.A. Hutton v Worcs (Leeds)	1969
	Benson & Hedges Cup	6-27 A.G. Nicholson v Minor Counties (North) (Middlesbrough)	1972

VALETE

The following players appeared for counties in 1984 but at the time of going to press were not expected to play in 1985. Their records are included to bring them up to date and in case they do re-appear.

Terrance Michael ALDERMAN (Aquinas College, Perth). B Subiaco, Western Australia 12/6/1956. RHB, RFM. Debut for Western Australia 1974-75. Debut for Kent 1984. Tests: 19 for Australia between 1981 and 1983-84. One-day Internationals: 18 for Australia. Tours: Australians to England 1981, New Zealand 1981-82, Pakistan 1982-83, West Indies 1983-84. *Wisden* 1981. HS: 52* v Sussex (Hastings) 1984. HSTC: 21* Australia v West Indies 1983-84. HSJPL: 11 v Lancs (Maidstone) 1984. BB: 7-28 Western Australia v New South Wales (Perth) 1981-82. BBTC: 6-135 Australia v England (Leeds) 1984. BBNW: 4-21 v Hants (Southampton) 1984. BBJPL: 5-36 v Lancs (Maidstone) 1984.

Martin John BAMBER (Carshalton HS; Millfield) B Cheam, Surrey 7/1/1961. RHB, RM. Debut for Northants 1982. HS: 77 v Cambridge U (Cambridge) 1983. HSJPL: 71 v Surrey (East Molesey) 1983. HSBH: 40 v Yorks (Bradford) 1984.

Dennis BREAKWELL (Ounsdale Comprehensive, Wombourne) B Brierley Hill, Staffs 2/7/1948. LHB, SLA. Played for Northants 1969-1972. Debut for Somerset 1973. Cap 1976. HS: 100* v New Zealanders (Taunton) 1978. HSGC/NW: 19* v Essex (Westcliff) 1974. HSJPL: 44* v Notts (Nottingham) 1976. HSBH: 36* v Glamorgan (Taunton) 1979. BB: 8-39 Northants v Kent (Dover) 1970. BBC: 6-38 v Oxford U (Oxford) 1981. BBJPL: 4-10 Northants v Derby (Northampton) 1970.

Colin Roy COOK (Merchant Taylor's School, Northwood) B Edgware 11/1/1960. RHB. Debut for Middlesex 1981. HS: 79 v Lancs (Southport) 1981 in debut match. HSJPL: 73 v Glos (Lord's) 1981.

Ian James CURTIS (Whitgift School and Oxford) B Purley 13/5/1959. LHB, SLA/SLC. Debut for Oxford U 1980. Blue 1980 and 1982. Debut for Surrey 1983. HS: 20* Oxford U v Warwicks (Oxford) 1982. BB: 6-28 v Oxford U (Oxford) 1983.

Christopher Stephen DALE B Canterbury, Kent 15/12/1961. RHB, OB. Debut for Glos 1984. HS: 49 v Yorks (Bradford) 1984. BB: 3-10 v Oxford U (Oxford) 1984.

Winston Walter DAVIS B St. Vincent 18/9/1958. RHB, RFM. Debut for Combined Islands 1979-80. Windward Islands 1981-82. Tours: Young West Indies to Zimbabwe 1981-82. Debut for Glamorgan 1982. BH Gold Award: 1. Tests: 9 for West Indies between 1982-83 and 1984. One-day Internationals: 12 for West Indies. HS: 77 West Indies v England (Manchester) 1984. HSC: 50 v Notts (Nottingham) 1984. BB: 7-70 v Notts (Ebbw Vale) 1983. BBTC: 3-21 West Indies v India (Ahmedabad) 1983-84. BBNW: 3-26 Glamorgan v Norfolk (Norwich) 1983. BBJPL: 4-24 Glamorgan v Derby (Derby) 1982. BBBH: 5-29 Glamorgan v Middlesex (Cardiff) 1984.

Peter William DENNING (Millfield School) B Chewton Mendip (Somerset) 16/12/1949. LHB, OB. Debut for Somerset 1969. Cap 1973. 1,000 runs (6) – 1,222 runs (av. 42.13) in 1979 best. Scored 122 and 107 v Glos (Taunton) 1977. Shared in 4th wkt partnership record for county, 310 with I.T. Botham v Glos (Taunton) 1980. Benefit 1981. Gillette Man of Match: 4. BH Gold Awards: 3. HS: 184 v Notts

(Nottingham) 1980. HSGC/NW: 145 v Glamorgan (Cardiff) 1978. HSJPL: 112* v Warwicks (Birmingham) 1982. HSBH: 129 v Glos (Taunton) 1982.

Richard James DOUGHTY (Scarborough College) B Bridlington, Yorkshire 17/11/1960. RHB, RM. Debut for Glos 1981. HS: 32* v Worcs (Bristol) 1983. HSJPL: 50* v Kent (Bristol) 1983. HSBH: 31 v Essex (Chelmsford) 1984. BB: 6-43 v Glamorgan (Bristol) 1982. BBJPL: 3-34 v Somerset (Bristol) 1982.

Kevin St John Dennis EMERY (St. Joseph's Comprehensive, Swindon; Bristol U) B Swindon, Wiltshire 28/11/1960, RHB, RFM. Debut for Hants 1982. HS: 18* v Derby (Derby) 1982. BB: 6-51 v Glamorgan (Portsmouth) 1982. BBJPL: 4-21 v Leics (Leicester) 1982. BBBH: 5-24 v Essex (Chelmsford) 1982.

David Arthur FRANCIS (Cwmtawe Comprehensive, Pontardawe) B Clydach 29/11/1953. RHB, OB. Debut for Glamorgan 1973. Cap 1982. 1,000 runs (1) – 1,076 (av. 38.42) in 1982. HS: 142* v Kent (Canterbury) 1982. HSGC/NW: 62* v Worcs (Worcester) 1977. HSJPL: 101* v Warwicks (Birmingham) 1980. HSBH: 59 v Warwicks (Birmingham) 1977.

Russell Christopher GREEN B St Alban's, Herts 30/7/1959. RHB, RFM. Debut for Glamorgan 1984.

John Harry HAMPSHIRE (Oakwood Technical HS, Rotherham) B Thurnscoe, Yorks 10/2/1941. Son of J. Hampshire (Yorks 1937). RHB, LB. Played for Yorks 1961-81. Cap 1963. Captain 1979-80. Debut for Derby and cap 1982. Played for Tasmania in 1967-68, 1968-69, 1977-78 and 1978-79. Benefit (£28,425) in 1976. Tests: 8 between 1969 and 1975. Scored 107 on debut v West Indies (Lord's). One-day Internationals: 3. Tours: Cavaliers in West Indies 1964-65; Commonwealth in Pakistan 1967-68; MCC in Ceylon 1969-70; MCC in Australia and New Zealand 1970-71, D.H. Robins in South Africa 1972-73, and West Indies 1974-75, Leics XI in Zimbabwe 1980-81. 1,000 runs (15) – 1,596 (av. 53.20) in 1978 best. Gillette Man of the Match: 4. Benson & Hedges Gold Awards: 3. HS: 183* Yorks v Sussex (Hove) 1971. HSTC: 107 v West Indies (Lord's) 1969. HSGC/NW: 110 Yorks v Durham (Middlesbrough) 1978. HSJPL: 119 Yorks v Leics (Hull) 1971. HSBH: 85 Yorks v Warwicks (Leeds) 1980. BB: 7-52 Yorks v Glamorgan (Cardiff) 1963.

Rupert William HANLEY (Grey HS; St. Andrew's College, Grahamstown) B Port Elizabeth 29/1/1952. RHB, RF. Son of A.W.D. Hanley (Border). Played for Eastern Province in 1970-71 and 1972-73 to 1974-75, Orange Free State in 1975-76 and Transvaal 1976-77 to date. Debut for Northants 1984. Played for D.H. Robins XI v Warwicks (Northampton) 1984. HS: 33* v Warwicks (Northampton) 1984. BB: 6-27 Orange Free State v Transvaal B (Stilfontein) 1975-76. BBUK: 6-21 v Lancs (Southport) 1984. BBJPL: 4-50 v Somerset (Northampton) 1984. BBBH: 3-37 v Scotland (Northampton) 1984.

Frank Charles HAYES (De la Salle College, Salford; Sheffield U) B Preston 6/12/1946. RHB, RM. Debut for Lancs 1970 scoring 94 and 99 in first two matches. Cap 1972. County Captain 1978 to 1980. Tests: 9 between 1973 and 1976. One-day Internationals: 6. Tours: D.H. Robins to South Africa 1972-73 and 1975-76, West Indies 1973-74, International Wanderers to South Africa 1975-76, International team to Pakistan 1981-82. Also played for Overseas XI v Board President's XI (Calcutta) 1980-81. 1,000 runs (6) – 1,311 runs (av. 35.43) in 1974 best. Scored 34 in one over (6 4 6 6 6 6) off M.A. Nash v Glamorgan (Swansea) 1977. Benefit 1983. Gillette Man of the Match Awards: 1. BH Gold Awards: 2. HS: 187 v Indians

(Manchester) 1974. HSTC: 106* v West Indies (Oval) 1973 in second innings on Test debut. HSGC/NW: 93 v Warwickshire (Birmingham) 1976. HSJPL: 87 v Essex (Manchester) 1982. HSBH: 102 v Minor Counties (North) (Manchester) 1973. Amateur soccer player.

Michael Donald HAYSMAN (Brighton HS; Adelaide). B Adelaide, Australia 22/4/1961. RHB, OB. Debut for South Australia v Queensland (Adelaide) scoring 106. Debut for Leics 1984. Tour: Young Australians to Zimbabwe 1982-83. HS: 153 South Australia v Victoria (Melbourne) 1982-83. HSUK: 102* v Cambridge U (Cambridge) 1984. HSBH: 28* v Scotland (Glasgow) 1984.

Michael HENDRICK B Darley Dale (Derbyshire) 22/10/1948. RHB, RFM. Played for Derbyshire 1969 to 1981. Cap 1972. *Wisden* 1977. Benefit (£36,050) in 1980. Debut for Notts 1982. Tests: 30 between 1974 and 1981. Tours: West Indies 1973-74. Australia and New Zealand 1974-75, D.H. Robins to South Africa 1975-76, Pakistan and New Zealand 1977-78, Australia 1978-79, Australia (returned home early through injury) 1979-80. SAB to South Africa 1981-82. Banned from Test cricket for 3 years. Hat-trick Derby v West Indians (Derby) 1980. Gillette Man of the Match: 1 (for Derby). BH Gold Awards: 3 (for Derby). HS: 46 Derby v Essex (Chelmsford) 1973. HSTC: 15 v Australia (Oval) 1977. HSNW: 18 v Worcs (Worcester) 1983. HSJPL: 21 Derby v Warwicks (Buxton) 1974. HSBH: 32 Derby v Notts (Chesterfield) 1973. BB: 8-45 Derby v Warwicks (Chesterfield) 1973. BBTC: 4-28 v India (Birmingham) 1974. BBGC/NW: 4-15 Derby v Middlesex (Chesterfield) 1975. BBJPL: 6-7 Derby v Notts (Nottingham) 1972. BBBH: 6-33 v Northants (Northampton) 1982.

Mervyn Gregory HUGHES B Euroa, Victoria, Australia 23/11/1961. RHB, RFM. Debut for Victoria 1981-82. Debut for Essex 1983. HS: 17 Victoria v New South Wales (St Kilda) 1981-82. HSUK: 10 v New Zealanders (Chelmsford) 1983. BB: 4-69 Victoria v Queensland (Geelong) 1981-82. BBUK: 4-71 v New Zealanders (Chelmsford) 1983.

Eifion Wyn JONES B Swansea 25/6/1942. Brother of A. Jones. RHB, WK. Debut for Glamorgan 1961. Cap 1967. Benefit 1975 (£17,000). Tour: Glamorgan in West Indies 1969-70. BH Gold Award: 1. HS: 146* v Sussex (Hove) 1968. HSGC/NW: 67* v Herts (Swansea) 1969. HSJPL: 48 v Hants (Cardiff) 1971. HSBH: 39* v Minor Counties (West) (Amersham) 1977.

Roger David Verdon KNIGHT (Dulwich College and Cambridge) B Streatham 6/9/1946. LHB, RM. Debut for Cambridge U 1967. Blue 1967-68-69-70. Debut for Surrey 1968. Debut for Glos 1971. Cap 1971. Debut for Sussex and Cap 1976. Rejoined Surrey 1978 as county captain. Cap 1978. Relinquished captaincy 1984. 1,000 runs (13) – 1,350 runs (av. 38.57) in 1974 best. Gillette Man of the Match: 5 (3 for Glos). BH Gold Awards: 5 (1 for Sussex, 2 for Glos). HS: 165* Sussex v Middlesex (Hove) 1976. HSC: 132 v Lancs (Oval) 1980. HSGC/NW: 75 Glos v Glamorgan (Cardiff) 1973. HSJPL: 127 Sussex v Hants (Hove) 1976. HSBH: 117 Sussex v Surrey (Oval) 1977. BB: 6-44 Glos v Northants (Northampton) 1974. BBC: 5-44 v Glos (Cheltenham) 1979. BBGC/NW: 5-39 Glos v Surrey (Bristol) 1971. BBJPL: 5-42 Sussex v Notts (Nottingham) 1977. BBBH: 3-19 Sussex v Surrey (Oval) 1977.

For players who have now joined another county, see page 168.

Barry John LLOYD (Llangatwg Comprehensive, Cadoxton, Bangor Normal College) B Neath 6/9/1953. RHB, OB. Debut for Glamorgan 1972. Cap 1982. HS: 48 v Sussex (Cardiff) 1982. HSNW: 12 v Warwicks (Cardiff) 1982. HSJPL: 32 v Northants (Northampton) 1983. HSBH: 28* v Somerset (Swansea) 1982. BB: 8-70 v Lancs (Cardiff) 1981. BBJPL: 3-22 v Derby (Derby) 1980. BBBH: 4-26 v Combined Universities (Cardiff) 1982.

Richard Graham LUMB (Mexborough GS; Percy Jackson GS) B Doncaster 27/2/1950. RHB, RM. Debut for Yorks 1970. Cap 1974. Benefit 1983. 1,000 runs (5) – 1,532 runs (av. 41.40) in 1975 best. HS: 165* v Glos (Bradford) 1984. HSGC/NW: 56 v Shropshire (Wellington) 1976. HSJPL: 101 v Notts (Scarborough) 1976. HSBH: 90 v Northants (Bradford) 1980.

Steven John MALONE (King's School, Ely) B Chelmsford 19/10/1953. RHB, RM. Debut for Essex 1975. Debut for Hants 1980. HS: 23 v Kent (Bournemouth) 1981. HSBH: 16 v Essex (Southampton) 1983. BB: 7-55 v Oxford U (Oxford) 1982. BBNW: 5-34 v Cheshire (Southampton) 1981. BBJPL: 4-39 v Yorks (Basingstoke) 1980. BBBH: 4-25 v Minor Counties (Bournemouth) 1983.

Michael Stephen Anthony McEVOY (Colchester RGS; Borough Road College) B Jorhat, Assam 25/1/1956. RHB, RM. Played for Essex 1976 to 1981. Debut for Worcs 1983. HS: 103 v Warwicks (Birmingham) 1983. HSJPL: 27* v Yorks (Bradford) 1984. HSBH: 24 v Glos (Gloucester) 1983. BB: 3-20 Essex v Middlesex (Lord's) 1981.

Steven Robert MEE (Ellis Guilford CS) B Nottingham 6/4/1965. RHB, RM. Debut for Notts 1984.

Peter MOORES (King Edward VI School, Macclesfield) B Macclesfield, Cheshire 18/12/1962. RHB, WK. Debut for Worcs 1983. HS: 45 v Somerset (Weston-super-Mare) 1984. HSJPL: 14* v Northants (Wellingborough) 1984.

Ian Roger PAYNE (Emanuel School) B Lambeth Hospital, Kennington 9/5/1958. RHB, RM. Debut for Surrey 1977. BH Gold Award: 1. HS: 43 v Essex (Oval) 1983. HSNW: 56* v Lincolnshire (Sleaford) 1983. HSJPL: 33* v Glamorgan (Swansea) 1983. BB: 5-13 v Glos (Oval) 1983. BBNW: 5-36 v Lincolnshire (Sleaford) 1983. BBJPL: 5-21 v Derby (Derby) 1982. BBBH: 3-20 v Leics (Oval) 1981.

Nicholas Edward Julian POCOCK (Shrewsbury School) B Maracaibo, Venezuela 15/12/1951. RHB, LM. Debut for Hants 1976. Captain 1980. Cap 1980. HS: 164 v Lancs (Southampton) 1982. HSGC/NW: 73* v Derby (Derby) 1980. HSJPL: 53* v Northants (Northampton) 1978. HSBH: 43* v Minor Counties (Bournemouth) 1983.

Elvis Leroy REIFER (St. George's School, Barbados) B St. Michael, Barbados 21/3/1961. LHB, LFM. Debut for Hants 1984. HS: 47 v Somerset (Southampton) 1984. HSJPL: 10* v Surrey (Oval) 1984. HSBH: 14* v Glos (Bristol) 1984. BB: 4-43 v Cambridge U (Cambridge) 1984. HSNW: 4-46 v Kent (Southampton) 1984. BBBH: 3-19 v Surrey (Oval) 1984.

Anderson Montgomery Everton ROBERTS (Princess Margaret School, Antigua) B Antigua 29/1/1951, RHB, RF. Played for Leeward Islands and Combined Islands from 1969-70 to date. Played for Hants 1973 to 1978. Cap 1974. *Wisden* 1974. Played for New South Wales in 1976-77. Debut for Leics 1981. Tests: 47 for West Indies between 1973-74 and 1983-84. One-day Internationals: 56 for West Indies.

Tours: West Indies to India, Sri Lanka and Pakistan 1974-75, Australia 1975-76, 1981-82, England 1976 and 1980, Australia and New Zealand 1979-80, India 1983-84. Took 100th wkt in Test cricket in 1976 in then record time of 2 years 142 days. Took 119 wkts (av. 13.62) in 1974. Hat-trick for Combined Islands v Jamaica (St Kitts) 1980-81. BH Gold Award: 1 (for Hants). HS: 89 v Glamorgan (Swansea) 1984. HSTC: 68 West Indies v India (Calcutta) 1983-84. HSNW: 46 v Somerset (Taunton) 1982. HSJPL: 59* v Somerset (Leicester) 1981. HSBH: 29 Hants v Glos (Bristol) 1975 and 29 v Surrey (Oval) 1981. BB: 8-47 Hants v Glamorgan (Cardiff) 1974. BBC: 8-56 v Glamorgan (Leicester) 1982. BBTC: 7-54 West Indies v Australia (Perth) 1975-76. BBGC/NW: 3-17 Hants v Glamorgan (Southampton) 1975. BBJPL: 5-13 Hants v Sussex (Hove) 1974. BBBH: 4-12 Hants v Somerset (Bournemouth) 1975.

Christopher James Castell ROWE (King's School, Canterbury) B Hong Kong 27/11/1951. RHB, OB. Played for Kent 1974 to 1981. Cap 1977. Joined Glamorgan 1982. Cap 1983. 1,000 runs (2) – 1,071 (av. 32.45) in 1982 best. HS: 147* Kent v Sussex (Canterbury) 1979. HSC: 105 v Somerset (Taunton) 1982. HSNW: 30 v Notts (Swansea) 1984. HSJPL: 81 Kent v Somerset (Canterbury) 1980. HSBH: 54 v Somerset (Swansea) 1982. BB: 6-46 Kent v Derby (Dover) 1976. BBC: 4-29 v Notts (Ebbw Vale) 1993. BBJPL: 5-32 Kent v Worcs (Worcester) 1976.

Michael Walter William SELVEY (Battersea GS, Manchester U, Cambridge U) B Chiswick 25/4/1948. RHB, RFM. Played for Surrey 1968 and 1971, Cambridge U (Blue) 1971, Middlesex 1972-82. Cap 1973. Transferred to Glamorgan as captain 1983. Cap 1983. Played for Orange Free State 1973-74. Tours: India, Sri Lanka and Australia 1976-77, Middlesex in Zimbabwe 1980-81, International XI in Pakistan 1981-82. 101 wkts (av. 19.09) in 1978. BH Gold Award: 1. HS: 67 Middlesex v Zimbabwe (Bulawayo) 1980-81. HSUK: 63 v Essex (Cardiff) 1983. HSGC/NW: 14 Middlesex v Derby (Derby) 1978. HSJPL: 38* Middlesex v Essex (Chelmsford) 1979. HSBH: 27* Middlesex v Surrey (Lord's) 1973. BB: 7-20 Middlesex v Glos (Gloucester) 1976. BBC: 6-47 v Oxford U (Oxford) 1983. BBGC/NW: 3-32 Middlesex v Somerset (Lord's) 1977. BBJPL: 5-18 Middlesex v Glamorgan (Cardiff) 1975. BBBH: 5-39 Middlesex v Glos (Lord's) 1972.

David Stanley STEELE (Enden SM) B Stoke-on-Trent 29/9/1941. Elder brother of J.F. Steele of Leics and cousin of B.S. Crump, former Northants player. Wears glasses. RHB, SLA. Debut for Northants 1963. Cap 1965. Benefit (£25,500) in 1975. *Wisden* 1975. Transferred to Derbyshire in 1979 as county captain. Relinquished post during season. Cap 1979. Rejoined Northants 1982. Tests: 8 in 1975 and 1976. One-day Internationals: 1. Tours: D.H. Robins to South Africa 1975-76, Leics to Zimbabwe 1980-81. 1,000 runs (10) – 1,756 (av. 48.77) in 1975 best. Hat-trick v Glamorgan (Derby) 1980. Had match double of 100 runs and 10 wkts (130, 6-36 and 5-39) v Derbyshire (Northampton) 1978. Gillette Man of the Match: 1. NW Man of the Match: 1 (for Derbyshire). HS: 140* v Worcs (Worcester) 1971. HSTC: 106 v West Indies (Nottingham) 1976. HSGC/NW: 109 v Cambs (March) 1975. HSJPL: 76 v Sussex (Hove) 1974. HSBH: 71 Derby v Notts (Nottingham) 1980. BB: 8-29 v Lancs (Northampton) 1966. BBNW: 3-23 Derby v Suffolk (Bury St. Edmunds) 1981. BBJPL: 4-21 Derby v Notts (Derby) 1979. BBBH: 4-35 v Warwicks (Northampton) 1984.

Robert William TAYLOR B Stoke-on-Trent 17/7/1941. RHB, WK, RM. Debut 1960 for Minor Counties v South Africans. Debut for Derby 1961. Cap 1962. Captain 1975-76. Testimonial (£6,672) 1973 and 1981. *Wisden* 1976. MBE 1981. Tests: 57 between 1970-71 and 1983-84. Tours: Ceylon 1969-70, Australia and New Zealand 1970-71, 1974-75 and 1982-83, Rest of the World in Australia 1971-72,

West Indies 1973-74, International Wanderers in South Africa 1975-76, Pakistan and New Zealand 1977-78, Australia 1978-79, Australia and India 1979-80, India and Sri Lanka 1981-82, New Zealand and Pakistan 1983-84. Dismissed 7 batsmen in an innings (equals Test record) and 10 batsmen in match (all caught) for Test record v India (Bombay) 1979-80. Dismissed 10 batsmen in a match (all ct) v Hants (Chesterfield) 1963 and 7 in an innings (all ct) v Glamorgan (Derby) 1966. Broke world record for dismissals by a wicket-keeper in 1982-83. Gillette Man of the Match: 1. Benson & Hedges Gold Award: 1. HS: 100 v Yorks (Sheffield) 1981. HSTC: 97 v Australia (Adelaide) 1978-79. HSGC/NW: 53* v Middlesex (Lord's) 1975. HSJPL: 43* v Glos (Burton-on-Trent) 1969. HSBH: 31* v Hants (Southampton) 1976.

Colin John TUNNICLIFFE B Derby 11/8/1951. RHB, LFM. Debut for Derby 1973. Cap 1977. Hat-trick in JPL v Worcs (Derby) 1979. HS: 91 v Hants (Portsmouth) 1983. HSNW: 14* v Northants (Lord's) 1981. HSJPL: 51* v Northants (Milton Keynes) 1982. HSBH: 28 v Warwicks (Birmingham) 1979. BB: 7-36 v Essex (Chelmsford) 1980. BBNW: 5-50 v Worcs (Worcester) 1981. BBJPL: 5-24 v Northants (Derby) 1981. BBBH: 5-24 v Yorks (Derby) 1981.

Robert George Dylan WILLIS (Guildford RGS) B Sunderland 30/5/1949. RHB, RF. Debut for Surrey 1969. Debut for Warwickshire in 1972. Cap 1972. *Wisden* 1977. County Captain 1980. Benefit 1981. Awarded MBE 1982. Tests: 90 between 1970-71 and 1983-84. Captain in 19 Tests. Has taken 325 Test wickets – the most for England. One-day Internationals: 64. Tours: Australia and New Zealand 1970-71 (flown out as replacement for A. Ward) and 1974-75, D.H. Robins to South Africa 1972-73. West Indies 1973-74 and 1980-81, India, Sri Lanka and Australia 1976-77, Pakistan and New Zealand 1977-78, Australia 1978-79, Australia and India 1979-80, India and Sri Lanka 1981-82, Australia 1982-83 (captain), New Zealand and Pakistan 1983-84. Hat-tricks (2) v Derby (Birmingham) 1972 and West Indies (Birmingham) 1976. Also in John Player League v Yorks (Birmingham) 1972. Gillette Man of the Match: 1 (for Surrey). BH Gold Awards: 5. HS: 72 v Indians (Birmingham) 1982. HSTC: 28* v Pakistan (Birmingham) 1982. HSGC/NW: 12* Surrey v Sussex (Oval) 1970. HSJPL: 52* v Derby (Birmingham) 1975. HSBH: 37 v Notts (Nottingham) 1982. BB: 8-32 v Glos (Bristol) 1977. BBTC: 8-43 v Australia (Leeds) 1981. BBGC/NW: 6-49 Surrey v Middlesex (Oval) 1970. BBJPL: 4-12 v Middlesex (Lord's) 1973. BBBH: 7-32 v Yorkshire (Birmingham) 1981. Played soccer (goalkeeper) for Guildford City.

Peter Hugh L'Estrange WILSON (Wellington College) B Guildford 17/8/1958. 6ft 5in tall. RHB. Played for Surrey 1978 to 1982. Joined Somerset 1983. Played for Northern Transvaal in 1979-80. HS: 29 Northern Transvaal v Transvaal (Pretoria) 1979-80. HSUK: 25 v Glos (Bristol) 1983. HSJPL: 18* Surrey v Worcs (Oval) 1979. BB: 5-36 Northern Transvaal v Eastern Province (Pretoria) 1979-80. BBUK: 4-39 Surrey v Warwicks (Oval) 1979. BBGC/NW: 3-59 Surrey v Essex (Colchester) 1978. BBJPL: 4-32 Surrey v Middlesex (Oval) 1979. BBBH: 5-21 Surrey v Combined Universities (Oval) 1979.

David John WOOD (Oathall CS) B Cuckfield, Sussex. LHB, SLA. Debut for Sussex 1984. HS: 15 v Surrey (Guildford) 1984.

Robert Andrew WOOLMER (Skinner's School) B Kanpur, India 14/5/1948. RHB, RM. Debut for Kent 1968. Cap 1970. *Wisden* 1975. Played for Natal between 1973-74 and 1975-76 and for Western Province in 1980-81. Benefit 1984. Tests: 19 between 1975 and 1981. One-day Internationals: 6. Tours: India, Sri Lanka and Australia 1976-77, SAB to South Africa 1981-82. Banned from Test cricket for 3 years. 1,000 runs (5) – 1,749 (av. 47.27) in 1976 best. Hat-trick for MCC v Australians (Lord's) 1975. Gillette Man of the Match Awards: 2. BH Gold Awards: 5. HS: 203 v Sussex (Tunbridge Wells) 1982. HSTC: 149 England v Australia (Oval) 1975. HSGC/NW: 91 v Yorks (Leeds) 1980. HSJPL: 112* v Notts (Nottingham) 1980. HSBH: 79* v Essex (Dartford) 1981. BB: 7-47 v Sussex (Canterbury) 1969. BBGC/NW: 4-28 v Somerset (Taunton) 1979. BBJPL: 6-9 v Derby (Chesterfield) 1979. BBBH: 4-14 v Sussex (Tunbridge Wells) 1972.

Syed Mohammad NASIR ZAIDI B Karachi 25/3/1961. RHB, LB. Debut for Lancs 1983. HS: 51 v Somerset (Manchester) 1983. BB: 3-27 v Sussex (Hove) 1983.

HAVE JOINED ANOTHER COUNTY

TO GLOUCESTERSHIRE

Brian Fettes DAVISON (Gifford HS, Rhodesia) B Bulawayo, Rhodesia 21/12/1946. RHB, RM. Played for Rhodesia 1967-68 to 1978-79. Debut for Leics 1970 after having played for International Cavaliers. Cap 1971. Captain in 1980. Played for Tasmania from 1979-80 to date. Benefit 1982. 1,000 (13) – 1,818 runs (av. 56.81) in 1976 best. Gillette Man of the Match: 1. NW Man of the Match: 1. BH Gold Awards: 6. HS: 189 Leics v Australians (Leicester) 1975. HSGC/NW: 99 Leics v Essex (Southend) 1977. HSJPL: 85* Leics v Glamorgan (Cardiff) 1974. HSBH: 158 Leics v Warwicks (Coventry) 1972. BB: 5-52 Rhodesia v Griqualand West (Bulawayo) 1967-68. BBUK: 4-99 Leics v Northants (Leicester) 1970. BBJPL: 4-29 Leics v Glamorgan (Neath) 1971. Has played hockey for Rhodesia.

TO SURREY

Trevor Edward JESTY (Privet County SM, Gosport) B Gosport 2/6/1948. RHB, RM. Debut for Hants 1966. Cap 1971. Played for Border in 1973-74 and Griqualand West in 1974-75, 1975-76 and 1980-81. Played for Canterbury in 1979-80. Benefit in 1982. *Wisden* 1982. Tours: Australia and New Zealand 1982-83. International XI in Jamaica 1982-83. One-day Internationals: 10. 1,000 runs (7) – 1,645 (av. 58.75) in 1982 best. Gillette Man of the Match: 3. NW Man of the Match: 2. BH Gold Awards: 7. HS: 187 v Derby (Derby) 1983. HSGC/NW: 118 v Derby (Derby) 1980. HSJPL: 166* v Surrey (Portsmouth) 1983. HSBH: 105 v Glamorgan (Swansea) 1977. BB: 7-75 v Worcs (Southampton) 1976. BBGC/NW: 6-46 v Glos (Bristol) 1979. BBJPL: 6-20 v Glamorgan (Cardiff) 1976. BBBH: 4-22 v Minor Counties (Southampton) 1981.

NOTTINGHAMSHIRE *Continued from page 129.*

Peter Mark SUCH (Harry Carlton Comprehensive) B Helensburgh, Scotland 12/6/1964. RHB, OB. Debut 1982. HS: 16 v Middlesex (Lord's) 1984. BB: 6-123 v Kent (Nottingham) 1983.

N.B. The following player whose figures appeared in the 1984 Annual has been omitted: M. Hendricks.

CAMBRIDGE UNIVERSITY

Captain: C.R. Andrew.

Christopher Robert ANDREW (Barnard Castle School and St. John's) B Richmond, Yorks 18/2/1963. LHB, OB. Debut and Blue 1984. HS: 101* v Notts (Nottingham) 1984. BB: 3-77 v Leics (Cambridge) 1984.

Martin Nicholas BREDDY (Cheltenham GS and Fitzwilliam) B Torquay, Devon 23/9/1961. RHB. Debut and Blue 1984. HS: 61 v Oxford U (Lord's) 1984.

Ian David BURNLEY (Hummersknott School; QE College, Darlington and Churchill) B Darlington, Co Durham 11/3/1963. RHB. Debut and Blue 1984. HS: 86 v Oxford U (Lord's) 1984.

Thomas Archibald COTTERELL (Downside and Peterhouse) B London 12/5/1963. RHB, SLA. Debut 1983. Blue 1983-84. HS: 52 v Notts (Nottingham) 1984. BB: 5-89 v Essex (Cambridge) 1983.

Andrew George DAVIES (Birkenhead School and Robinson) B Altrincham, Cheshire 5/5/1962. RHB, WK. Debut 1982. Blue 1984. HS: 69 v Surrey (Banstead) 1984.

Paul Lawrence GARLICK (Sherborne School and Jesus) B Chiswick, London 2/8/1964. RHB, RFM. Debut and Blue 1984.

Andrew Kenneth GOLDING (See Essex section).

Alexander David Hugh GRIMES (Tonbridge School and Pembroke) B Beirut, Lebanon 8/1/1965. RHB, RM. Debut and Blue 1984. HS: 13 v Surrey (Banstead) 1984.

Steven Guy Paul HEWITT (Bradford GS and Peterhouse) B Radcliffe, Lancs 6/4/1963. RHB, WK. Debut and Blue 1983. HS: 14* v Hants (Cambridge) 1984.

Antony Edward LEA (High Arcal School and Churchill) B Wolverhampton, Staffs 29/9/1962. RHB, LB. Debut and Blue 1984. HS: 119 v Essex (Cambridge) 1984.

Guy Francis Henry McDONNELL (Kevii School, Lytham and St. John's) B Lytham, Lancs 24/1/1963. LHB, OB. Debut 1984.

Ian George PECK (Bedford School and Magdalene) B Great Staughton, Hunts 18/10/1957. RHB. Debut for Cambridge U 1978. Blue and captain 1980-81. Debut for Northants 1980. HS: 49* v Hants (Cambridge) 1984. Rugby Blue.

Angus John POLLOCK (Shrewsbury and Trinity) B Liversedge, Yorks 19/4/1962. RHB, RM. Debut 1982. Blue 1982-83-84. Captain 1984. HS: 32 v Essex (Cambridge) 1984. BB: 5-107 v Worcs (Worcester) 1983. Soccer Blue.

CAMBRIDGE UNIVERSITY

David Gregory PRICE (Haberdashers' Aske's, Elstree and Homerton) B Luton, Beds 7/2/1965. RHB, OB. Debut and Blue 1984. HS: 49 v Warwicks (Cambridge) 1984.

Philip Charles RICHARDSON (Humphry Davy GS and Magdalene) B Paddington, London 12/6/1965. RHB, OB. Debut 1984.

Paul Gerrard Peter ROEBUCK (See Glos section).

Ian Edward Wakefield SANDERS (Cheltenham College; Bristol U and St. John's) B Edinburgh 26/2/1961. RHB, RFM. Debut 1984.

Shaw Naweed SIDDIQI (City of London School; St. Bartholomew's Hospital and Hughes Hall) B London 13/9/1959. RHB, RM. Debut 1984. HS: 52 v Sussex (Cambridge) 1984. BB: 5-90 v Warwicks (Cambridge) 1984.

Neill Peter THOMAS (Sevenoaks School and Downing) B Tenterden, Kent 26/5/1964. LHB, SLA. Debut 1984.

Timothy James TRAVERS (Wimbledon College and Churchill) B Wimbledon, Surrey 28/12/1962. RHB, OB. Debut 1984. HS: 15 v Warwicks (Cambridge) 1984.

University Records

Highest Innings	For	703-9d v Sussex (Hove)	1890
Totals:	Agst	703-3 by West Indians (Cambridge)	1950
Lowest Innings	For	30 v Yorks (Cambridge)	1928
Totals:	Agst	32 by Oxford U (Lord's)	1878
Highest Individual Innings:	For	254* K.S. Duleepsinhji v Middlesex (Cambridge)	1927
	Agst	304* E.D. Weekes for West Indies (Cambridge)	1950
Best Bowling in an Innings:	For	10-69 S.M.J. Woods v C.I. Thornton's XI (Cambridge)	1890
	Agst	10-38 S.E. Butler for Oxford U (Lord's)	1871
Best Bowling in a Match:	For	15-88 S.M.J. Woods v C.I. Thornton's XI (Cambridge)	1890
	Agst	15-95 S.E. Butler for Oxford U (Lord's)	1871
Most runs in a season:		1581 (av. 79.05) D.S. Sheppard	1952
runs in a career:		4310 (av.38.48) J.M. Brearley	1961-1968
100s in a season:		7 by D.S. Sheppard	1952
100s in a career:		14 by D.S. Sheppard	1950-1952
wickets in a season:		80 (av. 17.63) O.S. Wheatley	1958
wickets in a career:		208 (av. 21.82) G. Goonesena	1954-1957

RECORD WICKET STANDS

1st	349	J.G. Dewes & D.S. Sheppard v Sussex (Hove)	1950
2nd	429*	J.G. Dewes & G.H.G. Doggart v Essex (Cambridge)	1949
3rd	284	E.T. Killick & G.C. Grant v Essex (Cambridge)	1929
4th	275	R. de W.K. Winlaw & J.H. Human v Essex (Cambridge)	1934
5th	220	R. Subba Row & F.C.M. Alexander v Notts (Nottingham)	1953
6th	245	J.L. Bryan & C.T. Ashton v Surrey (Oval)	1921
7th	289	G. Goonesena & G.W. Cook v Oxford U (Lord's)	1957
8th	145	H. Ashton & A.E.R. Gilligan v Free Foresters (Cambridge)	1920
9th	200	G.W. Cook & C.S. Smith v Lancs (Liverpool)	1957
10th	177	A.E.R. Gilligan & J.H. Naumann v Sussex (Hove)	1919

CAMBRIDGE UNIVERSITY
Averages

All first-class matches: Played 10, Won 0, Drawn 3, Lost 7.

BATTING AND FIELDING

	M	I	NO	RUNS	HS	Avge	100	50	Ct	St
†I.D. Burnley	3	6	0	232	86	38.66	—	2	1	—
†A.G. Davies	7	14	5	308	69	34.22	—	3	9	2
†P.G.P. Roebuck	5	10	2	261	62	32.62	—	2	2	—
†C.R. Andrew	9	18	1	405	101*	23.82	1	1	2	—
†A.E. Lea	9	18	0	395	119	21.94	1	1	2	—
†D.G. Price	7	11	0	239	49	21.72	—	—	3	—
S.G.P. Hewitt	3	5	4	20	14*	20.00	—	—	3	1
S.N. Siddiqi	6	12	0	219	52	18.25	—	1	1	—
†M.N. Breddy	10	20	1	339	61	17.84	—	1	2	—
†T.A. Cotterell	10	16	1	247	52	16.46	—	1	3	—
†I.G. Peck	4	7	1	97	49*	16.16	—	—	2	—
†A.K. Golding	8	13	0	189	44	14.53	—	—	2	—
†A.J. Pollock	6	9	0	97	32	10.77	—	—	3	—
†A.D.H. Grimes	7	11	2	58	13	6.44	—	—	2	—
G.F.H. McDonnell	2	4	0	7	5	1.75	—	—	—	—
†P.L. Garlick	10	15	6	13	6*	1.44	—	—	1	—

Played in one match: P.C. Richardson 7; I.E.W. Sanders 0, 9; N.P. Thomas 0, 0 (1 ct); T.J. Travers 5, 15.

†denotes played in Varsity match.

BOWLING

	Type	O	M	R	W	Avge	Best	5 wI	10 wM
A.J. Pollock	RM	161.2	32	620	14	44.28	4-104	—	—
T.A. Cotterell	SLA	293.4	43	1074	13	82.61	3-95	—	—
P.L. Garlick	RFM	253	31	1092	12	91.00	2-69	—	—
C.R. Andrew	OB	158.3	25	568	6	94.66	3-77	—	—
A.K. Golding	SLA	185.1	17	822	6	137.00	2-100	—	—

Also bowled: A.D.H. Grimes 123-22-427-3; A.E. Lea 19-5-92-2; P.C. Richardson 21-0-122-1; I.E.W.Sanders25-5-93-3. S.N.Siddiqi23-6-90-5.

OXFORD UNIVERSITY

Captain: A.J.T. Miller.

James Gordon BRETTELL (Cheltenham College and Lincoln) B Woking, Surrey 19/12/1962. RHB, SLA. Brother of D.N. Brettell (Oxford U). Debut 1984.

William Robert BRISTOWE (Charterhouse and St. Edmund Hall) B Woking, Surrey 17/11/1963. RHB, OB. Debut and Blue 1984. HS: 30* v Glos (Oxford) 1984.

John Donald CARR (See Middlesex section).

Mark Ronald CULLINAN (Hilton College, Natal; Cape Town U and Worcester) B Johannesburg 3/4/1957. RHB, WK. Debut for South African Universities v Transvaal (Johannesburg) 1979-80. Debut for Oxford U 1983. Blue 1983-84. HS: 59 v Somerset (Oxford) 1984.

Roger Michael EDBROOKE (Queen Elizabeth's Hospital, Bristol and Hertford) B Bristol 30/12/1960. RHB. Debut 1982. Blue 1984. HS: 84* v Glamorgan (Swansea). Soccer Blue.

Jonathan Guy FRANKS (Stamford School and St. Edmund Hall) B Stamford, Lincs 23/9/1962. RHB, WK. Debut 1983. Blue 1984. HS: 42* v Middlesex (Oxford) 1984.

Kevin Anthony HAYES (See Lancs section).

Simon Mark HEWITT (Bradford GS and Wadham) B Radcliffe, Lancs 30/7/1961. RHB, RM. Debut 1984. Brother of S.G.P. Hewitt (Cambridge U). HS: 22 v Somerset (Oxford) 1984.

Mark Philip LAWRENCE (Manchester GS and Merton) B Warrington, Cheshire 6/5/1962. LHB, SLA. Debut 1982. Blue 1984. HS: 18 v Middlesex (Oxford) 1982. BB: 3-79 v Kent (Oxford) 1984.

Adrian Alexander Graham MEE (St. Alban's College, Pretoria; Merchant Taylors', Northwood and Oriel) B Johannesburg, SA 29/5/1963. RHB. Debut 1984.

Andrew John Trevor MILLER (See Middlesex section).

Michael David PETCHEY (Latymer Upper School, Sussex U and Christ Church) B London 16/12/1958. RHB, RM. Debut and Blue 1983. HS: 18 v Surrey (Oval) 1983. BB: 4-65 v Middlesex (Oxford) 1983.

Henry Thomas RAWLINSON (Eton College and Christ Church) B Edgware, Middlesex 21/1/1963. RHB, RM. Debut 1982. Blue 1983-84. HS: 24 v Worcs (Oxford) 1983. BB: 5-123 v Worcs (Oxford) 1983. Brother of J.L. Rawlinson who played for University 1979-80.

David Anthony THORNE (See Warwicks section).

Giles John TOOGOOD (North Bromsgrove HS and Lincoln) B West Bromwich, Staffs 19/11/1961. RHB, OB. Debut 1982. Blue 1982-83-84. Captain 1983. HS: 109 v Cambridge U (Lord's) 1984.

Jonathan Richard TURNBULL (Merchant Taylors' School, Northwood and Jesus) B Northwood, Middlesex 13/11/1962. RHB, RM. Debut 1983. BB: 4-51 v Sussex (Oxford) 1983.

University Records

Highest Innings	For	651 v Sussex (Hove)	1895
Totals:	Agst	679-7d by Australians (Oxford)	1938
Lowest Innings	For	12 v MCC (Oxford)	1877
Totals:	Agst	24 by MCC (Oxford)	1846
Highest Indi-	For	281 K.J. Key v Middlesex (Chiswick Park)	1887
vidual Innings:	Agst	338 W.W. Read for Surrey (Oval)	1888
Best Bowling	For	10-38 S.E. Butler v Cambridge U (Lord's)	1871
in an Innings:	Agst	10-49 W.G. Grace for MCC (Oxford)	1886
Best Bowling	For	15-95 S.E. Butler v Cambridge U (Lord's)	1871
in a Match:	Agst	16-225 J.E. Walsh for Leics (Oxford)	1953
Most runs in a season:		1307 (av. 93.35) Nawab of Pataudi (Snr.)	1931
runs in a career:		3319 (av. 47.41) N.S. Mitchell-Innes	1934-1937
100s in a season:		6 by Nawab of Pataudi (Snr.)	1931
100s in a career:		9 by A.M. Crawley	1927-1930
		Nawab of Pataudi (Snr.)	1928-31
		N.S. Mitchell-Innes	1934-37
		M.P. Donnelly	1946-47
wickets in a season:		70 (av. 18.15) I.A.R. Peebles	1930
wickets in a career:		182 (av. 19.38) R.H.B. Bettington	1920-1923

RECORD WICKET STANDS

1st	338	T. Bowring & H. Teesdale v Gents of England (Oxford)	1908
2nd	226	W.G. Keighley & H.A. Pawson v Cambridge U (Lord's)	1947
3rd	273	F.C. de Saram & N.S. Mitchell-Innes v Glos (Oxford)	1934
4th	276	P.G.T. Kingsley & N.M. Ford v Surrey (Oval)	1930
5th	256*	A.A. Baig & C.A. Fry v Free Foresters (Oxford)	1959
6th	270	D.R. Walsh & S.A. Westley v Warwicks (Oxford)	1969
7th	340	K.J. Key & H. Philipson v Middlesex (Chiswick Park)	1887
8th	160	H. Philipson & A.C.M. Croome v MCC (Lord's)	1889
9th	157	H.M. Garland-Wells & C.K.H. Hill-Wood v Kent (Oxford)	1928
10th	149	F.H. Hollins & B.A. Collins v MCC (Oxford)	1901

OXFORD UNIVERSITY
Averages

All first-class matches: Played 8, won 1, drawn 2, lost 5.

BATTING AND FIELDING

	M	I	NO	RUNS	HS	Avge	100	50	Ct	St
†J.D. Carr	7	12	0	468	123	39.00	2	2	9	—
†G.J. Toogood	8	15	1	425	109	30.35	1	2	3	—
†R.M.Edbrooke	8	16	1	420	66	28.00	—	2	4	—
†A.J.T. Miller	5	10	1	196	128*	21.77	1	—	1	—
†W.R. Bristowe	5	8	3	104	30*	20.80	—	—	2	—
†D.A. Thorne	8	14	2	237	69*	19.75	—	1	6	—
†J.G. Franks	8	13	2	170	42*	15.45	—	—	8	1
†K.A. Hayes	8	14	1	194	37	14.92	—	—	4	—
†M.R. Cullinan	7	12	0	155	59	12.91	—	2	4	1
S.M. Hewitt	4	6	1	60	22	12.00	—	—	2	—
†H.T. Rawlinson	4	6	1	35	19*	7.00	—	—	2	—
†M.P. Lawrence	8	11	3	49	17*	6.12	—	—	4	—
J.R. Turnbull	5	9	3	12	6	2.00	—	—	2	—

Played in one match: J.G. Brettell 0†, 0 (1 ct); A.A.G. Mee 2 (1 ct); M.D. Petchey did not bat.
† denotes played in the Varsity match.

BOWLING

	Type	O	M	R	W	Avge	Best	5 wI	10 wM
K.A. Hayes	RM	95	28	259	9	28.77	4-58	—	—
D.A. Thorne	LM	200.1	41	556	15	37.06	5-39	1	—
J.D. Carr	OB	313	89	812	18	45.11	5-57	2	—
M.P. Lawrence	SLA	291.1	59	869	13	66.84	3-79	—	—

Also bowled: J.G. Brettell 15-3-74-1; M.R. Cullinan 2-1-4-1; S.M. Hewitt 64.5-8-232-4; A.J.T. Miller 1-0-4-1; M.D. Petchey 34-7-82-4; H.T. Rawlinson 95.5-18-346-4; G.J. Toogood 54.5-9-199-3; J.R. Turnbull 91-16-354-3.

THE FIRST-CLASS
UMPIRES FOR 1985

N.B. The abbreviations used below are as for 'The Counties and their Players'.

Harold Denis BIRD B Barnsley 19/4/1933. RHB, RM. Played for Yorks from 1956 to 1959 and for Leics from 1960 to 1964. Was subsequently professional at Paignton CC. HS: 181* Yorks v Glamorgan (Bradford) 1959. Career record: 3,315 runs (av. 20.71), 2 centuries. Appointed 1970. Umpired in 29 Tests between 1973 and 1984.

Jack BIRKENSHAW B Rothwell (Yorks) 13/11/1940. LHB, OB. Played for Yorks from 1958 to 1960, for Leics from 1961 to 1980 and for Worcs in 1981. Benefit (£13,000) in 1974. Tests: 5 in 1972-73 and 1973-74. Tours: India, Pakistan and Sri Lanka 1972-73, West Indies 1973-74. Gillette Man of Match Awards: 1 (for Leics). HS: 131 Leics v Surrey (Guildford) 1969. BB: 8-94 Leics v Somerset (Taunton) 1972. Career Record: 12,780 runs (av. 23.57), 4 centuries, 1,073 wkts (av. 27.28). Appointed 1982.

David John CONSTANT B Bradford-on-Avon (Wilts) 9/11/1941. LHB, SLA. Played for Kent from 1961 to 1963 and for Leics from 1965 to 1968. HS: 80 v Glos (Bristol) 1966. Career record: 1,517 runs (av. 19.20), 1 wkt (36.00). Appointed 1969. Umpired in 28 Tests between 1971 and 1984.

Cecil (Sam) COOK B Tetbury (Glos) 23/8/1921. RHB, SLA. Played for Gloucestershire from 1946 to 1964. Benefit (£3,067) in 1957. Took wicket with first ball in first-class cricket. Tests: 1 v SA 1947. HS: 35* v Sussex (Hove) 1957. BB: 9-42 v Yorks (Bristol) 1947. Career record: 1,964 runs (av. 5.39), 1,782 wkts (av. 20.52). Appointed 1971, after having withdrawn from appointment in 1966.

Barry DUDLESTON B Bebington, Cheshire 16/7/1945. RHB, SLA. Played for Leics from 1966 to 1980, Glos from 1980 to 1983. Also played for Rhodesia 1976-77 to 1979-80. HS: 202 Leics v Derby (Leicester) 1979. BB: 4-6 Leics v Surrey (Leicester) 1972. Career record: 14,747 runs (av. 32.48), 32 centuries, 47 wkts (av. 29.04). Appointed 1984.

David Gwilliam Lloyd EVANS B Lambeth, London 27/7/1933. RHB, WK. Played for Glamorgan from 1956 to 1969. Benefit (£3,500) in 1969. HS: 46* v Oxford U (Oxford) 1961. Career record: 2,875 runs (av. 10.53), 558 dismissals (502 ct, 56 st). Appointed 1971. Umpired in 8 Tests between 1981 and 1984.

John Harry HAMPSHIRE Appointed 1985. (See Valete section).

John Humphrey HARRIS B Taunton 13/2/1936. LHB, RFM. Played for Somerset from 1952 to 1959. HS: 41 v Worcs (Taunton) 1957. Career record: 154 runs (av. 11.00), 19 wkts (av. 32.05). Appointed 1983.

John Wakefield HOLDER B St George Barbados 19/3/1945. RHB, RFM. Played for Hants from 1968 to 1972. HS: 33 v Sussex (Hove) 1971. BB: 7-79 v Glos (Gloucester) 1972. Career record: 374 runs (av. 10.68), 139 wkts (av. 24.56). Appointed 1983.

John Alexander JAMESON B Bombay 30/6/1941. RHB, RM/OB, WK. Played for Warwicks from 1960 to 1976. Tours: International XI to South Africa 1972-73, West Indies 1973-74. HS: 240* v Glos (Birmingham) 1974 sharing world-record 2nd wicket partnership of 465* with R.B. Kanhai. BB: 4-22 v Oxford U (Oxford) 1971. Career record: 18,941 runs (av. 43.17), 33 centuries, 89 wkts (av. 42.49). Appointed 1984.

Allan Arthur JONES B Horley, Surrey 9/12/1947. RHB, RFM. Played for Sussex 1966-69; Somerset 1970-75; Northern Transvaal 1972-73; Middlesex 1976-79; Orange Free State 1976-77 and Glamorgan 1980-81. HS: 33 Middlesex v Kent (Canterbury) 1978. BB: 9-51 Somerset v Sussex (Hove) 1972. Career record: 799 runs (av. 5.39), 549 wkts (av. 28.07). Appointed 1985.

Raymond JULIEN B Cosby (Leics) 23/8/1936. RHB, WK. Played for Leicestershire from 1953 (debut at age of 16) to 1971, but lost regular place in side to R.W. Tolchard in 1966. HS: 51 v Worcs (Worcester) 1962. Career record: 2,581 runs (av. 9.73), 421 dismissals (382 ct, 39 st). Appointed 1972.

Mervyn John KITCHEN B Nailsea (Somerset) 1/8/1940. LHB, RM. Played for Somerset from 1960 to 1979. Testimonial (£6,000) in 1973. Gillette Man of Match Awards: 2. Benson & Hedges Gold Awards: 1. HS: 189 v Pakistanis (Taunton) 1967. Career record: 15,230 runs (av. 26.25), 17 centuries, 2 wkts (av. 54.50). Appointed 1982.

Barrie LEADBEATER B Harehills, Leeds 14/8/1943. RHB, RM. Played for Yorkshire from 1966 to 1979. Joint benefit in 1980 with G.A. Cope. Gillette Man of Match Awards: 1 (in 1969 Cup Final). HS: 140* v Hants (Portsmouth) 1976. Career record: 5,373 runs (av. 25.34), 1 century, 1 wkt (av. 5.00). Appointed 1981.

Kevin James LYONS B Cardiff 18/12/1946. RHB. Played for Glamorgan 1967-77. HS: 92 v Cambridge U (Cambridge) 1972. Career record: 1,673 runs (av. 19.68), 2 wkts (av. 126.00). Appointed 1985.

Barrie John MEYER B Bournemouth 21/8/1932. RHB, WK. Played for Gloucestershire from 1957 to 1971. Benefit 1971. HS: 63 v Indians (Cheltenham) 1959, v Oxford U (Bristol) 1962 and v Sussex (Bristol) 1964. Career record: 5,367 runs (av. 14.19), 826 dismissals (707 ct, 119 st). Soccer for Bristol Rovers, Plymouth Argyle, Newport County and Bristol City. Appointed 1973. Umpired in 16 Tests between 1978 and 1984.

Donald Osmund OSLEAR B Cleethorpes (Lincs) 3/3/1929. Has not played first-class cricket. Played soccer for Grimsby Town, Hull City and Oldham Athletic. Also played ice hockey. Has umpired in county second XI matches since 1972. Appointed 1975. Umpired in 5 Tests between 1980 and 1984.

Kenneth Ernest PALMER B Winchester 22/4/1937. RHB, RFM. Played for Somerset from 1955 to 1969. Testimonial (£4,000) in 1968. Tour: Pakistan with Commonwealth team 1963-64. Coached in Johannesburg 1964-65 and was called upon by MCC to play in final Test v South Africa owing to injuries to other bowlers. Tests 1 v South Africa 1964-65. HS: 125* v Northants (Northampton) 1961. BB: 9-57 v Notts (Nottingham) 1963. Career record: 7,771 runs (av. 20.66), 2 centuries, 866 wkts (av. 21.34). Appointed 1972. Umpired in 8 Tests between 1978 and 1981.

Roy PALMER B Devizes (Wilts) 12/7/1942. RHB, RFM. Younger brother of K.E. Palmer. Played for Somerset from 1965 to 1970. Gillette Man of Match Awards: 2. HS: 84 v Leics (Taunton) 1967. BB: 6-45 v Middlesex (Lord's) 1967. Career record: 1,037 runs (av. 13.29). 172 wkts (av. 31.62). Appointed 1980.

Nigel Trevor PLEWIS B Nottingham 5/9/1934. Former policeman. Has not played first-class cricket. Umpired in 2nd XI games since 1968. On Minor Counties reserve list 1980, and on list 1981. Appointed 1982.

David Robert SHEPHERD B Bideford (Devon) 27/12/1940. RHB, RM. Played for Gloucestershire from 1965 to 1979, scoring 108 in debut match v Oxford U. Joint benefit in 1978 with J. Davey. Gillette Man of Match Awards: 1. Benson & Hedges Gold Awards: 1. HS: 153 v Middlesex (Bristol) 1968. Career record: 10,672 runs (av. 24.47), 12 centuries, 2 wkts (av. 53.00). Appointed 1981.

Robert Arthur WHITE B Fulham 6/10/1936. LHB, OB. Played for Middlesex 1958 to 1965. Played for Notts 1966 to 1980. Benefit (£11,000) in 1974. HS: 116* Notts v Surrey (Oval) 1967. BB: 7-41 Notts v Derby (Ilkeston) 1971. Career record: 12,452 runs (av. 23.18), 5 centuries, 693 wkts (av. 30.50). Appointed 1983.

Alan Geoffrey Thomas WHITEHEAD B Butleigh (Somerset) 28/10/1940. LHB, SLA. Played for Somerset from 1957 to 1961. HS: 15 v Hants (Southampton) 1959 and 15 v Leics (Leicester) 1960. BB: 6-74 v Sussex (Eastbourne) 1959. Career record: 137 runs (av. 5.70), 67 wkts (av. 34.41). Served on Minor Counties list in 1969. Appointed 1970. Tests: 1 in 1982.

Peter Bernard WIGHT B Georgetown, British Guiana 25/6/1930. RHB, OB. Played for British Guiana in 1950-51 and for Somerset from 1953 to 1965. Benefit (£5,000) in 1963. HS: 222* v Kent (Taunton) 1959. BB: 6-29 v Derbyshire (Chesterfield) 1957. Career record: 17,773 runs (av. 33.09), 28 centuries, 68 wkts (av. 32.26). Appointed 1966.

Test Match Panel for 1985: H.D. Bird, D.J. Constant, D.G.L. Evans, B.J. Meyer and D.O. Oslear.

FIRST CLASS AVERAGES
1984
Compiled by Brian Croudy

The following are the averages for all players who appeared in first-class matches played in England in 1984.
† indicates left-hand batsman.

BATTING AND FIELDING

	Cap	M	I	NO	Runs	HS	Avge	100	50	Ct	St
†Abrahams, J. (La)	1982	23	39	6	1216	201*	36.84	3	4	19	—
Acfield, D.L. (Ex)	1970	24	22	9	41	7*	3.15	—	—	10	—
Afford, J.A. (Nt)	—	3	—	—	—	—	—	—	—	1	—
Agnew, J.P. (E/Le)	1984	23	23	7	156	30	9.75	—	—	4	—
Alderman, T.M. (K)	1984	20	27	13	220	52*	15.71	—	1	29	—
Allott, P.J.W. (E/La)	1981	19	25	4	326	50*	15.52	—	1	8	—
Amarnath, M. (DBC)	—	1	1	0	15	15	15.00	—	—	—	—
Amiss, D.L. (Wa)	1965	26	50	10	2239	122	55.97	6	14	16	—
Anderson, I.S. (D)	—	14	23	1	454	79	20.63	—	1	14	—
†Andrew C.R. (CU)	—	9	18	1	405	101*	23.82	1	1	2	—
Andrew, S.J.W. (H)	—	7	6	4	12	6*	6.00	—	—	1	—
Anurasiri, S.D. (SL)	—	4	3	1	5	5	2.50	—	—	2	—
Asif Din, M. (Wa)	—	6	9	2	99	35*	14.14	—	—	2	—
Aslett, D.G. (K)	1983	26	45	3	1491	221*	35.50	5	3	15	—
Athey, C.W.J. (Gs)	—	26	52	4	1812	114*	37.75	4	11	26	—
Bailey, R.J. (No)	—	25	45	8	1405	114	37.97	3	8	14	—
Bainbridge, P. (Gs)	1981	22	42	7	1133	134*	32.37	2	6	9	—
Bairstow, D.L. (Y/DBC)	1973	23	26	5	787	94	37.47	—	7	39	7
Balderstone, J.C. (Le)	1973	20	36	2	1260	181*	37.05	3	5	14	—
Bamber, M.J. (No)	—	5	10	1	220	51	24.44	—	1	1	—
Banks, D.A. (Wo)	—	6	9	0	132	43	14.66	—	—	3	—
Baptiste, E.A.E. (WI)	—	10	9	1	196	87*	24.50	—	1	1	—
Barclay, J.R.T. (Sx)	1976	26	35	3	761	82	23.78	—	4	21	—
†Barlow, G.D. (M)	1976	19	36	2	903	96	26.55	—	5	10	—
Barnett, K.J. (D)	1982	24	41	3	1734	144	45.63	6	9	21	—
Barwick, S.R. (Gm)	—	20	19	9	105	25	10.50	—	—	6	—
†Benson, M.R. (K)	1981	14	26	2	914	127	38.08	3	4	7	—
Birch, J.D. (Nt)	1981	22	33	5	905	110*	32.32	1	5	20	—
Boon, T.J. (Le)	—	21	37	6	1233	144	39.77	4	4	9	—
†Booth, P.A. (Y)	—	10	13	3	78	26	7.80	—	—	2	—
Booth, S.C. (So)	—	12	14	7	100	42	14.28	—	—	13	—
Bore, M.K. (Nt)	1980	4	2	0	28	27	14.00	—	—	1	—
Botham, I.T. (E/So)	1976	17	26	1	797	90	31.88	—	7	7	—
Boycott, G. (Y)	1963	20	35	10	1567	153*	62.68	4	9	13	—
Boyd-Moss, R.J. (No)	1984	17	32	2	905	105	30.16	1	6	11	—
Brassington, A.J. (Gs)	—	2	3	1	22	22	11.00	—	—	2	1
Breddy, M.N. (CU)	—	10	20	1	339	61	17.84	—	1	2	—
Brettell, J.G. (OU)	—	1	2	1	0	0*	—	—	—	1	—

178

	Cap	M	I	NO	Runs	HS	Avge	100	50	Ct	St
Briers, N.E. (Le)	1981	22	37	3	616	73	18.11	—	1	9	—
Bristowe, W.R. (OU)	—	5	8	3	104	30*	20.80	—	—	2	—
†Broad, B.C. (E/Nt)	—	23	40	5	1549	108*	44.25	1	13	15	—
Broome, I (D)	—	2	4	3	35	26*	35.00	—	—	1	—
Brown, A. (Sc)	—	1	2	0	46	30	23.00	—	—	2	1
Brown, K.R. (M)	—	1	1	0	6	6	6.00	—	—	1	—
Burnley, I.D. (CU)	—	3	6	0	232	86	38.66	—	2	1	—
Burrows, D.A. (Gs)	—	1	1	0	0	0	0.00	—	—	—	—
†Butcher, A.R. (Sy)	1975	24	41	4	1415	135*	38.24	4	5	11	—
Butcher, I.P. (Le)	1984	24	42	1	1349	130	32.90	5	3	19	—
Butcher, R.O. (M)	1979	23	40	7	1326	116	40.18	2	10	17	—
Capel, D.J. (No)	—	17	28	5	789	81	34.30	—	6	8	—
†Carmichael, I.R. (Le)	—	7	6	3	6	4*	2.00	—	—	3	—
Carr, J.D. (M/OU)	—	9	14	0	468	123	33.42	2	2	9	—
Carrick, P. (Y)	1976	22	28	5	400	47*	17.39	—	—	13	—
Chadwick, M.R. (La)	—	7	14	0	293	61	20.92	—	2	2	—
†Childs, J.H. (Gs)	1977	7	6	2	12	4*	3.00	—	—	2	—
Clarke, S.T. (Sy)	1980	23	25	3	329	35	14.95	—	—	23	—
Clift, P.B. (Le)	1976	19	28	7	483	58	23.00	—	2	7	—
†Clinton, G.S. (Sy)	1980	19	28	6	948	192	43.09	2	5	6	—
†Close, D.B. (DBC)	—	1	1	1	15	15*	—	—	—	2	—
Cobb, R.A. (Le)	—	3	5	0	142	48	28.40	—	—	2	—
Cohen, M.F. (Ire)	—	1	1	0	0	0	0.00	—	—	—	—
Connor, C.A. (H)	—	21	23	9	65	13*	4.64	—	—	7	—
Cook, C.R. (M)	—	2	3	0	106	47	35.33	—	—	1	—
Cook, G. (No)	1975	22	43	4	1539	102	39.46	2	9	15	—
Cook, N.G.B. (E/Le/MCC)	1982	24	30	9	256	44	12.19	—	—	17	—
†Cooper, K.E. (Nt)	1980	24	19	6	117	19	9.00	—	—	10	—
Corlett, S.C. (Ire)	—	1	1	0	14	14	14.00	—	—	—	—
Cotterell, T.A. (CU)	—	10	16	1	247	52	16.46	—	1	3	—
Cowans, N.G. (E/M/MCC)	1984	21	25	1	269	66	11.20	—	1	9	—
Cowdrey, C.S. (K/MCC)	1979	22	37	3	1039	125*	30.55	2	5	22	—
Cowdrey, G.R. (K)	—	1	1	0	7	7	7.00	—	—	1	—
Cowley, N.G. (H)	1978	26	38	4	1042	80	30.64	—	6	9	—
Crowe, M.D. (So)	1984	25	41	6	1870	190	53.42	6	11	28	—
Cullinan, M.R. (OU)	—	7	12	0	155	59	12.91	—	2	2	1
†Cunningham, E.J. (Gs)	—	6	11	3	162	61*	20.25	—	1	—	—
Curtis, I.J. (Sy)	—	1	1	1	1	1*	—	—	—	—	—
Curtis T.S. (Wo)	1984	22	36	3	1405	129	42.57	3	8	13	—
Dale, C.S. (Gs)	—	8	8	2	100	49	16.66	—	—	1	—
Daniel, W.W. (M)	1977	21	24	14	87	16*	8.70	—	—	4	—
Davies, A.G. (CU)	—	7	14	5	308	69	34.22	—	3	9	2
Davies, T. (Gm)	—	27	35	7	398	43	14.21	—	—	43	10
†Davis, M.R. (So)	—	19	14	6	178	60*	22.25	—	1	6	—
Davis, W.W. (WI/Gm)	—	21	24	7	390	77	22.94	—	2	8	—
de Alwis, R.G. (SL)	—	2	1	0	74	74	74.00	—	1	3	—
de Mel, A.L.F. (SL)	—	6	7	1	117	37	19.50	—	—	3	—
de Silva, D.S. (SL)	—	5	4	1	55	37*	18.33	—	—	2	—
de Silva, P.A. (SL)	—	7	8	0	236	75	29.50	—	3	2	—
†Denning, P.W. (So)	1973	5	8	3	338	90	67.60	—	3	2	—

	Cap	M	I	NO	Runs	HS	Avge	100	50	Ct	St
Dennis, S.J. (Y)	1983	9	9	4	104	53*	20.80	—	1	1	—
Derrick, J. (Gm)	—	10	15	7	351	69*	43.87	—	3	8	—
Dias, R.L. (SL)	—	9	12	0	224	38	18.66	—	—	5	—
D'Oliveira, D.B. (Wo)	—	23	34	3	796	74	25.67	—	5	17	—
Donald, W.A. (Sc)	—	1	2	0	31	30	15.50	—	—	1	—
Doughty, R.J. (Gs)	—	1	1	0	4	4	4.00	—	—	—	—
Downton, P.R. (E/M/MCC)	1981	21	33	9	618	88	25.75	—	3	42	6
†Dredge, C.H. (So)	1978	21	26	8	214	25*	11.88	—	—	12	—
Dujon, P.J. (WI)	—	12	15	2	558	107	42.92	2	2	27	—
Duthie, P.G. (Sc)	—	1	2	0	64	34	32.00	—	1	—	—
Dyer, R.I.H.B. (Wa)	—	18	36	2	1187	106*	34.91	1	9	7	—
East, D.E. (Ex)	1982	27	37	2	510	81	14.57	—	3	76	1
East, R.E. (Ex)	1967	4	2	0	30	22	15.00	—	—	2	—
Edbrooke, R.M. (OU)	—	8	16	1	420	66	28.00	—	2	4	—
Edmonds, P.H. (M)	1974	25	33	4	600	142	20.68	1	2	20	—
Ellcock, R.M. (Wo)	—	9	8	3	134	45*	26.80	—	—	1	—
Ellis, R.G.P. (M)	—	2	3	0	54	33	18.00	—	—	—	—
†Ellison, R.M. (E/K)	1983	21	32	7	620	108	24.80	1	1	8	—
Emburey, J.E. (M)	1977	26	35	2	579	57	17.54	—	3	18	—
Evans, K.P. (Nt)	—	3	4	0	48	42	12.00	—	—	3	—
†Fairbrother, N.H. (La)	—	23	39	1	1201	102	31.60	1	10	19	—
Falkner, N.J. (Sy)	—	1	1	1	101	101*	—	—	1	—	—
Feltham, M.A. (Sy)	—	12	15	5	206	44	20.60	—	—	5	—
†Felton, N.A. (So)	—	14	24	1	499	101	21.69	1	3	5	—
Ferreira, A.M. (Wa)	1983	26	39	13	777	76*	29.88	—	4	12	—
Ferris, G.J.F. (Le)	—	1	1	0	0	0	0.00	—	—	—	—
Finney, R.J. (D)	—	24	37	5	679	78	21.21	—	4	5	—
Fletcher, K.W.R. (Ex)	1963	25	37	5	1056	131	33.00	3	4	22	—
Fletcher, S.D. (Y)	—	8	5	1	35	28*	8.75	—	—	—	—
Folley, I. (La)	—	17	28	9	194	22*	10.21	—	—	6	—
Foster, N.A. (E/Ex)	1983	22	27	8	356	54*	18.73	—	1	9	—
†Fowler, G. (E/La/DBC)	1981	17	29	0	1007	226	34.72	3	4	7	—
†Fowler, W.P. (D)	—	22	38	8	948	116	31.60	2	7	17	—
Francis, D.A. (Gm)	—	2	3	0	27	30	9.00	—	—	2	—
Franks, J.G. (OU)	—	8	13	2	170	42*	15.45	—	—	8	1
Fraser, A.R.C. (M)	—	1	—	—	—	—	—	—	—	—	—
Fraser-Darling, C.D. (Nt)	—	1	—	—	—	—	—	—	—	1	—
French, B.N. (Nt)	1980	26	32	6	697	98	26.80	—	3	76	11
Gard, T. (So)	1983	21	24	5	209	26	11.00	—	—	48	10
Garlick, P.L. (CU)	—	10	15	6	13	6*	1.44	—	—	1	—
Garner, J. (WI)	—	8	8	1	61	29	8.71	—	—	4	—
Garnham, M.A. (Le)	—	18	29	6	666	84	28.95	—	6	45	3
Gatting, M.W. (E/M/MCC)	1977	24	43	10	2257	258	68.39	8	10	24	—
†Gifford, N. (Wa)	1983	25	24	10	146	28*	10.42	—	—	10	—
†Gladwin, C. (Ex)	1984	26	45	3	1396	162	33.23	1	9	14	—
Goldie, C.F.E. (H)	—	1	—	—	—	—	—	—	—	2	1
Golding, A.K. (CU)	—	8	13	0	189	44	14.53	—	—	2	—

	Cap	M	I	NO	Runs	HS	Avge	100	50	Ct	St
Gomes, H.A. (WI)	—	12	17	5	841	143	70.08	4	3	2	—
Gooch G.A. (Ex)	1975	26	45	7	2559	227	67.34	8	13	27	—
†Gould, I.J. (Sx)	1981	23	27	4	529	84	23.00	—	2	62	6
†Gower, D.I. (E/Le/MCC)	1977	18	30	2	999	117*	35.67	2	6	17	—
Graveney, D.A. (Gs)	1976	26	40	13	430	33	15.72	—	—	18	—
Green, A.M. (Sx)	—	24	40	2	1006	81	26.47	—	4	12	—
Green, R.C. (Gm)	—	2	1	1	3	3*	—	—	—	1	—
Greenidge, C.G. (WI)	—	11	16	3	1069	223	82.23	4	3	5	—
Greig, I.A. (Sx)	1981	26	35	5	813	106*	27.10	1	2	17	—
Griffiths, B.J. (No)	1978	18	21	9	48	12	4.00	—	—	5	—
Grimes, A.D.H. (CU)	—	7	11	2	58	13	6.44	—	—	2	—
†Hadlee, R.J. (Nt)	1978	24	31	8	1179	210*	51.26	2	7	23	—
Hampshire, J.H. (D)	1982	21	32	4	792	101*	28.28	1	4	20	—
Hanley, R.W. (No)	—	17	21	7	131	33*	9.35	—	—	3	—
Hardie, B.R. (Ex)	1974	27	38	7	1077	99	34.74	—	6	27	—
†Hardy, J.J.E. (H)	—	13	20	6	513	95	36.64	—	4	9	—
Harper, R.A. (WI/DBC)	—	14	12	2	328	73	32.80	—	2	14	—
Hartley, S.N. (Y)	1981	13	21	4	437	104*	25.70	1	1	2	—
†Harrison, G.D. (Ire)	—	1	1	0	32	32	32.00	—	—	1	—
Hassan, S.B. (Nt)	1970	17	27	4	499	103*	21.69	1	1	23	—
Hayes, F.C. (La)	1972	1	1	0	11	11	11.00	—	—	—	—
Hayes, K.A. (La/OU)	—	9	16	1	209	37	13.93	—	—	4	—
Haynes, D.L. (WI/DBC)	—	13	18	1	743	125	43.70	2	5	10	—
Haysman, M.D. (Le)	—	5	10	4	230	102*	38.33	1	—	10	—
Hemmings, E.E. (Nt)	1980	24	24	7	248	35	14.58	—	—	7	—
†Henderson, S.P. (Gm)	—	10	17	1	487	108	30.43	1	3	4	—
Hendrick, M. (Nt)	—	3	—	—	—	—	—	—	—	2	—
Hewitt, S.G.P. (W)	—	3	5	4	20	14*	20.00	—	—	3	1
Hewitt, S.M. (OU)	—	4	6	1	60	22	12.00	—	—	—	—
Hick, G.A. (Wo)	—	1	1	1	82	82*	—	—	1	1	—
Hill, A. (D)	1976	25	44	3	1352	125	32.97	1	11	13	—
†Hinks, S.G. (K)	—	8	14	0	162	39	11.57	—	—	3	—
Holding, M.A. (WI)	—	7	7	0	189	69	27.00	—	2	3	—
Holmes, G.C. (Gm)	—	21	37	2	1039	90	29.68	—	6	10	—
Hopkins, J.A. (Gm)	1977	26	50	5	1500	128*	33.33	2	9	18	—
Howarth, G.P. (Sy)	1974	22	37	3	833	113	24.50	2	4	17	—
Hughes, D.P. (La)	1970	19	32	1	706	113	22.77	2	1	12	—
Hughes, S.P. (M)	1981	15	14	4	144	41*	14.40	—	—	5	—
Humpage, G.W. (Wa)	1976	26	47	8	1891	205	48.48	5	9	55	11
†Humphries, D.J. (Wo)	1978	22	32	9	644	133*	28.00	2	2	37	7
Illingworth, R.K. (Wo)	—	21	20	7	346	43*	26.61	—	—	9	—
Inchmore, J.D. (Wo)	1976	23	24	8	295	34	18.43	—	—	10	—
Jackson, P.B. (Ire)	—	1	1	0	10	10	10.00	—	—	7	—
†James, K.D. (M)	—	2	2	1	30	28*	30.00	—	—	—	—
Jarvis, K.B.S. (K)	1977	23	25	13	41	19	3.41	—	—	6	—
Jarvis, P.W. (Y)	—	12	14	4	157	37	15.70	—	—	2	—
Javed Miandad (Gm)	1980	8	15	2	832	212*	64.00	2	3	4	—
†Jefferies, S.T. (La)	—	18	28	3	633	65	25.32	—	2	4	—
Jesty, T.E. (H)	1971	25	44	4	1625	248	40.62	5	4	16	—
John, V.B. (SL)	—	5	3	1	4	4	2.00	—	—	1	—

181

	Cap	M	I	NO	Runs	HS	Avge	100	50	Ct	St
Johnson, G.W. (K)	1970	25	39	5	726	84	21.35	—	3	26	—
Johnson, P. (Nt)	—	10	14	1	647	133	49.76	2	3	7	1
†Jones, A.L. (Gm)	1983	27	51	2	1811	132	36.95	5	7	30	—
†Jones, A.N. (Sx)	—	10	7	4	73	35	24.33	—	—	3	—
†Kallicharran, A.I. (Wa)	1972	26	50	6	2301	200*	52.29	9	7	17	—
Kapil Dev (Wo)	—	12	19	4	640	95	42.66	—	6	10	—
Ker, A.B.M. (Sc)	—	1	2	0	8	6	4.00	—	—	1	—
Ker, J.E. (Sc)	—	1	2	1	34	20*	—	—	—	—	—
†Knight, R.D.V. (Sy)	1978	21	35	3	1254	142	39.18	3	8	19	—
Knott, A.P.E. (K)	1965	14	22	2	295	43	14.75	—	—	29	1
Kuruppu, D.S.B.P. (SL)	—	3	4	0	38	25	9.50	—	—	4	1
Lamb, A.J. (E/No)	1978	18	34	4	1209	133*	40.30	5	5	14	—
Larkins, W. (No)	1976	25	49	3	1656	183*	36.00	3	7	11	—
Lawrence, D.V. (Gs)	—	19	25	4	135	17	6.42	—	—	2	—
†Lawrence, M.P. (OU)	—	8	11	3	49	17*	6.12	—	—	4	—
Le Roux, G.S. (Sx)	1981	24	24	6	321	68*	17.83	—	2	4	—
Lea, A.E. (CU)	—	9	18	0	395	119	21.94	1	1	2	—
Lenham, N.J. (Sx)	—	1	1	0	31	31	31.00	—	—	1	—
Lethbridge, C. (Wa)	—	15	17	3	324	46	23.14	—	—	6	—
Lever, J.K. (Ex)	1970	24	22	7	182	37	12.13	—	—	10	—
Lilley, A.W. (Ex)	—	1	—	—	—	—	—	—	—	—	—
†Lloyd, C.H. (WI)	—	9	9	2	364	72	52.00	—	3	12	—
†Lloyd, T.A. (E/Wa)	1980	8	14	2	590	110	49.16	2	4	3	—
†Lloyds, J.W. (So)	1982	20	30	10	812	113*	40.60	1	5	22	—
Logie, A.L. (WI)	—	8	10	2	585	141	73.12	2	4	3	—
†Lord, G.J. (Wa)	—	4	6	0	83	55	13.83	—	1	3	—
Love, J.D. (Y)	1980	15	23	2	568	112	27.04	1	3	7	—
Lumb, R.G. (Y)	1974	10	17	2	534	165*	35.60	2	1	2	—
Lynch, M.A. (Sy)	1982	25	41	1	1546	144	38.65	4	8	32	—
Madugalle, R.S. (SL)	—	7	12	4	336	87*	42.00	—	3	3	—
Maher, B.J.M. (D)	—	7	11	2	146	66	16.22	—	1	17	—
Makinson, D.J. (La)	—	4	5	2	18	9	6.00	—	—	—	—
Malcolm, D.E. (D)	—	7	8	1	40	23	5.71	—	—	4	—
Mallender, N.A. (No)	1984	20	30	5	261	33*	10.44	—	—	7	—
Malone, S.J. (H)	—	3	2	0	4	4	2.00	—	—	2	—
Marks, V.J. (So)	1979	24	34	10	1262	134	52.58	3	6	16	—
Marsh, S.A. (K)	—	5	7	1	106	48	17.66	—	—	11	—
Marshall, M.D. (WI)	—	8	9	0	103	34	11.44	—	—	3	—
Maru, R.J. (H)	—	17	20	4	246	36	15.37	—	—	22	—
†Masters, K.D. (K)	—	2	3	1	0	0*	0.00	—	—	—	—
Maynard, C. (La)	—	15	21	5	402	50*	25.12	—	1	29	5
†McDonnell, G.F.H. (CU)	—	2	4	0	7	5	1.75	—	—	—	—
McEvoy, M.S.A. (Wo)	—	10	13	0	188	46	14.46	—	—	11	—
McEwan, K.S. (Ex)	1974	27	44	6	1755	142*	46.18	4	10	20	—
McFarlane, L.L. (La)	—	12	15	7	41	15*	5.12	—	—	2	—
McPate, W.A. (Sc)	—	1	2	1	12	12*	12.00	—	—	—	—
Medlycott, K.T. (Sy)	—	6	6	5	128	117*	128.00	1	—	4	—
Mee, A.A.G. (OU)	—	1	1	0	2	2	2.00	—	—	1	—
Mee, S.R. (Nt)	—	1	—	—	—	—	—	—	—	—	—
Mendis, G.D. (Sx)	1980	23	36	2	1141	209*	33.55	3	4	9	—
Mendis, L.R.D. (SL)	—	7	10	2	442	111	55.25	1	3	1	—

	Cap	M	I	NO	Runs	HS	Avge	100	50	Ct	St
Metcalfe, A.A. (Y)	—	9	13	0	216	60	16.61	—	2	5	—
Metson, C.P. (M)	—	12	17	5	300	96	25.00	—	2	28	2
Middleton, T.C. (H)	—	1	2	0	15	10	7.50	—	—	—	—
†Miller, A.J.T. (M/OU)	—	8	15	1	253	128*	18.07	1	—	2	—
Miller, G. (E/D)	1976	22	34	5	933	130	32.17	1	5	27	—
Moir, D.G. (D)	—	20	28	6	534	107	24.27	1	2	18	—
Monkhouse, G. (Sy)	1984	18	25	7	328	100*	18.22	1	1	8	—
Monteith, J.D. (Ire)	—	1	1	0	95	95	95.00	—	1	—	—
Moores, P. (Wo)	—	4	4	2	61	45	30.50	—	—	7	4
†Morris H. (Gm)	—	12	20	4	542	114*	33.87	1	4	2	—
Morris, J.E. (D)	—	15	28	1	948	135	35.11	3	3	4	—
Mortensen, O.H. (D)	—	8	8	4	63	40*	15.75	—	—	4	—
†Morton, W. (Wa)	—	8	8	2	39	13*	6.50	—	—	3	—
Moxon, M.D. (Y/DBC)	1984	19	32	1	1034	126*	35.65	2	6	19	—
Mushtaq Mohammed (DBC)	—	1	1	0	22	22	22.00	—	—	—	—
Neale, P.A. (Wo)	1978	25	43	7	1706	143	47.38	2	11	9	—
Needham, A. (Sy)	—	19	30	1	644	70	22.20	—	4	10	—
Newell, M. (Nt)	—	4	7	1	109	76	18.16	—	1	6	—
Newman, P.G. (D)	—	16	21	2	269	40	14.15	—	—	3	—
Newport, P.J. (Wo)	—	10	11	5	187	40*	31.16	—	—	2	—
Nicholas, M.C.J. (H/MCC)	1982	26	48	2	1559	158	33.89	4	6	16	—
†Old, C.M. (Wa)	—	18	21	4	393	70	23.11	—	2	8	—
Oldham, S. (Y)	—	8	6	3	85	22	28.33	—	—	2	—
†Ollis, R.L. (So)	—	6	12	1	112	22	10.18	—	—	8	—
Ontong, R.C. (Gm)	1979	25	45	8	1320	204*	35.67	1	7	15	—
O'Reilly, P.M. (Ire)	—	1	1	1	0	0*	—	—	—	—	—
Ormrod J.A. (La)	1984	23	40	3	1199	139*	32.40	1	7	10	—
O'Shaughnessy, S.J. (La)	—	21	38	4	1167	159*	34.32	3	3	11	—
Palmer, G.V. (So)	—	16	20	2	299	73*	16.61	—	1	15	—
Parker, P.W.G. (Sx)	1979	26	40	4	1692	181	47.00	6	6	23	—
Parks, R.J. (H)	1982	25	34	9	444	89	17.76	—	2	61	10
†Parsons, G.J. (Le)	1984	26	39	10	853	63	29.41	—	6	8	—
Patel, D.N. (Wo)	1979	25	41	1	1348	197	33.70	2	7	11	—
Patterson, B.P. (La)	—	1	2	0	10	10	5.00	—	—	—	—
†Patterson, T.J.T. (Ire)	—	1	1	0	23	23	23.00	—	—	1	—
Pauline, D.B. (Sy)	—	10	16	1	367	88	24.46	—	3	9	—
Payne, I.R. (Sy)	—	2	3	0	30	17	10.00	—	—	4	—
Payne, T.R.O. (WI)	—	7	8	3	191	44	38.20	—	—	4	1
Peck, I.G. (CU)	—	4	7	1	97	49*	16.16	—	—	2	—
†Penn, C. (K)	—	12	15	2	317	115	24.38	1	1	8	—
Petchey, M.D. (OU)	—	1	—	—	—	—	—	—	—	—	—
Phillip, N. (Ex)	1978	13	17	2	293	71	19.53	—	1	3	—
†Pick, R.A. (Nt)	—	12	10	5	96	27*	19.20	—	—	3	—
Pigott, A.C.S. (Sx)	1982	2	—	—	—	—	—	—	—	—	—
Pocock, N.E.J. (H)	1980	13	18	2	314	55	19.62	—	1	13	—
Pocock, P.I. (E/Sy)	1967	20	21	6	112	29*	7.46	—	—	8	—
Pollock, A.J. (CU)	—	6	9	0	97	32	10.77	—	—	3	—
Pont, K.R. (Ex)	1976	2	3	0	61	32	20.33	—	—	1	—
Popplewell, N.F.M. (So)	1983	22	36	2	1116	133	32.82	1	7	27	—
Potter, L. (K)	—	14	25	1	574	117	23.91	1	2	7	—

	Cap	M	I	NO	Runs	HS	Avge	100	50	Ct	St
Price, D.G. (CU)	—	7	11	0	239	49	21.72	—	—	3	—
Price, M.R. (Gm)	—	3	2	0	8	7	4.00	—	—	—	—
Prichard, P.J. (Ex)	—	20	29	2	888	100	32.88	1	6	10	—
Pridgeon, A.P. (Wo)	1980	24	23	7	211	67	13.18	—	1	14	—
Pringle, D.R. (E/Ex)	1982	21	35	7	658	96	23.50	—	4	14	—
Prior, J.A. (Ire)	—	1	1	0	87	87	87.00	—	1	—	—
Racionzer, T.B. (Sc)	—	1	2	0	58	51	29.00	—	1	—	—
Radford, N.V. (La)	—	4	5	1	53	36	13.25	—	—	—	—
Radley, C.T. (M)	1967	24	38	7	1072	128*	34.58	2	7	21	—
Ranatunga, A. (SL)	—	8	11	1	419	118	41.90	1	3	5	—
Randall, D.W. (E/Nt)	1973	25	40	3	1528	136	41.29	3	12	25	—
†Ratnayeke, J.R. (SL)	—	8	11	5	163	66	27.16	—	1	5	—
Rawlinson, H.T. (OU)	—	4	6	1	35	19*	7.00	—	—	2	—
Reeve, D.A. (Sx)	—	21	22	4	486	119	27.00	1	3	14	—
†Reifer, E.L. (H)	—	20	26	8	357	47	19.83	—	—	6	—
Rhodes, S.J. (Y)	—	2	2	1	41	35	41.00	—	—	3	—
Rice, C.E.B. (Nt)	1975	24	39	7	1553	152*	48.53	3	6	21	—
Richards, C.J. (Sy)	1978	25	38	8	908	109	30.26	2	4	46	6
Richards, I.V.A. (WI)	—	12	15	1	625	170	44.64	2	3	12	—
Richardson, P.C. (CU)	—	1	1	0	7	7	7.00	—	—	—	—
Richardson, R.B. (WI)	—	8	10	0	335	111	33.50	1	1	3	—
Ripley, D. (No)	—	14	21	3	281	61	15.61	—	1	26	12
Roberts, A.M.E. (Le)	—	8	12	4	188	89	23.50	—	1	2	—
Roberts, B. (D)	—	17	26	5	554	80	26.38	—	3	12	—
Robinson, P.E. (Y)	—	15	24	5	756	92	39.78	—	6	7	—
Robinson, R.T. (Nt)	1983	27	47	7	2032	171	50.80	5	11	16	—
†Roebuck, P.G.P. (Gs/CU)	—	6	12	2	286	62	28.60	—	2	2	—
Roebuck, P.M. (So)	1978	24	37	1	1702	159	47.27	7	4	4	—
Rolls, L.M. (Gs)	—	1	—	—	—	—	—	—	—	—	—
Romaines, P.W. (Gs)	1983	26	52	0	1844	141	35.46	4	10	12	—
†Rose, B.C. (So)	1975	20	33	4	856	123	29.51	1	4	5	—
Rowe, C.J.C. (Gm)	1983	6	11	2	155	60*	17.22	—	1	2	—
†Russell, R.C. (Gs)	—	21	27	6	513	63	24.42	—	1	26	9
Sainsbury, G.E. (Gs)	—	22	20	15	40	10*	8.00	—	—	8	—
Samaranayeke A.D.A. (SL)	—	5	5	1	14	9*	14.00	—	—	3	—
Sanders, I.E.W. (CU)	—	1	2	0	9	9	4.50	—	—	—	—
Saxelby, K. (Nt)	1984	20	19	8	196	27	17.81	—	—	2	—
Scott, C.W. (Nt)	—	2	2	1	26	15	26.00	—	—	6	—
Selvey, M.W.W. (Gm)	1983	15	18	8	111	20	11.10	—	—	9	—
Sharp, G. (No)	1973	11	12	0	168	28	14.00	—	—	15	2
†Sharp, K. (Y)	1982	24	39	2	1445	173	39.05	3	8	17	—
Shaw, C. (Y)	—	3	5	2	32	17	10.66	—	—	—	—
Shepherd, J.N. (Gs)	1983	24	39	7	885	87	27.65	—	6	13	—
Short, J.F. (Ire)	—	1	1	0	15	15	15.00	—	—	—	—
Siddiqi, S.N. (CU)	—	6	12	0	219	52	18.25	—	1	1	—
†Sidebottom, A. (Y/DBC)	1980	20	22	6	511	54*	31.93	—	2	1	—
†Silva, S.A.R. (SL)	—	7	12	3	558	161*	62.00	2	2	13	—
Simmons, J. (La)	1971	21	34	5	748	72*	25.79	—	6	15	—
Simpson D.J. (Sc)	—	1	2	0	12	9	6.00	—	—	—	—
†Slack, W.N. (M)	1981	25	46	8	1631	145	42.92	4	6	23	—

	Cap	M	I	NO	Runs	HS	Avge	100	50	Ct	St
Small, G.C. (Wa)	1982	24	30	8	400	41*	18.18	—	—	6	—
Small, M.A. (WI)	—	5	3	2	6	3*	6.00	—	—	1	—
Smith, C.L. (H/MCC)	1981	26	49	3	1298	125	28.21	4	3	13	—
†Smith, D.J. (Sx)	—	3	2	0	3	2	1.50	—	—	9	—
†Smith, D.M. (Wo)	—	17	31	5	1093	189*	42.03	2	6	12	—
Smith, K.D. (Wa)	1978	21	40	1	692	93	17.74	—	3	3	—
Smith, P.A. (Wa)	—	23	41	4	1040	89	28.10	—	8	10	—
Smith, R.A. (H)	—	7	13	3	483	132	48.30	1	2	4	—
Standing, D.K. (Sx)	—	2	2	1	12	7	12.00	—	—	1	—
Stanworth, J. (La)	—	10	10	3	18	6	2.57	—	—	16	1
Steele, D.S. (No)	1965	25	39	13	639	78*	24.57	—	3	29	—
Steele, J.F. (Gm)	1984	25	41	12	820	60*	28.27	—	1	33	—
Stevenson, G.B. (Y)	1978	14	16	1	180	27	12.00	—	—	5	—
Stewart, A.J. (Sy)	—	15	21	3	570	73	31.66	—	4	26	—
Stovold, A.W. (Gs)	1976	25	50	2	1524	139*	31.75	2	11	18	2
Such, P.M. (Nt)	—	15	10	5	29	16	5.80	—	—	6	—
Swallow, I.G. (Y)	—	11	9	3	136	34*	22.66	—	—	9	—
Swan, R.G. (Sc)	—	1	2	0	23	22	11.50	—	—	—	—
Tavaré, C.J. (E/K)	1978	24	41	0	1198	117	29.21	2	5	22	—
†Taylor, J.P. (D)	—	3	2	0	11	11	5.50	—	—	2	—
Taylor, L.B. (Le)	1981	7	5	1	37	16*	9.25	—	—	—	—
Taylor, N.R. (K)	1982	21	39	5	1098	139	32.29	2	5	8	—
Taylor, N.S. (Sy)	—	3	1	1	6	6*	—	—	—	2	—
Taylor, R.W. (D)	1962	18	22	7	303	46	20.20	—	—	27	5
Tedstone, G.A. (Wa)	—	1	1	1	0	0*	—	—	—	1	1
Terry, V.P. (E/H)	1983	16	28	3	1208	175*	48.32	5	6	17	—
†Thomas, D.J. (Sy)	1982	20	28	5	425	48	18.47	—	—	10	—
Thomas, J.G. (Gm)	—	20	26	5	314	36*	14.95	—	—	9	—
†Thomas, N.P. (CU)	—	1	2	0	0	0	0.00	—	—	1	—
Thomson, J. (Sc)	—	1	1	0	0	0	0.00	—	—	—	—
Thorne, D.A. (Wa/OU)	—	9	16	3	306	69*	23.53	—	1	7	—
Tomlins, K.P. (M)	1983	10	18	1	363	103*	21.35	1	—	8	—
Toogood, G.J. (OU)	—	8	15	1	425	109	30.35	1	2	3	—
Travers, T.J. (CU)	—	1	2	0	20	15	15.00	—	—	—	—
Trembath, C.R. (Gs)	—	2	3	2	25	17*	25.00	—	—	—	—
Tremlett, T.M. (H)	1983	23	31	7	438	74	18.25	—	2	4	—
Turnbull, J.R. (OU)	—	5	9	3	12	6	2.00	—	—	2	—
†Turner, D.R. (H)	1970	20	37	4	1365	153	41.36	3	7	7	—
Turner, M.S. (So)	—	1	2	0	1	1	0.50	—	—	—	—
Turner, S. (Ex)	1970	12	13	5	197	59*	24.62	—	2	4	—
†Turner, S.J. (So)	—	5	6	3	75	27*	25.00	—	—	12	3
Underwood D.L. (K)	1964	24	33	9	498	111	20.75	1	—	11	—
Varey, D.W. (La)	—	8	14	1	235	61	18.07	—	1	3	—
Vonhagt, D.M. (SL)	—	5	9	0	251	75	27.88	—	1	2	—
†Walker, A. (No)	—	13	15	4	64	19	5.81	—	—	4	—
Wall, S. (Wa)	—	7	9	4	47	19	9.40	—	—	1	—
Waller, C.E. (Sx)	1976	22	21	14	56	16*	8.00	—	—	13	—
Walsh, C.A. (WI/Gs)	—	14	15	3	98	30	8.16	—	—	1	—
Warke, S.J.S. (Ire)	—	1	1	0	54	54	54.00	—	1	2	—

	Cap	M	I	NO	Runs	HS	Avge	100	50	Ct	St
Warner, A.E. (Wo)	—	8	7	2	62	27	12.40	—	—	5	—
Warner, C.J. (Sc)	—	1	2	0	123	70	61.50	—	2	2	—
Wasim Raja (DBC)	—	1	1	1	48	48*	—	—	—	—	—
Waterman, P.A. (Sy)	3	2	1	0	0	0*	0.00	—	—	2	—
Waterton, S.N.V. (K)	—	7	10	1	193	50	21.44	—	1	11	4
Watkinson, M. (La/DBC)	—	17	29	6	668	77	29.04	—	4	7	—
Wells, A.P. (Sx)	—	25	39	7	1045	127	32.65	2	7	10	—
Wells C.M. (Sx)	1982	26	39	7	1389	203	43.40	5	4	4	—
Weston, M.J. (Wo)	—	24	41	3	1061	145*	27.92	1	7	15	—
Wettimuny, S. (SL)	—	7	11	1	505	190	50.50	2	1	2	—
Whitaker, J.J. (Le)	—	19	32	2	1097	160	36.56	2	6	20	—
Whitticase, P. (Le)	—	8	9	2	35	14	5.00	—	—	18	—
†Wild, D.J. (No)	—	15	27	2	855	144	34.20	2	2	5	—
Willey, P. (Le)	—	26	45	4	1472	167	35.90	6	2	17	—
Williams, N.F. (M/MCC)	1984	19	21	3	285	44	15.83	—	—	6	—
Williams, R.G. (No/MCC)	1979	20	37	4	1072	169	32.48	1	5	10	—
Willis, R.G.D. (E/Wa)	1972	8	8	5	56	22	18.66	—	—	3	—
Wills, R.T. (Ire)	—	1	1	0	17	17	17.00	—	—	—	—
Wilson, P.H.L. (So)	—	4	2	0	0	0	0.00	—	—	1	—
†Wood, D.J. (Sx)	—	2	3	0	32	15	10.66	—	—	—	—
Woolmer, R.A. (K)	1970	8	14	3	427	153	38.81	1	2	4	—
†Wootton, S.H. (Gs)	—	4	8	1	194	97	27.71	—	1	4	—
Wright, A.J. (Gs)	—	22	39	3	971	139	26.97	1	6	11	—
†Wright, J.G. (D)	1977	12	21	1	1201	177	60.05	2	9	10	—
Wyatt, J.G. (So)	—	16	28	0	666	103	23.78	1	3	8	—
†Younis Ahmed (Gm)	—	21	35	4	1369	158*	44.16	2	9	13	—
Yusuf, M.M. (SL)	—	4	1	1	2	2*	—	—	—	—	—
Zaheer Abbas (Gs)	1975	14	28	4	738	157*	30.75	1	4	2	—
Zaidi, S.M.N. (La)	—	6	6	3	98	36	32.66	—	—	6	—
Extras	—	—	—	—	12621	—		—	—	—	70	—
Total	5412	7971	1323	211289	258	31.78	328	929	3871	140

BOWLING

	Type	O	M	R	W	Avge	Best	5 wI	10 wM
†Abrahams, J. (La)	OB	88	19	247	4	61.75	2-25	—	—
Acfield, D.L. (Ex)	OB	577.4	174	1368	46	29.73	6-44	2	—
Afford, J.A. (Nt)	SLA	88.3	32	256	7	36.57	2-49	—	—
Agnew, J.P. (E/Le)	RF	670.1	127	2413	84	28.72	8-47	5	1
Alderman, T.M. (K)	RFM	559.4	149	1725	76	22.69	5-25	6	—
Allott, P.J.W. (E/La)	RFM	604.5	171	1496	79	18.93	7-72	6	—
Amarnath, M. (DBC)	RM	9	1	50	1	50.00	1-50	—	—
Anderson, I.S. (D)	OB	55	10	176	3	58.66	1-16	—	—
†Andrew, C.R. (CU)	OB	158.3	25	568	6	94.66	3-77	—	—
Andrew, S.J.W. (H)	RM	162.2	43	530	11	48.18	4-30	—	—
Anurasiri, S.D. (SL)	SLA	89.5	21	336	1	336.00	1-65	—	—
Asif Din, M. (Wa)	LB	11.3	1	55	5	11.00	3-49	—	—
Aslett, D.G. (K)	LB	18.4	1	92	0	—	—	—	—
Athey, C.W.J. (Gs)	RM	13	1	54	0	—	—	—	—
Bailey, R.J. (No)	OB	21	6	45	1	45.00	1-24	—	—
Bainbridge, P. (Gs)	RM	303.2	73	959	18	53.27	4-76	—	—
Bairstow, D.L. (Y/DBC)	RM	11	1	39	0	—	—	—	—
Balderstone, J.C. (Le)	SLA	19	5	69	2	34.50	2-3	—	—
Bamber, M.J. (No)	RM	2.3	1	3	0	—	—	—	—
Banks, D.A. (Wo)	—	4	0	17	0	—	—	—	—
Baptiste, E.A.E. (WI)	RFM	221.2	64	517	19	27.21	4-17	—	—
Barclay, J.R.T. (Sx)	OB	417	117	1023	36	28.41	4-32	—	—
Barnett, K.J. (D)	LB	43	6	162	0	—	—	—	—
Barwick, S.R. (Gm)	RM	473.4	127	1299	50	2598	7-38	2	—
Birch, J.D. (Nt)	RM	3	0	20	0	—	—	—	—
†Booth, P.A. (Y)	SLA	347	124	749	17	44.05	3-22	—	—
Booth, S.C. (So)	SLA	408.4	117	1172	38	30.84	4-50	—	—
Bore, M.K. (Nt)	LM	151.2	40	413	13	31.76	5-30	1	—
Botham, I.T. (E/So)	RFM	449.4	93	1562	59	26.47	8-103	4	—
Boycott, G. (Y)	RM	11	0	25	0	—	—	—	—
Boyd-Moss, R.J. (No)	SLA	55	12	268	1	268.00	1-68	—	—
Brettell, J.G. (OU)	SLA	15	3	74	1	74.00	1-74	—	—
Briers, N.E. (Le)	RM	109	24	264	12	22.00	3-48	—	—
†Broad, B.C. (E/Nt)	RM	31.2	6	131	2	65.50	2-23	—	—
Broome, I (D)	RFM	19.1	6	82	2	41.00	1-17	—	—
Burrows, D.A. (Gs)	RFM	15	0	76	0	—	—	—	—
†Butcher, A.R. (Sy)	SLA	38	9	134	4	33.50	3-65	—	—
Butcher, I.P. (Le)	—	2	1	13	0	—	—	—	—
Capel, D.J. (No)	RM	155	20	679	16	42.43	5-28	1	—
†Carmichael, I.R. (Le)	LFM	208	40	661	17	38.88	5-84	1	—
Carr, J.D. (M/OU)	OB	343	94	885	22	40.22	5-57	2	—
Carrick, P. (Y)	SLA	665.5	219	1606	44	36.50	6-32	3	1
†Childs, J.H. (Gs)	SLA	289	83	740	15	49.33	3-72	—	—
Clarke, S.T. (Sy)	RF	651	165	1687	78	21.62	6-62	2	—
Clift, P.B. (Le)	RM	620.1	165	1608	63	25.52	8-26	2	1
†Clinton, G.S. (Sy)	RM	6	1	30	0	—	—	—	—
†Close, D.B. (DBC)	OB	1.1	0	2	0	—	—	—	—
Connor, C.A. (H)	RFM	642.5	155	1949	62	31.43	7-37	1	—
Cook, G. (No)	SLA	15.1	1	99	0	—	—	—	—

	Type	O	M	R	W	Avge	Best	5 wI	10 wM
Cook, N.G.B. (E/Le/MCC)	SLA	769.3	209	2053	49	41.89	4-45	—	—
†Cooper, K.E. (Nt)	RFM	623.2	217	1364	51	26.74	8-44	1	—
Corlett, S.C. (Ire)	RM	58	21	98	5	19.60	3-42	—	—
Cotterell, T.A. (CU)	SLA	293.4	43	1074	13	82.61	3-95	—	—
Cowans, N.G. (E/M/MCC)	RF	493.1	76	1593	73	21.82	6-64	2	—
Cowdrey, C.S. (K/MCC)	RM	271.1	57	832	28	29.71	3-28	—	—
Cowdrey, G.R. (K)	RM	7	0	22	1	22.00	1-22	—	—
Cowley, N.G. (H)	OB	588.1	133	1779	56	31.76	4-33	—	—
Crowe, M.D. (So)	RM	435	101	1353	44	30.75	5-66	1	—
Cullinan, M.R. (OU)	—	2	1	4	1	4.00	1-4	—	—
†Cunningham, E.J. (Gs)	OB	21	3	70	0	—	—	—	—
Curtis, I.J. (Sy)	SLA	11.3	3	36	1	36.00	1-36	—	—
Curtis, T.S. (Wo)	LB	3.3	0	22	0	—	—	—	—
Dale, C.S. (Gs)	OB	125.1	22	467	7	66.71	3-10	—	—
Daniel, W.W. (M)	RF	462	86	1463	54	27.09	4-53	—	—
†Davis, M.R. (So)	LFM	500.4	108	1569	66	23.77	7-55	4	1
Davis, W.W. (WI/Gm)	RFM	547.5	118	1725	62	27.82	5-32	4	1
de Mel, A.L.F. (SL)	RFM	153.2	31	470	19	24.73	4-110	—	—
de Silva, D.S. (SL)	LBG	216	62	532	13	40.92	5-39	1	—
de Silva P.A. (SL)	RM	4	0	19	0	—	—	—	—
Dennis, S.J. (Y)	LFM	277.2	48	953	25	38.12	5-124	1	—
Derrick, J. (Gm)	RM	133.5	31	.441	8	55.12	3-42	—	—
Dias, R.L. (SL)	RM	6	3	18	1	18.00	1-9	—	—
D'Oliveira, D.B. (Wo)	RM/OB	113	24	341	10	34.10	2-50	—	—
†Dredge, C.H. (So)	RM	533	125	1534	53	28.94	4-48	—	—
Duthie, P.G. (Sc)	RM	23	3	73	1	73.00	1-73	—	—
Dyer, R.I.H.B. (Wa)	RM	5	0	39	0	—	—	—	—
East, D.E. (Ex)	—	3	0	11	0	—	—	—	—
East, R.E. (Ex)	SLA	152.4	48	324	11	29.45	3-24	—	—
Edmonds, P.H. (M)	SLA	823.3	233	2096	77	27.22	8-53	2	1
Ellcock, R.M. (Wo)	RF	221.2	32	714	29	24.62	4-34	—	—
†Ellison, R.M. (E/K)	RM	535.5	142	1323	59	22.42	5-27	1	—
Emburey, J.E. (M)	OB	865.3	255	1978	72	27.47	5-94	1	—
Evans, K.P. (Nt)	RFM	48	8	173	2	86.50	2-31	—	—
†Fairbrother, N.H. (La)	—	4.1	1	20	1	20.00	1-11	—	—
Feltham, M.A. (Sy)	RM	291.2	53	1012	32	31.62	5-62	1	—
†Felton, N.A. (So)	—	0.1	0	4	0	—	—	—	—
Ferreira, A.M. (Wa)	RM	772.1	156	2208	79	27.94	6-70	1	—
Ferris, G.J.F. (Le)	RFM	21	4	83	0	—	—	—	—
Finney, R.J. (D)	LM	584	130	1770	62	28.54	5-55	2	—
Fletcher, K.W.R. (Ex)	LB	9	2	28	0	—	—	—	—
Fletcher, S.D. (Y)	RM	162	35	471	14	33.64	4-24	—	—
Folley, I.J. (La)	LFM	369	91	1015	34	29.85	5-65	2	—
Foster, N.A. (E/Ex)	RM	687.1	153	2098	87	24.11	6-79	4	—
†Fowler, G. (E/La/DBC)	—	3.1	0	16	0	—	—	—	—
†Fowler, W.P. (D)	LM	117.3	27	398	5	79.60	2-53	—	—
Fraser, A.R.C. (M)	RFM	34	7	124	1	124.00	1-68	—	—
Fraser-Darling, C.D. (Nt)	RFM	29	9	55	3	18.33	2-14	—	—

188

	Type	O	M	R	W	Avge	Best	5 wI	10 wM
French, B.N. (Nt)	—	1	0	22	0	—	—	—	—
Garlick, P.L. (CU)	RFM	253	31	1092	12	91.00	2-69	—	—
Garner, J. (WI)	RF	270.5	81	624	39	16.00	5-19	2	—
Gatting, M.W. (E/M/MCC)	RM	87	20	205	8	25.62	3-16	—	—
†Gifford, N. (Wa)	SLA	812.4	238	1919	65	29.52	6-83	2	—
†Gladwin, C. (Ex)	RM	15	1	48	0	—	—	—	—
Golding, A.K. (CU)	SLA	185.1	17	822	6	137.00	2-100	—	—
Gomes, H.A. (WI)	RM	44	15	81	2	40.50	1-2	—	—
Gooch, G.A. (Ex)	RM	321.1	75	850	38	22.36	4-54	—	—
Graveney, D.A. (Gs)	SLA	667.4	202	1584	54	29.33	6-73	3	—
Green, A.M. (Sx)	RM	18	2	41	1	41.00	1-25	—	—
Green, R.C. (Gm)	RFM	31.5	9	92	2	46.00	2-65	—	—
Greenidge, C.G. (WI)	—	9	6	11	1	11.00	1-11	—	—
Greig, I.A. (Sx)	RM	648	153	1913	62	30.85	4-39	—	—
Griffiths, B.J. (No)	RFM	474	114	1332	43	30.97	5-52	2	—
Grimes, A.D.H. (CU)	RM	123	22	427	3	142.33	1-24	—	—
†Hadlee, R.J. (Nt)	RF	772.2	248	1645	117	14.05	7-35	6	1
Hampshire, J.H. (D)	LB	1	1	0	0	—	—	—	—
Hanley, R.W. (No)	RF	399.1	87	1182	37	31.94	6-21	3	—
†Hardy, J.J.E. (H)	—	1	0	3	0	—	—	—	—
Harper, R.A. (WI/DBC)	OB	314.1	109	676	37	18.27	6-57	3	—
Hartley, S.N. (Y)	RM	93	13	359	6	59.83	3-106	—	—
†Harrison, G.D. (Ire)	RFM	12	8	14	0	—	—	—	—
Hayes, K.A. (La/OU)	RM	99	28	284	9	31.55	4-58	—	—
Hemmings, E.E. (Nt)	OB	797.5	234	2220	94	23.61	7-47	7	1
Hendrick, M. (Nt)	RFM	72.1	33	86	8	10.75	5-17	1	—
Hewitt, S.M. (OU)	RM	64.5	8	232	4	58.00	2-52	—	—
Hick, G.A. (Wo)	OB	6	0	27	0	—	—	—	—
Hill, A. (D)	OB	50	10	191	3	63.66	1-22	—	—
†Hinks, S.G. (K)	RM	16	3	53	2	26.50	1-26	—	—
Holding, M.A. (WI)	RF	178.5	42	486	21	23.14	5-43	1	—
Holmes, G.C. (Gm)	RM	77	10	271	3	90.33	1-26	—	—
Hopkins, J.A. (Gm)	—	2.2	0	18	0	—	—	—	—
Howarth, G.P. (Sy)	OB	0.4	0	2	0	—	—	—	—
Hughes, D.P. (La)	SLA	105	34	261	4	65.25	3-42	—	—
Hughes, S.P. (M)	RFM	314.2	53	1051	35	30.02	4-27	—	—
Humpage, G.W. (Wa)	RM	14	0	57	2	28.50	2-44	—	—
Illingworth, R.K. (Wo)	SLA	744	220	1872	57	32.84	5-32	2	—
Inchmore, J.D. (Wo)	RFM	497	110	1364	44	31.00	4-37	—	—
†James, K.D. (M)	LM	41	16	106	4	26.50	2-9	—	—
Jarvis, K.B.S. (K)	RFM	570.5	128	1788	72	24.83	5-30	2	—
Jarvis, P.W. (Y)	RFM	304	53	1115	32	34.84	6-61	2	—
Javed Miandad (Gm)	LBG	51.2	9	187	6	31.16	2-26	—	—
†Jefferies, S.T. (La)	LFM	450.5	86	1392	43	32.37	6-67	2	—
Jesty, T.E. (H)	RM	220.1	50	668	19	35.15	3-15	—	—
John, V.B. (SL)	RFM	190.3	46	603	26	23.19	6-58	3	—
Johnson, G.W. (K)	OB	462.2	117	1220	39	31.28	5-38	2	—
Johnson, P. (Nt)	RM	4	0	23	2	11.50	1-9	—	—

189

	Type	O	M	R	W	Avge	Best	5 wI	10 wM
†Jones, A.L. (Gm)	—	10	0	86	1	86.00	1-60	—	—
†Jones, A.N. (Sx)	RFM	208.1	44	636	25	25.44	5-29	1	—
†Kallicharran, A.I. (Wa)	OB	10	5	12	0			—	—
Kapil Dev (Wo)	RFM	296.3	75	819	35	23.40	5-30	2	—
Kev, J.E. (Sc)	RM	20.3	4	69	3	23.00	3-69	—	—
†Knight, R.D.V. (Sy)	RM	349.4	99	925	27	34.25	4-7	—	—
Lamb, A.J. (E/No)	RM	1	0	6	0			—	—
Larkins, W. (No)	RM	68	19	175	6	29.16	5-59	1	—
Lawrence, D.V. (Gs)	RFM	455.1	80	1531	41	37.34	5-58	3	—
†Lawrence, M.P. (OU)	SLA	291.1	59	869	13	66.84	3-79	—	—
Le Roux, G.S. (Sx)	RF	604.2	154	1647	78	21.11	6-57	2	—
Lea, A.E. (CU)	LB	19	5	92	2	46.00	2-27	—	—
Lethbridge, C. (Wa)	RM	279.5	42	987	30	32.90	4-35	—	—
Lever, J.K. (Ex)	LFM	874.5	195	2550	116	21.98	8-37	8	3
Lilley, A.W. (Ex)	RM	5.2	2	11	2	5.50	2-11	—	—
†Lloyd, T.A. (E/Wa/MCC)	RM	8	2	41	1	41.00	1-6	—	—
†Lloyds, J.W. (So)	OB	240.2	69	697	14	49.78	3-62	—	—
Lumb, R.G. (Y)	RM	1	0	5	0			—	—
Lynch, M.A. (Sy)	RM/OB	22.3	3	89	4	22.25	3-10	—	—
Madugalle, R.S. (SL)	RM	31	6	75	2	37.50	1-18	—	—
Makinson, D.J. (La)	LFM	93	17	313	7	44.71	2-49	—	—
Malcolm, D.E. (D)	RF	156.2	24	674	16	42.12	3-78	—	—
Mallender, N.A. (No)	RFM	508	114	1533	47	32.61	4-45	—	—
Malone, S.J. (H)	RM	65	17	204	6	34.00	3-40	—	—
Marks, V.J. (So)	OB	808	231	2233	86	25.96	8-141	5	1
Marshall, M.D. (WI)	RF	260.4	75	646	40	16.15	7-53	4	—
Maru, R.J. (H)	SLA	549.4	129	1664	47	35.40	7-79	2	—
†Masters, K.D. (K)	RM	41.5	6	173	4	43.25	2-85	—	—
Maynard, C. (La)	—	2	0	8	0			—	—
McFarlane, L.L. (La)	RFM	272.5	45	875	31	28.22	4-65	—	—
McPate, W.A. (Sc)	RFM	23	8	70	2	35.00	2-70	—	—
Medlycott, K.T. (Sy)	SLA	98	34	186	7	26.57	2-15	—	—
Mee, S.R. (Nt)	RM	23	4	63	2	31.50	2-44	—	—
Mendis, L.R.D. (SL)	RM	1	0	2	0			—	—
†Miller, A.J.T. (M/OU)	—	1	0	4	1	4.00	1-4	—	—
Miller, G. (E/D)	OB	897.3	257	2233	87	25.70	6-30	6	—
Moir, D.G. (D)	SLA	822.5	206	2419	65	37.21	6-60	3	1
Monkhouse, G. (Sy)	RM	460.5	120	1273	50	25.46	4-41	—	—
Monteith, J.D. (Ire)	SLA	66	28	105	2	52.50	2-52	—	—
†Morris, H. (Gm)	—	9	1	45	1	45.00	1-45	—	—
Morris, J.E. (D)	RM	11	0	73	1	73.00	1-35	—	—
Mortensen, O.H. (D)	RFM	212.3	55	570	18	31.66	3-37	—	—
†Morton, W. (Wa)	SLA	189.5	45	549	14	39.21	4-85	—	—
Moxon, M.D. (Y/DBC)	RM	104	19	353	7	50.42	3-26	—	—
Mushtaq Mohammed (DBC)	LBG	6	1	27	0			—	—
Neale, P.A. (Wo)	RM	1.3	0	11	0			—	—
Needham, A. (Sy)	OB	328.5	79	1047	29	36.10	5-82	1	—

	Type	O	M	R	W	Avge	Best	5 wI	10 wM
Newell, M. (Nt)	LB	4	0	14	0	—	—	—	—
Newman, P.G. (D)	RFM	505.2	89	1717	50	34.34	7-104	1	—
Newport, P.J. (Wo)	RFM	204.4	36	689	21	32.80	5-51	1	—
Nicholas, M.C.J. (H/MCC)	RM	129	23	438	7	62.57	2-56	—	—
†Old, C.M. (Wa)	RFM	496	134	1306	45	29.02	6-46	3	1
Oldham, S. (D)	RFM	244.5	57	703	18	39.05	4-59	—	—
Ontong, R.C. (Gm)	RM	837.4	231	2155	74	29.12	7-96	4	—
O'Reilly, P.M. (Ire)	—	20	7	67	4	16.75	3-43	—	—
O'Shaughnessy, S.J. (La)	RM	214.3	40	753	19	39.63	3-76	—	—
Palmer, G.V. (So)	RM	320.3	56	1231	30	41.03	4-58	—	—
Parker, P.W.G. (Sx)	RM	11.1	2	40	2	20.00	2-21	—	—
†Parsons, G.J. (Le)	RM	662.1	140	2164	67	32.29	5-42	2	—
Patel, D.N. (Wo)	OB	770	219	2063	61	33.81	5-28	2	—
Patterson, B.P. (La)	RFM	21	3	51	0	—	—	—	—
†Patterson, T.J.T. (Ire)	LM	36	9	96	3	32.00	2-54	—	—
Pauline, D.B. (Sy)	RM	6	4	6	0	—	—	—	—
Payne, I.R. (Sy)	RM	42.5	18	102	3	34.00	2-24	—	—
†Penn, C. (K)	RFM	157	26	491	8	61.37	2-11	—	—
Petchey, M.D. (OU)	RM	34	7	82	4	20.50	4-65	—	—
Phillip, N. (Ex)	RFM	275,2	48	911	34	26.79	5-48	1	—
†Pick, R.A. (Nt)	RM	243.5	52	773	25	30.92	5-25	2	1
Pigott, A.C.S. (Sx)	RFM	32	5	96	2	48.00	1-24	—	—
Pocock, N.E.J. (H)	LM	11	1	61	0	—	—	—	—
Pocock, P.I. (E/Sy)	OB	638.5	167	1621	63	25.73	7-74	3	1
Pollock, A.J. (CU)	RM	161.2	32	620	14	44.28	4-104	—	—
Popplewell, N.F.M. (So)	RM	125.3	30	370	8	46.25	3-79	—	—
Potter, L. (K)	LM	63	18	196	5	39.20	2-31	—	—
Price, M.R. (Gm)	SLA	31	4	109	2	54.50	1-43	—	—
Prichard, P.J. (Ex)	—	1	0	5	0	—	—	—	—
Pridgeon, A.P. (Wo)	RM	719.5	168	1949	66	29.53	5-50	2	—
Pringle, D.R. (E/Ex)	RM	580.1	127	1784	64	27.87	7-53	3	—
Prior, J.A. (Ire)	RM	12.5	4	31	3	10.33	2-7	—	—
Racionzer, T.B. (Sc)	OB	3	0	19	0	—	—	—	—
Radford, N.V. (La)	RFM	106.4	17	390	10	39.00	5-95	1	—
Ranatunga, A. (SL)	RM	69	12	227	6	37.83	2-44	—	—
Randall, D.W. (E/Nt)	RM	9.4	0	43	3	14.33	3-43	—	—
†Ratnayeke, J.R. (SL)	RFM	227.2	43	730	16	45.62	4-93	—	—
Rawlinson, H.T. (OU)	RM	95.5	18	346	4	86.50	3-114	—	—
Reeve, D.A. (Sx)	RM	572.4	175	1420	55	25.81	5-22	1	—
†Reifer, E.L. (H)	LFM	524.5	100	1761	49	35.93	4-43	—	—
Rice, C.E.B. (Nt)	RM	206	54	569	19	29.94	4-61	—	—
Richards, C.J. (Sy)	—	4	0	20	0	—	—	—	—
Richards, I.V.A. (WI)	OB	74	20	185	3	61.66	2-60	—	—
Richardson, P.C. (CU)	OB	21	0	122	1	122.00	1-92	—	—
Roberts, A.M.E. (Le)	RF	265	70	769	33	23.30	7-74	3	—
Roberts, B. (D)	RM	277	43	1044	22	47.45	4-77	—	—
Robinson, P.E. (Y)	LM	2	0	12	0	—	—	—	—
Roebuck, P.M. (So)	OB	10.2	5	18	0	—	—	—	—
Rolls, L.M. (Gs)	OB	15	1	49	0	—	—	—	—

	Type	O	M	R	W	Avge	Best	5 wI	10 wM
Romaines, P.W. (Gs)	—	0.3	0	8	0				
Rowe, C.J.C. (Gm)	OB	135	41	356	12	29.66	3-20	—	—
Sainsbury, G.E. (Gs)	LM	566.2	141	1596	48	33.25	5-19	2	—
Samaranayeke, A.D.A. (SL)	RFM	143.2	24	499	9	55.44	4-142	—	—
Sanders, I.E.W. (CU)	RFM	25	5	93	3	31.00	2-78	—	—
Saxelby, K. (Nt)	RFM	516.5	140	1592	47	33.87	5-43	1	—
Selvey, M.W.W. (Gm)	RFM	311.3	69	997	25	39.88	6-31	1	—
Sharp, G. (No)	SLA	1	1	0	0				
†Sharp, K. (Y)	OB	71	18	229	7	32.71	2-13	—	—
Shaw, C. (Y)	RFM	53.4	5	177	5	35.40	4-68	—	—
Shepherd, J.N. (Gs)	RM	800.3	209	2225	72	30.90	5-30	2	—
Siddiqi, S.N. (CU)	RM	23	6	90	5	18.00	5-90	1	—
Sidebottom, A. (Y/DBC)	RFM	488.1	105	1292	63	20.50	6-41	3	—
Simmons, J. (La)	OB	619.4	177	1644	63	26.09	7-176	7	1
†Slack, W.N. (M)	RM	28	3	76	0				
Small, G.C. (Wa)	RFM	643.4	127	2027	71	28.54	5-41	2	—
Small, M.A. (WI)	—	100	17	321	13	24.69	4-52	—	—
Smith, C.L. (H/MCC)	OB	159	19	701	9	77.88	2-41	—	—
†Smith, D.M. (Wo)	RM	6	0	22	1	22.00	1-20	—	—
Smith, P.A. (Wa)	RFM	194.4	23	839	20	41.95	4-41	—	—
Steele, D.S. (No)	SLA	732	227	2100	61	34.42	5-86	2	—
Steele, J.F. (Gm)	SLA	674	175	1867	68	27.45	5-42	4	—
Stevenson, G.B. (Y)	RM	262.3	44	892	19	46.94	4-35	—	—
Such, P.M. (Nt)	RM	386.5	122	937	42	22.30	5-34	2	—
Swallow, I.G. (Y)	OB	229.1	62	620	15	41.33	4-52	—	—
Tavaré, C.J. (E,K)	RM	2	0	18	0				
†Taylor, J.P. (D)	LFM	49.2	6	188	2	94.00	2-92	—	—
Taylor, L.B. (Le)	RFM	142	42	369	10	36.90	2-22	—	—
Taylor, N.R. (K)	OB	15	3	54	0				
Taylor, N.S. (Sy)	RFM	80	20	254	10	25.40	3-38	—	—
Taylor, R.W. (D)	RM	6.2	1	23	1	23.00	1-23	—	—
†Thomas, D.J. (Sy)	LFM	505.4	114	1654	60	27.56	6-36	2	1
Thomas, J.G. (Gm)	RM	435.2	95	1575	47	33.51	5-56	2	1
Thomson, J. (Sc)	—	38	10	116	4	29.00	4-116	—	—
Thorne, D.A. (Wa/OU)	LM	203.1	42	565	15	37.66	5-39	1	—
Tomlins, K.P. (M)	RM	5	1	9	0				
Toogood, J.T. (OU)	OB	54.5	9	199	3	66.33	1-1	—	—
Trembath, C.R. (Gs)	RM	46.5	5	225	5	45.00	3-106	—	—
Tremlett, T.M. (H)	RM	669.5	210	1444	71	20.33	5-48	2	—
Turnbull, J.R. (OU)	RM	91	16	354	3	118.00	1-35	—	—
†Turner, D.R. (H)	RM	5	1	9	0				
Turner, M.S. (So)	RFM	29	8	85	0				
Turner, S. (Ex)	RM	285	95	617	21	29.38	3-29	—	—
Underwood, D.L. (K)	LM	676.4	250	1511	77	19.62	8-87	2	1
†Walker, A. (No)	RFM	308.5	52	1118	27	41.40	4-50	—	—
Wall, S. (Wa)	RFM	140.4	28	545	9	60.55	2-65	—	—
Waller, C.E. (Sx)	SLA	610.3	221	1349	53	25.45	6-75	1	—
Walsh, C.A. (WI/Gs)	RFM	341.3	80	1179	32	36.84	6-70	1	—

	Type	O	M	R	W	Avge	Best	5 wI	10 wM
Warner, A.E. (Wo)	RFM	186	33	632	15	42.13	5-27	1	—
Waterman, P.A. (Sy)	RM	58.2	7	194	5	38.80	2-16	—	—
Watkinson, M. (La/DBC)	RM	359.3	73	1229	29	42.37	6-39	1	—
Wells, C.M. (Sx)	RM	497.2	146	1396	59	23.66	5-25	2	—
Weston, M.J. (Wo)	RM	123.4	29	315	14	22.50	4-44	—	—
Wettimuny, S. (SL)	RM	5	1	7	1	7.00	1-7	—	—
†Wild, D.J. (No)	RM	91.4	18	329	10	32.90	3-15	—	—
Willey, P. (Le)	OB	544.1	163	1291	43	30.02	6-78	2	—
Williams, N.F. (M/MCC)	RFM	474.1	95	1653	49	33.73	4-19	—	—
Williams, R.G. (No/MCC)	OB	442.2	104	1348	32	42.12	4-22	—	—
Willis, R.G.D. (E/Wa)	RF	213	42	747	15	49.80	2-19	—	—
Wilson, P.H.L. (So)	RFM	56	14	176	5	35.20	3-36	—	—
Woolmer, R.A. (K)	RM	20	3	51	5	10.20	2-16	—	—
†Wright, J.G. (D)	RM	22	2	114	1	114.00	1-81	—	—
Wyatt, J.G. (So)	RM	3	1	4	1	4.00	1-0	—	—
†Younis Ahmed (Gm)	LM/SLA	12	3	34	0	—	—	—	—
Yusuf, M.M. (SL)	—	74	10	282	1	282.00	1-25	—	—
Zaheer Abbas (Gs)	OB	5.4	4	1	0	—	—	—	—
Zaidi, S.M.N. (La)	LB	80	12	297	3	99.00	2-10	—	—
Extras	—	—	—	12621	151	—	—	—	—
Total		68462.5	16637	211289	6648	31.78	8-26	221	20

CAREER RECORDS
Compiled by Brian Heald

The following career records are for all players who appeared in first-class cricket during the 1984 season. Some players who did not appear for their counties in 1984, but who may do so in 1985, are also included.

Aggregates of 1,000 runs overseas are preceded by a + sign, e.g. D.L. Amiss 20+1.

BATTING AND FIELDING

	M	I	NO	Runs	HS	Avge	100s	1000 runs in season	Ct	St
Abrahams, J.	191	294	40	7293	201*	28.71	9	3	127	—
Acfield, D.L.	376	377	191	1545	42	8.30	—	—	126	—
Afford, J.A.	3	—	—	—	—	—	—	—	1	—
Agnew, J.P.	81	79	14	600	56	9.23	—	—	23	—
Alderman, T.M.	110	121	61	537	52*	8.95	—	—	100	—
Allott, P.J.W.	112	111	29	1135	52*	13.84	—	—	34	—
Amarnath, M.	191	300	49	10425	207	41.53	22	3	133	—
Amiss, D.L.	581	1004	112	39118	262*	43.85	91	20+1	374	—
Anderson, I.S.	93	146	21	2994	112	23.95	2	1	78	—
Andrew, C.R.	9	18	1	405	101*	23.82	1	—	2	—
Andrew, S.J.W.	7	6	4	12	6*	6.00	—	—	1	—
Anurasiri, S.D.	4	3	1	5	5	2.50	—	—	2	—
Asif Din	65	101	11	2243	102	24.92	1	—	38	—
Aslett, D.G.	64	113	11	3910	221*	38.33	9	2	46	—
Athey, C.W.J.	189	320	25	8615	134	29.20	15	3	176	2
Bailey, R.J.	30	53	9	1515	114	34.43	3	1	20	—
Bainbridge, P.	122	213	34	5453	146	30.46	7	4	60	—
Bairstow, D.L.	357	508	97	10285	145	25.02	4	2	770	116
Balderstone, J.C.	351	556	55	17353	181*	34.63	29	10	197	—
Bamber, M.J.	13	26	2	638	77	26.58	—	—	6	—
Banks, D.A.	13	22	1	495	100	23.57	1	—	6	—
Baptiste, E.A.E.	71	99	18	2240	136*	27.65	2	—	39	—
Barclay, J.R.T.	250	414	38	9384	119	24.95	9	4	203	—
Barlow, G.D.	226	366	54	10850	177	34.77	19	6	128	—
Barnett, K.J.	130	199	22	5888	144	33.26	11	2	80	—
Barwick, S.R.	47	48	23	282	25	11.28	—	—	14	—
Benson, M.R.	83	142	15	4840	152*	38.11	12	3	40	—
Birch, J.D.	168	252	38	5856	125	27.36	5	2	129	—
Boon, T.J.	59	100	12	2383	144	27.07	4	1	19	—
Booth, P.A.	12	16	4	78	26	6.50	—	—	2	—
Booth, S.C.	22	26	12	124	42	8.85	—	—	20	—
Bore, M.K.	152	151	51	856	37*	8.56	—	—	50	—
Botham, I.T.	250	387	26	11907	228	32.98	24	3	229	—
Boycott, G.	575	960	149	45777	261*	56.44	143	22+3	250	—
Boyd-Moss, R.J.	98	171	13	4892	139	30.96	9	2	45	—
Brassington, A.J.	124	153	44	878	35	8.05	—	—	209	48
Breddy, M.N.	10	20	1	339	61	17.84	—	—	2	—

194

	M	I	NO	Runs	HS	Avge	100s	1000 runs in season	Ct	St
Brettell, J.G.	1	2	1	0	0*	0.00	—	—	1	—
Briers, N.E.	165	265	26	6672	201*	27.91	9	3	68	—
Bristowe, W.R.	5	8	3	104	30*	20.80	—	—	2	—
Broad, B.C.	112	199	14	6353	145	34.34	9	4	50	—
Broome, I.	2	4	3	35	26*	35.00	—	—	1	—
Brown, A.	6	9	0	110	30	12.22	—	—	9	1
Brown, K.R.	1	1	0	6	6	6.00	—	—	1	—
Burnley, I.D.	3	6	0	232	86	38.66	—	—	1	—
Burrows, D.A.	1	1	0	0	0	0.00	—	—	—	—
Butcher, A.R.	248	419	40	12693	216*	33.49	26	6	114	—
Butcher, I.P.	49	83	5	2560	139	32.82	8	1	41	—
Butcher, R.O.	176	278	25	7817	197	30.89	12	2	205	1
Capel, D.J.	49	76	15	1820	109*	29.83	1	—	28	—
Carmichael, I.R.	18	17	6	17	4*	1.54	—	—	5	—
Carr, J.D.	18	24	4	535	123	26.75	2	—	14	—
Carrick, P.	263	333	64	5826	131*	21.65	3	—	132	—
Chadwick, M.R.	8	16	0	295	61	18.43	—	—	3	—
Childs, J.H.	165	151	72	535	34*	6.77	—	—	63	—
Clarke, S.T.	166	186	30	2397	100*	15.36	1	—	96	—
Clift, P.B.	251	360	80	6652	100*	23.75	1	—	129	—
Clinton, G.S.	150	252	29	6802	192	30.50	11	3	45	—
Close, D.B.	784	1221	171	34926	198	33.26	52	20	811	1
Cobb, R.A.	44	68	1	1335	63	19.92	—	—	26	—
Cohen, M.F.	2	2	0	0	0	0.00	—	—	1	—
Connor, C.A.	21	23	9	65	13*	4.64	—	—	7	—
Cook, C.R.	11	18	2	393	79	24.56	—	—	8	—
Cook, G.	342	606	43	17618	172	31.29	26	9	348	3
Cook, N.G.B.	152	156	47	1293	75	11.86	—	—	91	—
Cooper, K.E.	159	157	36	1113	38*	9.19	—	—	54	—
Corlett, S.C.	30	42	7	534	60	15.25	—	—	24	—
Cotterell, T.A.	20	28	4	328	52	13.66	—	—	5	—
Cowans, N.G.	67	73	11	509	66	8.20	—	—	31	—
Cowdrey, C.S.	160	234	37	6163	125*	31.28	8	2	145	—
Cowdrey, G.R.	1	1	0	7	7	7.00	—	—	1	—
Cowley, N.G.	208	302	42	5767	109*	22.18	2	1	81	—
Crowe, M.D.	85	139	21	5359	190	45.41	17	1	94	—
Cullinan, M.R.	16	21	2	215	59	11.31	—	—	18	1
Cunningham, E.J.	14	23	6	271	61*	15.94	—	—	4	—
Curtis, I.J.	31	30	14	77	20*	4.81	—	—	7	—
Curtis, T.S.	60	104	14	2809	129	31.21	3	1	32	—
Dale, C.S.	8	8	2	100	49	16.66	—	—	1	—
Daniel, W.W.	205	189	85	1304	53*	12.53	—	—	47	—
Davies, A.G.	12	18	5	325	69	25.00	—	—	14	2
Davies, T.	50	68	15	956	69*	18.03	—	—	89	14
Davis, M.R.	42	43	13	368	60*	12.26	—	—	15	—
Davis, W.W.	82	99	38	906	77	14.85	—	—	28	—
de Alwis, R.G.	14	19	0	281	74	14.78	—	—	20	2
de Mel A.L.F.	29	40	7	747	100*	22.63	1	—	17	—
de Silva D.S.	64	95	16	1735	97	21.96	—	—	34	—

	M	I	NO	Runs	HS	Avge	100s	1000 runs in season	Ct	St
de Silva P.A.	9	10	1	259	75	28.77	—	—	3	—
Denning P.W.	269	447	44	11559	184	28.68	8	6	131	—
Dennis, S.J.	47	51	20	313	53*	10.09	—	—	12	—
Derrick, J.	15	20	10	403	69*	40.30	—	—	11	—
Dias, R.L.	64	105	11	2978	127	31.68	3	—	25	—
Dilley, G.R.	114	119	42	1205	81	15.64	—	—	53	—
D'Oliveira, D.B.	49	80	6	1833	102	24.77	1	—	32	—
Donald, W.A.	6	10	1	157	45	17.44	—	—	1	—
Doughty, R.J.	14	19	7	214	32*	17.83	—	—	2	—
Downton, P.R.	163	193	37	3055	90*	19.58	—	—	347	48
Dredge, C.H.	159	184	58	1749	56*	13.88	—	—	70	—
Dujon, P.J.	82	119	17	4340	135*	42.54	11	—	154	11
Duthie, P.G.	1	2	0	64	34	32.00	—	—	1	—
Dyer, R.I.H.B.	34	60	6	1510	106*	27.96	1	1	15	—
East, D.E.	90	118	17	1814	91	17.96	—	—	225	20
East, R.E.	410	517	112	7178	113	17.72	1	—	256	—
Edbrooke, R.M.	11	20	2	591	84*	32.83	—	—	5	—
Edmonds, P.H.	307	401	68	6566	142	19.71	3	—	286	—
Ellcock, R.M.	25	33	6	337	45*	13.48	—	—	4	—
Ellis, R.G.P.	39	71	3	1997	105*	29.36	2	—	19	—
Ellison, R.M.	57	75	23	1379	108	26.51	1	—	29	—
Emburey, J.E.	246	296	66	4703	133	20.44	2	—	220	—
Evans, K.P.	3	4	0	48	42	12.00	—	—	3	—
Fairbrother, N.H.	40	65	6	1960	102	33.22	1	1	27	—
Falkner, N.J.	1	1	1	101	101*	—	1	—	1	—
Feltham, M.A.	13	15	5	206	44	20.60	—	—	5	—
Felton, N.A.	29	48	2	1221	173*	26.54	2	—	11	—
Ferrerra A.M.	151	230	43	5016	112*	26.82	2	—	77	—
Ferris, G.J.F.	20	22	10	84	26	7.00	—	—	3	—
Finney, R.J.	45	73	7	1296	78	19.63	—	—	10	—
Fletcher, K.W.R.	651	1062	151	35013	228*	38.43	62	20	586	—
Fletcher, S.D.	11	9	3	49	28*	8.16	—	—	—	—
Folley, I.	46	52	17	450	36	12.85	—	—	12	—
Foster, N.A.	48	55	16	725	54*	18.58	—	—	18	—
Fowler, G.	109	183	9	6548	226	37.63	18	4	56	5
Fowler, W.P.	49	82	13	1823	116	26.42	2	—	34	—
Francis, D.A.	138	237	36	4938	142*	24.56	3	1	62	—
Franks, J.G.	13	20	2	268	42*	14.88	—	—	10	1
Fraser, A.R.C.	1	—	—	—	—	—	—	—	—	—
Fraser-Darling, C.D.	1	—	—	—	—	—	—	—	—	—
French, B.N.	170	221	44	3303	95	18.66	—	—	378	41
Gard, T.	64	73	15	827	51*	14.25	—	—	115	26
Garlick, P.L.	10	15	6	13	6*	1.44	—	—	1	—
Garner, J.	147	164	39	2176	104	17.40	1	—	98	—
Garnham, M.A.	52	78	14	1541	84	24.07	—	—	107	16
Gatting, M.A.	224	347	56	12833	258	44.09	30	6	207	—
Gifford, N.	617	715	226	6649	89	13.59	—	—	302	—
Gladwin, C.	36	60	3	1919	162	33.66	1	1	18	—

196

	M	I	NO	Runs	HS	Avge	100s	1000 runs in season	Ct	St
Goldie, C.F.E.	22	24	3	302	77	14.38	—	—	34	8
Golding, A.K.	9	15	2	197	44	15.15	—	—	2	—
Gomes, H.A.	191	310	44	11139	200*	41.87	25	1+2	67	—
Gooch, G.A.	292	493	43	18963	227	42.14	47	8+1	272	—
Gould, I.J.	183	245	34	4782	128	22.66	1	—	382	62
Gower, D.I.	236	378	35	13631	200*	39.74	28	5	149	—
Graveney, D.A.	265	365	95	5087	119	18.84	2	—	134	—
Green, A.M.	58	102	5	2441	99	25.16	—	1	30	—
Green, R.C.	2	1	1	3	3*	—	—	—	1	—
Greenidge, C.G.	374	641	55	26492	273*	45.20	62	12+1	386	—
Greig, I.A.	123	166	19	3739	147*	25.43	4	—	75	—
Griffiths, B.J.	154	123	44	255	16	3.22	—	—	32	—
Grimes, A.D.H.	7	11	2	58	13	6.44	—	—	2	—
Hadlee, R.J.	231	320	54	7787	210*	29.27	9	1	136	—
Hampshire, J.H.	577	924	112	28059	183	34.55	43	15	445	—
Hanley, R.W.	109	96	43	314	33*	5.92	—	—	39	—
Hardie, B.R.	261	421	51	12579	162	33.99	14	9	241	—
Hardy, J.J.E.	13	20	6	513	95	36.64	—	—	9	—
Harper, R.A.	48	60	3	1068	86	18.73	—	—	58	—
Harrison, G.D.	2	3	1	139	86	69.50	—	—	—	—
Hartley, S.N.	92	144	21	2970	114	24.14	3	—	37	—
Hassan, S.B.	329	544	53	14285	182*	29.09	15	5	304	1
Hayes, F.C.	272	421	58	13018	187	35.86	23	6	176	—
Hayes, K.A.	38	63	4	1268	152	21.49	1	—	12	—
Haynes, D.L.	117	190	16	7269	184	41.77	12	0+2	67	—
Haysman, M.D.	24	44	7	1520	153	41.08	4	—	33	—
Hemmings, E.E.	322	436	95	6845	127*	20.08	1	—	150	—
Henderson, S.P.	63	104	13	2305	209*	25.32	3	—	43	—
Hendrick, M.	267	267	109	1601	46	10.13	—	—	176	—
Hewitt, S.G.P.	9	12	6	29	14*	4.83	—	—	9	2
Hewitt, S.M.	4	6	1	60	22	12.00	—	—	—	—
Hick, G.A.	7	12	3	272	82*	30.22	—	—	11	—
Hill, A.	224	393	38	10585	160*	29.81	14	4	85	—
Hinks, S.G.	16	28	1	450	87	16.66	—	—	6	—
Holding, M.A.	123	152	25	1884	69	14.83	—	—	46	—
Holmes, G.C.	75	122	24	2435	100*	24.84	1	1	29	—
Hopkins, J.A.	239	426	27	11305	230	28.33	16	7	173	1
Howarth, G.P.	315	544	41	16615	183	33.03	32	4	222	—
Hughes, D.P.	344	447	82	8201	153	22.46	8	2	233	—
Hughes, S.P.	65	64	29	272	41*	7.82	—	—	16	—
Humpage, G.W.	223	367	45	11878	254	36.88	23	7	396	52
Humphries, D.J.	174	251	45	5054	133*	24.53	4	—	292	60
Illingworth, R.K.	57	71	17	810	55	15.00	—	—	21	—
Imran Khan	289	451	70	13307	170	34.92	22	3	93	—
Inchmore, J.D.	192	229	49	2982	113	16.56	1	—	65	—
Jackson, P.B.	4	5	1	106	46	26.50	—	—	11	1
James, K.D.	15	16	6	220	34	22.00	—	—	3	—
Jarvis, K.B.S.	205	150	65	275	19	3.23	—	—	50	—

	M	I	NO	Runs	HS	Avge	100s	1000 runs in season	Ct	St
Jarvis, P.W.	21	22	9	186	37	14.30	—	—	7	—
Javed Miandad	284	460	74	20416	311	52.89	56	448	268	3
Jefferies, S.T.	73	97	19	2016	75*	25.84	—	—	23	—
Jesty, T.E.	366	584	75	15970	248	31.37	27	7	213	1
John, V.B.	18	20	8	70	27*	5.83	—	—	3	—
Johnson, G.W.	374	582	73	12549	168	24.65	11	3	305	—
Johnson, P.	30	49	4	1349	133	29.97	3	—	16	1
Jones, A.L.	128	230	18	5483	132	25.86	5	2	86	—
Jones, A.N.	26	27	12	146	35	9.73	—	—	4	—
Kallicharran, A.I.	421	693	73	28096	243*	45.31	75	10+1	277	—
Kapil Dev	154	218	22	5762	193	29.39	8	—	102	—
Ker, A.B.M.	4	7	1	178	65	29.66	—	—	4	—
Ker, J.E.	8	12	5	147	50	21.00	—	—	3	—
Knight, R.D.V.	384	668	59	19518	165*	32.04	31	13	294	—
Knott, A.P.E.	492	721	129	17726	156	29.94	17	2	1158	132
Kuruppu, D.S.B.P.	9	15	0	249	55	16.60	—	—	10	2
Lamb, A.J.	217	374	64	15058	178	48.57	39	6	157	—
Larkins, W.	261	452	27	14665	252	34.50	34	7	128	—
Lawrence, D.V.	29	34	8	157	17	6.03	—	—	3	—
Lawrence, M.P.	13	16	5	69	18	6.27	—	—	5	—
Lea, A.E.	9	18	0	395	119	21.94	1	—	2	—
Lenham, N.J.	1	1	0	31	31	31.00	—	—	1	—
le Roux, G.S.	157	191	53	3364	83	24.37	—	—	59	—
Lethbridge, C.	47	55	12	949	87*	22.06	—	—	16	—
Lever, J.K.	442	453	171	3067	91	10.87	—	—	169	—
Lilley, A.W.	31	48	2	1175	100*	25.54	1	—	16	—
Lloyd, C.H.	469	699	92	29865	242*	49.20	76	10+4	367	—
Lloyd, T.A.	146	258	30	8365	208*	36.68	15	4	86	—
Lloyds, J.W.	101	163	21	4050	132*	28.52	5	—	85	—
Logie, A.L.	58	88	9	2894	171	36.63	8	—	19	—
Lord, G.J.	7	9	0	174	61*	19.33	—	—	4	—
Love, J.D.	158	259	38	6869	170*	31.08	11	2	85	—
Lumb, R.G.	245	406	30	11723	165*	31.17	22	5	131	—
Lynch, M.A.	140	239	25	6889	144	32.19	14	3	100	—
Madugalle, R.S.	47	70	8	1972	142*	31.80	1	—	32	—
Maher, B.J.M.	27	37	10	351	66	13.00	—	—	49	5
Makinson, D.J.	4	5	2	18	9	6.00	—	—	—	—
Malcolm, D.E.	7	8	1	40	23	5.71	—	—	4	—
Mallender, N.A.	96	109	34	887	71*	11.82	—	—	37	—
Malone, S.J.	48	40	14	178	23	6.84	—	—	11	—
Marks, V.J.	209	318	50	7789	134	29.06	4	1	94	—
Marsh, S.A.	8	10	2	121	48*	15.12	—	—	17	—
Marshall, M.D.	164	207	24	4005	116*	21.88	4	—	62	—
Maru, R.J.	33	36	7	393	36	13.55	—	—	36	—
Masters, K.D.	4	7	1	1	1	0.16	—	—	2	—
Maynard, C.	79	97	17	1613	85	20.16	—	—	115	17
McDonnell, G.F.H.	2	4	0	7	5	1.75	—	—	—	—
McEvoy, M.S.A.	69	113	2	2128	103	19.17	1	—	70	—

198

	M	I	NO	Runs	HS	Avge	100s	1000 runs in season	Ct	St
McEwan, K.S.	356	589	52	21842	218	40.67	58	11	318	7
McFarlane, L.L.	43	36	18	115	15*	6.38	—	—	9	—
McPate, W.A.	2	3	2	17	12*	17.00	—	—	—	—
Medlycott, K.T.	6	6	5	128	117*	128.00	1	—	—	—
Mee, A.A.G.	1	1	0	2	2	2.00	—	—	1	—
Mee, S.R.	1	—	—	—	—	—	—	—	—	—
Mendis, G.D.	181	320	27	9865	209*	33.66	17	5	83	1
Mendis, L.R.D.	82	138	13	4569	194	36.55	9	—	36	1
Metcalfe, A.A.	10	15	0	345	122	23.00	1	—	6	—
Metson, C.P.	13	18	6	338	96	28.16	—	—	29	2
Middleton, T.C.	1	2	0	15	10	7.50	—	—	—	—
Miller, A.J.T.	24	43	4	1275	128*	32.69	2	1	3	—
Miller, G.	276	411	67	9444	130	27.45	1	—	204	—
Moir, D.G.	64	77	11	990	107	15.00	1	—	57	—
Monkhouse, G.	48	59	21	793	100*	20.86	1	—	21	—
Monteith, J.D.	28	39	5	530	95	15.55	—	—	23	—
Moores, P.	11	15	3	215	45	17.91	—	—	18	6
Morris, H.	25	42	10	1004	114*	31.37	1	—	10	—
Morris, J.E.	26	50	2	1327	135	27.64	3	—	8	—
Mortensen, O.H.	26	31	19	139	40*	11.58	—	—	9	—
Morton, W.	10	10	2	47	13*	5.87	—	—	6	—
Moxon, M.D.	53	96	4	3135	153	34.07	6	1	37	—
Mushtaq Mohammad	501	841	104	31066	303*	42.15	72	12+3	346	—
Neale, P.A.	198	341	41	10514	163*	35.04	16	6	80	—
Needham, A.	55	78	10	1141	134*	16.77	1	—	24	—
Newell, M.	4	7	1	109	76	18.16	—	—	6	—
Newman, P.G.	61	67	13	640	40	11.85	—	—	16	—
Newport, P.J.	17	20	7	297	41*	22.84	—	—	3	—
Nicholas, M.C.J.	120	208	25	6003	206*	32.80	13	3	77	—
Old, C.M.	371	455	89	7634	116	20.85	6	—	213	—
Oldham, S.	127	96	40	640	50	11.42	—	—	37	—
Ollis, R.L.	22	40	3	691	99*	18.67	—	—	13	—
Ontong, R.C.	241	414	46	10477	204*	28.47	16	4	118	—
O'Reilly, P.M.	2	3	2	1	1*	1.00	—	—	—	—
Ormrod, J.A.	496	839	95	23151	204*	31.11	32	13	396	—
O'Shaughnessy, S.J.	68	108	18	2726	159*	30.28	5	1	22	—
Palmer, G.V.	27	35	4	451	78	14.54	—	—	23	—
Parker, P.W.G.	204	343	48	10251	215	34.74	24	6	132	—
Parks, R.J.	105	121	27	1537	89	16.35	—	—	243	33
Parsons, G.J.	110	142	33	2077	63	19.05	—	—	38	—
Patel, D.N.	188	295	19	7863	197	28.48	14	4	112	—
Patterson, B.P.	3	5	0	16	10	3.20	—	—	1	—
Patterson, T.J.T.	1	1	0	23	23	23.00	—	—	1	—
Pauline, D.B.	36	58	4	1411	115	26.12	1	—	14	—
Payne, I.R.	29	37	5	338	43	10.56	—	—	30	—
Payne, T.R.O.	34	53	8	1829	140	40.64	4	—	43	2
Peck, I.G.	29	43	5	507	49*	13.34	—	—	14	1
Penn, C.	21	24	6	395	115	21.94	1	—	13	—

	M	I	NO	Runs	HS	Avge	100s	1000 runs in season	Ct	St
Petchey, M.D.	7	6	0	21	18	3.50	—	—	3	—
Phillip, N.	221	321	37	6694	134	23.57	1	—	69	—
Pick, R.A.	18	18	5	180	27*	16.36	—	—	3	—
Pigott, A.C.S.	89	103	21	1228	63	14.97	—	—	35	—
Pocock, N.E.J.	127	186	22	3790	164	23.10	2	—	124	—
Pocock, P.I.	501	538	138	4543	75*	11.35	—	—	175	—
Pollock, A.J.	23	26	4	198	32	9.00	—	—	7	—
Pont, K.R.	181	277	40	6122	125*	25.83	7	—	87	—
Popplewell, N.F.M.	125	184	25	4006	143	25.19	3	1	100	—
Potter, L.	35	63	4	1706	118	28.91	3	—	17	—
Price, D.G.	7	11	0	239	49	21.72	—	—	3	—
Price, M.R.	3	2	0	8	7	4.00	—	—	—	—
Prichard, P.J.	20	29	2	888	100	32.88	1	—	10	—
Pridgeon, A.P.	187	185	75	1032	67	9.38	—	—	62	—
Pringle, D.R.	114	168	35	3965	127*	29.81	6	—	58	—
Prior, J.A.	4	6	0	186	87	31.00	—	—	1	—
Racionzer, T.B.	45	80	9	1552	115	21.85	1	—	35	—
Radford, N.V.	64	75	16	1148	76*	19.45	—	—	33	—
Radley, C.T.	498	796	113	23901	171	34.99	41	15	485	—
Ranatunga, A.	24	39	3	1186	118*	32.94	1	—	13	—
Randall, D.W.	324	549	48	18448	209	36.82	32	9	230	—
Ratnayeke, J.R.	31	44	14	551	66	18.36	—	—	10	—
Rawlinson, H.T.	16	21	3	156	24	8.66	—	—	5	—
Reeve, D.A.	38	42	9	678	119	20.54	1	—	21	—
Reifer, E.L.	20	26	8	357	47	19.83	—	—	6	—
Rhodes, S.J.	3	2	1	41	35	41.00	—	—	3	—
Rice, C.E.B.	347	559	84	19099	246	40.20	33	10	268	—
Richards, C.J.	190	242	54	4364	117*	23.21	3	—	360	50
Richards, I.V.A.	326	525	36	24089	291	49.26	74	10+3	309	1
Richardson, P.C.	1	1	0	7	7	7.00	—	—	—	—
Richardson, R.B.	30	46	1	1739	162	38.64	6	—	23	—
Ripley, D.	14	21	3	281	61	15.61	—	—	26	12
Roberts, A.M.E.	228	291	67	3516	89	15.69	—	—	52	—
Roberts, B.	29	48	7	1167	89	28.46	—	—	20	—
Robinson, P.E.	15	24	5	756	92	39.78	—	—	7	—
Robinson, R.T.	109	189	24	6117	207	37.07	9	2	55	—
Roebuck, P.G.P.	11	19	5	368	62	26.28	—	—	3	—
Roebuck, P.M.	206	342	49	9990	159	34.09	13	4	100	—
Rolls, L.M.	1	—								
Romaines, P.W.	69	126	7	3795	186	31.89	—	2	27	—
Rose, B.C.	248	412	44	12196	205	33.14	23	8	118	—
Rowe, C.J.C.	175	277	43	6173	147*	26.38	6	2	63	—
Russell, R.C.	50	66	17	1102	64*	22.48	—	—	83	29
Sainsbury, G.E.	48	45	25	112	15	5.60	—	—	9	—
Samaranayeke, A.D.A.	6	2	1	14	9*	14.00	—	—	3	—
Sanders, I.E.W.	1	2	0	9	9	4.50	—	—	—	—
Saxelby, K.	63	71	19	671	59*	12.90	—	—	10	—
Scott, C.W.	7	8	2	151	78	25.16	—	—	13	2
Selvey, M.W.W.	278	278	88	2405	67	12.65	—	—	79	—

	M	I	NO	Runs	HS	Avge	100s	1000 runs in season	Ct	St
Sharp, G.	295	383	80	6143	98	20.27	—	—	548	87
Sharp, K.	126	211	15	6245	173	31.86	11	1	57	—
Shaw, C.	3	5	2	32	17	10.66	—	—	—	—
Shephard, J.N.	421	611	106	13354	170	26.44	10	2	290	—
Short, J.F.	11	18	2	533	114	33.31	1	—	10	—
Siddiqi, S.N.	6	12	0	219	52	18.25	—	—	1	—
Sidebottom, A.	147	167	40	2987	124	23.51	1	—	36	—
Silva, S.A.R.	11	19	3	655	161*	40.93	2	—	22	1
Simmons, J.	365	454	117	7953	112	23.59	5	—	284	—
Simpson, D.J.	1	2	0	12	9	6.00	—	—	—	—
Slack, W.N.	129	219	23	7213	248*	36.80	12	4	95	—
Small, G.C.	92	112	26	1087	57*	12.63	—	—	24	—
Small, M.A.	11	10	5	17	3*	3.40	—	—	2	—
Smith, C.L.	115	205	21	6924	193	37.63	18	3	69	—
Smith, D.J.	14	14	2	29	13	2.41	—	—	25	—
Smith, D.M.	158	246	53	6313	189*	32.70	10	2	108	—
Smith, K.D.	192	337	28	8614	140	27.87	9	4	69	—
Smith, P.A.	46	74	8	1881	114	28.50	1	1	18	—
Smith, R.A.	36	64	11	2058	132	38.83	5	—	13	—
Standing, D.K.	6	10	4	252	60	42.00	—	—	3	—
Stanworth, J.	13	16	5	108	31*	9.81	—	—	18	1
Steele, D.S.	500	812	124	22346	140*	32.47	30	10	546	—
Steele, J.F.	356	576	77	14489	195	29.03	20	6	393	—
Stevenson, G.B.	181	220	31	3806	115*	20.13	2	—	72	—
Stewart, A.J.	27	42	7	1130	118*	32.28	1	—	37	1
Stovold, A.W.	249	450	24	13292	212*	31.20	15	6	283	45
Such, P.M.	33	34	12	45	16	2.04	—	—	19	—
Swallow, I.G.	13	12	5	155	34*	22.14	—	—	10	—
Swan, R.G.	5	10	1	203	66	22.55	—	—	3	—
Tavaré, C.J.	231	392	40	13460	168*	38.23	25	8	227	—
Taylor, J.P.	3	2	0	11	11	5.50	—	—	2	—
Taylor, L.B.	138	117	51	673	47	10.19	—	—	32	—
Taylor, N.R.	90	159	21	4615	155*	33.44	11	3	54	—
Taylor, N.S.	11	7	2	16	6*	3.20	—	—	4	—
Taylor, R.W.	637	878	167	12040	100	16.93	1	—	1471	175
Tedstone, G.A.	17	22	6	288	67*	18.00	—	—	28	6
Terry, V.P.	55	90	13	2673	175*	34.71	8	2	40	—
Thomas, D.J.	109	148	29	2380	119	20.05	2	—	41	—
Thomas, J.G.	51	68	9	865	84	14.66	—	—	26	—
Thomas, N.P.	1	2	0	0	0	0.00	—	—	1	—
Thomson, J.	2	2	1	1	1*	1.00	—	—	2	—
Thorne, D.A.	14	23	6	368	69*	21.64	—	—	10	—
Tomlins, K.P.	75	108	13	2529	146	26.62	4	—	57	—
Toogood, G.J.	22	39	5	865	109	25.44	1	—	7	—
Travers, T.J.	1	2	0	20	15	10.00	—	—	—	—
Trembath, C.R.	4	4	3	33	17*	33.00	—	—	1	—
Tremlett, T.M.	110	151	25	2516	88	19.96	—	—	51	—
Turnbull, J.R.	12	16	7	17	6	1.88	—	—	8	—
Turner, D.R.	352	581	53	15435	181*	29.23	24	7	172	—
Turner, M.S.	1	2	0	1	1	0.50	—	—	—	—

	M	I	NO	Runs	HS	Avge	100s	1000 runs in season	Ct	St
Turner, S.	354	502	100	9261	121	23.03	4	—	217	—
Turner, S.J.	5	6	3	75	27*	25.00	—	—	12	3
Underwood, D.L.	604	639	177	4630	111	10.02	1	—	248	—
Varey, D.W.	30	56	6	1206	156*	24.12	1	—	14	—
Vonhagt, D.M.	6	11	1	269	75	26.90	—	—	2	—
Walker, A.	19	19	7	82	19	6.83	—	—	7	—
Wall, S.	7	9	4	47	19	9.40	—	—	1	—
Waller, C.E.	251	257	108	1444	51*	9.69	—	—	131	—
Walsh, C.A.	30	41	7	259	30	7.61	—	—	11	—
Warke, S.J.S.	3	4	0	166	63	41.50	—	—	3	—
Warner, A.E.	28	39	9	480	67	16.00	—	—	10	—
Warner, C.J.	8	14	1	391	70	30.07	—	—	7	—
Wasim Raja	235	378	51	10897	165	33.32	16	0+1	147	—
Waterman, P.A.	5	4	2	6	6*	3.00	—	—	2	—
Waterton, S.N.V.	21	26	3	364	50	15.82	—	—	36	8
Watkinson, M.	33	49	10	836	77	21.43	—	—	9	—
Wells, A.P.	48	79	14	2021	127	31.09	2	1	24	—
Wells, C.M.	114	180	26	5115	203	33.21	10	3	32	—
Weston, M.J.	70	120	6	2764	145*	24.24	2	1	33	—
Wettimuny, S.	38	63	4	1933	190	32.76	4	—	12	—
Whitaker, J.J.	29	48	6	1402	160	33.38	2	1	24	—
Whitticase, P.	8	9	2	35	14	5.00	—	—	18	—
Wild, D.J.	34	55	7	1258	144	26.20	2	—	9	—
Willey, P.	397	656	95	16960	227	30.23	31	5	162	—
Williams, N.F.	67	75	17	1069	63	18.43	—	—	20	—
Williams, R.G.	182	296	36	7990	175*	30.73	13	6	72	—
Willis, R.G.D.	308	333	145	2690	72	14.30	—	—	134	—
Wills, R.T.	4	6	0	112	48	18.66	—	—	—	—
Wilson, P.H.L.	61	50	25	261	29	10.44	—	—	11	—
Wood, D.J.	2	3	0	32	15	10.66	—	—	—	—
Woolmer, R.A.	350	545	75	15771	203	33.55	34	5	238	1
Wootton, S.H.	15	24	3	558	104	26.57	1	—	8	—
Wright, A.J.	42	75	7	1750	139	25.73	1	—	19	—
Wright, J.G.	222	386	27	14582	190	40.61	34	6	139	—
Wyatt, J.G.	22	40	2	1018	103	26.78	1	—	9	—
Younis Ahmed	413	693	104	23122	221*	39.25	38	12	232	—
Yusuf, M.M.	5	1	1	2	2*		—	—	—	—
Zaheer Abbas	436	733	85	338+4	274	52.47	106	11+6	260	—
Zaidi, S.M.N.	19	22	9	313	51	24.07	—	—	15	—

BOWLING

	Runs	Wkts	Avge	BB	5 wI	10 wM	100 wkts in season
Abrahams, J.	2472	47	52.59	3-27	—	—	—
Acfield, D.L.	24214	876	27.64	8-55	32	4	—
Afford, J.A.	256	7	36.57	2-49	—	—	—
Agnew, J.P.	6446	209	30.84	8-47	7	1	—
Alderman, T.M.	10006	414	24.16	7-28	22	3	—
Allott, P.J.W.	8018	303	26.46	8-48	15	—	—
Amarnath, M.	8386	261	32.13	7-27	7	1	—
Amiss, D.L.	718	18	39.88	3-21	—	—	—
Anderson, I.S.	1281	20	64.05	4-35	—	—	—
Andrew, C.R.	568	6	94.66	3-77	—	—	—
Andrew, S.J.W.	530	11	48.18	4-30	—	—	—
Anurasiri, S.D.	336	1	336.00	1-65	—	—	—
Asif Din	1845	33	55.90	5-100	1	—	—
Aslett, D.G.	653	10	65.30	4-119	—	—	—
Athey, C.W.J.	1114	21	53.04	3-38	—	—	—
Bailey, R.J.	80	4	20.00	3-33	—	—	—
Bainbridge, P.	4885	122	40.04	6-59	2	—	—
Bairstow, D.L.	247	6	41.16	3-82	—	—	—
Balderstone, J.C.	7949	307	25.89	6-25	5	—	—
Bamber, M.J.	3	0	—	—	—	—	—
Banks, D.A.	17	0	—	—	—	—	—
Baptiste, E.A.E.	4788	174	27.51	5-37	5	—	—
Barclay, J.R.T.	8958	293	30.57	6-61	7	1	—
Barlow, G.D.	54	3	18.00	1-6	—	—	—
Barnett, K.J.	1527	18	84.83	4-76	—	—	—
Barwick, S.R.	2945	100	29.45	8-42	4	—	—
Benson, M.R.	72	0	—	—	—	—	—
Birch, J.D.	1856	38	48.84	6-64	1	—	—
Boon, T.J.	57	0	—	—	—	—	—
Booth, P.A.	821	17	48.29	3-22	—	—	—
Booth, S.C.	2021	59	34.25	4-26	—	—	—
Bore, M.K.	10858	359	30.24	8-89	9	—	—
Botham, I.T.	21581	852	25.32	8-34	49	7	1
Boycott, G.	1430	45	31.77	4-14	—	—	—
Boyd-Moss, R.J.	1499	33	45.42	5-27	1	—	—
Brassington, A.J.	10	0	—	—	—	—	—
Brettel, J.G.	74	1	74.00	1-74	—	—	—
Briers, N.E.	607	22	27.59	3-43	—	—	—
Broad, B.C.	787	13	60.53	2-14	—	—	—
Broome, I.	82	2	41.00	1-17	—	—	—
Burrows, D.A.	76	0	—	—	—	—	—
Butcher, A.R.	4054	103	39.35	6-48	1	—	—
Butcher, I.P.	15	1	15.00	1-2	—	—	—
Butcher, R.O.	76	0	—	—	—	—	—
Capel, D.J.	1343	25	53.72	5-28	1	—	—
Carmichael, I.R.	2107	58	36.32	6-112	4	—	—
Carr, J.D.	1361	31	43.90	5-57	2	—	—
Carrick, P.	19307	656	29.43	8-33	33	4	—

203

	Runs	Wkts	Avge	BB	5 wI	10 wM	100 wkts in season
Childs, J.H.	13468	421	31.99	9-56	21	2	—
Clarke, S.T.	13236	634	20.87	7-34	36	5	—
Clift, P.B.	17170	699	24.56	8-17	22	2	—
Clinton, G.S.	127	4	31.75	2-8	—	—	—
Close, D.B.	30843	1168	26.40	8-41	43	3	2
Cobb, R.A.	5	0			—	—	—
Connor, C.A.	1949	62	31.43	7-37	1	—	—
Cook, G.	669	14	47.78	3-47	—	—	—
Cook, N.G.B.	12109	427	28.35	7-63	18	2	—
Cooper, K.E.	10301	371	27.76	8-44	12	—	—
Corlett, S.C.	2126	70	30.37	7-82	4	—	—
Cotterell, T.A.	1832	30	61.06	5-89	1	—	—
Cowans, N.G.	4715	190	24.81	6-64	8	—	—
Cowdrey, C.S.	2775	73	38.01	3-17	—	—	—
Cowdrey, G.R.	22	1	22.00	1-22	—	—	—
Cowley, N.G.	11092	327	33.92	6-48	4	—	—
Crowe, M.D.	2604	84	31.00	5-18	3	—	—
Cullinan, M.R.	4	1	4.00	1-4	—	—	—
Cunningham, E.J.	264	4	66.00	2-55	—	—	—
Curtis, I.J.	2109	51	41.35	6-28	2	—	—
Curtis, T.S.	194	4	48.50	2-58	—	—	—
Dale, C.S.	467	7	66.71	3-10	—	—	—
Daniel, W.W.	14222	670	21.22	9-61	27	7	—
Davis, M.R.	2923	103	28.37	7-55	4	1	—
Davis, W.W.	7637	273	27.97	7-70	13	2	—
de Mel, A.L.F.	2693	72	37.40	5-68	1	—	—
de Silva D.S.	6714	238	28.21	8-46	15	5	—
de Silva, P.A.	19	0			—	—	—
Denning, P.W.	96	1	96.00	1-4	—	—	—
Dennis, S.J.	4152	136	30.52	5-35	4	—	—
Derrick, J.	472	8	59.00	3-42	—	—	—
Dias, R.L.	24	1	24.00	1-9	—	—	—
Dilley, G.R.	7722	270	28.60	6-66	9	1	—
D'Oliveira, D.B.	603	14	43.07	2-50	—	—	—
Donald, W.A.	64	1	64.00	1-46	—	—	—
Doughty, R.J.	939	23	40.82	6-43	1	—	—
Dredge, C.H.	11033	380	29.03	6-37	11	—	—
Dujon, P.J.	1	0			—	—	—
Duthie, P.G.	73	1	73.00	1-73	—	—	—
Dyer, R.I.H.B.	41	0			—	—	—
East, D.E.	11	0			—	—	—
East, R.E.	26210	1019	25.72	8-30	49	10	—
Edmonds, P.H.	25245	1021	24.72	8-53	45	9	—
Ellcock, R.M.	1920	63	30.47	4-34	—	—	—
Ellis, R.G.P.	264	4	66.00	2-40	—	—	—
Ellison, R.M.	3391	130	26.08	5-27	2	—	—
Emburey, J.E.	19634	834	23.54	7-36	43	8	1
Evans, K.P.	173	2	86.50	2-31	—	—	—

204

	Runs	Wkts	Avge	BB	5 wI	10 wM	100 wkts in season
Fairbrother, N.H.	21	1	21.00	1-11	—	—	—
Feltham, M.A.	1056	34	31.05	5-62	1	—	—
Felton, N.A.	4	0	—	—	—	—	—
Ferreira, A.M.	12469	414	30.11	8-38	15	1	—
Ferris, G.J.F.	1657	67	24.73	7-42	3	1	—
Finney, R.J.	2780	93	29.89	5-55	3	—	—
Fletcher, K.W.R.	2252	50	45.04	5-41	1	—	—
Fletcher, S.D.	657	22	29.86	4-24	—	—	—
Folley, I.	2295	68	33.75	5-65	2	—	—
Foster, N.A.	4523	175	25.84	6-30	7	—	—
Fowler, G.	94	2	47.00	2-43	—	—	—
Fowler, W.P.	1059	14	75.64	2-44	—	—	—
Francis, D.A.	31	0	—	—	—	—	—
Fraser, A.R.C.	124	1	124.00	1-68	—	—	—
Fraser-Darling, C.D.	55	3	18.33	2-14	—	—	—
French, B.N.	22	0	—	—	—	—	—
Gard, T.	8	0	—	—	—	—	—
Garlick, P.L.	1092	12	91.00	2-69	—	—	—
Garner, J.	11801	665	17.74	8-31	41	7	—
Gatting, M.A.	2642	103	25.65	5-34	2	—	—
Gifford, N.	43556	1889	23.05	8-28	88	14	4
Gladwin, C.	59	0	—	—	—	—	—
Golding, A.K.	919	8	114.87	2-100	—	—	—
Gomes, H.A.	3866	98	39.44	4-22	—	—	—
Gooch, G.A.	4549	140	32.49	7-14	2	—	—
Gould, I.J.	35	0	—	—	—	—	—
Gower, D.I.	180	4	45.00	3-47	—	—	—
Graveney, D.A.	17146	594	28.86	8-85	28	4	—
Green, A.M.	563	13	43.30	2-30	—	—	—
Green, R.C.	92	2	46.00	2-65	—	—	—
Greenidge, C.G.	449	17	26.41	5-49	1	—	—
Greig, I.A.	7812	276	28.30	7-43	7	2	—
Griffiths, B.J.	11240	391	28.74	8-50	12	—	—
Grimes, A.D.H.	427	3	142.33	1-24	—	—	—
Hadlee, R.J.	18341	977	18.77	7-23	55	8	2
Hampshire, J.H.	1637	30	54.56	7-52	2	—	—
Hanley, R.W.	8326	398	20.91	7-31	23	3	—
Hardie, B.R.	80	2	40.00	2-39	—	—	—
Hardy, J.J.E.	3	0	—	—	—	—	—
Harper, R.A.	3822	157	24.34	6-57	11	1	—
Harrison, G.D.	54	2	27.00	2-30	—	—	—
Hartley, S.N.	1552	33	47.03	3-40	—	—	—
Hassan, S.B.	407	6	67.83	3-33	—	—	—
Hayes, F.C.	15	0	—	—	—	—	—
Hayes, K.A.	537	17	31.58	6-58	1	—	—
Haynes, D.L.	27	2	13.50	1-2	—	—	—
Haysman, M.D.	219	0	—	—	—	—	—
Hemmings, E.E.	26635	932	28.58	10-175	45	11	—
Henderson, S.P.	185	3	61.66	2-48	—	—	—

205

	Runs	Wkts	Avge	BB	5 wI	10 wM	100 wkts in season
Hendrick, M.	15785	770	20.50	8-45	30	3	—
Hewitt, S.M.	232	4	58.00	2-52	—	—	—
Hick, G.A.	196	3	65.33	3-39	—	—	—
Hill, A.	343	8	42.87	3-5	—	—	—
Hinks, S.G.	58	2	29.00	1-26	—	—	—
Holding, M.A.	10586	448	23.62	8-92	25	3	—
Holmes, G.C.	1288	29	44.41	5-86	1	—	—
Hopkins, J.A.	68	0	—	—	—	—	—
Howarth, G.P.	3543	112	31.63	5-32	1	—	—
Hughes, D.P.	18228	609	29.93	7-24	20	2	—
Hughes, S.P.	4989	184	27.11	6-32	6	—	—
Humpage, G.W.	444	10	44.40	2-13	—	—	—
Illingworth, R.K.	4513	123	36.69	5-26	3	—	—
Imran Khan	21999	995	22.10	8-58	56	11	—
Inchmore, J.D.	13371	464	28.81	8-58	18	1	—
James, K.D.	494	25	19.76	5-28	1	—	—
Jarvis, K.B.S.	15718	543	28.94	8-97	16	3	—
Jarvis, P.W.	1778	43	41.34	6-61	2	—	—
Javed Miandad	6192	187	33.11	7-39	6	—	—
Jefferies, S.T.	6788	251	27.04	8-46	10	1	—
Jesty, T.E.	15065	555	27.14	7-75	18	—	—
John, V.B.	1681	67	25.08	6-55	5	—	—
Johnson, G.W.	17058	555	30.73	7-76	22	3	—
Johnson, P.	23	2	11.50	1-9	—	—	—
Jones, A.L.	128	1	128.00	1-60	—	—	—
Jones, A.N.	1485	54	27.50	5-29	1	—	—
Kallicharran, A.I.	3280	74	44.32	5-45	1	—	—
Kapil Dev	13322	499	26.69	9-83	29	3	—
Ker, J.E.	313	11	28.45	3-45	—	—	—
Knight, R.D.V.	13252	369	35.91	6-44	4	—	—
Knott, A.P.E.	87	2	43.50	1-5	—	—	—
Lamb, A.J.	99	4	24.75	1-1	—	—	—
Larkins, W.	1360	38	35.78	5-59	1	—	—
Lawrence, D.V.	2304	50	46.08	5-58	3	—	—
Lawrence, M.P.	1271	15	84.73	3-79	—	—	—
Lea, A.E.	92	2	46.00	2-27	—	—	—
le Roux, G.S.	11892	587	20.25	8-107	29	3	—
Lethbridge, C.	2733	72	37.95	5-68	1	—	—
Lever, J.K.	34400	1458	23.59	8-37	73	12	4
Lilley, A.W.	21	2	10.50	2-11	—	—	—
Lloyd, C.H.	4104	114	36.00	4-48	—	—	—
Lloyd, T.A.	740	9	82.22	2-29	—	—	—
Lloyds, J.W.	4667	135	34.57	7-88	6	1	—
Logie, A.L.	99	2	49.50	1-2	—	—	—
Lord, G.J.	12	0	—	—	—	—	—
Love, J.D.	233	1	233.00	1-46	—	—	—
Lumb, R.G.	5	0	—	—	—	—	—

206

	Runs	Wkts	Avge	BB	5 wI	10 wM	100 wkts in season
Lynch, M.A.	663	15	44.20	3-6	—	—	—
Madugalle, R.S.	107	2	53.50	1-18	—	—	—
Makinson, D.J.	313	7	44.71	2-49	—	—	—
Malcolm, D.E.	674	16	42.12	3-78	—	—	—
Mallender, N.A.	7115	234	30.40	7-41	5	1	—
Malone, S.J.	3582	105	34.11	7-55	2	1	—
Marks, V.J.	16152	498	32.43	8-141	24	1	—
Marshall, M.D.	12966	709	18.28	8-71	46	6	1
Maru, R.J.	2430	70	34.71	7-79	2	—	—
Masters, K.D.	294	6	49.00	2-26	—	—	—
Maynard, C.	8	0	—	—	—	—	—
McEvoy, M.S.A.	103	3	34.33	3-20	—	—	—
McEwan, K.S.	309	4	77.25	1-0	—	—	—
McFarlane, L.L.	3132	86	36.41	6-59	1	—	—
McPate, W.A.	115	3	38.33	2-70	—	—	—
Medlycott, K.T.	186	7	26.57	2-15	—	—	—
Mee, S.R.	63	2	31.50	2-44	—	—	—
Mendis, G.D.	11	0	—	—	—	—	—
Mendis, L.R.D.	32	1	32.00	1-4	—	—	—
Metcalfe, A.A.	6	0	—	—	—	—	—
Miller, A.J.T.	4	1	4.00	1-4	—	—	—
Miller, G.	18300	711	25.73	8-70	33	6	—
Moir, D.G.	6161	187	32.94	6-60	9	1	—
Monkhouse, G.	2932	116	25.27	7-51	1	—	—
Monteith, J.D.	1941	94	20.64	7-38	7	1	—
Morris, H.	68	1	68.00	1-45	—	—	—
Morris, J.E.	73	1	73.00	1-35	—	—	—
Mortensen, O.H.	2175	84	25.89	6-27	3	1	—
Morton, W.	765	23	33.26	4-40	—	—	—
Moxon, M.D.	659	10	65.90	3-26	—	—	—
Mushtaq Mohammad	22785	936	24.34	7-18	39	2	—
Neale, P.A.	201	1	201.00	1-15	—	—	—
Needham, A.	3185	80	39.81	6-30	4	—	—
Newell, M.	14	0	—	—	—	—	—
Newman, P.G.	5046	151	33.41	7-104	2	—	—
Newport, P.J.	1045	30	34.83	5-51	1	—	—
Nicholas, M.C.J.	1297	36	36.02	5-45	1	—	—
Old, C.M.	24615	1057	23.28	7-20	38	2	—
Oldham, S.	8817	269	32.77	7-78	4	—	—
Ollis, R.L.	2	0	—	—	—	—	—
Ontong, R.C.	16530	555	29.78	7-60	21	1	—
O'Reilly, P.M.	81	5	16.20	3-43	—	—	—
Ormrod, J.A.	1094	25	43.76	5-27	1	—	—
O'Shaughnessy, S.J.	2708	83	32.62	4-66	—	—	—
Palmer, G.V.	1918	50	38.36	5-38	1	—	—
Parker, P.W.G.	541	10	54.10	2-21	—	—	—
Parks, R.J.	0	0	—	—	—	—	—

207

	Runs	Wkts	Avge	BB	5 wI	10 wM	100 wkts in season
Parsons, G.J.	7913	252	31.40	5-25	4	—	—
Patel, D.N.	10767	300	35.89	7-46	12	—	—
Patterson, B.P.	180	4	45.00	2-26	—	—	—
Patterson, T.J.T.	96	3	32.00	2-54	—	—	—
Pauline, D.B.	28	0	—	—	—	—	—
Payne, I.R.	1127	26	43.34	5-13	1	—	—
Penn, C.	934	17	54.94	2-11	—	—	—
Petchey, M.D.	886	16	55.37	4-65	—	—	—
Phillip, N.	16395	668	24.54	7-33	29	2	—
Pick, R.A.	1273	32	39.78	5-25	2	1	—
Pigott, A.C.S.	6363	230	27.66	7-74	10	1	—
Pocock, N.E.J.	396	4	99.00	1-4	—	—	—
Pocock, P.I.	38989	1506	25.88	9-57	59	7	1
Pollock, A.J.	1853	49	37.81	5-107	2	—	—
Pont, K.R.	2689	83	32.39	5-17	2	—	—
Popplewell, N.F.M.	4284	103	41.59	5-33	1	—	—
Potter, L.	243	7	34.71	2-31	—	—	—
Price, M.R.	109	2	54.50	1-43	—	—	—
Prichard, P.J.	5	0	—	—	—	—	—
Pridgeon, A.P.	14226	417	34.11	7-35	8	1	—
Pringle, D.R.	7312	260	28.12	7-32	8	1	—
Prior, J.A.	111	3	37.00	2-7	—	—	—
Racionzer, T.B.	71	2	35.50	2-11	—	—	—
Radford, N.V.	5366	175	30.66	6-41	7	1	—
Radley, C.T.	117	6	19.50	1-0	—	—	—
Ranatunga, A.	560	15	37.33	2-17	—	—	—
Randall, D.W.	185	6	30.83	3-15	—	—	—
Ratnayeke, J.R.	2221	59	37.64	5-42	2	—	—
Rawlinson, H.T.	1407	23	61.17	5-123	1	—	—
Reeve, D.A.	2653	97	27.35	5-22	1	—	—
Reifer, E.L.	1761	49	35.93	4-43	—	—	—
Rice, C.E.B.	15645	712	21.97	7-62	20	1	—
Richards, C.J.	44	0	—	—	—	—	—
Richards, I.V.A.	6161	146	42.19	5-88	1	—	—
Richardson, P.C.	122	1	122.00	1-92	—	—	—
Richardson, R.B.	2	0	—	—	—	—	—
Roberts, A.M.E.	18679	889	21.01	8-47	47	7	1
Roberts, B.	1613	48	33.60	4-32	—	—	—
Robinson, P.E.	12	0	—	—	—	—	—
Robinson, R.T.	94	2	47.00	1-22	—	—	—
Roebuck, P.G.P.	269	6	44.83	2-44	—	—	—
Roebuck, P.M.	2022	42	48.14	6-50	1	—	—
Rolls, L.M.	49	0	—	—	—	—	—
Romaines, P.W.	17	0	—	—	—	—	—
Rose, B.C.	224	6	37.33	3-9	—	—	—
Rowe, C.J.C.	5127	128	40.05	6-46	3	1	—
Sainsbury, G.C.	3801	114	33.34	6-66	5	—	—
Samaranayeke, A.D.A.	499	9	55.44	4-142	—	—	—
Sanders, I.E.W.	93	3	31.00	2-78	—	—	—

	Runs	Wkts	Avge	BB	5 wI	10 wM	100 wkts in season
Saxelby, K.	4223	148	28.53	5-43	3	—	—
Selvey, M.W.W.	20582	772	26.66	7-20	38	4	1
Sharp, G.	68	1	68.00	1-47	—	—	—
Sharp, K.	321	7	45.85	2-13	—	—	—
Shaw, C.	177	5	35.40	4-63	—	—	—
Shepherd, J.N.	31935	1155	27.64	8-40	54	2	—
Siddiqi, S.N.	90	5	18.00	5-90	1	—	—
Sidebottom, A.	8544	364	23.47	7-18	14	2	—
Simmons, J.	22482	822	27.35	7-59	33	4	—
Slack, W.N.	462	18	25.66	3-17	—	—	—
Small, G.C.	6966	214	32.55	7-68	4	—	—
Small, M.A.	866	33	26.24	5-57	1	—	—
Smith, C.L.	1661	31	53.58	3-35	—	—	—
Smith, D.M.	1485	28	53.03	3-40	—	—	—
Smith, K.D.	3	0	—	—	—	—	—
Smith, P.A.	2219	51	43.50	4-41	—	—	—
Smith, R.A.	30	0	—	—	—	—	—
Standing, D.K.	32	0	—	—	—	—	—
Steele, D.S.	15511	623	24.89	8-29	26	3	—
Steele, J.F.	14629	564	25.93	7-29	16	—	—
Stevenson, G.B.	13681	478	28.62	8-57	18	2	—
Stovold, A.W.	86	2	43.00	1-0	—	—	—
Such, P.M.	2441	87	28.05	6-123	4	—	—
Swallow, I.G.	702	17	41.29	4-52	—	—	—
Swan, R.G.	0	0	—	—	—	—	—
Tavaré, C.J.	293	2	146.50	1-20	—	—	—
Taylor, J.P.	188	2	94.00	2-92	—	—	—
Taylor, L.B.	9787	401	24.40	7-28	12	1	—
Taylor, N.R.	288	5	57.60	2-58	—	—	—
Taylor, N.S.	974	32	30.43	5-49	1	—	—
Taylor, R.W.	75	1	75.00	1-23	—	—	—
Terry, V.P.	39	0	—	—	—	—	—
Thomas, D.J.	8237	252	32.68	6-36	5	1	—
Thomas, J.G.	3778	128	29.51	5-56	5	1	—
Thomson, J.	154	4	38.50	4-116	—	—	—
Thorne, D.A.	754	17	44.35	5-39	1	—	—
Tomlins, K.P.	317	4	79.25	2-28	—	—	—
Toogood, G.J.	221	3	73.66	1-1	—	—	—
Trembath, C.R.	441	11	40.36	5-91	1	—	—
Tremlett, T.M.	5031	214	23.50	6-82	5	—	—
Turnbull, J.R.	778	15	51.86	4-51	—	—	—
Turner, D.R.	332	9	36.88	2-7	—	—	—
Turner, M.S.	85	0	—	—	—	—	—
Turner, S.	20892	808	25.85	6-26	27	1	—
Underwood, D.L.	45525	2301	19.78	9-28	150	46	10
Varey, D.W.	4	0	—	—	—	—	—

209

	Runs	Wkts	Avge	BB	5 wI	10 wM	100 wkts in season
Walker, A.	1696	49	34.61	4-50	—	—	—
Wall, S.	545	9	60.55	2-65	—	—	—
Waller, C.E.	17430	610	28.57	7-64	21	1	—
Walsh, C.A.	2826	100	28.26	6-35	6	—	—
Warner, A.E.	1947	61	31.91	5-27	1	—	—
Wasim Raja	15306	529	28.93	8-65	31	7	—
Waterman, P.A.	345	6	57.50	2-16	—	—	—
Watkinson, M.	2203	65	33.89	6-39	3	—	—
Wells, A.P.	42	0	—	—	—	—	—
Wells, C.M.	3980	126	31.55	5-25	2	—	—
Weston, M.J.	760	22	34.54	4-44	—	—	—
Wettimuny, S.	46	2	23.00	1-7	—	—	—
Whitaker, J.J.	88	0	—	—	—	—	—
Wild, D.J.	945	19	49.73	3-15	—	—	—
Willey, P.	17506	593	29.52	7-37	22	3	—
Williams, N.F.	5339	174	30.68	5-77	1	—	—
Williams, R.G.	8225	246	33.43	7-73	6	—	—
Willis, R.G.D.	22468	899	24.99	8-32	34	2	—
Wilson, P.H.L.	3394	110	30.85	5-36	1	—	—
Woolmer, R.A.	10868	420	25.87	7-47	12	1	—
Wootton, S.H.	7	0	—	—	—	—	—
Wright, A.J.	3	0	—	—	—	—	—
Wright, J.G.	181	2	90.50	1-4	—	—	—
Wyatt, J.G.	4	1	4.00	1-0	—	—	—
Younis Ahmed	1639	39	42.02	4-10	—	—	—
Yusuf, M.M.	282	1	282.00	1-25	—	—	—
Zaheer Abbas	1020	26	39.23	5-15	1	—	—
Zaidi, S.M.N.	827	19	43.52	3-27	—	—	—

THE 1984 FIRST CLASS SEASON
STATISTICAL HIGHLIGHTS
Compiled by Brian Croudy

HIGHEST INNINGS TOTALS

606	West Indies v England at Birmingham
524-7d	Essex v Yorkshire at Leeds
518-5d	Surrey v Yorkshire at The Oval
516	Somerset v Middlesex at Bath
508	Somerset v Derbyshire at Taunton
506-5d	West Indies v Leicestershire at Leicester
501-5d	Somerset v Northamptonshire at Weston-Super-Mare
500	West Indies v England at Manchester
495-7d	Lancashire v Oxford University at Oxford
494	Somerset v Kent at Taunton
491-7d	Sri Lanka v England at Lord's
489-6d	West Indies v Glamorgan at Swansea
475	Derbyshire v Sussex at Derby
473-7d	Middlesex v Somerset at Bath
472-7d	Somerset v Worcestershire at Weston-Super-Mare
472	Warwickshire v Hampshire at Birmingham
468-7d	Essex v Derbyshire at Chesterfield
466-6d	Worcestershire v Glamorgan at Swansea
463-4d	Essex v Cambridge University at Cambridge
459	West Indies v Derbyshire at Derby
456	Leicestershire v Gloucestershire at Leicester
450-7d	Nottinghamshire v Northamptonshire at Nottingham
450-9	Sussex v Hampshire at Hove
449-5d	Essex v Hampshire at Southampton
448-3d	Hampshire v Cambridge University at Cambridge
446	Essex v Lancashire at Manchester
445-7d	Worcestershire v Warwickshire at Worcester
444-8d	Warwickshire v Derbyshire at Chesterfield
439	Derbyshire v Yorkshire at Harrogate
439	Yorkshire v Derbyshire at Chesterfield
438-5d	Warwickshire v Northamptonshire at Birmingham
438-7d	Warwickshire v Glamorgan at Cardiff
438-9d	Middlesex v Glamorgan at Swansea
436-6d	Worcestershire v Kent at Worcester
436-9d	Sussex v Nottinghamshire at Hove
432-8d	Derbyshire v Warwickshire at Chesterfield
431	Derbyshire v Leicestershire at Leicester
427-4d	Glamorgan v Leicestershire at Swansea
425-7d	Glamorgan v Hampshire at Cardiff
420-5d	Kent v Sri Lanka at Canterbury
419	Kent v Oxford University at Oxford
417-3d	Sussex v Somerset at Hove
417	Essex v Northamptonshire at Chelmsford
415-9d	Yorkshire v Glamorgan at Cardiff
412-7d	Kent v Gloucestershire at Bristol

412-9d	West Indies v Worcestershire at Worcester
404-4d	Lancashire v Kent at Maidstone
404	Nottinghamshire v Leicestershire at Leicester
402	Worcestershire v Yorkshire at Scarborough
401	Surrey v Somerset at The Oval
401	Yorkshire v Hampshire at Basingstoke
400-6d	Worcestershire v Derbyshire at Worcester
400-9d	Warwickshire v Northamptonshire at Northampton

LOWEST INNINGS TOTALS

56	Hampshire v Kent at Canterbury
65†	Cambridge University v Leicestershire at Cambridge
70	Kent v Gloucestershire at Canterbury
70	Lancashire v Northamptonshire at Southport
72	Gloucestershire v Somerset at Taunton
72	Oxford University v Gloucestershire at Oxford
73	Gloucestershire v Somerset at Bristol
76	Lancashire v Essex at Southend
88	Glamorgan v West Indies at Bristol
89	Derbyshire v West Indies at Derby
90	Essex v Kent at Colchester
90	Gloucestershire v Essex at Bristol
90	Middlesex v Surrey at The Oval
90	Oxford University v Lancashire at Oxford
92	Kent v Sussex at Hastings
93	Essex v Nottinghamshire at Chelmsford
94	Middlesex v Warwickshire at Lord's

†indicates batted one short

DOUBLE CENTURIES

258	M.W. Gatting for Middlesex v Somerset at Bath
248	T.E. Jesty for Hampshire v Cambridge University at Cambridge
227	G.A. Gooch for Essex v Derbyshire at Chesterfield
226	G. Fowler for Lancashire v Kent at Maidstone
223	C.G. Greenidge for West Indies v England at Manchester
221*	D.G. Aslett for Kent v Sri Lanka at Canterbury
220	G.A. Gooch for Essex v Hampshire at Southampton
214*	C.G. Greenidge for West Indies v England at Lord's
212*	Javed Miandad for Glamorgan v Leicestershire at Swansea
210*	R.J. Hadlee for Nottinghamshire v Middlesex at Lord's
209*	G.D. Mendis for Sussex v Somerset at Hove
205	G.W. Humpage for Warwickshire v Derbyshire at Chesterfield
204*	R.C. Ontong for Glamorgan v Middlesex at Swansea
203	C.M. Wells for Sussex v Hampshire at Hove
201*	J. Abrahams for Lancashire v Warwickshire at Nuneaton
200*	A.I. Kallicharran for Warwickshire v Northamptonshire at Birmingham

OPENING BATSMAN CARRYING HIS BAT

113* (260)	G.S. Clinton for Surrey v Derbyshire at The Oval
55* (183)	G. Boycott for Yorkshire v Warwickshire at Leeds
48* (127)	A. Hill for Derbyshire v Kent at Maidstone

CENTURY IN EACH INNINGS

117* & 114   A.R. Butcher for Surrey v Glamorgan at The Oval
143* & 141   T.E. Jesty for Hampshire v Worcestershire at Worcester
200* & 117*   A.I. Kallicharran for Warwickshire v Northamptonshire at
             Birmingham

CENTURY BEFORE LUNCH

K.J. Barnett (103) for Derbyshire v Somerset at Taunton (0 to 103) 1st Day
A.I. Kallicharran (155) for Warwickshire v Glamorgan at Cardiff (0 to 100*) 1st
Day
A.I. Kallicharran (115) for Warwickshire v Leicester at Leicester (17* to 132*) 2nd
Day

CENTURY WICKET PARTNERSHIPS

319	3rd	M.D. Crowe and P.M. Roebuck for Somerset v Leicestershire at Taunton (County Record)
302	2nd	V.P. Terry and T.E. Jesty for Hampshire v Cambridge University at Cambridge
290*	4th	P. Willey and T.J. Boon for Leicestershire v Warwickshire at Leicester (County Record)
290	4th	H.A. Gomes and A.L. Logie for West Indies v Leicestershire at Leicester
287*	2nd	C.G. Greenidge and H.A. Gomes for West Indies v England at Lord's
277	1st	G.S. Clinton and A.R. Butcher for Surrey v Yorkshire at The Oval
272	3rd	A.L. Jones and Javed Miandad for Glamorgan v Hampshire at Cardiff
265	2nd	R.T. Robinson and D.W. Randall for Nottinghamshire v Yorkshire at Nottingham
260	2nd	R.G. Lumb and K. Sharp for Yorkshire v Glamorgan at Cardiff
260	4th	C.E.B. Rice and P. Johnson for Nottinghamshire v Kent at Folkestone
259*	3rd	J.C. Balderstone and T.J. Boon for Leicestershire v Derbyshire at Leicester
249	2nd	A.I. Kallicharran and K.D. Smith for Warwickshire v Leicestershire at Leicester
249	3rd	N.F.M. Popplewell and M.D. Crowe for Somerset v Middlesex at Bath
247*	4th	R.G. Lumb and S.N. Hartley for Yorkshire v Gloucestershire at Bradford
246	1st	J.G. Wyatt and P.M. Roebuck for Somerset v Yorkshire at Taunton
242	3rd	J.C. Balderstone and T.J. Boon for Leicestershire v Gloucestershire at Leicester
240	1st	A.L. Jones and J.A. Hopkins for Glamorgan v Gloucestershire at Cardiff
238	3rd	M.C.J. Nicholas and T.E. Jesty for Hampshire v Worcestershire at Worcester
231	2nd	C.L. Smith and D.R. Turner for Hampshire v Derbyshire at Derby
229	3rd	C.G. Greenidge and H.A. Gomes for West Indies v Lancashire at Liverpool
227*	2nd	R.I.H.B. Dyer and D.L. Amiss for Warwickshire v Glamorgan at Cardiff
226	2nd	T.S. Curtis and D.N. Patel for Worcestershire v Cambridge University at Worcester

224*	6th	J. Abrahams and J. Simmons for Lancashire v Warwickshire at Nuneaton
223	1st	V.P. Terry and C.L. Smith for Hampshire v Gloucestershire at Southampton
220*	1st	R.T. Robinson and B.C. Broad for Nottinghamshire v Oxford University at Oxford
220	4th	P.W.G. Parker and C.M. Wells for Sussex v Gloucestershire at Hove
217	2nd	A.I. Kallicharran and R.I.H.B. Dyer for Warwickshire v Lancashire at Manchester
216	4th	D.R. Turner and J.J.E. Hardy for Hampshire v Warwickshire at Birmingham
216	4th	S.J. O'Shaughnessy and D.P. Hughes for Lancashire v Somerset at Bath
215	2nd	T.A. Lloyd and A.I. Kallicharran for Warwickshire v Northamptonshire at Birmingham
214*	2nd	J.A. Ormrod and S.J. O'Shaughnessy for Lancashire v Hampshire at Portsmouth
211	3rd	C.J. Tavare and D.G. Aslett for Kent v Worcestershire at Worcester
209	4th	I.V.A. Richards and A.L. Logie for West Indies v Glamorgan at Swansea
207	3rd	M.W. Gatting and C.T. Radley for Middlesex v Northamptonshire at Northampton
207	3rd	R.A. Woolmer and D.G. Aslett for Kent v Gloucestershire at Bristol
206	1st	C.G. Greenidge and D.L. Haynes for West Indies v Worcestershire at Worcester
206	3rd	H.A. Gomes and I.V.A. Richards for West Indies v England at Birmingham
205	1st	G. Fowler and J.A. Ormrod for Lancashire v Kent at Maidstone
203*	5th	A.I. Kallicharran and G.W. Humpage for Warwickshire v Northamptonshire at Birmingham
201	3rd	R.J. Boyd-Moss and D.J. Wild for Northamptonshire v Lancashire at Southport
200	4th	G.D. Mendis and C.M. Wells for Sussex v Northamptonshire at Horsham
189	8th	K.T. Medlycott and N.J. Falkner for Surrey v Cambridge University at Banstead
150	9th	E.A.E. Baptiste and M.A. Holding for West Indies v England at Birmingham
113	8th	B. Roberts and D.G. Moir for Derbyshire v Gloucestershire at Gloucester

CENTURY PARTNERSHIPS IN BOTH INNINGS

163 & 120	S.A.R. Silva and D.M. Vonhagt for Sri Lanka v Warwickshire at Birmingham

TWO CENTURIES ON DEBUT IN SAME INNINGS

K.T. Medlycott and N.J. Falkner for Surrey v Cambridge University at Banstead – first occasion in this country

EIGHT WICKETS IN AN INNINGS

8-26	P.B. Clift for Leicestershire v Warwickshire at Birmingham
8-37	J.K. Lever for Essex v Gloucestershire at Bristol
8-44	K.E. Cooper for Nottinghamshire v Middlesex at Lord's
8-47	J.P. Agnew for Leicestershire v Cambridge University at Cambridge

8-53   P.H. Edmonds for Middlesex v Hampshire at Bournemouth
8-87   D.L. Underwood for Kent v Hampshire at Bournemouth
8-103   I.T. Botham for England v West Indies at Lord's
8-141   V.J. Marks for Somerset v Kent at Taunton

HAT-TRICK

E.E. Hemmings for Nottinghamshire v Northamptonshire at Nottingham

SIX DISMISSALS IN AN INNINGS BY A WICKET-KEEPER

(6c)   D.L. Bairstow for Yorkshire v Derbyshire at Chesterfield
(6c)   B.N. French for Nottinghamshire v Somerset at Taunton
(6c)   P.B. Jackson for Ireland v Scotland at Glasgow
(6c)   R.J. Parks for Hampshire v Essex at Colchester

TEN DISMISSALS IN A MATCH BY A WICKET-KEEPER

(7c 3st)   B.N. French for Nottinghamshire v Oxford University at Oxford

FIRST TO TARGETS

1000 runs: A.I. Kallicharran on June 14th
2000 runs: G.A. Gooch on August 18th
100 wickets: J.K. Lever on August 18th

THE DOUBLE

1179 runs and 117 wickets - R.J. Hadlee. First time since 1967 when F.J. Titmus
achieved the feat and the only time since the reduction of the County Championship

TIED MATCHES

Kent 92 and 243 tied with Sussex 143 and 292 at Hastings
Northamptonshire 124 and 330 tied with Kent 250 and 204 at Northampton

WIN AFTER FOLLOWING ON

Essex 114 and 374 beat Warwickshire 334 and 119 at Ilford
Derbyshire 139 and 381 beat Nottinghamshire 361 and 131 at Nottingham

PERCENTAGE OF RUNS IN BOUNDARIES

84% D.G. Moir (7×6 and 12×4) for Derbyshire v Warwickshire at Chesterfield

PERCENTAGE OF RUNS SCORED IN AN INNINGS

74.34% G.A. Gooch 84 out of 113 for Essex v Kent at Canterbury

MOST EXTRAS IN AN INNINGS

53 West Indies v England at Birmingham
50 Somerset v Middlesex at Bath

FIRST-CLASS CRICKET RECORDS

COMPLETE TO END OF 1984 SEASON

Highest Innings Totals

1107	Victoria v New South Wales (Melbourne)	1926-27
1059	Victoria v Tasmania (Melbourne)	1922-23
951-7d	Sind v Baluchistan (Karachi)	1973-74
918	New South Wales v South Australia (Sydney)	1900-01
912-8d	Holkar v Mysore (Indore)	1945-46
910-6d	Railways v Dera Ismail Khan (Lahore)	1964-65
903-7d	England v Australia (Oval)	1938
887	Yorkshire v Warwickshire (Birmingham)	1896
849	England v West Indies (Kingston)	1929-30

NB. There are 22 instances of a side making 800 runs or more in an innings, the last occasion being 951-7 declared by Sind as above.

Lowest Innings Totals

12*	Oxford University v MCC and Ground (Oxford)	1877
12	Northamptonshire v Gloucestershire (Gloucester)	1907
13	Auckland v Canterbury (Auckland)	1877-78
13	Nottinghamshire v Yorkshire (Nottingham)	1901
14	Surrey v Essex (Chelmsford)	1983
15	MCC v Surrey (Lord's)	1839
15*	Victoria v MCC (Melbourne)	1903-04
15*	Northamptonshire v Yorkshire (Northampton)	1908
15	Hampshire v Warwickshire (Birmingham)	1922
16	MCC and Ground v Surrey (Lord's)	1872
16	Derbyshire v Nottinghamshire (Nottingham)	1879
16	Surrey v Nottinghamshire (Oval)	1880
16	Warwickshire v Kent (Tonbridge)	1913
16	Trinidad v Barbados (Bridgetown)	1941-42
16	Border v Natal (East London)	1959-60

*Batted one man short

NB. There are 26 instances of a side making less than 20 in an innings, the last occasion being 16 and 18 by Border v Natal at East London in 1959-60. The total of 34 is the lowest by one side in a match.

Highest Aggregates in a Match

2376	(38)	Bombay v Maharashtra (Poona)	1948-49
2078	(40)	Bombay v Holkar (Bombay)	1944-45
1981	(35)	South Africa v England (Durban)	1938-39
1929	(39)	New South Wales v South Australia (Sydney)	1925-26
1911	(34)	New South Wales v Victoria (Sydney)	1908-09
1905	(40)	Otago v Wellington (Dunedin)	1923-24

In England the highest are:

1723	(31)	England v Australia (Leeds) 5 day match	1948
1601	(29)	England v Australia (Lord's) 4 day match	1930
1507	(28)	England v West Indies (Oval) 5 day match	1976
1502	(28)	MCC v New Zealanders (Lord's)	1927
1499	(31)	T.N. Pearce's XI v Australians (Scarborough)	1961
1496	(24)	England v Australia (Nottingham) 4 day match	1938
1494	(37)	England v Australia (Oval) 4 day match	1934
1492	(33)	Worcestershire v Oxford U (Worcester)	1904
1477	(32)	Hampshire v Oxford U (Southampton)	1913
1477	(33)	England v South Africa (Oval) 4 day match	1947
1475	(27)	Northamptonshire v Surrey (Northampton)	1920

Lowest Aggregate in a Match

105	(31)	MCC v Australia (Lord's)	1878
134	(30)	England v The B's (Lord's)	1831
147	(40)	Kent v Sussex (Sevenoaks)	1828
149	(30)	England v Kent (Lord's)	1858
150	(30)	Cambridge Town v MCC (Chatteris)	1832
151	(30)	Canterbury v Otago (Christchurch)	1866-67
153	(37)	MCC v Sussex (Lord's)	1843
153	(31)	Otago v Canterbury (Dunedin)	1896-97
156	(30)	Nelson v Wellington (Nelson)	1885-86
158	(22)	Surrey v Worcestershire (Oval)	1954

Wickets that fell are given in parentheses.

Tie Matches

Due to the change of law made in 1948 for tie matches, a tie is now a rarity. The law states that only if the match is played out and the scores are equal is the result a tie.
The most recent tied matches are as follows:

Yorkshire (351-4d & 113) v Leicestershire (328 & 136) at Huddersfield	1954
Sussex (172 & 120) v Hampshire (153 & 139) at Eastbourne	1955
Victoria (244 & 197) v New South Wales (281 & 160) at Melbourne (St. Kilda)	1956-57

(The first tie in Sheffield Shield cricket)

T.N. Pearce's XI (313-7d & 258) v New Zealanders (268 & 303-8d) at Scarborough	1958
Essex (364-6d & 176-8d) v Gloucestershire (329 & 211) at Leyton	1959
Australia (505 & 232) v West Indies (453 & 284) at Brisbane	1960-61

(The first tie in Test cricket)

Bahawalpur (123 & 282) v Lahore B (127 & 278) at Bahawalpur	1961-62
Middlesex (327-5d & 123-9d v Hampshire (277 & 173) at Portsmouth	1967
England XI (312-8d & 190-3d) v England Under-25 XI (320-9d & 182) at Scarborough	1968
Yorkshire (106-9d & 207) v Middlesex (102 & 211) at Bradford	1973
Sussex (245 & 173-5d) v Essex (200-8d & 218) at Hove	1974
South Australia (431 & 171-7d) v Queensland (340-8d & 262) at Adelaide	1976-77
England XI (296-6d & 104) v Central Districts (198 & 202) at New Plymouth	1977-78
Peshawar (139 & 188) v Allied Bank (240 & 87) at Peshawar	1979-80
Victoria (230-5d & 245) v New Zealanders (301-9d & 174-3d) at Melbourne	1982-83

Tie Matches (continued)

Muslim Commercial Bank (229 & 238) v Railways (149 & 318)
  at Sialkot   1983-84
Kent (92 & 243) v Sussex (143 & 192) at Hastings   1984
Northamptonshire (124 & 330) v Kent (250 & 204) at
  Northampton   1984

Highest Individual Scores

499	Hanif Mohammad, Karachi v Bahawalpur (Karachi)	1958-59
452*	D.G. Bradman, New South Wales v Queensland (Sydney)	1929-30
443*	B.B. Nimbalkar, Maharashtra v Kathiawar (Poona)	1948-49
437	W.H. Ponsford, Victoria v Queensland (Melbourne)	1927-28
429	W.H. Ponsford, Victoria v Tasmania (Melbourne)	1922-23
428	Aftab Baloch, Sind v Baluchistan (Karachi)	1973-74
424	A.C. MacLaren, Lancashire v Somerset (Taunton)	1895
385	B. Sutcliffe, Otago v Canterbury (Christchurch)	1952-53
383	C.W. Gregory, New South Wales v Queensland (Brisbane)	1906-07
369	D.G. Bradman, South Australia v Tasmania (Adelaide)	1935-36
365*	C. Hill, South Australia v New South Wales (Adelaide)	1900-01
365*	G.S. Sobers, West Indies v Pakistan (Kingston)	1957-58
364	L. Hutton, England v Australia (Oval)	1938
359*	V.M. Merchant, Bombay v Maharashtra (Bombay)	1943-44
359	R.B. Simpson, New South Wales v Queensland (Brisbane)	1963-64
357*	R. Abel, Surrey v Somerset (Oval)	1899
357	D.G. Bradman, South Australia v Victoria (Melbourne)	1935-36
356	B.A. Richards, South Australia v Western Australia (Perth)	1970-71
355	B. Sutcliffe, Otago v Auckland (Dunedin)	1949-50
352	W.H. Ponsford, Victoria v New South Wales (Melbourne)	1926-27
350	Rashid Israr, Habib Bank v National Bank (Lahore)	1976-77

NB. There are 93 instances of a batsman scoring 300 or more in an innings, the last occasion being 311* by G.M. Turner for Worcestershire v Warwickshire (Worcester) 1982.

Most Centuries in a Season

18	D.C.S. Compton	1947
16	J.B. Hobbs	1925
15	W.R. Hammond	1938
14	H. Sutcliffe	1932

Most Centuries in an Innings

6	for Holkar v Mysore (Indore)	1945-46
5	for New South Wales v South Australia (Sydney)	1900-01
5	for Australia v West Indies (Kingston)	1954-55

Most Centuries in Successive Innings

6	C.B. Fry	1901
6	D.G. Bradman	1938-39
6	M.J. Procter	1970-71
5	E.D. Weekes	1955-56

Two Double Centuries in a Match

A.E. Fagg, 244 and 202* for Kent v Essex (Colchester)   1938

A Double Century and a Century in a Match

C.B. Fry, 125 and 229, Sussex v Surrey (Hove)	1900
W.W. Armstrong, 157* and 245, Victoria v South Australia (Melbourne)	1920-21
H.T.W. Hardinge, 207 and 102* for Kent v Surrey (Blackheath)	1921
C.P. Mead, 113 and 224, Hampshire v Sussex (Horsham)	1921
K.S. Duleepsinhji, 115 and 246, Sussex v Kent (Hastings)	1929
D.G. Bradman, 124 and 225, Woodfull's XI v Ryder's XI (Sydney)	1929-30
B. Sutcliffe, 243 and 100*, New Zealanders v Essex (Southend)	1949
M.R. Hallam, 210* and 157, Leicestershire v Glamorgan (Leicester)	1959
M.R. Hallam, 203* and 143* Leicestershire v Sussex (Worthing)	1961
Hanumant Singh, 109 and 213*, Rajasthan v Bombay (Bombay)	1966-67
Salahuddin, 256 and 102*, Karachi v East Pakistan (Karachi)	1968-69
K.D. Walters, 242 and 103, Australia v West Indies (Sydney)	1968-69
S.M. Gavaskar, 124 and 220, India v West Indies (Port of Spain)	1970-71
L.G. Rowe, 214 and 100*, West Indies v New Zealand (Kingston)	1971-72
G.S. Chappell, 247* and 133, Australia v New Zealand (Wellington)	1973-74
L. Baichan, 216* and 102, Berbice v Demerara (Georgetown)	1973-74
Zaheer Abbas, 216* and 156*, Gloucestershire v Surrey (Oval)	1976
Zaheer Abbas, 230* and 104*, Gloucestershire v Kent (Canterbury)	1976
Zaheer Abbas, 205* and 108*, Gloucestershire v Sussex (Cheltenham)	1977
Saadat Ali, 141 and 222, Income Tax v Multan (Multan)	1977-78
Talat Ali, 214* and 104, Pakistan International Airways v Punjab (Lahore)	1978-79
Shafiq Ahmed, 129 and 217*, National Bank v Muslim Commercial Bank (Karachi)	1978-79
D.W. Randall, 209 and 146, Nottinghamshire v Middlesex (Nottingham)	1979
Zaheer Abbas, 215* and 150*, Gloucestershire v Somerset (Bath)	1981
Qasim Omar, 210* and 110, Muslim Commercial Bank v Lahore (Lahore)	1982-83

Two Centuries in a Match on Most Occasions

8   Zaheer Abbas   7   W.R. Hammond   6   J.B. Hobbs, G.M. Turner

Most Centuries

J.B. Hobbs, 197 (175 in England); E.H. Hendren, 170 (151); W.R. Hammond, 167 (134); C.P. Mead, 153 (145); H. Sutcliffe, 149 (135); F.E. Woolley, 145 (135); G. Boycott, 143 (112); L. Hutton, 129 (105); W.G. Grace, 126 (125); D.C.S. Compton, 123 (92); T.W. Graveney, 122 (91); D.G. Bradman, 117 (41); M.C. Cowdrey, 107 (80); A. Sandham, 107 (87); Zaheer Abbas, 106 (59); T.W. Hayward, 104 (100); J.H. Edrich, 103 (90); G.M. Turner, 103 (78); L.E.G. Ames, 102 (89); G.E. Tyldesley, 102 (94).

Highest Individual Batting Aggregate in a Season

Runs		Season	M	Innings	NO	HS	Avge	100s
3,816	D.C.S. Compton	1947	30	50	8	246	90.85	18
3,539	W.J. Edrich	1947	30	52	8	267*	80.43	12

NB. The feat of scoring 3,000 runs in a season has been achieved on 28 occasions, the last instance being by W.E. Alley (3,019 runs, av. 59.96) in 1961.
Since the reduction of the matches in the County Championship in 1969, the highest aggregate in a season is 2,559 runs (av. 67.34) by G.A. Gooch in 1984.

Partnerships for First Wicket

561	Waheed Mirza and Mansoor Akhtar, Karachi Whites v Quetta (Karachi)	1976-77
555	H. Sutcliffe and P. Holmes, Yorkshire v Essex (Leyton)	1932
554	J.T. Brown and J. Tunnicliffe, Yorkshire v Derbyshire (Chesterfield)	1898
490	E.H. Bowley and J.G. Langridge, Sussex v Middlesex (Hove)	1933
456	W.H. Ponsford and E.R. Mayne, Victoria v Queensland (Melbourne)	1923-24
451*	S. Desai and R.M.H. Binny, Karnataka v Kerala (Chikmagalur)	1977-78
428	J.B. Hobbs and A. Sandham, Surrey v Oxford U (Oval)	1926
424	J.F.W. Nicholson and I.J. Siedle, Natal v Orange Free State (Bloemfontein)	1926-27
421	S.M. Gavaskar and G.A. Parkar, Bombay v Bengal (Bombay)	1981-82
418	Kamal Najamuddin and Khalid Alvi, Karachi v Railways (Karachi)	1980-81
413	V. Mankad and P. Roy, India v New Zealand (Madras)	1955-56
405	C.P.S. Chauhan and M. Gupte, Maharashtra v Vidarbha (Poona)	1972-73

Partnerships for Second Wicket

465*	J.A. Jameson and R.B. Kanhai, Warwickshire v Gloucestershire (Birmingham)	1974
455	K.V. Bhandarkar and B.B. Nimbalkar, Maharashtra v Kathiawar (Poona)	1948-49
451	D.G. Bradman and W.H. Ponsford, Australia v England (Oval)	1934
446	C.C. Hunte and G.S. Sobers, West Indies v Pakistan (Kingston)	1957-58
429*	J.G. Dewes and G.H.G. Doggart, Cambridge U v Essex (Cambridge)	1949
426	Arshad Pervez and Mohsin Khan, Habib Bank v Income Tax Department (Lahore)	1977-78
398	W. Gunn and A. Shrewsbury, Nottinghamshire v Sussex (Nottingham)	1890

Partnerships for Third Wicket

456	Aslam Ali and Khalid Irtiza, United Bank v Multan (Karachi)	1975-76
451	Mudassar Nazar and Javed Miandad, Pakistan v India (Hyderabad)	1982-83
445	P.E. Whitelaw and W.N. Carson, Auckland v Otago (Dunedin)	1936-37
434	J.B. Stollmeyer and G.E. Gomez, Trinidad v British Guiana (Port of Spain)	1946-47
424*	W.J. Edrich and D.C.S. Compton, Middlesex v Somerset (Lord's)	1948
410	R.S. Modi and L. Amarnath, India v Rest (Calcutta)	1946-47
399	R.T. Simpson and D.C.S. Compton, MCC v NE Transvaal (Benoni)	1948-49

Partnerships for Fourth Wicket

577	Gul Mahomed and V.S. Hazare, Baroda v Holkar (Baroda)	1946-47
574*	C.L. Walcott and F.M.M. Worrell, Barbados v Trinidad (Port of Spain)	1945-46
502*	F.M.M. Worrell and J.D.C. Goddard, Barbados v Trinidad (Bridgetown)	1943-44
470	A.I. Kallicharran and G.W. Humpage, Warwickshire v Lancashire (Southport)	1982
448	R. Abel and T.W. Hayward, Surrey v Yorkshire (Oval)	1899
424	I.S. Lee and S.O. Quin, Victoria v Tasmania (Melbourne)	1933-34
411	P.B.H. May and M.C. Cowdrey, England v West Indies (Birmingham)	1957
410	G. Abraham and B. Pandit, Kerala v Andhra (Palghat)	1959-60
402	W. Watson and T.W. Graveney, MCC v British Guiana (Georgetown)	1953-54
402	R.B. Kanhai and K. Ibadulla, Warwickshire v Nottinghamshire (Nottingham)	1968

Partnerships for Fifth Wicket

405	D.G. Bradman and S.G. Barnes, Australia v England (Sydney)	1946-47
397	W. Bardsley and C. Kellaway, New South Wales v South Australia (Sydney)	1920-21
393	E.G. Arnold and W.B. Burns, Worcestershire v Warwickshire (Birmingham)	1909
360	U.M. Merchant and M.N. Raiji, Bombay v Hyderabad (Bombay)	1947-48
355	Altaf Shah and Tanq Bashir, HBFC v Multan (Multan)	1976-77

Partnerships for Sixth Wicket

487*	G.A. Headley and C.C. Passailaigue, Jamaica v Lord Tennyson's XI (Kingston)	1931-32
428	W.W. Armstrong and M.A. Noble, Australians v Sussex (Hove)	1902
411	R.M. Poore and E.G. Wynyard, Hampshire v Somerset (Taunton)	1899
376	R. Subba Row and A. Lightfoot, Northamptonshire v Surrey (Oval)	1958
371	V.M. Merchant and R.S. Modi, Bombay v Maharashtra (Bombay)	1943-44

Partnerships for Seventh Wicket

347	D.S. Atkinson and C.C. Depeiza, West Indies v Australia (Bridgetown)	1954-55
344	K.S. Ranjitsinhji and W. Newham, Sussex v Essex (Leyton)	1902
340	K.J. Key and H. Philipson, Oxford U v Middlesex (Chiswick Park)	1887
336	F.C.W. Newman and C.R. Maxwell, Cahn's XI v Leicestershire (Nottingham)	1935
335	C.W. Andrews and E.C. Bensted, Queensland v New South Wales (Sydney)	1934-35

Partnerships for Eighth Wicket

433	V.T. Trumper and A. Sims, Australians v Canterbury (Christchurch)	1913-14
292	R. Peel and Lord Hawke, Yorkshire v Warwickshire (Birmingham)	1896
270	V.T. Trumper and E.P. Barbour, New South Wales v Victoria (Sydney)	1912-13
263	D.R. Wilcox and R.M. Taylor, Essex v Warwickshire (Southend)	1946
255	E.A.V. Williams and E.A. Martindale, Barbados v Trinidad (Bridgetown)	1935-36

Partnerships for Ninth Wicket

283	A.R. Warren and J. Chapman, Derbyshire v Warwickshire (Blackwell)	1910
251	J.W.H.T. Douglas and S.N. Hare, Essex v Derbyshire (Leyton)	1921
245	V.S. Hazare and N.D. Nagarwalla, Maharashtra v Baroda (Poona)	1939-40
239	H.B. Cave and I.B. Leggat, Central Districts v Otago (Dunedin)	1952-53
232	C. Hill and E. Walkley, South Australia v New South Wales (Adelaide)	1900-01

Partnerships for Tenth Wicket

307	A.F. Kippax and J.E.H. Hooker, New South Wales v Victoria (Melbourne)	1928-29
249	C.T. Sarwate and S.N. Bannerjee, Indians v Surrey (Oval)	1946
235	F.E. Woolley and A. Fielder, Kent v Worcestershire (Stourbridge)	1909
230	R.W. Nicholls and W. Roche, Middlesex v Kent (Lord's)	1899
228	R. Illingworth and K. Higgs, Leicestershire v Northamptonshire (Leicester)	1977
218	F.H. Vigar and T.P.B. Smith, Essex v Derbyshire (Chesterfield)	1947

BOWLING

Most Wickets in a Season

W		Season	O	M	R	Avge
304	A.P. Freeman	1928	37 1976.1	423	5489	18.05
298	A.P. Freeman	1933	33 2039	651	4549	15.26

NB. The feat of taking 250 wickets in a season has been achieved on 12 occasions, the last instance being by A.P. Freeman in 1933 as above. 200 or more wickets in a season have been taken on 59 occasions, the last instance being by G.A.R. Lock (212 wkts, avge 12.02) in 1957.

The most wickets taken in a season since the reduction of County Championship matches in 1969 are as follows.

W		Season	M	O	M	R	Avge
134	M.D. Marshall	1982	22	822	225	2108	15.73
131	L.R. Gibbs	1971	23	1024.1	295	2475	18.89
121	R.D. Jackman	1980	23	746.2	220	1864	15.40

NB. 100 wickets in a season have been taken on 36 occasions since 1969.

All Ten Wickets in an Innings

The feat has been achieved on 71 occasions.

On three occasions: A.P. Freeman, 1929, 1930 and 1931.

On two occasions: J.C. Laker, 1956, H. Verity, 1931 and 1932, V.E. Walker, 1859 and 1865.

Instances since the war:

W.E. Hollies, Warwickshire v Nottinghamshire (Birmingham) 1946; J.M. Sims of Middlesex playing for East v West (Kingston) 1948; J.K.R. Graveney, Gloucestershire v Derbyshire (Chesterfield) 1949; T.E. Bailey, Essex v Lancashire (Clacton) 1949; R. Berry, Lancashire v Worcestershire (Blackpool) 1953; S.P. Gupte, Bombay v Pakistan Services (Bombay), 1954-55; J.C. Laker, Surrey v Australians (Oval) 1956; J.C. Laker, England v Australia (Manchester) 1956; G.A.R. Lock, Surrey v Kent (Blackheath) 1956; K. Smales, Nottinghamshire v Gloucestershire (Stroud) 1956; P. Chatterjee, Bengal v Assam (Jorhat) 1956-57; J.D. Bannister, Warwickshire v Combined Services (Birmingham) 1959; A.J.G. Pearson, Cambridge U v Leicestershire (Loughborough) 1961; N.I. Thomson, Sussex v Warwickshire (Worthing) 1964; P.J. Allan, Queensland v Victoria (Melbourne) 1965-66; I. Brayshaw, Western Australia v Victoria (Perth) 1967-68; Shahid Mahmood, Karachi Whites v Khairpur (Karachi) 1969-70; E.E. Hemmings, International XI v West Indies XI (Kingston) 1982-83.

Nineteen Wickets in a Match

J.C. Laker 19-90 (9-37 and 10-53), England v Australia (Manchester) 1956.

Seventeen Wickets in a Match

In addition to Laker's 19 wickets the feat has been achieved on 18 occasions. Instances between the two wars were: A.P. Freeman (for 67 runs), Kent v Sussex (Hove) 1922; F.C.L. Matthews (89 runs), Nottinghamshire v Northamptonshire (Nottingham) 1923; C.W.L. Parker (56 runs), Gloucestershire v Essex (Gloucester 1925; G.R. Cox (106 runs), Sussex v Warwickshire (Horsham) 1926; A.P. Freeman (92 runs), Kent v Warwickshire (Folkestone)1932; H. Verity (91 runs), Yorkshire v Essex (Leyton) 1933; J.C. Clay (212 runs) Glamorgan v Worcestershire (Swansea) 1937; T.W.J. Goddard (106 runs), Gloucestershire v Kent (Bristol) 1939. There has been no instance since the last war.

Most Hat-tricks in a Career

7 D.V.P. Wright.
6 T.W.J. Goddard, C.W.L. Parker.
5 S. Haigh, V.W.C. Jupp, A.E.G. Rhodes, F.A. Tarrant.

The 'Double' Event

3,000 runs and 100 wickets: J.H. Parks, 1937.
2,000 runs and 200 wickets: G.H. Hirst, 1906.
2,000 runs and 100 wickets: F.E. Woolley (4), J.W. Hearne (3), G.H. Hirst (2), W. Rhodes (2), T.E. Bailey, D.E. Davies, W.G. Grace, G.L. Jessop, V.W.C. Jupp, James Langridge, F.A. Tarrant, C.L. Townsend, L.F. Townsend.
1,000 runs and 200 wickets: M.W. Tate (3), A.E. Trott (2), A.S. Kennedy.
Most 'Doubles': W. Rhodes (16), G.H. Hirst (14), V.W.C. Jupp (10).
'Double' in first season: D.B. Close, 1949. At the age of 18, Close is the youngest player ever to perform this feat.
The feat of scoring 1,000 runs and taking 100 wickets has been achieved on 303 occasions, the last instance being R.J. Hadlee in 1984.

FIELDING

Most catches in a season:	78 W.R. Hammond	1928
	77 M.J. Stewart	1957
Most catches in a match:	10 W.R. Hammond, Gloucestershire v Surrey (Cheltenham)	1928
Most catches in an innings:	7 M.J. Stewart, Surrey v Northamptonshire (Northampton)	1957
	7 A.S. Brown, Gloucestershire v Nottinghamshire (Nottingham)	1966

WICKET-KEEPING

Most dismissals in a season:	127 (79ct, 48st), L.E.G. Ames	1929

NB. The feat of making 100 dismissals in a season has been achieved on 12 occasions, the last instance being by R. Booth (100 dismissals–91ct, 9st) in 1964.

Most dismissals in a match:	12 E. Pooley (8 ct, 4 st) Surrey v Sussex (Oval)	1868
	12 D. Tallon (9 ct, 3 st), Queensland v New South Wales (Sydney)	1938-39
	12 H.B. Taber (9 ct, 3 st), New South Wales v South Australia (Adelaide)	1968-69
Most catches in a match:	11 A. Long, Surrey v Sussex (Hove)	1964
	11 R.W. Marsh, Western Australia v Victoria (Perth)	1975-76
	11 D.L. Bairstow, Yorkshire v Derbyshire (Scarborough)	1982
Most dismissals in an innings:	8 A.T.W. Grout (8 ct), Queensland v W. Australia (Brisbane)	1959-60

TEST CRICKET RECORDS

The following series in 1984-85 are included: Pakistan v India; Australia v West Indies; Pakistan v New Zealand; India v England.

HIGHEST INNINGS TOTALS

903-7d	England v Australia (Oval)	1938
849	England v West Indies (Kingston)	1929-30
790-3d	West Indies v Pakistan (Kingston)	1957-58
758-8d	Australia v West Indies (Kingston)	1954-55
729-6d	Australia v England (Lord's)	1930
701	Australia v England (Oval)	1934
695	Australia v England (Oval)	1930
687-8d	West Indies v England (Oval)	1976
681-8d	West Indies v England (Port of Spain)	1953-54
674	Australia v India (Adelaide)	1947-48
668	Australia v West Indies (Bridgetown)	1954-55
659-8d	Australia v England (Sydney)	1946-47
658-8d	England v Australia (Nottingham)	1938
657-8d	Pakistan v West Indies (Bridgetown)	1957-58
656-8d	Australia v England (Manchester)	1964
654-5	England v South Africa (Durban)	1938-39
652	Pakistan v India (Faisalabad)	1982-83
652-8d	West Indies v England (Lord's)	1973
652-7d	England v India (Madras)	1984-85
650-6d	Australia v West Indies (Bridgetown)	1964-65

The highest innings for the countries not mentioned above are:

644-7d	India v West Indies (Kanpur)	1978-79
622-9d	South Africa v Australia (Durban)	1969-70
551-9d	New Zealand v England (Lord's)	1973
491-7d	Sri Lanka v England (Lord's)	1984

LOWEST INNINGS TOTALS

26	New Zealand v England (Auckland)	1954-55
30	South Africa v England (Port Elizabeth)	1895-96
30	South Africa v England (Birmingham)	1924
35	South Africa v England (Cape Town)	1898-99
36	Australia v England (Birmingham)	1902
36	South Africa v Australia (Melbourne)	1931-32
42	Australia v England (Sydney)	1887-88
42	New Zealand v Australia (Wellington)	1945-46
42†	India v England (Lord's) †*Batted one man short*	1974
43	South Africa v England (Cape Town)	1888-89
44	Australia v England (Oval)	1896
45	England v Australia (Sydney)	1886-87
45	South Africa v Australia (Melbourne)	1931-32
47	South Africa v England (Cape Town)	1888-89
47	New Zealand v England (Lord's)	1958

The lowest innings for the countries not mentioned above are:

62	Pakistan v Australia (Perth)	1981-82
76	West Indies v Pakistan (Dacca)	1958-59
93	Sri Lanka v New Zealand (Wellington)	1982-83

HIGHEST INDIVIDUAL INNINGS

365* G.S. Sobers, West Indies v Pakistan (Kingston) 1957-58
364 L. Hutton, England v Australia (Oval) 1938
337 Hanif Mohammad, Pakistan v West Indies (Bridgetown) 1957-58
336* W.R. Hammond, England v New Zealand (Auckland) 1932-33
334 D.G. Bradman, Australia v England (Leeds) 1930
325 A. Sandham, England v West Indies (Kingston) 1929-30
311 R.B. Simpson, Australia v England (Manchester) 1964
310* J.H. Edrich, England v New Zealand (Leeds) 1965
307 R.M. Cowper, Australia v England (Melbourne) 1965-66
304 D.G. Bradman, Australia v England (Leeds) 1934
302 L.G. Rowe, West Indies v England (Bridgetown) 1973-74
299* D.G. Bradman, Australia v South Africa (Adelaide) 1931-32
291 I.V.A. Richards, West Indies v England (Oval) 1976
287 R.E. Foster, England v Australia (Sydney) 1903-04
285* P.B.H. May, England v West Indies (Birmingham) 1957
280* Javed Miandad, Pakistan v India (Hyderabad) 1982-83
278 D.C.S. Compton, England v Pakistan (Nottingham) 1954
274 R.G. Pollock, South Africa v Australia (Durban) 1969-70
274 Zaheer Abbas, Pakistan v England (Birmingham) 1971
270* G.A. Headley, West Indies v England (Kingston) 1934-35
270 D.G. Bradman, Australia v England (Melbourne) 1936-37
268 G.N. Yallop, Australia v Pakistan (Melbourne) 1983-84
266 W.H. Ponsford, Australia v England (Oval) 1934
262* D.L. Amiss, England v West Indies (Kingston) 1973-74
261 F.M.M. Worrell, West Indies v England (Nottingham) 1950
260 C.C. Hunte, West Indies v Pakistan (Kingston) 1957-58
259 G.M. Turner, New Zealand v West Indies (Georgetown) 1971-72
258 T.W. Graveney, England v West Indies (Nottingham) 1957
258 S.M. Nurse, West Indies v New Zealand (Christchurch) 1968-69
256 R.B. Kanhai, West Indies v India (Calcutta) 1958-59
256 K.F. Barrington, England v Australia (Manchester) 1964
255* D.J. McGlew, South Africa v New Zealand (Wellington) 1952-53
254 D.G. Bradman, Australia v England (Lord's) 1930
251 W.R. Hammond, England v Australia (Sydney) 1928-29
250 K.D. Walters, Australia v New Zealand (Christchurch) 1976-77
250 S.F.A.F. Bacchus, West Indies v India (Kanpur) 1978-79

The highest individual innings for other countries are:

236* S.M. Gavaskar, India v West Indies (Madras) 1983-84
190 S. Wettimuny, Sri Lanka v England (Lord's) 1984

HIGHEST RUN AGGREGATES IN A TEST RUBBER

R		Season	T	I	NO	HS	Avge	100s	50s
974	D.G. Bradman (A v E)	1930	5	7	0	334	139.14	4	—
905	W.R. Hammond (E v A)	1928-29	5	9	1	251	113.12	4	—
834	R.N. Harvey (A v SA)	1952-53	5	9	0	205	92.66	4	3
829	I.V.A. Richards (WI v E)	1976	4	7	0	291	118.42	3	2
827	C.L. Walcott (WI v A)	1954-55	5	10	0	155	82.70	5	2
824	G.S. Sobers (WI v P)	1957-58	5	8	2	365*	137.33	3	3
810	D.G. Bradman (A v E)	1936-37	5	9	0	270	90.00	3	1
806	D.G. Bradman (A v SA)	1931-32	5	5	1	299*	201.50	4	—
779	E.D. Weekes (WI v I)	1948-49	5	7	0	194	111.28	4	2
774	S.M. Gavaskar (I v WI)	1970-71	4	8	3	220	154.80	4	3
761	Mudassar Nazar (P v I)	1982-83	6	8	2	231	126.83	4	1
758	D.G. Bradman (A v E)	1934	5	8	0	304	94.75	2	1
753	D.C.S. Compton (E v SA)	1947	5	8	0	208	94.12	4	2

225

RECORD WICKET PARTNERSHIPS—ALL TEST CRICKET

1st	413	V. Mankad & P. Roy, I v NZ (Madras)	1955-56
2nd	451	W.H. Ponsford & D.G. Bradman, A v E (Oval)	1934
3rd	451	Mudassar Nazar & Javed Miandad, P v I (Hyderabad)	1982-83
4th	411	P.B.H. May & M.C. Cowdrey, E v WI (Birmingham)	1957
5th	405	S.G. Barnes & D.G. Bradman, A v E (Sydney)	1946-47
6th	346	J.H. Fingleton & D.G. Bradman, A v E (Melbourne)	1936-37
7th	347	D.S. Atkinson & C.C. Depeiza, WI v A (Bridgetown)	1954-55
8th	246	L.E.G. Ames & G.O. Allen, E v NZ (Lord's)	1931
9th	190	Asif Iqbal & Intikhab Alam, P v E (Oval)	1967
10th	151	B.F. Hastings & R.O. Collinge, NZ v P (Auckland)	1972-73

WICKET PARTNERSHIPS OF OVER 300

451	3rd W.H. Ponsford & D.G. Bradman, A v E (Oval)	1934
451	3rd Mudassar Nazar & Javed Miandad, P v I (Hyderabad)	1982-83
446	2nd C.C. Hunte & G.S. Sobers, WI v P (Kingston)	1957-58
413	1st V. Mankad & P. Roy, I v NZ (Madras)	1955-56
411	4th P.B.H. May & M.C. Cowdrey, E v WI (Birmingham)	1957
405	5th S.G. Barnes & D.B. Bradman, A v E (Sydney)	1946-47
399	4th G.S. Sobers & F.M.M. Worrell, WI v E (Bridgetown)	1959-60
388	4th W.H. Ponsford & D.G. Bradman, A v E (Leeds)	1934
387	1st G.M. Turner & T.W. Jarvis, NZ v WI (Georgetown)	1971-72
382	2nd L. Hutton & M. Leyland, E v A (Oval)	1938
382	1st W.M. Lawry & R.B. Simpson, A v WI (Bridgetown)	1964-65
370	3rd W.J. Edrich & D.C.S. Compton, E v SA (Lord's)	1947
369	2nd J.H. Edrich & K.F. Barrington, E v NZ (Leeds)	1965
359	1st L. Hutton & C. Washbrook, E v SA (Johannesburg)	1948-49
350	4th Mushtaq Mohammad & Asif Iqbal, P v NZ (Dunedin)	1972-73
347	7th D.S. Atkinson & C.C. Depeiza, WI v A (Bridgetown)	1954-55
346	6th J.H. Fingleton & D.G. Bradman, A v E (Melbourne)	1936-37
344*	2nd S.M. Gavaskar & D.B. Vengsarkar, I v WI (Calcutta)	1978-79
341	3rd E.J. Barlow & R.G. Pollock, SA v A (Adelaide)	1963-64
338	3rd E.D. Weekes & F.M.M. Worrell, WI v E (Port of Spain)	1953-54
336	4th W.M. Lawry & K.D. Walters, A v WI (Sydney)	1968-69
323	1st J.B. Hobbs & W. Rhodes, E v A (Melbourne)	1911-12
319	3rd A. Melville & A.D. Nourse, SA v E (Nottingham)	1947
316†	3rd G.R. Viswanath & Yashpal Sharma, I v E (Madras)	1981-82
308	7th Waqar Hasan & Imtiaz Ahmed, P v NZ (Lahore)	1955-56
303	3rd I.V.A. Richards & A.I. Kallicharran, WI v E (Nottingham)	1976
301	2nd A.R. Morris & D.G. Bradman, A v E (Leeds)	1948

†415 runs were added for this wicket in two separate partnerships. D.B. Vengsarkar retired hurt and was replaced by Yashpal Sharma after 99 runs had been added.

NINE OR TEN WICKETS IN AN INNINGS

10-53	J.C. Laker, England v Australia (Manchester)	1956
9-28	G.A. Lohmann, England v South Africa (Johannesburg)	1895-96
9-37	J.C. Laker, England v Australia (Manchester)	1956
9-69	J.M. Patel, India v Australia (Kanpur)	1959-60
9-83	Kapil Dev, India v West Indies (Ahmedabad)	1983-84
9-86	Sarfraz Nawaz, Pakistan v Australia (Melbourne)	1978-79
9-95	J.M. Noreiga, West Indies v India (Port of Spain)	1970-71
9-102	S.P. Gupte, India v West Indies (Kanpur)	1958-59
9-103	S.F. Barnes, England v South Africa (Johannesburg)	1913-14
9-113	H.J. Tayfield, South Africa v England (Johannesburg)	1956-57
9-121	A.A. Mailey, Australia v England (Melbourne)	1920-21

FIFTEEN OR MORE WICKETS IN A MATCH

19-90	J.C. Laker, England v Australia (Manchester)	1956
17-159	S.F. Barnes, England v South Africa (Johannesburg)	1913-14
16-137	R.A.L. Massie, Australia v England (Lord's)	1972
15-28	J. Briggs, England v South Africa (Cape Town)	1888-89
15-45	G.A. Lohmann, England v South Africa (Port Elizabeth)	1895-96
15-99	C. Blythe, England v South Africa (Leeds)	1907
15-104	H. Verity, England v Australia (Lord's)	1934
15-124	W. Rhodes, England v Australia (Melbourne)	1903-04

HIGHEST WICKET AGGREGATES IN A TEST RUBBER

Wkts		Season	Tests	Balls	Mdns	Runs	Avge	5 wI	10 M
49	S.F. Barnes (E v SA)	1913-14	4	1356	56	536	10.93	7	3
46	J.C. Laker (E v A)	1956	5	1703	127	442	9.60	4	2
44	C.V. Grimmett (A v SA)	1935-36	5	2077	140	642	14.59	5	3
42	T.M. Alderman (A v E)	1981	6	1950	76	893	21.26	4	—
41	R.M. Hogg (A v E)	1978-79	6	1740	60	527	12.85	5	2
40	Imran Khan (P v I)	1982-83	6	1339	69	558	13.95	4	2
39	D.K. Lillee (A v E)	1981	6	1870	81	870	22.30	2	1
39	A.V. Bedser (E v A)	1953	5	1591	58	682	17.48	5	1
38	M.W. Tate (E v A)	1924-25	5	2528	62	881	23.18	5	1
37	W.J. Whitty (A v SA)	1910-11	5	1395	55	632	17.08	2	—
37	H.J. Tayfield (SA v E)	1956-57	5	2280	105	636	17.18	4	1
36	A.E.E. Vogler (SA v E)	1909-10	5	1349	33	783	21.75	4	1
36	A.A. Mailey (A v E)	1920-21	5	1465	27	946	26.27	4	2
35	G.A. Lohmann (E v SA)	1895-96	3	520	38	203	5.80	4	2
35	B.S. Chandrasekhar (I v E)	1972-73	5	1747	83	662	18.91	4	—

MOST WICKET-KEEPING DISMISSALS IN AN INNINGS

7 (7 ct)	Wasim Bari, Pakistan v New Zealand (Auckland)	1978-79
7 (7 ct)	R.W. Taylor, England v India (Bombay)	1979-80
6 (6 ct)	A.T.W. Grout, Australia v South Africa (Johannesburg)	1957-58
6 (6 ct)	D.T. Lindsay, South Africa v Australia (Johannesburg)	1966-67
6 (6 ct)	J.T. Murray, England v India (Lord's)	1967
6 (5 ct, 1 st)	S.M.H. Kirmani, India v New Zealand (Christchurch)	1975-76

MOST WICKET-KEEPING DISMISSALS IN A MATCH

10 (10 ct)	R.W. Taylor, England v India (Bombay)	1979-80

MOST WICKET-KEEPING DISMISSALS IN A SERIES

28 (28 ct)	R.W. Marsh, Australia v England	1982-83
26 (23 ct, 3 st)	J.H.B. Waite, South Africa v New Zealand	1961-62
26 (26 ct)	R.W. Marsh, Australia v West Indies	1975-76
24 (22 ct, 2 st)	D.L. Murray, West Indies v England	1963
24 (24 ct)	D.T. Lindsay, South Africa v Australia	1966-67
24 (21 ct, 3 st)	A.P.E. Knott, England v Australia	1970-71

HAT-TRICKS

F.R. Spofforth	Australia v England (Melbourne)	1878-79
W. Bates	England v Australia (Melbourne)	1882-83
J. Briggs	England v Australia (Sydney)	1891-92
G.A. Lohmann	England v South Africa (Port Elizabeth)	1895-96
J.T. Hearne	England v Australia (Leeds)	1899
H. Trumble	Australia v England (Melbourne)	1901-02
H. Trumble	Australia v England (Melbourne)	1903-04
T.J. Matthews (2)*	Australia v South Africa (Manchester)	1912
M.J.C. Allom†	England v New Zealand (Christchurch)	1929-30
T.W.J. Goddard	England v South Africa (Johannesburg)	1938-39
P.J. Loader	England v West Indies (Leeds)	1957
L.F. Kline	Australia v South Africa (Cape Town)	1957-58
W.W. Hall	West Indies v Pakistan (Lahore)	1958-59
G.M. Griffin	South Africa v England (Lord's)	1960
L.R. Gibbs	West Indies v Australia (Adelaide)	1960-61
P.J. Petherick	New Zealand v Pakistan (Lahore)	1976-77

In each innings.   †Four wickets in five balls.

HIGHEST WICKET AGGREGATES

Wkts			Tests	Balls	Runs	Avge	5 wI	10 wM
355	D.K. Lillee	(A)	70	18467	8493	23.92	23	7
325	R.G.D. Willis	(E)	90	17357	8190	25.20	16	—
312	I.T. Botham	(E)	73	16881	8191	26.25	24	4
309	L.R. Gibbs	(WI)	79	27115	8989	29.09	18	2
307	F.S. Trueman	(E)	67	15178	6625	21.57	17	3
297	D.L. Underwood	(E)	86	21860	7674	25.83	17	6
266	B.S. Bedi	(I)	67	21364	7637	28.71	14	1
258	Kapil Dev	(I)	68	14523	7406	28.70	18	2
252	J.B. Statham	(E)	70	16056	6261	24.84	9	1
248	R. Benaud	(A)	63	19108	6704	27.03	16	1
246	G.D. McKenzie	(A)	60	17681	7328	29.78	16	3
242	B.S. Chandrasekhar	(I)	58	15963	7199	29.74	16	2
236	A.V. Bedser	(E)	51	15918	5876	24.89	15	3
235	R.J. Hadlee	(NZ)	50	12721	5626	23.94	18	4
235	G.S. Sobers	(WI)	93	21599	7999	34.03	6	—
232	Imran Khan	(P)	51	12551	5316	22.91	16	4
228	R.R. Lindwall	(A)	61	13650	5251	23.03	12	—
224	M.A. Holding	(WI)	52	11350	5194	23.18	13	2
216	C.V. Grimmett	(A)	37	14513	5231	24.21	21	7
210	J. Garner	(WI)	47	10952	4490	21.38	6	—
202	A.M.E. Roberts	(WI)	47	11135	5173	25.61	11	2
202	J.A. Snow	(E)	49	12021	5387	26.66	8	1

MOST TEST APPEARANCES FOR EACH COUNTRY

The abandoned match at Melbourne in 1970–71 is excluded from these figures

England		Australia	
M.C. Cowdrey	114	R.W. Marsh	96
G. Boycott	108	G.S. Chappell	87
A.P.E. Knott	95	R.N. Harvey	79
T.G. Evans	91	I.M. Chappell	75
R.G.D. Willis	90	K.D. Walters	74
D.L. Underwood	86	K.J. Hughes	70
W.R. Hammond	85	D.K. Lillee	70
K.F. Barrington	82	W.M. Lawry	67
T.W. Graveney	79	A.R. Border	66
L. Hutton	79	I.R. Redpath	66

South Africa		West Indies	
J.H.B. Waite	50	C.H. Lloyd	110
A.W. Nourse	45	G.S. Sobers	93
B. Mitchell	42	L.R. Gibbs	79
H.W. Taylor	42	R.B. Kanhai	79
T.L. Goddard	41	I.V.A. Richards	73
R.A. McLean	40	A.I. Kallicharran	66
H.J. Tayfield	37	C.G. Greenidge	62
D.J. McGlew	34	D.L. Murray	62
A.D. Nourse	34	R.C. Fredericks	59
E.J. Barlow	30	M.A. Holding	52

New Zealand		Pakistan	
B.E. Congdon	61	Wasim Bari	81
J.R. Reid	58	Zaheer Abbas	74
M.G. Burgess	50	Javed Miandad	65
R.J. Hadlee	50	Majid Khan	63
B. Sutcliffe	42	Asif Iqbal	58
G.M. Turner	41	Mushtaq Mohammad	57
G.P. Howarth	40	Hanif Mohammad	55
G.T. Dowling	39	Sarfraz Nawaz	55
B.L. Cairns	37	Wasim Raja	55
J.M. Parker	36	Imran Khan	51

India			
S.M. Gavaskar	106	P.R. Umrigar	59
G.R. Viswanath	91	B.S. Chandrasekhar	58
S.M.H. Kirmani	85	S. Venkataraghavan	57
D.B. Vengsarkar	76	C.G. Borde	55
Kapil Dev	68	V.L. Manjrekar	55
B.S. Bedi	67		

MOST CATCHES

Total		Tests
122	G.S. Chappell (A)	87
120	M.C. Cowdrey (E)	114
110	W.R. Hammond (E)	85
110	R.B. Simpson (A)	62
109	G.S. Sobers (WI)	93
105	I.M. Chappell (A)	75

HIGHEST WICKET-KEEPING DISMISSAL AGGREGATES

Total		Tests	Ct	St
355	R.W. Marsh (A)	96	343	12
269	A.P.E. Knott (E)	95	250	19
228	Wasim Bari (P)	81	201	27
219	T.G. Evans (E)	91	173	46
193	S.M.H. Kirmani (I)	85	157	36
187	A.T.W. Grout (A)	51	163	24
174	R.W. Taylor (E)	57	167	7
141	J.H.B. Waite (SA)	50	124	17
130	W.A. Oldfield (A)	54	78	52
114	J.M. Parks (E)	46	103	11

N.B. Park's figures include 2 catches as a fielder.

HIGHEST RUN AGGREGATES

Runs			Tests	Inns	NO	HS	Avge	100s	50s
8654	S.M. Gavaskar	(I)	106	185	14	236*	50.60	30	37
8114	G. Boycott	(E)	108	193	23	246*	47.72	22	42
8032	G.S. Sobers	(WI)	93	160	21	365*	57.78	26	30
7624	M.C. Cowdrey	(E)	114	188	15	182	44.06	22	38
7515	C.H. Lloyd	(WI)	110	175	14	242*	46.67	19	39
7249	W.R. Hammond	(E)	85	140	16	336*	58.45	22	24
7110	G.S. Chappel	(A)	87	151	19	247*	53.86	24	31
6996	D.G. Bradman	(A)	52	80	10	334	99.94	29	13
6971	L. Hutton	(E)	79	138	15	364*	56.67	19	33
6806	K.F. Barrington	(E)	82	131	15	256	58.67	20	35
6227	R.B. Hanhai	(WI)	79	137	6	256	47.53	15	28
6149	R.N. Harvey	(A)	79	137	10	205	48.41	21	24
6080	G.R. Viswanath	(I)	91	155	10	222	41.93	14	35
5807	D.C.S. Compton	(E)	78	131	15	278	50.06	17	28
5579	I.V.A. Richards	(WI)	73	110	6	291	53.64	18	23
5410	J.B. Hobbs	(E)	61	102	7	211	56.94	15	28
5357	K.D. Walters	(A)	74	125	14	250	48.26	15	33
5345	I.M. Chappel	(A)	75	136	10	196	42.42	14	26
5234	W.M. Lawry	(A)	67	123	12	210	47.15	13	27
5138	J.H. Edrich	(E)	77	127	9	310*	43.54	12	24
5034	Zaheer Abbas	(P)	74	119	11	274	46.61	12	20
4906	Javed Miandad	(P)	65	103	16	280*	56.39	13	26
4882	T.W. Graveney	(E)	79	123	13	258	44.38	11	20
4869	R.B. Simpson	(A)	62	111	7	311	46.81	10	27
4737	I.R. Redpath	(A)	66	120	11	171	43.45	8	31
4735	A.R. Border	(A)	66	116	20	162	49.32	12	28
4653	D.I. Gower	(E)	70	120	11	200*	42.68	9	24
4555	H. Sutcliffe	(E)	54	84	9	194	60.73	16	23
4552	C.G. Greenidge	(WI)	62	104	11	223	48.94	11	25
4537	P.B.H. May	(E)	66	106	9	285*	46.77	13	22
4502	E.R. Dexter	(E)	62	102	8	205	47.89	9	27

230

TEST CAREER RECORDS

FIGURES include the following series in 1984–85: Pakistan v India, Pakistan v New Zealand in Pakistan, Australia v West Indies, India v England

Compiled by Brian Heald

NEW ZEALAND

BATTING AND FIELDING

	M	I	NO	Runs	HS	Avge	100	50	Ct	St
S.L. Boock	19	29	8	116	35	5.52	—	—	10	—
B.P. Bracewell	5	10	2	17	8	2.12	—	—	1	—
J.G. Bracewell	12	19	2	138	30	8.11	—	—	11	—
B.L. Cairns	37	58	7	852	64*	16.70	—	2	26	—
E.J. Chatfield	16	22	12	86	13*	8.60	—	—	2	—
J.V. Coney	33	56	9	1627	174*	34.61	1	11	41	—
J.J. Crowe	13	21	0	625	128	29.76	1	4	15	—
M.D. Crowe	16	26	1	602	100	24.08	1	1	16	—
B.A. Edgar	30	53	3	1577	161	31.54	3	8	13	—
T.J. Franklin	1	2	0	9	7	4.50	—	—	—	—
E.J. Gray	4	8	0	86	25	10.75	—	—	2	—
R.J. Hadlee	50	85	11	1820	103	24.59	1	9	28	—
G.P. Howarth	40	71	5	2270	147	34.39	6	10	27	—
W.K. Lees	21	37	4	778	152	23.57	1	1	52	7
P.E. McEwan	4	7	1	96	40*	16.00	—	—	5	—
J.M. Parker	36	63	2	1498	121	24.55	3	5	30	—
J.F. Reid	10	17	1	744	180	46.50	3	2	5	—
I.D.S. Smith	18	26	7	508	113*	26.73	1	—	51	2
M.C. Snedden	10	12	2	147	32	14.70	—	—	2	—
D.A. Stirling	3	5	1	55	16	13.75	—	—	—	—
G.B. Troup	12	15	6	43	13*	4.77	—	—	2	—
J.G. Wright	34	59	2	1799	141	31.56	4	6	19	—

BOWLING

	Balls	Runs	Wkts	Avge	Best	5 wI	10 wM
S.L. Boock	4328	1534	54	28.40	7-87	3	—
B.P. Bracewell	838	456	10	45.60	3-110	—	—
J.G. Bracewell	2320	1027	29	35.41	5-75	1	—
B.L. Cairns	9096	3550	115	30.86	7-74	6	1
E.J. Chatfield	3757	1533	48	31.93	5-63	2	—
J.V. Coney	1785	546	15	36.40	3-28	—	—
J.J. Crowe	18	9	0				
M.D. Crowe	765	390	9	43.33	2-29	—	—
B.A. Edgar	18	3	0				
E.J. Gray	642	311	8	38.87	3-73	—	—
R.J. Hadlee	12721	5626	235	23.94	7-23	18	4
G.P. Howarth	560	254	3	84.66	1-13	—	—
W.K. Lees	5	4	0				
P.E. McEwan	36	13	0				
J.M. Parker	40	24	1	24.00	1-24	—	—

J.F. Reid	12	7	0	—	—	—	—	—	—
M.C. Snedden	1698	819	23	35.60	3-21	—	—		
D.A. Stirling	553	338	8	42.25	4-88	—	—		
G.B. Troup	2601	1114	34	32.76	6-95	1	1		
J.G. Wright	12	3	0	—	—	—	—		

PAKISTAN

BATTING AND FIELDING

	M	I	NO	Runs	HS	Avge	100	50	Ct	St
Abdul Qadir	31	37	4	486	50	14.72	—	1	8	—
Anil Dalpat	6	7	1	102	52	17.00	—	1	15	3
Ashraf Ali	4	5	3	206	65	103.00	—	2	8	2
Azeem Hafeez	15	16	5	97	24	8.81	—	—	1	—
Ehteshamuddin	5	3	1	2	2	1.00	—	—	2	—
Ejaz Fakih	2	4	0	63	34	15.75	—	—	—	—
Haroon Rashid	23	36	1	1217	153	34.77	3	5	16	—
Imran Khan	51	77	12	2033	123	31.12	2	7	16	—
Iqbal Qasim	40	45	13	353	56	11.03	—	1	31	—
Jalaluddin	5	3	2	3	2	3.00	—	—	1	—
Javed Miandad	65	103	16	4906	280*	56.39	13	26	54	1
Mansoor Akhtar	13	22	3	484	111	25.47	1	2	7	—
Manzoor Elahi	2	3	1	49	26	24.50	—	—	2	—
Mohammad Nazir	14	18	10	144	29*	18.00	—	—	4	—
Mohsin Kamal	1	1	0	0	0	0.00	—	—	—	—
Mohsin Khan	37	60	5	2335	200	42.45	7	8	28	—
Mudassar Nazar	49	76	5	2937	231	41.36	8	11	35	—
Qasim Omar	14	24	1	880	210	38.26	2	2	10	—
Ramiz Raja	2	4	1	34	26	11.33	—	—	4	—
Rashid Khan	3	4	3	118	59	118.00	—	1	1	—
Rizwan-uz-Zaman	3	6	0	112	42	18.66	—	—	1	—
Saleem Yousuf	1	1	0	4	4	4.00	—	—	5	2
Salim Malik	21	29	5	1126	119*	46.91	5	5	26	—
Sarfraz Nawaz	55	72	13	1045	90	17.71	—	4	26	—
Shoaib Mohammad	4	7	1	173	80	28.83	—	1	—	—
Sikander Bakht	26	35	12	146	22*	6.34	—	—	7	—
Tahir Naqqash	14	17	5	299	57	24.91	—	1	2	—
Taslim Arif	6	10	2	501	210*	62.62	1	2	6	3
Tauseef Ahmed	10	7	4	51	18*	17.00	—	—	4	—
Wasim Raja	55	89	14	2792	125	37.22	4	18	19	—
Zaheer Abbas	74	119	11	5034	274	46.61	12	20	34	—

BOWLING

	Balls	Runs	Wkts	Avge	Best	5 wI	10 wM
Abdul Qadir	8291	3791	112	33.84	7-142	8	2
Azeem Hafeez	3379	1719	51	33.70	6-46	3	—
Ehteshamuddin	940	375	14	23.43	5-47	1	—
Ejaz Fakih	156	85	1	85.00	1-76	—	—
Haroon Rashid	8	3	0	—	—	—	—
Imran Khan	12551	5316	232	22.91	8-58	16	4
Iqbal Qasim	10445	3871	133	29.10	7-49	5	2

Jalaluddin	966	449	10	44.90	3-77	—	—
Javed Miandad	1428	665	17	39.11	3-74	—	—
Manzoor Elahi	162	76	1	76.00	1-74	—	—
Mohammad Nazir	3262	1123	34	33.02	7-99	3	—
Mohsin Kamal	192	125	2	62.50	1-59	—	—
Mohsin Khan	86	30	0	—	—	—	—
Mudassan Nazar	3652	1596	41	38.92	6-32	1	—
Qasim Omar	6	0	0	—	—	—	—
Rashid Khan	546	263	6	43.83	3-129	—	—
Rizwan-uz-Zaman	102	39	3	13.00	3-26	—	—
Salim Malik	72	27	3	9.00	1-3	—	—
Sarfraz Nawaz	13926	5798	177	32.75	9-86	4	1
Sikander Bakht	4870	2411	67	35.98	8-69	3	1
Tahir Naqqash	2600	1317	31	42.48	5-40	2	—
Taslim Arif	30	28	1	28.00	1-28	—	—
Tauseef Ahmed	2310	924	29	31.86	4-58	—	—
Wasim Raja	4074	1813	51	35.54	4-50	—	—
Zaheer Abbas	370	132	3	44.00	2.21	—	—

SRI LANKA

BATTING AND FIELDING

	M	I	NO	Runs	HS	Avge	100	50	Ct	St
A.M.J.G. Amerasinghe	2	4	1	54	34	18.00	—	—	3	—
R.G. de Alwis	5	10	0	102	28	10.20	—	—	9	1
A.L.F. de Mel	7	14	3	188	34	17.09	—	—	5	—
D.S. de Silva	12	22	3	406	61	21.36	—	2	5	—
P.A. de Silva	1	2	0	19	16	9.50	—	—	—	—
R.L. Dias	9	17	0	747	109	43.94	2	5	6	—
E.R.N.S. Fernando	5	10	0	112	46	11.20	—	—	—	—
Y. Goonasekera	2	4	0	48	23	12.00	—	—	6	—
R.P.W. Guneratne	1	2	2	0	0*	—	—	—	—	—
R.S.A. Jayasekera	1	2	0	2	2	1.00	—	—	—	—
S. Jeganathan	2	4	0	19	8	4.75	—	—	—	—
V.B. John	6	10	5	53	27*	10.60	—	—	2	—
S.M.S. Kaluperuma	3	6	0	82	23	13.66	—	—	6	—
R.S. Madugalle	12	24	3	681	91*	32.42	—	4	7	—
L.R.D. Mendis	10	20	0	726	111	36.30	3	3	4	—
A. Ranatunga	9	18	0	521	90	28.94	—	5	3	—
R.J. Ratnayake	4	8	0	76	30	9.50	—	—	1	—
J.R. Ratnayeke	8	16	4	150	29*	12.50	—	—	1	—
S.A.R. Silva	2	4	1	118	102*	39.33	1	—	5	—
M.D. Wettimuny	2	4	0	28	17	7.00	—	—	2	—
S. Wettimuny	11	22	1	819	190	39.00	2	4	4	—
R.G.C.E. Wijesuriya	1	2	0	3	3	1.50	—	—	—	—

BOWLING

	Balls	Runs	Wkts	Avge	Best	5 wI	10 wM
A.M.J.G. Amerasinghe	300	150	3	50.00	2-73	—	—
A.L.F. de Mel	1515	1015	29	35.00	5-68	1	—
D.S. de Silva	3031	1347	37	36.40	5-59	1	—

R.P.W. Guneratne	102	84	0	—	—	—	—
S. Jeganathan	30	12	0	—	—	—	—
V.B. John	1281	614	28	21.92	5-60	2	—
S.M.S. Kaluperuma	162	62	2	31.00	2-17	—	—
R.S. Madugalle	24	4	0	—	—	—	—
A. Ranatunga	432	173	5	34.60	2-17	—	—
R.J. Ratnayake	678	405	8	50.62	4-81	—	—
J.R. Ratnayeke	1385	687	17	40.41	5-42	1	—
S. Wettimuny	12	21	0	—	—	—	—
R.G.C.E. Wijesuriya	144	105	0	—	—	—	—

AUSTRALIA

BATTING AND FIELDING

	M	I	NO	Runs	HS	Avge	100	50	Ct	St
T.M. Alderman	22	33	15	113	23	6.27	—	—	17	—
M.J. Bennett	2	3	2	48	23	48.00	—	—	4	—
D.C. Boon	3	5	0	132	51	26.40	—	1	2	—
A.R. Border	66	116	20	4735	162	49.32	12	28	70	—
R.J. Bright	16	27	5	303	33	13.77	—	—	8	—
T.M. Chappell	3	6	1	79	27	15.80	—	—	2	—
J. Dyson	30	58	7	1359	127*	26.64	2	5	10	—
A.M.J. Hilditch	11	21	0	637	113	30.33	1	5	10	—
T.G. Hogan	7	12	1	205	42*	18.63	—	—	2	—
R.M. Hogg	38	58	13	439	52	9.75	—	1	7	—
R.G. Holland	3	4	1	15	7*	5.00	—	—	1	—
D.W. Hookes	19	34	2	1171	143*	36.95	1	8	8	—
K.J. Hughes	70	124	6	4415	213	37.41	9	22	50	—
D.M. Jones	2	4	0	65	48	16.25	—	—	1	—
B.M. Laird	21	40	2	1341	92	35.28	—	11	16	—
G.F. Lawson	28	46	9	577	57*	15.59	—	2	7	—
C.J. McDermott	2	2	0	4	4	2.00	—	—	1	—
J.N. Maguire	3	5	1	28	15*	7.00	—	—	2	—
G.R.J. Matthews	4	6	1	118	75	23.60	—	1	1	—
W.B. Phillips	12	21	1	756	159	37.80	2	3	24	—
C.G. Rackemann	5	5	0	16	12	3.20	—	—	2	—
G.M. Ritchie	9	17	1	449	106*	28.06	1	2	5	—
S.J. Rixon	13	24	3	394	54	18.76	—	2	42	5
S.B. Smith	3	5	0	41	12	8.20	—	—	1	—
J.R. Thomson	49	69	16	641	49	12.09	—	—	19	—
D.M. Wellham	4	7	0	221	103	31.57	1	—	1	—
K.C. Wessels	17	29	1	1320	179	47.14	4	5	15	—
M.R. Whitney	2	4	0	4	4	1.00	—	—	—	—
G.M. Wood	48	92	5	2849	126	32.74	7	13	37	—
R.D. Woolley	2	2	0	21	13	10.50	—	—	7	—
G.N. Yallop	39	70	3	2756	268	41.13	8	9	23	—

234

BOWLING

	Balls	Runs	Wkts	Avge	Best	5 wI	10 wM
T.M. Alderman	5373	2597	79	32.87	6-128	5	—
M.J. Bennett	472	214	5	42.80	3-79	—	—
A.R. Border	1516	588	15	39.20	3-20	—	—
R.J. Bright	3598	1343	37	36.29	7-87	3	1
T.G. Hogan	1436	706	15	47.06	5-66	1	—
R.M. Hogg	7633	3499	123	28.24	6-74	6	2
R.G. Holland	783	404	14	28.85	6-54	1	1
D.W. Hookes	78	35	0	—	—	—	—
K.J. Hughes	85	28	0	—	—	—	—
B.M. Laird	18	12	0	—	—	—	—
G.F. Lawson	6300	3210	118	27.20	8-112	9	2
C.J. McDermott	414	273	10	27.30	3-118	—	—
J.N. Maguire	616	324	10	32.40	4-57	—	—
G.R.J. Matthews	547	296	7	42.28	2-48	—	—
C.G. Rackemann	936	539	23	23.43	6-86	3	1
J.R. Thomson	10199	5326	197	27.03	6-46	8	—
K.C. Wessels	48	17	0	—	—	—	—
M.R. Whitney	468	246	5	49.20	2-50	—	—
G.N. Yallop	192	116	1	116.00	1-21	—	—

WEST INDIES

BATTING AND FIELDING

	M	I	NO	Runs	HS	Avge	100	50	Ct	St
E.A.E. Baptiste	9	10	1	224	87*	24.88	—	1	2	—
W.W. Daniel	10	11	4	46	11	6.57	—	—	4	—
W.W. Davis	9	10	4	141	77	23.50	—	1	6	—
P.J. Dujon	29	38	3	1608	139	45.94	4	6	97	2
J. Garner	47	57	11	560	60	12.17	—	1	34	—
H.A. Gomes	45	69	10	2683	143	45.47	9	11	13	—
C.G. Greenidge	62	104	11	4552	223	48.94	11	25	59	—
R.A. Harper	13	15	1	192	39*	13.71	—	—	17	—
D.L. Haynes	50	80	5	2890	184	38.53	7	16	28	—
M.A. Holding	52	68	10	765	69	13.18	—	5	17	—
C.H. Lloyd	110	175	14	7515	242*	46.67	19	39	90	—
A.L. Logie	9	11	0	327	130	29.72	1	2	3	—
M.D. Marshall	36	44	3	710	92	17.31	—	4	16	—
I.V.A. Richards	73	110	6	5579	291	53.64	18	23	75	—
R.B. Richardson	11	16	1	589	154	39.26	3	1	14	—
A.M.E. Roberts	47	62	11	762	68	14.94	—	3	9	—
M.A. Small	2	1	1	3	3*	—	—	—	—	—
C.A. Walsh	5	6	3	32	18*	10.66	—	—	1	—

BOWLING

	Balls	Runs	Wkts	Avge	Best	5 wI	10 wM
E.A.E. Baptiste	1224	486	15	32.40	3-31	—	—
W.W. Daniel	1754	910	36	25.27	5-39	1	—
W.W. Davis	1719	894	22	40.63	3-21	—	—

J. Garner	10952	4490	210	21.38	6-56	6	—
H.A. Gomes	2107	823	13	63.30	2-20	—	—
C.G. Greenidge	26	4	0	—	—	—	—
R.A. Harper	2332	914	32	28.56	6-57	1	—
D.L. Haynes	18	8	1	8.00	1-2	—	—
M.A. Holding	11350	5194	224	23.18	8-92	13	2
C.H. Lloyd	1716	622	10	62.20	2-13	—	—
A.L. Logie	1	4	0	—	—	—	—
M.D. Marshall	7855	3671	161	22.80	7-53	12	1
I.V.A. Richards	2578	936	18	52.00	2-20	—	—
A.M.E. Roberts	11135	5174	202	25.61	7-54	11	2
M.A. Small	270	153	4	38.25	3-40	—	—
C.A. Walsh	878	432	13	33.23	3-55	—	—

INDIA

BATTING AND FIELDING

	M	I	NO	Runs	HS	Avge	100	50	Ct	St
M. Amarnath	49	83	7	3241	120	42.64	8	19	37	—
Arun Lal	4	7	0	164	63	23.42	—	2	5	—
M. Azharuddin	3	5	1	439	122	109.75	3	1	1	—
R. Bhatt	2	3	1	6	6	3.00	—	—	—	—
R.M.H. Binny	18	30	3	618	83*	22.88	—	4	7	—
C.P.S. Chauhan	40	68	2	2084	97	31.57	—	16	38	—
Chetan Sharma	5	6	4	62	18*	31.00	—	—	1	—
D.R. Doshi	33	38	10	129	20	4.60	—	—	10	—
A.D. Gaekwad	40	70	4	1985	201	30.07	2	10	15	—
S.M. Gavaskar	106	185	14	8654	236*	50.60	30	37	92	—
K.D. Ghavri	39	57	14	913	86	21.23	—	2	16	—
Gopal Sharma	1	—	—	—	—	—	—	—	1	—
Kapil Dev	68	101	9	2788	126*	30.30	3	15	26	—
S.M.H. Kirmani	85	122	22	2717	102	27.17	2	12	157	36
Kirti Azad	7	12	0	135	24	11.25	—	—	3	—
S. Madan Lal	38	60	16	1000	74	22.75	—	5	15	—
A. Malhotra	7	10	1	226	72*	25.11	—	1	2	—
Maninder Singh	13	15	5	58	15	5.80	—	—	3	—
S.V. Nayak	2	3	1	19	11	9.50	—	—	1	—
G.A. Parkar	1	2	0	7	6	3.50	—	—	1	—
S.M. Patil	29	47	4	1588	174	36.93	4	7	12	—
M. Prabhakar	2	4	1	86	35*	28.66	—	—	1	—
P. Roy	2	3	1	71	60*	35.50	—	1	1	—
B.S. Sandu	8	11	4	214	71	30.57	—	2	1	—
T.A. Sekar	2	1	1	0	0*	—	—	—	—	—
R.J. Shastri	34	53	8	1676	142	37.24	5	7	15	—
R. Shukla	1	—	—	—	—	—	—	—	—	—
N.S. Sidhu	2	3	0	39	20	13.00	—	—	1	—
L. Sivaramakrishnan	6	6	1	76	25	15.20	—	—	2	—
L. Srikkanth	8	13	1	288	84	24.00	—	2	3	—
D.B. Vengsarkar	76	124	11	4328	159	38.30	9	22	52	—
G.R. Viswanath	91	155	10	6080	222	41.93	14	35	63	—
N.S. Yadav	23	30	9	308	43	14.66	—	—	7	—
Yashpal Sharma	37	59	11	1606	140	33.45	2	9	16	—

BOWLING

	Balls	Runs	Wkts	Avge	Best	5 wI	10 wM
M. Amarnath	3275	1629	29	56.17	4-63	—	—
Arun Lal	7	6	0	—	—	—	—
M. Azharuddin	6	8	0	—	—	—	—
R. Bhatt	438	151	4	37.75	2-65	—	—
R.M.H. Binny	1817	1041	24	43.37	3-18	—	—
C.P.S. Chauhan	174	106	2	53.00	1-4	—	—
Chetan Sharma	669	433	8	54.12	4-38	—	—
D.R. Doshi	9322	3502	114	30.71	6-102	6	—
A.D. Gaekwad	334	187	2	93.50	1-4	—	—
S.M. Gavaskar	350	187	1	187.00	1-34	—	—
K.D. Ghauri	7042	3656	109	33.54	5-33	4	—
Gopal Sharma	426	132	3	44.00	3-115	—	—
Kapil Dev	14523	7406	258	28.70	9-83	18	2
S.M.H. Kumani	18	13	1	13.00	1-9	—	—
Kuti Azad	750	373	3	124.33	2-84	—	—
S. Madan Lal	5872	2798	68	41.14	5-23	4	—
A. Malhotra	18	3	0	—	—	—	—
Maninder Singh	2568	1060	16	66.25	4-85	—	—
S.V. Nayak	231	132	1	132.00	1-16	—	—
S.M. Patil	645	240	9	26.66	2-26	—	—
M. Prabhakar	174	102	1	102.00	1-68	—	—
B.S. Sandhu	1020	557	10	55.70	3-87	—	—
T.A. Sekar	204	129	0	—	—	—	—
R.J. Shastri	7683	2947	73	40.36	5-75	2	—
R. Shukla	294	152	2	76.00	2-82	—	—
N.S. Sidhu	6	9	0	—	—	—	—
L. Sivaramakrishnan	1797	818	23	35.56	6-64	3	1
K. Srikkanth	48	21	0	—	—	—	—
D.B. Vengsarkar	47	36	0	—	—	—	—
G.R. Viswanath	70	46	1	46.00	1-11	—	—
N.S. Yadav	5052	2336	60	38.93	5-131	1	—
Yashpal Sharma	30	17	1	17.00	1-6	—	—

ENGLAND

BATTING AND FIELDING

	M	I	NO	Runs	HS	Avge	100	50	Ct	St
J.P. Agnew	2	3	2	8	5	8.00	—	—	—	—
P.J.W. Allott	9	13	2	186	52*	16.90	—	1	4	—
C.W.J. Athey	3	6	0	17	9	2.83	—	—	2	—
D.L. Amiss	50	88	10	3612	262*	46.30	11	11	24	—
D.L. Bairstow	4	7	1	125	59	20.83	—	1	12	1
I.T. Botham	73	117	3	4159	208	36.48	13	18	84	—
G. Boycott	108	193	23	8114	246*	47.72	22	42	33	—
B.C. Broad	5	9	0	281	86	31.22	—	2	1	—
A.R. Butcher	1	2	0	34	20	17.00	—	—	—	—
R.O. Butcher	3	5	0	71	32	14.20	—	—	3	—
G. Cook	7	13	0	203	66	15.61	—	2	9	—
N.G.B. Cook	9	15	1	101	26	7.21	—	—	5	—
N.G. Cowans	18	28	6	153	36	6.95	—	—	9	—

						100	50	Ct	St
C.S. Cowdrey	5	6	1	96	38	19.20	—	—	5	—
G.R. Dilley	18	28	8	330	56	16.50	—	2	5	—
P.R. Downton	15	24	5	462	74	24.31	—	3	35	2
P.H. Edmonds	28	34	6	605	64	21.60	—	2	23	—
R.M. Ellison	5	7	1	86	41	14.33	—	—	1	—
J.E. Emburey	22	33	6	326	57	12.07	—	1	15	—
K.W.R. Fletcher	59	96	14	3272	216	39.90	7	19	54	—
N.A. Foster	8	10	2	75	18*	9.37	—	—	3	—
G. Fowler	21	37	0	1307	201	35.32	3	8	10	—
M.W. Gatting	35	61	7	1719	207	31.83	2	10	35	—
G.A. Gooch	42	75	4	2540	153	35.77	4	15	36	—
D.I. Gower	70	120	11	4653	200*	42.68	9	24	49	—
I.A. Greig	2	4	0	26	14	6.50	—	—	—	—
E.E. Hemmings	5	10	1	198	95	22.00	—	1	4	—
A.P.E. Knott	95	149	15	4389	135	32.75	5	30	250	19
A.J. Lamb	32	56	5	1955	137*	38.33	7	8	34	—
W. Larkins	6	11	0	176	34	16.00	—	—	3	—
J.K. Lever	20	29	4	306	53	12.24	—	1	11	—
T.A. Lloyd	1	1	1	10	10*	—	—	—	—	—
V.J. Marks	6	10	1	249	83	27.66	—	3	—	—
G. Miller	34	51	4	1213	98*	25.80	—	7	17	—
C.M. Old	46	66	9	845	65	14.82	—	2	22	—
P.W.G. Parker	1	2	0	13	13	6.50	—	—	—	—
A.C.S. Pigott	1	2	1	12	8*	12.00	—	—	—	—
P.I. Pocock	25	37	4	206	33	6.24	—	—	15	—
D.R. Pringle	10	17	3	247	47*	17.64	—	—	3	—
D.W. Randall	47	79	5	2470	174	33.37	7	12	31	—
R.T. Robinson	5	9	2	444	160	63.42	1	2	—	—
C.L. Smith	7	12	1	358	91	32.54	—	2	5	—
G.B. Stevenson	2	2	1	28	27*	28.00	—	—	—	—
C.J. Tavaré	30	55	2	1753	149	33.07	2	12	20	—
R.W. Taylor	57	83	12	1156	97	16.26	—	3	167	7
V.P. Terry	2	3	0	16	8	5.33	—	—	2	—
D.L. Underwood	86	116	35	937	45*	11.56	—	—	44	—
P. Willey	20	38	5	923	102*	27.96	2	4	3	—
R.G.D. Willis	90	128	55	840	28*	11.50	—	—	39	—

BOWLING

	Balls	Runs	Wkts	Avge	Best	5 wI	10 wM
J.P. Agnew	414	274	4	68.50	2-51	—	—
P.J.W. Allott	1547	787	21	37.47	6-61	1	—
I.T. Botham	16881	8191	312	26.25	8-34	24	4
G. Boycott	944	382	7	54.57	3-47	—	—
A.R. Butcher	12	9	0	—	—	—	—
G. Cook	42	27	0	—	—	—	—
N.G.B. Cook	2990	1212	40	30.30	6-65	4	1
N.G. Cowans	3254	1875	49	38.26	6-77	2	—
C.S. Cowdrey	366	288	4	72.00	2-65	—	—
G.R. Dilley	3130	1595	50	31.90	4-24	—	—
P.H. Edmonds	6877	2317	73	31.73	7-66	2	—
R.M. Ellison	1104	489	10	48.90	4-66	—	—
J.E. Emburey	4981	1696	56	30.28	6-33	2	—
K.W.R. Fletcher	285	193	2	96.50	1-6	—	—
N.A. Foster	1836	902	26	34.69	6-104	3	1

Continued on page 245.

ONE-DAY INTERNATIONALS
CAREER RECORDS

The following are the career records in One-Day Internationals for those likely to play for English counties in 1985 and are complete to the end of the 1984 English season.

BATTING AND FIELDING

	M	I	NO	Runs	HS	Avge	100s	Ct	St
Alderman, T.M. (A)	18	7	3	19	9*	4.75	—	8	—
Allott, P.J.W.	10	5	1	13	8	3.25	—	1	—
Amiss, D.L.	18	18	0	859	137	47.72	4	2	—
Athey, C.W.J.	2	2	0	83	51	41.50	—	1	—
Bairstow, D.L.	21	20	6	206	23*	14.71	—	17	4
Baptiste, E.A.E. (WI)	23	9	2	111	28*	15.85	—	3	—
Barlow, G.D.	6	6	1	149	80*	29.80	—	4	—
Botham, I.T.	72	64	8	1147	65	20.48	—	25	—
Boycott, G.	36	34	4	1082	105	36.06	1	5	—
Butcher, A.R.	1	1	0	14	14	14.00	—	—	—
Butcher, R.O.	3	3	0	58	52	19.33	—	1	—
Clarke, S.T. (WI)	10	8	2	60	20	10.00	—	4	—
Cook, G	6	6	0	106	32	17.66	—	2	—
Cook, N.G.B.	1	—	—	—	—	—	—	1	—
Cowans, N.G.	13	5	2	9	4*	3.00	—	3	—
Crowe, M.D. (NZ)	18	17	3	547	105*	39.07	1	6	—
Daniel, W.W. (WI)	18	5	4	49	16*	49.00	—	5	—
Davis, W.W. (WI)	12	2	2	7	7*	—	—	—	—
Dilley, G.R.	18	11	3	96	31*	12.00	—	1	—
Downton, P.R.	1	—	—	—	—	—	—	1	—
Edmonds, P.H.	11	6	2	31	15	7.75	—	2	—
Emburey, J.E.	8	7	1	31	18	5.16	—	3	—
Fletcher, K.W.R.	24	22	3	757	131	39.84	1	4	—
Foster, N.A.	8	5	2	35	24	11.66	—	5	—
Fowler, G.	13	13	2	488	81*	44.36	—	1	2
Garner, J. (WI)	55	28	12	154	37	9.62	—	12	—
Gatting, M.W.	31	29	8	604	96	28.76	—	5	—
Gooch, G.A.	37	36	1	1046	108	29.88	1	15	—
Gould, I.J.	18	14	2	155	42	12.91	—	15	3
Gower, D.I.	66	63	7	2172	158	38.78	6	27	—
Greenidge, C.G. (WI)	60	60	6	2545	115	47.12	5	20	—
Hadlee, R.J. (NZ)	63	52	4	798	79	16.62	—	19	—
Harper, R.A. (WI)	10	1	0	0	0	0.00	—	4	—
Hemmings, E.E.	5	2	0	4	3	2.00	—	1	—
Hendrick, M.	22	10	5	6	2*	1.20	—	5	—

239

Holding, M.A. (WI)	66	31	8	198	64	8.60	—	20	—
Howarth, G.P. (NZ)	57	54	4	1235	76	24.70	—	13	—
Humpage, G.W.	3	2	0	11	6	5.50	—	2	—
Javed Miandad (P)	58	56	11	1641	119*	36.46	2	14	—
Jesty, T.E.	10	10	4	127	52*	21.16	—	5	—
Kallicharran A.I. (WI)	31	28	4	826	78	34.41	—	8	—
Kapil Dev (I)	47	46	6	1048	175*	26.20	1	19	—
Knott, A.P.E.	20	14	4	200	50	20.00	—	15	1
Lamb, A.J.	32	31	5	1235	118	47.50	3	10	—
Larkins, W.	6	6	0	84	34	14.00	—	2	—
Lever, J.K.	22	11	4	56	27*	8.00	—	6	—
Lloyd, C.H. (WI)	73	59	14	1609	102	35.75	1	39	—
Lloyd, T.A.	3	3	0	101	49	33.66	—	—	—
Love, J.D.	3	3	0	61	43	20.33	—	1	—
Marks, V.J.	25	16	3	160	28	12.30	—	7	—
Marshall, M.D. (WI)	44	26	8	281	56*	15.61	—	8	—
Miller, G.	25	18	2	136	46	8.50	—	4	—
Old, C.M.	32	25	7	338	51*	18.77	—	8	—
Phillip, N. (WI)	1	1	0	0	0	0.00	—	—	—
Pringle, D.R.	7	5	2	61	34*	20.33	—	3	—
Radley, C.T.	4	4	1	250	117*	83.33	1	1	—
Randall, D.W.	48	44	5	1048	88	26.87	—	25	—
Richards, C.J.	3	2	0	3	3	1.50	—	1	—
Richards, I.V.A. (WI)	76	71	9	3175	189*	51.20	7	28	—
Rose, B.C.	2	2	0	99	54	49.50	—	1	—
Smith, C.L.	4	4	0	109	70	27.25	—	—	—
Stevenson, G.B.	4	4	3	43	28*	43.00	—	2	—
Tavaré, C.J.	29	28	2	720	83*	27.69	—	7	—
Underwood, D.L.	26	13	4	53	17	5.88	—	6	—
Willey, P.	19	18	1	475	64	27.94	—	3	—
Wright, J.G. (NZ)	52	52	1	1465	84	28.72	—	23	—
Zaheer Abbas (P)	49	49	6	2177	123	50.62	7	13	—

BOWLING

	Balls	Runs	Wkts	Avge	B/B	4wI
Alderman, T.M. (A)	1020	598	25	23.92	5-17	1
Allott, P.J.W.	651	420	13	32.30	3-41	—
Baptiste, E.A.E. (WI)	1218	786	23	34.17	2-10	—
Botham, I.T.	3762	2533	96	26.38	4-56	1

Boycott, G	168	105	5	21.00	2-14	—
Clarke, S.T.	524	245	13	18.84	3-22	—
Cook, N.G.B.	48	34	1	34.00	1-34	—
Cowans, N.G.	699	496	11	45.09	2-20	—
Crowe, M.D. (NZ)	312	262	9	29.11	2-9	—
Daniel, W.W. (WI)	912	595	23	25.86	3-27	—
Davis, W.W. (WI)	729	489	12	40.75	7-51	1
Dilley, G.R.	972	595	18	33.05	4-45	1
Edmonds, P.H.	484	230	11	20.90	3-39	—
Emburey, J.E.	435	262	5	52.40	2-22	—
Foster, N.A.	448	302	5	60.40	2-19	—
Garner, J. (WI)	3116	1618	85	19.03	5-31	3
Gatting, M.W.	128	95	4	23.75	3-32	—
Gooch, G.A.	799	612	16	38.25	2-12	—
Greenidge, C.G. (WI)	60	45	1	45.00	1-21	—
Hadlee, R.J. (NZ)	3481	1817	86	21.12	5-25	4
Harper, R.A. (WI)	516	386	12	32.16	3-34	—
Hemmings, E.E.	249	175	5	35.00	3-11	—
Hendrick, M.	1248	681	35	19.45	5-31	3
Holding, M.A. (WI)	3630	1998	98	20.38	4-17	4
Javed Miandad (P)	352	209	5	41.80	2-22	—
Jesty, T.E.	108	93	1	93.00	1-23	—
Kallicharran A.I. (WI)	105	64	3	21.33	2-10	—
Kapil Dev (I)	2553	1536	55	27.92	5-43	1
Lever, J.K.	1152	713	24	29.70	4-29	1
Lloyd, C.H. (WI)	357	210	7	30.00	2-4	—
Marks, V.J.	1404	796	36	22.11	5-20	2
Marshall, M.D. (WI)	2382	1259	58	21.70	4-34	1
Miller, G.	1268	813	25	32.52	3-27	—
Old, C.M.	1755	999	45	22.20	4-8	2
Phillip, N. (WI)	42	22	1	22.00	1-22	—
Pringle, D.R.	390	320	8	40.00	3-21	—
Randall, D.W.	2	2	1	2.00	1-2	—
Richards, I.V.A. (WI)	2206	1690	45	37.55	3-41	—
Smith, C.L.	36	28	2	14.00	2-8	—
Stevenson, G.B.	192	125	7	17.85	4-33	1
Tavaré, C.J.	12	3	0	—	—	—
Underwood, D.L.	1278	734	32	22.93	4-44	1

Willey, P.	756	481	9	53.44	3-33	—
Wright, J.G.	18	2	0	—	—	—
Zaheer Abbas	175	129	6	21.50	2-14	—

TEXACO CUP

31 MAY
Played at Old Trafford
West Indies 272-9 in 55 overs (Richards 189*, Miller 3-32)
England 168 in 50 overs (Lamb 75, Garner 3-18)
West Indies won by 104 runs

2 JUNE
Played at Trent Bridge
West Indies 179 in 48.3 overs (Lloyd 52, Pringle 3-21)
England 180-7 in 47.5 overs
England won by 3 wickets

4 JUNE
Played at Lord's
England 196-9 in 55 overs (Marshall 3-38)
West Indies 197-2 in 46.5 overs (Richards 84*, Gomes 56*)
West Indies won by 8 wickets

WARWICKSHIRE *Continued from page 149.*

Kenneth <u>David</u> SMITH (Heaton GS) B Jesmond, Newcastle-upon-Tyne 9/7/1956. RHB. Son of Kenneth D. Smith (Leics). Brother of P.A. Smith. Debut 1973. Cap 1978. 1,000 runs (4) – 1,582 runs (av. 36.79) in 1980 best. NW Man of the Match: 1. BH Gold Awards: 1. HS: 140 v Worcs (Worcester) 1980. HSNW: 113 v Yorks (Birmingham) 1982. HSJPL: 73 v Essex (Colchester) 1982. HSBH: 84 v Worcs (Worcester) 1980.

Paul Andrew SMITH (Heaton GS) B Newcastle-upon-Tyne 15/4/1964. Son of K.D. Smith (Leics). Brother of K.D. Smith Junior. RHB, RM. Debut 1982. Scored 1,040 runs (av. 28.10) in 1984. HS: 114 v Oxford U (Birmingham) 1983. HSNW: 41* v Oxfordshire (Birmingham) 1984. HSJPL: 49* v Surrey (Birmingham) 1984. HSBH: 37 v Somerset (Birmingham) 1984. BB: 4-41 v Worcs (Birmingham) 1984. BBNW: 3-10 v Shropshire (Birmingham) 1984. BBJPL: 4-23 v Notts (Birmingham) 1983.

Geoffrey Alan TEDSTONE (Warwick School; St Paul's College, Cheltenham) B Southport, Lancs 19/1/1961. RHB, WK. Debut 1982. HS: 67* v Cambridge U (Cambridge) 1983. HSJPL: 23 v Middlesex (Birmingham) 1982.

David Anthony THORNE B Coventry 12/12/1964. RHB, LM. Debut for Warwicks 1983. Debut for Oxford U and Blue 1984. HS: 69* Oxford U v Kent (Oxford) 1984. HSC: 49 v Yorks (Leeds) 1984. HSJPL: 42 v Glos (Moreton-in-the-Marsh) 1983. BB: 5-39 Oxford U v Cambridge U (Lord's) 1984.

Stephen WALL (Dondales School) B Ulverston, Lancs 10/12/1959. RHB, RFM. Debut 1984. HS: 19 v Hants (Birmingham) 1984.

NB. The following player whose particulars appeared in the 1984 Annual has been omitted: R.G.D. Willis.

MINOR COUNTIES FIXTURES, 1985

(E) *Eastern Division*   (W) *Western Division*

MAY		**MCCA Representative Match**
Sun 19	Arundel	Lavinia, Duchess of Norfolk's XI v MCCA (One day)
		English Estates Trophy, *Qualifying Round*
Sun 19	Market Rasen	Lincolnshire v Northumberland
	Watford	Hertfordshire v Bedfordshire
	Bridgnorth	Shropshire v Oxfordshire
		United Friendly Insurance Championship
Sun 26	Sleaford	(E) Lincolnshire v Hertfordshire
	Jesmond	(E) Northumberland v Bedfordshire
Tue 28	Netherfield, Kendal	(E) Cumberland v Bedfordshire
	Hartlepool	(E) Durham v Hertfordshire
Thu 30	West Bromwich	(E) Staffordshire v Hertfordshire
JUNE		**English Estates Trophy,** *First Round*
Sun 2	Chester-le-Street	Durham v Lincolnshire or Northumberland
	Exeter	Devon v Wiltshire
	Fenner's	Cambridgeshire v Suffolk
	Workington	Cumberland v Cheshire
	Potter's Bar or (t.b.a.)	Hertfordshire or Bedfordshire v Norfolk
	Bracknell	Berkshire v Shropshire or Oxfordshire
	Dean Park	Dorset v Cornwall
	Longton	Staffordshire v Buckinghamshire
		United Friendly Insurance Championship
Sun 9	Millom	(E) Cumberland v Cambridgeshire
Mon 10	Henlow	(E) Bedfordshire v Staffordshire
	Nantwich	(W) Cheshire v Cornwall
Tue 11	Jesmond	(E) Northumberland v Cambridgeshire
Wed 12	Newport	(W) Shropshire v Cornwall
Sun 16		**English Estates Trophy** *Quarter-Final*
		United Friendly Insurance Championship
Wed 19	Wisbech	(E) Cambridgeshire v Norfolk
	Leek	(E) Staffordshire v Lincolnshire
Sun 23	Bourne	(E) Lincolnshire v Cumberland
	Jesmond	(E) Northumberland v Norfolk
	Chester, Boughton Hall	(W) Cheshire v Somerset II
Tue 25	South Shields	(E) Durham v Norfolk
	Hitchin	(E) Hertfordshire v Cumberland
	Wellington	(W) Shropshire v Somerset II
Thu 27	Street (Victoria Club)	(W) Somerset II v Buckinghamshire
		MCCA Representative Match
Sat 29	Cleethorpes	MCCA v Zimbabwe (Three days)
Sun 30		**English Estates Trophy** *Semi-Final*
JULY		**United Friendly Insurance Championship**
Sat 6	St Albans	(E) Hertfordshire v Bedfordshire
Sun 7	Burghley Park	(E) Lincolnshire v Durham
	Slough	(W) Buckinghamshire v Shropshire

	Oxford Morris Motors	(W) Oxfordshire v Cheshire
Mon 8	Bishops Stortford	(E) Hertfordshire v Cambridgeshire
Tue 9	Chippenham	(W) Wiltshire v Cheshire
Wed 10	Newcastle-under-Lyme	(E) Staffordshire v Northumberland
Sun 14	Fenner's	**English Estates Trophy** *Final*

United Friendly Insurance Championship

Sun 14	Troon	(W) Cornwall v Devon
	Bournemouth S.C.	(W) Dorset v Buckinghamshire
	Morris Motors	(W) Oxfordshire v Berkshire

MCCA Representative Match

| Thu 18 | Jesmond | MCCA v Australians (One day) |

United Friendly Insurance Championship

Thu 18	Bury St Edmunds	(E) Suffolk v Cambridgeshire
	Sidmouth	(W) Devon v Dorset
Sun 21	Barrow	(E) Cumberland v Staffordshire
	Chester-le-Street	(E) Durham v Northumberland
	Lincoln Lindum	(E) Lincolnshire v Norfolk
	Toft	(W) Cheshire v Dorset
	Falmouth	(W) Cornwall v Berkshire
	St Edward's School	(W) Oxfordshire v Buckinghamshire
Mon 22	Devizes	(W) Wiltshire v Somerset II
Tue 23	Ipswich (G.R.E.)	(E) Suffolk v Hertfordshire
	Newton Abbott	(W) Devon v Berkshire
	St George's Oakengates	(W) Shropshire v Dorset
Wed 24	Stone	(E) Staffordshire v Durham
Sun 28	Jesmond	(E) Northumberland v Lincolnshire
	Framlingham College	(E) Suffolk v Cumberland
	Falkland CC Newbury	(W) Berkshire v Wiltshire
	Banbury XX Ground	(W) Oxfordshire v Shropshire
Mon 29	Truro	(W) Cornwall v Buckinghamshire
Tue 30	Lakenham	(E) Norfolk v Cumberland
	Swindon	(W) Wiltshire v Shropshire
Wed 31	March	(E) Cambridgeshire v Bedfordshire
	Exmouth	(W) Devon v Buckinghamshire

AUGUST

Thu 1	Reading (Kensington Road)	(W) Berkshire v Dorset
Fri 2	Lakenham	(E) Norfolk v Bedfordshire
Sun 4	Shrewsbury	(W) Shropshire v Cheshire
Mon 5	Lakenham	(E) Norfolk v Staffordshire
	Yeovil (Westland's)	(W) Somerset II v Devon
Wed 7	Lakenham	(E) Norfolk v Hertfordshire
	Mildenhall	(E) Suffolk v Staffordshire
	Sherborne School	(W) Dorset v Somerset II
	Trowbridge	(W) Wiltshire v Oxfordshire
Fri 9	Lakenham	(E) Norfolk v Suffolk
Sun 11	Bedford Town	(E) Bedfordshire v Lincolnshire
	Carlisle	(E) Cumberland v Durham
	Reading School	(W) Berkshire v Shropshire

G. Fowler	18	11	0	—	—	—	—
M.W. Gatting	302	151	2	75.50	1-14	—	—
G.A. Gooch	937	348	8	43.50	2-12	—	—
D.I. Gower	30	15	1	15.00	1-1	—	—
I.A. Greig	188	114	4	28.50	4-53	—	—
E.E. Hemmings	1468	558	12	46.50	3-68	—	—
A.J. Lamb	18	12	1	12.00	1-6	—	—
J.K. Lever	4115	1785	67	26.64	7-46	3	1
V.J. Marks	1082	484	11	44.00	3-78	—	—
G. Miller	5149	1859	60	30.98	5-44	1	—
C.M. Old	8858	4020	143	28.11	7-50	4	—
A.C.S. Pigott	102	75	2	37.50	2-75	—	—
P.I. Pocock	6650	2976	67	44.41	6-79	3	—
D.R. Pringle	1520	752	16	47.00	5-108	1	—
D.W. Randall	16	3	0	—	—	—	—
R.T. Robinson	6	0	0	—	—	—	—
C.L. Smith	102	39	3	13.00	2-31	—	—
G.B. Stevenson	312	183	5	36.60	3-111	—	—
C.J. Tavaré	30	11	0	—	—	—	—
R.W. Taylor	12	6	0	—	—	—	—
D.L. Underwood	21860	7674	297	25.83	8-51	17	6
P. Willey	1067	441	6	73.50	2-73	—	—
R.G.D. Willis	17357	8190	325	25.20	8-43	16	—

UNITED FRIENDLY CHAMPIONSHIP
FINAL TABLE 1984

EASTERN DIVISION		Played	Won	Tied	Lost	W 1st Inns	T 1st Inns	L 1st Inns	No Result	Points
Durham	NW	9	4	—	2(1)	2	—	1	—	50
Staffordshire	NW	9	4	—	1	—	—	2	2	46
Norfolk	NW	9	3	—	3(2)	2	—	1	—	43
Hertfordshire	NW	9	3	—	3	2	—	—	1	38
Suffolk	NW	9	2	—	3(3)	1	—	2	1	36
Cumberland	NW	9	2	—	1	4	—	2	—	34
Bedfordshire	NW	9	2	—	3(2)	—	—	4	—	30
Lincolnshire		9	2	—	3	1	—	2	2	26
Cambridgeshire		9	1	—	3(1)	4	—	1	—	26
Northumberland		9	1	—	2(1)	2	—	2	2	25
WESTERN DIVISION										
Cheshire	NW	9	6	—	—	2	—	1	—	67
Buckinghamshire	NW	9	3	—	2	1	—	3	—	36
Shropshire	NW	9	2	—	2(1)	2	—	2	1	33
Somerset II		9	2	—	3(1)	2	—	2	—	31
Devon	NW	9	2	—	1	1	—	4	1	29
Berkshire	NW	9	1	—	—	5	—	3	—	28
Oxfordshire	NW	9	1	—	3(1)	4	—	1	—	26
Dorset	NW	9	1	—	1(1)	3	—	4	—	26
Wiltshire		9	2	—	5(1)	—	—	2	—	25
Cornwall		9	1	—	4	3	—	1	—	20

(1) 1st Innings points in 1 match lost
(2) 1st Innings points in 2 matches lost
(3) 1st Innings points in 3 matches lost

Oxfordshire take precedence over Dorset through a superior nett batting average

PRINCIPAL FIXTURES 1985

Including play on Sunday

Saturday 20 April

Cambridge: Cambridge U v Essex
Oxford: Oxford U v Somerset

Wednesday 24 April

Cambridge: Cambridge U v
   Nottinghamshire
Oxford: Oxford U v Glamorgan
Lord's: MCC v Essex (three days)

Saturday 27 April

Britannic Assurance Championship
Derby: Derbys v Northants
Chelmsford:* Essex v Warwicks
Southampton:* Hants v Kent
Old Trafford:* Lancs v Sussex
Leicester: Leics v Yorks
Lord's: Middx v Worcs
Taunton:* Somerset v Notts
The Oval:* Surrey v Glam
Other Match
Cambridge: Cambridge U v
   Gloucestershire

Wednesday 1 May

Britannic Assurance Championship
Bristol: Glos v Lancs
Canterbury: Kent v Surrey
Trent Bridge: Notts v Essex
Taunton: Somerset v Glam
Other Matches
Cambridge: Cambridge U v Middx
Oxford: Oxford U v Leics

Saturday 4 May

Benson & Hedges Cup
Chelmsford: Essex v Sussex
Cardiff: Glam v Kent
Bristol: Glos v Notts
Old Trafford: Lancs v Leics
The Oval: Surrey v Combined U
Worcester: Worcs v Warwicks
Aberdeen (Mannofield): Scotland v
   Derbys
Shrewsbury: Minor Counties v
   Somerset

Britannic Assurance Championship
Northampton: Northants v Hants
Headingley: Yorks v Middx

Sunday 5 May

John Player Special League
Chelmsford: Essex v Sussex
Cardiff: Glam v Kent
Bristol: Glos v Notts
Old Trafford: Lancs v Leics
Northampton: Northants v Hants
The Oval: Surrey v Warwicks
Worcester: Worcs v Somerset
Bradford: Yorks v Middx
Tourist Match
Arundel: Lavinia, Duchess of
   Norfolk's XI v Australia (one day)

Wednesday 8 May

Britannic Assurance Championship
Leicester: Leics v Derbys
Lord's: Middx v Kent
The Oval: Surrey v Lancs
Edgbaston: Warwicks v Glam
Worcester: Worcs v Glos
Tourist Match
Taunton: Somerset v Australia
Other Matches
Cambridge: Cambridge U v Sussex
Oxford: Oxford U v Hampshire

Saturday 11 May

Benson & Hedges Cup
Swansea: Glam v Minor Counties
Canterbury: Kent v Hants
Leicester: Leics v Yorks
Northampton: Northants v Glos
Hove: Sussex v Surrey
Edgbaston: Warwicks v Lancs
Cambridge: Combined U v Middx
Glasgow (Titwood): Scotland v Notts
Tourist Match
Worcester:* Worcs v Australia

Sunday 12 May

John Player Special League
Derby: Derbys v Northants
Canterbury: Kent v Hants

247

Leicester: Leics v Yorks
Lord's: Middx v Glos
Taunton: Somerset v Glam
Hove: Sussex v Surrey
Edgbaston: Warwicks v Lancs

Tuesday 14 May

Benson & Hedges Cup
Derby: Derbys v Northants
Bristol: Glos v Scotland
Southampton: Hants v Glam
Old Trafford: Lancs v Yorks
Leicester: Leics v Worcs
Taunton: Somerset v Kent
The Oval: Surrey v Essex
Hove: Sussex v Middx
Tourist Match
Trent Bridge: Notts v Australia (one day)

Thursday 16 May

Benson & Hedges Cup
Southampton: Hants v Somerset
Canterbury: Kent v Minor Counties
Lord's: Middx v Essex
Northampton: Northants v Scotland
Trent Bridge: Notts v Derbys
Worcester: Worcs v Lancs
Headingley: Yorks v Warwicks
Oxford: Combined U v Sussex
Tourist Match
The Oval: Surrey v Australia (one day)

Saturday 18 May

Benson & Hedges Cup
Chesterfield: Derbys v Glos
Chelmsford: Essex v Combined U
Lord's: Middx v Surrey
Trent Bridge: Notts v Northants
Taunton: Somerset v Glam
Edgbaston: Warwicks v Leics
Bradford: Yorks v Worcs
Reading: Minor Counties v Hants
Tourist Match
Hove:* Sussex v Australia (four days)

Sunday 19 May

John Player Special League
Southampton: Hants v Surrey
Old Trafford: Lancs v Glos

Lord's: Middx v Glam
Trent Bridge: Notts v Leics
Scarborough: Yorks v Derbys

Wednesday 22 May

Britannic Assurance Championship
Chesterfield: Derbys v Lancs
Cardiff: Glam v Middx
Leicester: Leics v Notts
Northampton: Northants v Kent
Taunton: Somerset v Hants
Hove: Sussex v Glos
Edgbaston: Warwicks v Surrey
Sheffield: Yorks v Essex
Tourist Match
Lord's: MCC v Australia
Other Match
Oxford: Oxford U v Worcs

Saturday 25 May

Britannic Assurance Championship
Bristol: Glos v Somerset
Southampton: Hants v Glam
Old Trafford:* Lancs v Yorks
Leicester: Leics v Northants
Lord's: Middx v Sussex
The Oval: Surrey v Essex
Worcester:* Worcs v Warwicks
Tourist Match
Derby:* Derbys v Australia (four days)

Sunday 26 May

John Player Special League
Bristol: Glos v Kent
Basingstoke: Hants v Glam
Leicester: Leics v Northants
Lord's: Middx v Sussex
Trent Bridge: Notts v Somerset
The Oval: Surrey v Essex

Wednesday 29 May

Britannic Assurance Championship
Basingstoke: Hants v Derbyshire
Northampton: Northants v Warwicks
Trent Bridge: Notts v Leics
The Oval: Surrey v Middx
Hove: Sussex v Glam
Headingley: Yorks v Somerset
Other Match
Oxford: Oxford U v Kent

248

Thursday 30 May

TEXACO TROPHY
Old Trafford: ENGLAND v
   AUSTRALIA
   (First One-day International)

Saturday 1 June

TEXACO TROPHY
Edgbaston: ENGLAND v
   AUSTRALIA
   (Second One-day International)
Britannic Assurance Championship
Derby: Derbys v Glos
Chelmsford: Essex v Leics
Canterbury: Kent v Worcs
Taunton: Somerset v Warwicks
Horsham: Sussex v Surrey
Middlesbrough: Yorks v Hants
Other Match
Oxford: Oxford U v Lancs

Sunday 2 June

John Player Special League
Derby: Derbys v Glos
Chelmsford: Essex v Leics
Canterbury: Kent v Worcs
Northampton: Northants v Lancs
Taunton: Somerset v Warwicks
Horsham: Sussex v Notts
Middlesbrough: Yorks v Hampshire

Monday 3 June

TEXACO TROPHY
Lord's: ENGLAND v AUSTRALIA
   (Third One-day International)

Wednesday 5 June

Benson & Hedges Cup Quarter-Finals
Tourist Match
Headingley: Yorks v Australia
(or Warwicks or Lancashire)

Saturday 8 June

Britannic Assurance Championship
Ilford: Essex v Lancs
Abergavenny: Glam v Worcs
Tunbridge Wells: Kent v Notts
Lord's: Middx v Derbys
Northampton: Northants v Sussex
Bath: Somerset v Glos
Edgbaston: Warwicks v Hants

Tourist Matches
Leicester:* Leics v Australia (four
   days)
Oxford: Oxford U v Zimbabwe
Other Match
Cambridge: Cambridge U v Surrey

Sunday 9 June

John Player Special League
Ilford: Essex v Lancs
Ebbw Vale: Glam v Worcs
Lord's: Middx v Derbys
Bath: Somerset v Glos
Edgbaston: Warwicks v Hants
Sheffield: Yorks v Sussex

Wednesday 12 June

Britannic Assurance Championship
Derby: Derbys v Sussex
Ilford: Essex v Northants
Bournemouth: Hants v Middx
Tunbridge Wells: Kent v Glos
Hinckley: Leics v Warwicks
Bath: Somerset v Lancs
The Oval: Surrey v Notts
Other Matches
Cambridge: Cambridge U v Worcs
Oxford: Oxford U v Yorks

Thursday 13 June

CORNHILL INSURANCE TEST
   SERIES
Headingley: ENGLAND v
   AUSTRALIA
   (First Test Match)

Saturday 15 June

Britannic Assurance Championship
Swansea: Glam v Essex
Old Trafford: Lancs v Derbys
Lord's: Middx v Leics
Northampton: Northants v Glos
Trent Bridge: Notts v Kent
Hove: Sussex v Hants
Worcester: Worcs v Surrey
Tourist Match
Bath: Somerset v Zimbabwe (one-day)
Other Matches
Oxford: Oxford U v Warwicks
Cambridge:* Cambridge U v M.C.C.
   (three days)

249

Sunday 16 June

John Player Special League
Swansea: Glam v Essex
Old Trafford: Lancs v Derbys
Lord's: Middx v Leics
Northampton: Northants v Glos
Trent Bridge: Notts v Kent
Bath: Somerset v Yorks
Hove: Sussex v Hants
Worcester: Worcs v Surrey

Wednesday 19 June
Benson & Hedges Cup Semi-Finals
Other Matches
First-Class County not in B. & H. Cup
Semi-finals v Zimbabwe
Harrogate: Tilcon Trophy
(three days)

Thursday 20 June

Tourist Match
Cambridge: Combined U v Australia
(one day)

Saturday 22 June

Britannic Assurance Championship
Bristol: Glos v Sussex
Old Trafford: Lancs v Kent
Leicester: Leics v Glam
Northampton: Northants v Essex
Trent Bridge: Notts v Middx
The Oval: Surrey v Somerset
Harrogate:* Yorks v Worcs
Tourist Matches
Southampton:* Hants v Australia
(four days)
Edgbaston: Warwicks v Zimbabwe
Other Match
Oxford: Oxford U v M.C.C. (three
days)

Sunday 23 June

John Player Special League
Bristol: Glos v Sussex
Old Trafford: Lancs v Kent
Leicester: Leics v Glam
Luton: Northants v Essex
Trent Bridge: Notts v Middlesex
The Oval: Surrey v Somerset

Wednesday 26 June

Britannic Assurance Championship
Derby: Derbys v Notts
Chelmsford: Essex v Kent
Cardiff: Glam v Somerset
Bristol: Glos v Hants
Old Trafford: Lancs v Warwicks
Northampton: Northants v Surrey
Worcester: Worcs v Middx
Bradford: Yorks v Leics
Tourist Match
Coatbridge: Scotland v Zimbabwe
(three days)

Thursday 27 June

**CORNHILL INSURANCE TEST
SERIES**
Lord's: ENGLAND v AUSTRALIA
(Second Test Match)

Saturday 29 June

Britannic Assurance Championship
Derby: Derbys v Glam
Southampton: Hants v Essex
Leicester: Leics v Surrey
Trent Bridge:* Notts v Glos
Hastings: Sussex v Lancs
Edgbaston: Warwicks v Northants
Worcester: Worcs v Yorks
Tourist Match
Cleethorpes:* Minor Counties v
Zimbabwe (three days)
Other Match
Taunton: Somerset v Cambridge U

Sunday 30 June

John Player Special League
Derby: Derbys v Glam
Bournemouth: Hants v Essex
Canterbury: Kent v Middx
Leicester: Leics v Surrey
Hastings: Sussex v Lancs
Edgbaston: Warwicks v Northants
Worcester: Worcs v Yorks

Wednesday 3 July

NatWest Bank Trophy (First Round)
Luton (Wardown Pk): Beds v Glos
Birkenhead (Oxton): Cheshire v Yorks
Derby: Derbys v Durham
Chelmsford: Essex v Oxon

Southampton: Hants v Berks
Hitchin: Herts v Worcs
Canterbury: Kent v Surrey
Uxbridge: Middx v Cumberland
Norwich: Norfolk v Leics
Trent Bridge: Notts v Staffs
Edinburgh (M'side): Scotland v Glam
Telford (St. George): Shropshire v
  Northants
Taunton: Somerset v Bucks
Bury St. Edmunds: Suffolk v Lancs
Hove: Sussex v Ireland
Edgbaston: Warwicks v Devon
Other Match
Lord's: Oxford U v Cambridge U
  (three days)

Saturday 6 July

Britannic Assurance Championship
Swansea: Glam v Notts
Gloucester: Glos v Yorks
Liverpool: Lancs v Hants
Northampton: Northants v Middx
Taunton: Somerset v Leics
The Oval: Surrey v Kent
Hove: Sussex v Warwicks
Worcester: Worcs v Derbys
Tourist Match
Chelmsford:* Essex v Australia (four
  days)

Sunday 7 July

John Player Special League
Knypersley: Derbys v Worcs
Swansea: Glam v Notts
Gloucester: Glos v Yorks
Old Trafford: Lancs v Hants
Tring: Northants v Middx
Taunton: Somerset v Leics
The Oval: Surrey v Kent
Hove: Sussex v Warwicks

Wednesday 10 July

Britannic Assurance Championship
Southend: Essex v Somerset
Swansea: Glam v Leics
Gloucester: Glos v Worcs
Portsmouth: Hants v Sussex
Maidstone: Kent v Yorks
Lord's: Middx v Notts
Northampton: Northants v Derbys
Edgbaston: Warwicks v Lancs

Tourist Match
League Cricket Conference v
  Zimbabwe (two or three days)

Thursday 11 July

**CORNHILL INSURANCE TEST
SERIES**
**Trent Bridge: ENGLAND v
  AUSTRALIA
  (Third Test Match)**

Saturday 13 July

Britannic Assurance Championship
Chesterfield: Derbys v Leics
Southend: Essex v Glos
Portsmouth: Hants v Worcs
Maidstone: Kent v Northants
Old Trafford: Lancs v Glam
Lord's: Middx v Somerset
Nuneaton: Warwicks v Notts
Sheffield: Yorks v Surrey
Tourist match
Hove: Sussex v Zimbabwe (one day)

Sunday 14 July

John Player Special League
Southend: Essex v Glos
Portsmouth: Hants v Worcs
Maidstone: Kent v Northants
Old Trafford: Lancs v Glam
Lord's: Middx v Somerset
Edgbaston: Warwicks v Notts
Hull or Bradford: Yorks v Surrey
Other Match
Arundel: Lavinia, Duchess of
  Norfolk's XI v Zimbabwe (one day)

Wednesday 17 July

*NatWest Bank Trophy (Second
  Round)*
Bedford (Town Gd.) or Bristol: Beds
  or Glos v Shropshire or Northants
Birkenhead (Oxton) or Headingley:
  Cheshire or Yorks v Somerset or
  Bucks
Chelmsford or Oxford: Essex or Oxon
  v Middx or Cumberland
Southampton or Reading: Hants or
  Berks v Norfolk or Leics
Canterbury or The Oval: Kent or
  Surrey v Derbys or Durham

Trent Bridge or Stone: Notts or Staffs
v Warwicks or Devon
Glasgow or Cardiff: Scotland or Glam
v Sussex or Ireland
T.B.A. or Old Trafford: Suffolk or
Lancs v Herts or Worcs
Tourist Match
Kent or Surrey v Zimbabwe

Thursday 18 July

Tourist Match
Jesmond: Minor Counties v Australia
(one day)

Saturday 20 July

**Lord's: BENSON & HEDGES CUP
FINAL**
Tourist Matches
Neath:* Glam v Australia (or
Warwicks if Glam in B. & H. Final)
Bristol: Glos v Zimbabwe (will start
on Sun 21 if Glos in B. & H. Final)

Sunday, 21 July

John Player Special League
Derby: Derbys v Somerset
Chelmsford: Essex v Kent
Leicester: Leics v Warwicks
Northampton: Northants v Sussex
Guildford: Surrey v Notts
Worcester: Worcs v Middx

Wednesday 24 July

Britannic Assurance Championship
Chesterfield: Derbys v Yorks
Dartford: Kent v Essex
Southport: Lancs v Surrey
Uxbridge: Middx v Northants
Trent Bridge: Notts v Sussex
Edgbaston: Warwicks v Somerset
Hereford: Worcs v Glam
Tourist Matches
Bristol: Glos v Australia
Leicester: Leics v Zimbabwe

Saturday 27 July

Britannic Assurance Championship
Bristol: Glos v Glam
Leicester: Leics v Kent
Uxbridge: Middx v Lancs
Worksop: Notts v Yorks

Taunton: Somerset v Essex
Guildford: Surrey v Hants
Eastbourne: Sussex v Worcs
Edgbaston: Warwicks v Derbyshire
Tourist Match
Northampton:* Northants v Australia
(four days)

Sunday 28 July

John Player Special League
Bristol: Glos v Glam
Leicester: Leics v Kent
Lord's: Middx v Lancs
Trent Bridge: Notts v Yorks
Taunton: Somerset v Essex
Eastbourne: Sussex v Worcs
Edgbaston: Warwicks v Derbys

Wednesday 31 July

Britannic Assurance Championship
Leicester: Leics v Lancs
Lord's: Middx v Glos
The Oval: Surrey v Warwicks
Eastbourne: Sussex v Kent
Bradford: Yorks v Derbys

Thursday 1 August

**CORNHILL INSURANCE TEST
SERIES**
**Old Trafford: ENGLAND v
AUSTRALIA
(Fourth Test Match)**

Saturday 3 August

Britannic Assurance Championship
Derby: Derbys v Surrey
Chelmsford: Essex v Middx
Swansea:* Glam v Kent
Bournemouth: Hants v Somerset
Northampton: Northants v Notts
Edgbaston: Warwicks v Yorks
Worcester: Worcs v Lancs

Sunday 4 August

John Player Special League
Derby: Derbys v Surrey
Chelmsford: Essex v Middx
Southampton: Hants v Somerset
Northampton: Northants v Notts
Edgbaston: Warwicks v Yorks
Worcester: Worcs v Lancs

Wednesday 7 August

*NatWest Bank Trophy (Quarter-
    Finals)*

Thursday 8 August

Tourist Match
Downpatrick: Ireland v Australia (one
    day)

Saturday 10 August

Britannic Assurance Championship
Colchester: Essex v Derbys
Cardiff: Glam v Warwicks
Cheltenham: Glos v Leics
Southampton: Hants v Surrey
Canterbury: Kent v Sussex
Trent Bridge: Notts v Worcs
Weston-s-Mare: Somerset v Northants
Headingley: Yorks v Lancs
Tourist Match
Lord's:* Middx v Australia (four days)

Sunday 11 August

John Player Special League
Colchester: Essex v Derbys
Cardiff: Glam v Warwicks
Cheltenham: Glos v Leics
Canterbury: Kent v Sussex
Trent Bridge: Notts v Worcs
Weston-s-Mare: Somerset v Northants
Headingley: Yorks v Lancs
Other Matches
Warwick Under-25 Semi-Finals (one
    day) (or Sunday, 18 August)

Wednesday 14 August

Britannic Assurance Championship
Buxton: Derbys v Worcs
Colchester: Essex v Sussex
Cardiff: Glam v Hants
Cheltenham: Glos v Notts
Canterbury: Kent v Warwicks
Lytham: Lancs v Northants
Weston-s-Mare: Somerset v Middx
The Oval: Surrey v Yorks

Thursday 15 August

**CORNHILL INSURANCE TEST
    SERIES**
Edgbaston: **ENGLAND v
    AUSTRALIA (Fifth Test Match)**

Saturday 17 August

Britannic Assurance Championship
Cheltenham: Glos v Warwicks
Old Trafford: Lancs v Notts
Leicester: Leics v Hants
Lord's: Middx v Surrey
Wellingborough: Northants v Glam
Hove: Sussex v Derbys
Worcester: Worcs v Essex
Scarborough: Yorks v Kent

Sunday 18 August

John Player Special League
Cheltenham: Glos v Warwicks
Old Trafford: Lancs v Notts
Leicester: Leics v Hants
Lord's: Middx v Surrey
Wellingborough: Northants v Glam
Hove: Sussex v Derbys
Worcester: Worcs v Essex
Scarborough: Yorks v Kent
Other Match
Warwick Under-25 Semi-Finals (one
    day) (If not played on Sunday 11
    August)

Wednesday 21 August

NatWest Bank Trophy (Semi-Finals)
Other Match
Glasgow (Titwood): Scotland v
    M.C.C. (three days)

Saturday 24 August

Britannic Assurance Championship
Chelmsford: Essex v Surrey
Swansea: Glam v Yorks
Bournemouth: Hants v Glos
Old Trafford: Lancs v Somerset
Northampton: Northants v Leics
Trent Bridge: Notts v Derbys
Hove: Sussex v Middx
Edgbaston: Warwicks v Worcs
Tourist Match
Canterbury:* Kent v Australia (four
    days)

Sunday 25 August

John Player Special League
Heanor: Derbys v Notts
Swansea: Glam v Yorks
Bournemouth: Hants v Glos

253

Old Trafford: Lancs v Somerset
The Oval: Surrey v Northants
Worcester: Worcs v Warwicks
Other Match
Edgbaston: Warwick Under-25 Final
  (one day)

Wednesday 28 August

Britannic Assurance Championship
Derby: Derbys v Somerset
Bristol: Glos v Essex
Bournemouth: Hants v Leics
Trent Bridge: Notts v Glam
Hove: Sussex v Yorks
Worcester: Worcs v Kent

Thursday 29 August

**CORNHILL INSURANCE TEST
  SERIES**
**The Oval: ENGLAND v AUSTRALIA
  (Sixth Test Match)**

Saturday 31 August

Britannic Assurance Championship
Cardiff: Glam v Glos
Folkestone: Kent v Derbys
Leicester: Leics v Worcs
Trent Bridge: Notts v Lancs
Taunton: Somerset v Sussex
Edgbaston: Warwicks v Essex
Headingley: Yorks v Northants

Sunday 1 September

John Player Special League
Cardiff: Glam v Surrey
Southampton: Hants v Middx
Folkestone: Kent v Derbys
Leicester: Leics v Worcs
Taunton: Somerset v Sussex
Edgbaston: Warwicks v Essex
Headingley: Yorks v Northants

Wednesday 4 September

Britannic Assurance Championship
Bristol: Glos v Northants
Folkestone: Kent v Hants
Leicester: Leics v Middx
The Oval: Surrey v Sussex
Worcester: Worcs v Somerset

Other Matches
Scarborough: *ASDA Cricket
  Challenge*
Derbys v Yorks (one day)

Thursday 5 September

Scarborough: *ASDA Cricket
  Challenge*
Lancs v Notts (one day)

Friday 6 September

Scarborough: *ASDA Cricket
  Challenge Final* (one day)

Saturday 7 September

**Lord's: NATWEST BANK TROPHY
  FINAL**
Britannic Assurance Championship
Hove: Sussex v Leics
(Will be played on 11 Sept if either
  County in NatWest Bank Trophy
  Final)

Sunday 8 September

John Player Special League
Moreton-in-Marsh: Glos v Worcs
Southampton: Hants v Derbys
Canterbury: Kent v Warwicks
Trent Bridge: Notts v Essex
The Oval: Surrey v Lancs
Hove: Sussex v Leics
Other Match
Scarborough: International Match
  (three days)

Wednesday 11 September

Britannic Assurance Championship
Chesterfield: Derbys v Warwicks
Southampton: Hants v Northants
Lord's: Middx v Essex
Taunton: Somerset v Worcs
Hove: Sussex v Leics (if not played on
  7 Sept)
Scarborough: Yorks v Notts

Saturday 14 September

Britannic Assurance Championship
Chelmsford: Essex v Yorks
Cardiff: Glam v Sussex
Canterbury: Kent v Somerset
Old Trafford: Lancs v Leics

254

Trent Bridge: Notts v Hants
The Oval: Surrey v Glos
Edgbaston: Warwicks v Middx
Worcester: Worcs v Northants

Sunday 15 September

John Player Special League
Chesterfield: Derbys v Leics
Chelmsford: Essex v Yorks

Cardiff: Glam v Sussex
Canterbury: Kent v Somerset
Trent Bridge: Notts v Hants
The Oval: Surrey v Glos
Edgbaston: Warwicks v Middx
Worcester: Worcs v Northants

©Test and County Cricket Board 1985

MINOR COUNTIES CHAMPIONS

1895	Norfolk	1924	Berkshire
	Durham	1925	Buckinghamshire
	Worcestershire	1926	Durham
1896	Worcestershire	1927	Staffordshire
1897	Worcestershire	1928	Berkshire
1898	Worcestershire	1929	Oxfordshire
1899	Northamptonshire	1930	Durham
	Buckinghamshire	1931	Leicestershire II
1900	Glamorgan	1932	Buckinghamshire
	Durham	1933	Undecided
	Northamptonshire	1934	Lancashire II
1901	Durham	1935	Middlesex II
1902	Wiltshire	1936	Hertfordshire
1903	Northamptonshire	1937	Lancashire II
1904	Northamptonshire	1938	Buckinghamshire
1905	Norfolk	1939	Surrey II
1906	Staffordshire	1946	Suffolk
1907	Lancashire II	1947	Yorkshire II
1908	Staffordshire	1948	Lancashire II
1909	Wiltshire	1949	Lancashire II
1910	Norfolk	1950	Surrey II
1911	Staffordshire	1951	Kent II
1912	In abeyance	1952	Buckinghamshire
1913	Norfolk	1953	Berkshire
1920	Staffordshire	1954	Surrey II
1921	Staffordshire	1955	Surrey II
1922	Buckinghamshire	1956	Kent II
1923	Buckinghamshire	1957	Yorkshire II

1958	Yorkshire II		
1959	Warwickshire II		
1960	Lancashire II		
1961	Somerset II		
1962	Warwickshire II		
1963	Cambridgeshire		
1964	Lancashire II		
1965	Somerset II		
1966	Lincolnshire		
1967	Cheshire		
1968	Yorkshire II		
1969	Buckinghamshire		
1970	Bedfordshire		
1971	Yorkshire II		
1972	Bedfordshire		
1973	Shropshire		
1974	Oxfordshire		
1975	Hertfordshire		
1976	Durham		
1977	Suffolk		
1978	Devon		
1979	Suffolk		
1980	Durham		
1981	Durham		
1982	Oxfordshire		
1983	Hertfordshire		
1984	Durham		

A *Queen Anne Press* Book

© Queen Anne Press 1985

Cover photograph: Paul Downton by Adrian Murrell
                          All-Sport Photographic

First published in Great Britain in 1985 by
Queen Anne Press, Macdonald & Co (Publishers) Ltd,
A BPCC plc Company

All rights reserved. No part of this publication
may be reproduced, stored in a retrieval system,
or transmitted, in any form or by any means,
without the prior permission in writing of
the publisher, nor be otherwise circulated
in any form of binding or cover other than that in
which it is published and without a similar
condition including this condition being imposed
on the subsequent publisher.

British Library Cataloguing in Publication Data

Playfair cricket annual.—38th ed. (1985)
   1. Cricket—Periodicals
   796.35′05   GV911

ISBN 0-356-10741-8

Typeset, printed and bound in Great Britain by
Hazell Watson & Viney Limited,
Member of the BPCC Group,
Aylesbury, Bucks